Détente

DÉTENTE

edited by G. R. URBAN

UNIVERSE BOOKS
New York

Published in the United States of America 1976
by Universe Books
381 Park Avenue South, New York, N.Y.10016

Library of Congress Catalog Card Number: 75–33483

ISBN 0 87663 271 1

Printed in Great Britain

Contents

Editor's note

This symposium originated in a series of Radio Free Europe broadcasts transmitted, in several instalments, between December 1973 and August 1975. They are reproduced here, with minor editorial alterations, in chronological order. I have, in most cases, resisted the temptation to bring them up to date for fear of disturbing the chain of the argument. Also, I feel there is some insight to be gained from the unfolding story of détente.

Although the Conference on Security and Co-operation in Europe has provided the topics for most of the discussions, the issues covered range substantially beyond both the Conference and the document which has emerged from it. More particularly, western interest in promoting the free flow of people and ideas has given us a chance to examine the rationale of the whole spectrum of East/West relations. The symposium ends in a three-cornered conversation of somewhat speculative character, adding, as I hope, a predictive element to the preceding, and predominantly historical, dialogues.

The contributors have been drawn from the policy-making, policy-interpreting and policy-studying communities in several western countries. They speak, of course, exclusively for themselves. Their controversial commitments on this or that side of the debate may help to clarify some of those profound political and moral issues which underly the policy of détente but have not always been adequately articulated.

September 1975   G. R. URBAN

Acknowledgements

The editor would like to acknowledge a debt of deep gratitude to J. F. Brown and Charles András who helped him to design this symposium and took the trouble of discussing with him its various arguments in a spirit of meticulous and friendly criticism.

BRUNO PITTERMANN

The moral factor in the conduct of foreign affairs

URBAN: I have before me two definitions of the word détente: 'an easing of strained relations, especially between states', which is the definition given by the *Concise Oxford Dictionary*, and another which goes back to the French connotations of the word and has to do with the use of firearms. Here détente means the release of the strained string of the crossbow and the discharge of the bolt. There is a French phrase for this kind of exercise: *reculer pour mieux sauter*—taking a step back for a better leap forward.

While both definitions may be correct in their respective political and linguistic environments, complications arise if in the present context of East-West détente one side is pursuing détente in the *Oxford Dictionary's* sense of the word, whereas the other acts on the French definition.

PITTERMANN: The conflict exists, and it is pretty clear to me which of the two definitions supplies the key to Soviet practice. The Soviet leaders and the Soviet press never tire of telling us that the concept of peaceful co-existence between states and nations—and that is their definition of détente—excludes any idea of peaceful co-existence between political systems and ideologies. As a social democrat (and you do not have to be a social democrat to agree with me) I do not believe that you can have one without the other. You cannot have confidence between states and governments unless they live, at the very least, in a state of détente with their own populations, for if they suppress minorities, silence dissidents, cut their peoples off from contact with the world and, worse, become prisoners of their own propaganda—have they the moral authority to pursue détente in the democratic sense of the word? Can we be sure that they speak for the peoples to whom we want to move closer and who, I believe, want to move closer to us? And can we rely on their word to respect their commitments in any accord we may sign with them on security, co-operation and the free flow of people and ideas? I think not. That is why we ought to heed the warnings of Solzhenitsyn, Sakharov and the other Russian dissidents.

Sakharov has repeatedly made the point that détente without

democratization inside Russia and Eastern Europe would be extremely dangerous, for it would mean the acceptance by the western democracies of the Soviet rules of the game. It would be dangerous for the world's present balance of power, too, for it would mean bolstering up Russia's stagnant economy with western loans and technology, solving problems for her which she cannot solve for herself, and allowing her to accumulate power which a weakened or disarmed West would one day have to face.

URBAN: Détente has been rather vaguely associated with two words in German: *Entspannung* and *Gewaltverzicht*; they carry very different connotations.

PITTERMANN: When we talk of détente we are thinking of a relaxation of tension—*Entspannung*. A renunciation of the use of force—*Gewaltverzicht*—falls distinctly short of that. Yet I believe that is all the Russians really want. They want to have the status quo in Eastern Europe fully guaranteed, they want what amounts to indirect western subsidies to continue their military build-up, *and* they want to keep their hands free to do exactly as they please in stirring up trouble in the West and the Third World.

Brezhnev cannot be faulted for not having warned us: 'The Soviet Union is on the offensive and the West on the defensive: the impact of our ideology is tremendous; it is mounting every day, undermining the mainstay of the non-Soviet system from within.' Of course, Brezhnev took care not to say things of this sort within earshot of American senators and businessmen.

Entspannung for us, social democrats, means the freedom of individual people *within* the same country to assert their rights as autonomous, adult human beings, and to communicate with each other and the outside world.

Solzhenitsyn and Sakharov are only the tip of the iceberg. There may well be a great many people in the Soviet Union, even important groups within the Soviet Communist Party, who would endorse the ideas of Solzhenitsyn, Sakharov and the other articulate (and as yet unarrested) dissidents.

The eastern interpretation of détente comes exclusively from the Soviet Presidium and the Party leadership, and this interpretation limits détente to a renunciation of force between states. It takes no account of what Solzhenitsyn has aptly called the 'steady, permanent violence by the state' against the people.

URBAN: It seems to me that even the renunciation of force is not clearly spelled out in the Soviet conception of peaceful co-existence. One of Czechoslovakia's conservative ideological pundits, J. Kucera, said in June 1973 that the 'ideological offensive' against the West need not restrict itself to cheering on the proletariat. 'To defeat bourgeois ideology', he wrote, 'it must be attacked in its own lair, in which it lives and reproduces itself and from which it reaches into our midst with its tentacles . . . Revolution cannot be exported . . . but there is no reason why we should hesitate to assist in this process.'

PITTERMANN: I would not take this as entirely typical. Despite a good deal of re-Stalinization, Eastern Europe is not the monolith it used to be. This kind of sentiment is committed to paper to tranquilize the Stalinist old-guard in Czechoslovakia, to defend the party leaders against the disgruntled die-hards, and—generally—against internal opposition. At the moment the Soviet Government and the Communist Party are committed to the renunciation of force as an instrument of foreign policy. Whether in a critical situation they would stand by that decision is another matter.

That brings us back to the importance I attach to peaceful co-existence between people and government, the ruled and the rulers, especially in the USSR. As the decision to forego the use of force has been made by a small body of men in isolation from the public, we don't know what credibility to attach to it. The same small body of men may change that decision overnight; it may be replaced by another oligarchy or a single dictator who may act as it or he pleases. If political organizations representing different points of view were free to pursue their policies in the Soviet Union, and the Soviet Government's decision to work for a détente with the democratic western world rested on the consensus or majority view of these political organizations, then we in the western democracies would have every reason to believe that détente was sincerely meant because it would have the backing of the majority of the Soviet people and could not be changed with a stroke of the pen. There would be checks and balances to prevent any such thing from happening.

But as there is no such freedom in Russia, we cannot be sure whether or not we are being tricked into a false sense of security—into, in fact, possibly underwriting our own future unfreedom. I am not saying that this need be so, but we cannot be sure that it won't be so, and it is at least doubtful whether we can afford to take the risk.

Now the same is, of course, true of the dictatorships in the western world, but Spain, for example, is at least not threatening to make war on anyone or support revolutions.

URBAN: Senator Jackson and his supporters are in the process of denying the Soviet Union most-favoured-nation status in its economic relations with the United States unless the Soviet

Government permits the free emigration of its citizens. The Amendment raises a highly controversial issue: is an instrument of foreign policy a legitimate means of influencing the domestic affairs of a sovereign state? Senator Jackson, like you, believes that East-West détente without an internal human détente is phoney, but Secretary Kissinger has stated quite categorically that although one could not be indifferent to the denial of human rights in the Soviet Union, the United States could not so insist on the transformation of the domestic structure of the Soviet Union as to give up the general evolution towards détente. This view is shared by many professional diplomats on both sides of the Atlantic: you deal with, and you try to make the best deal with, the government in power, not the one you would like to see in power.

PITTERMANN: Before answering your comment, let me insert a personal note here. I have been pushing for the freedom of Soviet Jews to leave their country for many years in the Council of Europe and elsewhere, but I always warned my Israeli friends that it was impossible to interfere. Kosygin, the Soviet Prime Minister, made resounding promises both in Paris and in Canada that Jewish families separated by the second world war would be allowed to reunite. Yet, for a long time, these promises were not kept, although here was the Soviet Prime Minister himself telling the world in front of hundreds of journalists that these divided families would be allowed to reunite. How can we believe anything the Russians say if they do not keep their word in a matter so simple and easy to verify?

We told the Soviet leaders: you have ratified the United Nations instruments outlawing racial discrimination and racial persecution, yet you are practising these very things when you discriminate against Jews. How can we trust any Soviet signature when you flagrantly violate one of the cardinal principles of the United Nations?

URBAN: Surely the Russians would not admit that there was racial discrimination in the Soviet Union?

PITTERMANN: No, but neither could they totally deny it. They could not counter our argument that Yiddish and Hebrew schools no longer exist in the Soviet Union. There had been such schools in Tsarist Russia, and in the early years of Soviet rule they were encouraged and enlarged. But after the second world war they were closed down and have never been allowed to reopen—all this in violation of the Soviet constitution which lays down that every nation has a right to have its children educated in its own language.

Well, the Soviet answer was: true, there had been Yiddish schools in Tsarist Russia, but the vast majority of Tsarist education was conducted at a pitifully low level. Today Jewish children have the whole gamut of sophisticated Soviet education at their disposal at the secondary and higher levels; they can improve themselves and equip themselves as far as their talents will carry them, exactly like the children of all the other Soviet nationalities.

But this is a specious argument, for why, for example, have the Latvians and Lithuanians been allowed to have their young educated in their own languages, but not the Jews? The Russians know that they are on very weak ground here.

But the Soviets are violating the Universal Declaration of Human Rights, too, for this stipulates that the signatories respect their citizens' right to leave their country *and* to return to it. Let me add, however, that, as far as Jewish emigration to Israel is concerned, the Soviet Union has to some extent opened its frontiers, and a considerable number of Jews have been allowed to leave. Whether this policy is here to stay is another matter.

URBAN: Isn't this an advance on the earlier position, especially at a time when Israel is anxious to increase her manpower resources and the Soviet Union is helping her to do so at the risk—indeed the certainty—of incurring Arab displeasure?

PITTERMANN: It is an advance made under the pressure of world public opinion, but the Soviet Jews, when they leave, have to give up their citizenship and, with few exceptions, are not allowed to return. This is a violation of the Universal Declaration of Human Rights. It is a racist measure.

URBAN: The Jackson Amendment does not ask the Soviet Government to give Soviet Jews preferential treatment. It urges the United States Executive not to grant the Soviet Union most-favoured-nation treatment unless the Soviet Government permits any citizen who so desires to leave the country.

PITTERMANN: But free exit (even if it were commonly granted, which it is not) is not enough. The Russians are also under an obligation to facilitate free re-entry. Look at the cases of Valerie Chalidze and Zhores Medvedev. Neither is a Jew; both have been allowed to leave and, while abroad, both have been stripped of their citizenship. Their return to Soviet Russia has been made virtually impossible.

As Sozhenitsyn put it in August 1973: 'Citizenship in our country is not an inalienable natural right for every human being born on its soil, but it is a kind of coupon which is kept by an exclusive clique of people who in no way and by nothing have proved that they have a greater right to the Russian soil. And this clique can, if it doesn't approve of some citizen's convictions, declare him deprived of his homeland.'

It is a great pity that the United States herself is not in a strong position to lecture the Soviet Government on this point. Entry into the United States is subject to visa requirements which are not easy to satisfy if, for instance, you have a communist—even a remote communist—background. And one remembers the deplorable entry, exit, and travel restrictions which applied during the McCarthy era and after.

URBAN: Let me take you back to the legal and moral issues raised by the Jackson Amendment, for these pose the perennial dilemma: when is an internal policy an internal policy? *Are* there domestic affairs in a rapidly shrinking world?

In his Nobel Prize oration Solzhenistyn said: 'There are no *internal affairs* left on this cramped globe of ours. And mankind can only be saved if everybody takes an interest in everybody else's affairs, if the people of the West cease to be indifferent to what is happening in the East.'

These are impeccably libertarian sentiments, and no-one has a more profound right to voice them and to deserve our respect than Solzhenitsyn. Yet, if you, as a former Vice-Chancellor, had to ask yourself, as Kissinger has, how to make a highly volatile world safe for peace, wouldn't you, too, accept the unsavoury nature of the power with whom you had to strike a bargain? Wouldn't you, too, in all likelihood choose a policy of détente, knowing full well that your choice was, as it almost always is in the murky art of politics, a choice between highly unpleasant alternatives?

I know how firmly Solzhenitsyn would reject this appeal to *raison d'état* from the way he condemned the United Nations for 'obsequiously' voting 'to reject the examination of *private petitions*—the groans, cries and implorations of individual *mere people*—as the buzz of insects too insignificant for such a great organization'. But when the alternative is nuclear confrontation, with millions of lives and the future of western civilization at stake, isn't it at least defensible to argue that in certain circumstances the ends justify the means?

PITTERMANN: We have to conceive of this issue in a lower key and at a more practical level. The Soviet Union wants certain commercial advantages or, to be more precise, the abolition of certain commercial disadvantages, from the United States, which the latter can grant or withhold. The Soviet Union, hard-pressed in its economy and technology in a number of well-known ways, wants to make a business deal on the usual Soviet principle 'what is mine is mine, what is yours is negotiable'. In other words, Moscow wants something for nothing.

The United States and the Soviet Union are sovereign states, and it is entirely for them to decide under what conditions they agree to co-operate with each other. I cannot think of any international agreement—whether it is about the export of shoes, or the pricing policy of the Wagon Lits sleeper service, or sugar imports—that does not have, directly or indirectly, domestic repercussions. Foreign relations are in no essential respect different from relations between individuals, groups or business companies. There is give and take in both. Now this, now the other party has the greater leverage, and if you decide, as the Americans appear to have decided, to use your enormous leverage with moderation, the least you can do is to make sure that any agreement you sign serves the interests of both sides—that there is reciprocity in your dealings. The Jackson Amendment seems to be trying to do just that: the Russians want something from America, and the American Senate wants something in return. The Russians want loans, investment, technical assistance and security on their European border, not least as a reassurance against China. The Americans, who are in a position of being able to give or deny these things to them, have every right to say that they will not play the game unless the word détente is filled out with practical meaning—that is to say, unless the Soviet Union honours the obligations she has accepted in the Universal Declaration of Human Rights, making provisions for the free movement of people and ideas across national frontiers.

I don't think the Jackson Amendment is the kind of instrument that could decide war and peace, and it would be wrong to place it on that level. It is an amendment to a proposed business deal which both the Russians and certain American capitalists badly want. And Senator Jackson and his supporters are entirely right in tying this business deal to the fulfilment, as I say, of certain international commitments which the Russians have accepted and ought to be honouring anyway. It all boils down to a matter of priorities: does profit override considerations of human freedom or should it be the other way around?

It isn't that the United States has a record of cashing in on Russia's economic embarrassments. The 1972 wheat deal with the Soviet Union was indeed so generous that the bill for the mismanagement of Soviet agriculture was in effect paid by the American taxpayer to the tune of some 300 million dollars, for the Russians were allowed to buy the wheat at a subsidized price of 1.60 dollars per bushel, whereas in 1973 the price went up to 4.30 dollars.

URBAN: I'm reminded of Senator Jackson's lapidary statement: 'Fifty years ago Lenin promised the Soviet people bread and freedom. If American farmers are to provide the bread, is it too much to ask that the Soviet leaders provide their own people a measure of freedom?'

The grain deal was not a very shrewd move, and to make things worse, some of the American wheat was eventually shipped off to drought-stricken India as *Soviet* aid. Having caused a world shortage of grain and driven up the price of beef, the United States was subsequently buying back, through world market channels, some of the wheat she had sold cheaply to Russia, at high prices.

PITTERMANN: Senator Jackson is, to my knowledge, not a social democrat, but he put his finger on the problem when he mockingly said of his opponents in an interview: 'We are so anxious to do business—any kind of business—that we'll agree to anything'. And he went on to quote Lenin's famous words to Radek to the effect that if the communists gave the bourgeoisie enough rope, they would hang themselves—with the rope supplied by bourgeois businessmen.

Well, Kissinger has written about Metternich and I believe he is a great admirer of this erstwhile arbiter of Europe. Metternich came from the Rheinland, Kissinger comes from Bavaria; some people in Vienna claim to have discovered a streak of Metternichian finesse in Kissinger's balancing acts on the world stage, and call him, perhaps not unflatteringly, 'Metternichinger'. I am sure Metternich would agree with Kissinger's policies, but we social democrats don't: trade relations are foreign relations, domestic relations are foreign relations. There is ultimately only one circuit on which the various currents, bearing this or that label, can move.

URBAN: I'm sure you are making a valid point, but can a responsible minister of the world's leading power take a chance to prove it?

PITTERMANN: I cannot answer that question directly. It was at the initiative of the socialist group in the European Parliament that Western Europe's relations with the extreme right-wing governments of Spain, and (as they then were) of Portugal and Greece, were frozen. At a time when the West European countries were making economic sacrifices in order to harmonize their policies, it would have been absurd to expect them to subsidize fascist governments. Now as then we are talking of business, not war and peace, and I can see no reason why we should sacrifice socialist principles vis-à-vis the Soviet Union for the sake of commercial advantage, any more than we sacrificed them in our relationship with Spain or the Greece of the colonels.

URBAN: Are you implying that the Soviet regime is fascist by your standards?

PITTERMANN: The differences between fascist and Soviet rule are less significant than the similarities between them, especially in the matter of human rights. One claims to be fighting to free the working class from exploitation, and the other claims to be freeing society from communist subversion; but to achieve their respective goals, both imprison, torture and execute their opponents and regiment the rest of society.

Soviet society may now be slowly veering away from this form of totalitarianism. The sociological structure of the Soviet élite has changed; there are more highly educated people in leading positions, and the technological revolution is probably also impressing its rationale on the decision-making process. So I believe the Soviet type of dictatorship may become economically more rational.

URBAN: You were implying that if the Jackson Amendment and détente *did* involve questions of war and peace, a Metternichian balance-of-power policy would have to take priority over all other considerations. My impression is that if your argument were put to Kissinger he would say that détente, linked as it is to the talks on force reductions and SALT, *is* about war and peace, for these three building stones mutually condition and support one another, and if you take away one, the whole edifice collapses.

PITTERMANN: I am not at all persuaded. The cardinal element in Soviet détente policy is Russia's need of western investment, know-how, and loans—in short, it is about the Soviet economy. I have nothing against mutually profitable economic relations between western and eastern countries. In 1963, when I was Vice-Chancellor, I signed two important trade agreements with the Soviet Union and China. This was the time when the American embargo on certain 'sensitive' products was hitting the communist countries very hard. I opened Austria's frontiers to the East: we had perfected in Austria techniques for the production of high-quality steel, and our agreements with the Russians and Chinese provided for the construction of Soviet and Chinese steelworks, using Austrian technology, on a co-production basis.

So I was not, and I am not, against trade and co-operation. But I think we should call a spade a spade. It is business that détente is about and business we should call it. Why dress it up in ideological language? Why talk about European security? I should imagine Kissinger could safely put it to the American people that what he is talking about is a commercial deal. The American people have a keen sense of business, and they would not feel that there was anything derogatory in striking a commercial bargain with the Soviet Union provided the advantages were mutual. Let me say it again: The Russians have a stagnant economy, they have trouble with their consumer industry, they need vast investments and technology to exploit their oil and mineral deposits. If the American Government feels that the assistance which the Soviet Union requires would not be used to free Soviet resources for a further military build-up, and that therefore assistance could be safely given, why not say so?

What I am against is presenting the issue as something of critical importance to the world's peace.

URBAN: There is complete silence in Russia and Eastern Europe about the Soviet needs you have just mentioned. It is nowhere admitted that the Soviet economy is in trouble and that Russian hopes are pinned on American, West German and Japanese assistance. Détente is presented as a great victory for the might of the USSR. Capitalism is being *forced* to the conference table in the Soviet presentation.

PITTERMANN: This is the line taken by communist propaganda, but no-one believes it in the communist countries. The dedicated few in the Party may go along with it, but the population as a whole has a pretty shrewd idea what is happening. The universities and major libraries carry foreign papers and periodicals, trades unionists and other official visitors take information back from abroad, there is foreign broadcasting—in a word, the curtain isn't sound-proof. And those who have no means of gaining outside information have taught themselves to read between the lines of the official press.

URBAN: My impression is that the news blackout in Russia is much more effective than in Eastern Europe, and the really sad thing is that while the dissenting intellectual in Czechoslovakia, Poland or Hungary is helped and respected as the conscience of his nation, his opposite number in the Soviet Union is treated very differently. For the ordinary Russian Sakharov is an eccentric who has more pay, better housing and greater all-round privileges than the man in the street—and yet has the temerity to complain! I am reminded of David Bonavia's penetrating description of Soviet attitudes to dissent. 'It can be argued', he writes (in *Fat Sasha and the Urban Guerrilla*) 'that the present system suits the Soviet people reasonably well, bearing in mind their checkered political development and their need to concentrate on certain economic priorities before others. In such an argument, the protestors are simply the gadflies of society, products of a law which states that any social system will engender such and such a minimum percentage of malcontents. In that case, the Soviet authorities are perfectly right to suppress protest, and even to treat it as a form of schizophrenia. As social engineers, they are merely clearing a few molehills which impede the construction of a pyramid. When a pyramid is built, there will be no more molehills, because all the moles will come to live in it happily ever afterwards.'

PITTERMANN: There is, unfortunately, a great deal of truth in this. Soviet behaviour at the popular level is explained by Russia's historical background: Byzantium, the Greek-Orthodox cultural tradition, the long union between State and Church, the absence of a Renaissance from Russian life and letters, have all contributed to the docility of the masses and their non-comprehension and distrust of the individual. The word itself is a term of near-abuse in the Russian language.

The Soviet system, with its doctrine of egalitarianism at the lower levels of society and its insistence that the Leninist vision of history vests the leaders of the Party with special authority to guide the fortunes of the Russian people, meshes rather well with Russian traditions. That is why the Poles, Czechs and Hungarians, belonging as they do to the western-Christian tradition, repudiated in 1956 and 1968 the Russian, as much as the Soviet, type of dictatorship. The historical split in Europe has been between Rome and Constantinople, and it basically remains there to this day.

URBAN: The first European book on Russia was written by the representative of the Habsburgs at the Russian Court, Count Herberstein, in 1551. He was observing Russia after the fall of Byzantium when the Church of Constantinople was said to have fled to the 'Third Rome'—Moscow. In his discussion of the quasi-divine power of Tsar Wassili III he described how the Russian people almost worshipped their Tsar as God incarnate: 'It is not clear whether the Prince has to be a tyrant because the people are brutish and uncultured or whether they are made as uncultured, harsh and cruel as they are because the Prince is such a tyrant.'

PITTERMANN: Mutatis mutandis, the dilemma has lost none of its relevance.

URBAN: Social democracy is special anathema in Soviet eyes. Soviet and East European writers on détente seldom miss an opportunity to show social democrats, including yourself as one of their leaders, in the darkest colours as supporters of a refined form of anti-communism. Bruno Kreisky, the Austrian Chancellor, has remarked that the main challenge to the Soviet system is posed by democratic socialism. He observed that the social democratic governments now in power in various European countries have caused Moscow a great deal of anxiety because the Soviet leaders would much prefer an ideological confrontation with capitalism to a dialogue with social democrats, for which they are poorly equipped.

But parallel with their attacks on western social democracy, Soviet spokesmen are putting pressure on western social democrats to co-operate with the communist parties in forming electoral alliances with them. If this policy were to succeed, wouldn't there be a danger that the social democratic movement might lose its ideological identity and political independence?

PITTERMANN: This danger would exist, and it may well be part of the Politburo's détente policy that it should exist. By linking western social democrats with western communists and blurring the differences between them the Politburo hopes that the communists will reach the first ledges of power standing, as it were, on the backs of social democrats. The West European communists are told to work for the triumph of communism from within the social democratic parties, and the jointly controlled socialist-communist trades unions wherever this is politically convenient or necessary.

The Soviet leaders know that, in the western countries, communist electoral programmes modelled on the Soviet system would have no chance of winning elections. If you read the speeches of the French and Italian communist leaders, there is absolutely no mention in them of the Soviet model; on the contrary, all the emphasis is on more democracy, workers' codetermination, self-management, ending the alienation of the individual and so on. And why not? Electoral strategies of this kind have worked before—in the Weimar Republic, in favour of Hitler, for example—and may do so again, or so the Soviet leaders hope. If the social democratic-communist electoral alliance were to become a fact in the West European democracies, Moscow's problem with pressing home its conception of détente would automatically fall away, because the Russians would be talking to communist-controlled governments.

One difficulty I have with Moscow's strategy is that it is a little one-sided. I have often told the Soviet leaders: 'You want us to make alliances with you in the West, but you are not allowing social democratic parties to exist in Eastern Europe. Why?'

The real answer to this question is quite simple: the Soviet leaders rightly suspect that, in a free vote, the social democrats might prove very strong indeed, but, of course, they cannot say so. Therefore their official answer is that the social democrats have been happily and voluntarily absorbed in the party of the working class, which is the Communist Party, and if here and there remnants of the old social democratic movement survive, these are a small and historically insignificant minority.

'Very well', I then say to them, 'if the social democrats are a small minority, what have you to fear? Why make martyrs of them by persecuting them? You have a monopoly of the printing presses, of the media, of education, of every form of state power—after almost six decades of Soviet rule your people are either convinced by now of the blessings of the Soviet system, in which case they would not vote for the social democrats, or they are not so convinced, in which case you will not convince them now.'

URBAN: Have you openly made these points to the Soviet leaders?

PITTERMANN: Oh, certainly, and I have made them very angry. Kreisky is right: the Russians' Achilles heel is social democracy; they don't usually answer our criticisms—they attack us instead.

One diversionary tactic they employ against us is to accuse us of flirting with the Chinese—a heinous crime in Soviet eyes. On 4 August 1973 *Pravda* published a strongly worded and very long attack against the Socialist International, and especially against its two leaders: Pietro Nenni, the veteran Italian socialist and Lenin Prize-winner, and myself as Chairman of the International.

I had just made a visit to China—not as Chairman of the Socialist International but as President of the Austro-Chinese Research Institute, which is a bipartisan socialist-conservative enterprise. The charge against me was that I had gone to China as head of an anti-Soviet organization. A few days later, having seen only translated extracts from the *Pravda* article, I was interviewed in [the non-socialist Vienna paper] *Die Presse*, where I made a number of points about the relationship between social democracy and communism similar to those I have made in this discussion. I spoke of the continued suppression of the social democratic movement in Eastern Europe at a time when the Soviets were urging social democrats to share electoral platforms with communists in the West European countries. Three days after my interview *Tass* came back to the charge that the Socialist International was an anti-Soviet organization looking for support in Mao's China, and I was depicted as the principal villain.

URBAN: Knowing little more of the matter than what you have just told me, I would say that, seen from the Soviet angle, the suspicion was at least plausible, even though it may have been unjustified. The Chinese are supporting the European Community, they are against any weakening of Nato, they oppose détente, and incite the East European governments against Moscow. So, in Soviet eyes, a working alliance between China and the Socialist International would not be out of key with Chinese thinking.

PITTERMANN: This may be so, but talking to the Chinese I did not get the impression that the policy they were pursuing vis-à-vis the social democratic parties was in any way different from their attitude to other western democratic parties. Of course, the fact that the Chinese have no sizable fraternal parties, for example, in France or Italy, and that they are not in the business of trying to promote alliances between western social democrats and western communists, does make it easier for us, social democrats, to talk to them. But my visit to China had nothing to do with the machinations attributed to us by *Pravda* and *Tass*.

URBAN: Don't you feel that too much outspokenness on the part of the Social Democratic Party of a small and neutral country such as Austria is taking a risk with neutrality and Soviet goodwill? For example, Chancellor Kreisky gave an emphatic warning at the Vienna meeting of Amnesty International (14 September 1973) that the Soviet treatment of Sakharov, Solzhenitsyn and other dissidents was not conducive to co-operation in the cultural and scientific fields but was, on the contrary, bound to have a damaging overall effect on détente.

PITTERMANN: No, I don't feel that. Our experience with the Soviet leaders has always been that if we, social democrats, speak our minds freely and sincerely, our views are listened to and respected though not necessarily acted upon. The Russians know that when we complain about the restriction of civil rights in the Soviet Union, we also protest against similar restrictions in Greece, Spain, Portugal and Chile. In fact, we raised this very problem early in the security discussions: if the western democracies are for a free flow of ideas and people with Russia and Eastern Europe, why not urge the same freedoms on the South European dictatorships too? Restrictions are restrictions and a dictatorship is a dictatorship whatever the label. Therefore it is very difficult for the Soviet side not to pay attention to what we are saying. Also, Austria is a predominantly socialist country with seventy per cent of industrial shares in public ownership (and, incidentally, profitable public ownership); hence our voice carries special weight with the Soviet leaders. Our moral authority in international questions is certainly respected, and I am sure that Chancellor Kreisky's words, or those of Willy Brandt, do have some influence. Naturally, as Austrian Chancellor, Kreisky cannot speak with the same freedom as I can, but our views are identical.

URBAN: You have not quite stilled my anxiety that if electoral alliances were to be made between socialists and communists in Western Europe, the all-important ideological demarcation line between the two might not be blurred by commission or omission. Is there a single, easily identifiable principle that distinguishes the philosophy of your party from that of the communist party?

The answer to this question is not self-evident. Most European socialist parties profess to be, or have until recently professed to be, Marxist parties, so neither right-wing propaganda, nor communist propaganda has found it difficult to show that the differences between social democrats and communists are negligible, if indeed not imaginary: the extreme right of the Right wants to identify the two because it has an interest in branding all parties of the Left as communist, and the communists want to do likewise because *they* want to absorb the social democrats on grounds of ideological identity. It has been done before, it might be done again.

PITTERMANN: The ideological frontier is simple and crystal clear—it is personal freedom in all its manifestations, and on this principle we must stand. That is why I am always pressing communist parties and governments for the practical application of the Universal Declaration of Human Rights. I am, I can assure you, pretty outspoken when I talk to them: 'You have abolished all private property, you have nationalized all the means of production, and you say you have ended the exploitation of man by man. For more than half a century you have had the first phase of socialism, the dictatorship of the proletariat, which was never meant by Marx to be more than a temporary phase. If, as you claim, the dictatorship of the proletariat has been a success, the Soviet society is by now a classless society and the Soviet people are emancipated; and if you are, as you say you are, true Marxists, then you should now go over from socialism to communism and give the people their freedom.' This is the sort of thing I tell the Soviet leaders.

URBAN: What kind of reception do you get?

PITTERMANN: Oh, a pretty rough one. They tell me that the Soviet people would have no truck with social democracy, that they would not understand it, that there is no need for social democrats, that the development of history has overtaken social democracy and so on.

Well, the West European social democratic parties have more or less successfully injected socialism into a free society. It is now the turn of the communist parties in Eastern Europe to inject freedom into the fabric of socialism. It is as simple as that. And I can assure you that when that has happened, we shall have détente at the drop of a hat.

URBAN: The European Security Conference* has three main problem areas on its agenda (we can neglect the fourth for the purposes of this discussion): security in terms of the present European status quo, economic and scientific co-operation, and Basket Three—the free flow of people and ideas across ideological frontiers. Can agreement on the first two of these lead to a genuine détente without agreement also being reached on the free flow of persons and ideas?

PITTERMANN: Détente would certainly lack credibility if the

* The 1973–75 Conference on Security and Co-operation in Europe (CSCE) is referred to throughout for convenience as the European Security Conference or the Security Conference.

first two conditions were met but the third wasn't, for how could we trust the words of a power that has renounced the use of force in its 'foreign' relations but goes on using it internally? Nevertheless, one should aim high but be content with the best bargain one can strike in the circumstances. Stability in Europe *will* mean a certain progress. We are asked to underwrite the status quo in Eastern Europe. But isn't this a fact of life anyway? Could we change it short of going to war? And would anyone want to risk universal destruction so that Kaliningrad may revert back to Königsberg?

It may well be that the Security Conference will, in effect, not be able to progress beyond dealing with the first 'basket' of problems, in which case we shall simply be putting our names to Europe's present frontiers and going home, knowing perfectly well that not much has been achieved. However, it is possible and highly desirable, that the Conference should proceed to finding answers to the second and third 'baskets' of problems. But these are inter-related. If the Soviet side is serious about wanting both peace and loans, investment, know-how and all the rest of the things it needs, it must be prepared to match the free flow of western capital and technology with the free flow of people, information and ideas. Progress in one must bring with it progress in the other.

URBAN: But wouldn't a free flow of people, books, newspapers, radio and television programmes undermine Basket One— that is to say, the security of the Soviet system—by altering Russia's and Eastern Europe's present social order, and thereby changing the status quo? This is what the Soviet spokesmen really mean when they protest that they will not permit the nefarious products of bourgeois culture to be smuggled in under Basket Three. In a sense, I can see their point: you can't ask a partner, with whom you are negotiating a declaration of security and co-operation, to sign his own death warrant.

PITTERMANN: A free flow of people and ideas would surely change the Soviet system; the people would press for more freedom and democracy. But for this change to happen you need no declaration on security or anything else for that matter—it is happening anyhow, and it will be happening faster as the Soviet system gets technologically more sophisticated. You can't run computer-based industries with morons. A successful implementation of Basket Three would, of course, further accelerate this process, which is desirable.

The effects of a declaration on European security and co-operation would, of course, be a long time in coming. But it is not delay—it is much rather undue haste—that gives me cause for concern. The main danger that I see emerging from an ill-considered and over-hasty détente is an unholy alliance between capitalists and commissars. The capitalists are so anxious to do business with the commissars that they may conveniently forget to make the necessary conditions.

Göring said he preferred guns to butter. Capitalist businessmen are now telling us that they prefer a quick killing to morality and even long-term self-interest: they want to make money—no matter how, with whom and at what cost to human freedom. The multinational companies are a case in point; they would do exceptionally well in a dictatorship where they would have a strike-free and regimented labour force, with wage stability guaranteed by the state-controlled 'unions'. One can see why American business has been lobbying against the Jackson Amendment.

URBAN: With all that said, you are nevertheless for détente rather than against it?

PITTERMANN: I most definitely am, but we must have our wits about us. There is a negro proverb I have seen quoted in an American congressional testimony: 'Cheat me once—shame on you; cheat me twice—shame on me.' That sums it up.

SIR WILLIAM HAYTER

Sovereignty, appeasement and détente

URBAN: Détente raises the classic question about how far moral principles are appropriate to the conduct of foreign policy. To put it crudely: can one have good neighbourly relations with a man who beats his wife and batters his children without becoming an accomplice? Should one invite him home?

By the same token: can we reach genuine agreement with a system which has deliberately abandoned, in its domestic policies, the conventions of civilized life as we know them—a system which is asking for western co-operation in the short term but is telling us at the same time that its long-term objective continues to be our destruction?

In the first of this series of discussions Bruno Pittermann, a former socialist Vice-Chancellor of Austria, said that it was impossible to conceive of a genuine and lasting détente so long as internal repression prevailed in Russia, and as—he insisted—the Russians were the ones who needed investment and technology and were, in effect, asking for a kind of Marshall Plan financed by American and West German private sources, the West, and especially the United States, was in a good and morally justifiable position to exact concessions in return.

Pittermann's argument echoes a good deal of political liberalism. 'The world cannot exist half slave, half free', Abraham Lincoln said; or, nearer our time, one remembers President Kennedy's words: 'The line dividing domestic and foreign affairs has become as indistinct as a line drawn in water. All that happens to us abroad has a direct and intimate bearing on what we can and must do at home. . . . For, in a real sense, all of us, as individuals and as public officials, now belong simultaneously to a national and international constituency.'

Traditionally, America's foreign policy makers have perceived the world in such moral terms, but these conceptions are now in retreat, and even those who can see that some linkage between détente, ideology and domestic policies is inescapable, point out

26

that each side must take care not to overload the political processes of the other, that is to say, not to demand concessions which may seem sound and reasonable from one's own point of view, but which may seem intolerable to the other side.

How do you, as a former British Ambassador to the USSR, see the rights and wrongs of tying foreign policy to moral considerations?

HAYTER: This is a very complex question, and I cannot answer your particular formulation of it by yes or no, but if we look at some of the ideas you have quoted, we can deduce certain conclusions from them. When Lincoln said: 'The world cannot exist half slave, half free', he was uttering a very noble sentiment, but what he was saying was, and is to this day, not true. The world *is* in fact now half slave, half free; the division exists, and there is no reason to suppose that it is going to change in the near future. As far as I can see the world is likely to go on being half slave and half free for a long time.

Again, when you quote the analogy of the next-door neighbour who beats his wife and maltreats his children, and ask: can we have good relations with him and invite him home?—well, no, you don't *want* to invite him home. On the other hand he *lives* there; he is the owner of the house, you probably can't turn him out, so it is much better to work out some kind of a modus vivendi with him rather than throw things across the fence at him.

The whole argument which says that, because you can't approve of the policies of the person with whom you are working for a détente, you can't *have* a détente, is based on a series of false analogies.

I am quite sure that to have really intimate, long-term good relations with the Soviet Union is impossible as long as the Soviet Union maintains its present internal structure, and to this extent I agree with Pittermann. But I draw from this reading of the long-term prospects of the East-West situation very different conclusions from those of Pittermann. I agree with him that the Soviet aim of détente is not to settle down to having cosy relations with us, but to gain certain technological advantages.

One is reminded of the Aesopian fable of the sun and the wind who had a bet about getting a man's cloak off: the more the wind tried to do it by huffing and puffing, the tighter and tighter the man clasped the cloak around him; then the sun smiled, and the man took his cloak off. Détente is an alternative way of getting the West to take its cloak off. The Soviet leaders make very little bones about the fact that their intention is to weaken our position. It is perfectly plain from everything they say that peaceful co-existence does not mean what the man-in-the-street in the West would take it to mean; in fact it means the continuation of the Cold War by other means.

Peaceful co-existence in the Soviet interpretation is a neither-peace-nor-war kind of situation, but it seems to me preferable to the Cold War we had in Stalin's time when tensions, mutual hostility and the danger of actual warfare were present in everyone's mind. There is now a conscious attempt by the Russians to avoid a Berlin blockade or a Korean war type of confrontation; they are trying to work out a modus vivendi.

But the fact that the Russians' motives may not be particularly friendly to us—as I believe they are not—should not take away from the value of what they and we are trying to do. It may well be that it suits us as it suits them to lower the temperature, and it may also be that the resulting détente will be favourable to us. We have as much to gain as the Russians have by agreeing to a process of this kind provided that we realize what we are doing, don't take our cloak off, don't lower our defences, remain on guard and watch to see what happens.

URBAN: But is it, I wonder, psychologically possible for a democracy to remain on its guard if the taxpayer sees that a security document has been signed with the Soviet Union, that the credibility of American protection is undermined, and our relations with the Soviet side are increasingly conducted in an atmosphere of economic co-operation and the joint management of international crises?

Already we have seen French and German students putting pressure on their Governments against armaments and conscription. Would it be possible to sustain public support for large armed forces and long military service under conditions of détente? Wouldn't western governments be much more likely to reduce force levels than their East European counterparts in response to short-term trends? Wouldn't Soviet capabilities thus grow and ours diminish? I would have thought the likelihood of all these things happening was very real, in which case the political impact of Soviet armed superiority would be enough to change the whole pattern of West European behaviour towards the USSR. That is what negotiating from strength means, and it might very well lead to a slow Finlandization of Western Europe. It would be quite unnecessary to invade Europe, and I don't think the Russians have any intention of invading it.

HAYTER: The idea that we must keep up an atmosphere of tension because otherwise we are going to weaken our capacity to resist is a rather cynical way of conducting one's affairs. One maintains, you are implying, artificially an air of tension in order to persuade parliaments and people to vote for military credits: I don't feel that is a way in which one can operate in a free country. Nor does it do justice to the intelligence of people in the western democracies.

Given the nature of modern warfare we are able to make the kind of provisions that make attacking or putting pressure on the West a highly dangerous proposition. So I do not see the military danger— the danger of an all-out war—as a great one, as long as the Americans, on whom all such matters depend, maintain the kind of armaments they have, and I see no likelihood of their varying that.

Now a lowering of tension could very well work both ways: it could make the Russian people—little influence as they have over their Government—begin to wonder whether they need to spend quite so much time and money on military preparations, and that might have a kind of impact in the Soviet Union which would be more valuable than anything *we* could hope to achieve by trying to tie détente to concessions in Soviet domestic policies.

But let me come back to the problem of moral attitudes. Pittermann and others who think like him are saying: because we don't like the way in which the Russians run their society, we won't deal with them unless they change their regime. This seems to me a highly dangerous and indeed paradoxical doctrine. After all, I don't suppose the Russians like our regimes very much, but they are not suggesting that they won't deal with us unless we install communist governments everywhere, making it a condition of détente that we change our regime.

The basic problem here is the belief that it is morally wrong to do business with countries of whose policies one disapproves. It may be, indeed it is, distasteful to negotiate with a tyrannical regime, whether of the Right or of the Left. But if the tyrannical regime is firmly in power, and if its actions, interests and objectives clash with our own in a way which threatens the peace of the world, then one must overcome one's distaste. The moral wrong lies not in dealing with tyrants but in allowing one's distaste for such dealings to prevent one from taking steps to avert a major catastrophe to mankind. There are certain tyrannical regimes, for example, those of General Amin, of Albania and of Bulgaria, with which one is not obliged to have any relations if one does not want to, because their power and importance are not such that to ignore them would bring world peace in peril. But the Soviet Union is not in that category. It is there, it is very powerful, it crops up everywhere. We cannot ignore a country like that simply because, for very good reasons, we detest its internal regime. We cannot alter its regime; we cannot even, as the affair of the Soviet-American Trade Agreement shows, influence its conduct in a matter which is not really central to its policies.

Nowadays we are all complaining bitterly of the economic pressure the Arabs are putting on us through the oil sanctions to change our policy towards Israel. This is almost exactly what it is suggested we should do to the Russians; but at least the Arabs are pressing us in the defence—as they see it—of Arab interests; they are not saying to us: 'Unless you convert yourself to Islam you won't get any more oil.' Yet this is more or less what Pittermann is suggesting we should say to the Russians. This is of course, a *reductio ad absurdum*, but it is not as remote as all that from the conditions Pittermann would like to have the Russians meet.

I notice Pittermann complained that Kissinger was behaving like Metternich and that he himself was taking a much more moral line insisting that moral elements ought to come into foreign policy. But of course it is Pittermann and people who think like him who are behaving like Metternich. Metternich organized his Holy Alliance to see to it that liberalism did not spread to Austria, Prussia, France and Spain, etc. Well, this is almost exactly what Pittermann wants us to do in relation to Russia. I think it is ultimately as meaningless and unacceptable to liberal opinion as Metternich's policy was.

URBAN: I am not sure if your analogy is clear to me. Are you equating western social democracy of the 1970s with the Holy Alliance, and the Soviet Union with liberalism? I would be reluctant to see any parallel between nineteenth century liberalism and the single-party and ideologically intolerant system of the Soviet Union unless we agreed with Soviet propaganda that Soviet communism *is* the liberating wave of the future.

HAYTER: Of course I am not equating western social democracy with Metternichian autocracy. My point was that Pittermann, like that other Austrian, Metternich, seemed to be trying to organize a league of like-minded states seeking to impose their political ideas on the rest of Europe. But the political ideas in question, in the two leagues, are, of course, entirely different ones.

URBAN: You seem to be taking a slightly neutral view of the differences between the western type of democracies and the communist regimes. You are saying: the Russians are not making it a condition of détente that we change our governments, so why should we try to make it a condition that they change theirs before we will deal with them? But can we weigh the two systems on the same pair of scales? We have on our side a collection of broadly like-minded parliamentary democracies; they are highly imperfect, disputatious and often seemingly ungovernable. But with all their grave faults, they are not institutionally oppressive or unmindful of the needs and dignity of the individual. On the Soviet side, however, you have a system that is a dictatorship by its own definition, moreover one that has—as we know from Khrushchev—deported, imprisoned, starved and killed millions, not in the first heat of the revolution, but systematically, in cold blood, over a large number of years. Aren't we, as states and human beings, under some obligation to demonstrate our revulsion at the regime that has caused all this suffering, even though we may want to achieve a détente with it for fear of calling down upon ourselves the even greater evil of a nuclear war?

HAYTER: There is, indeed, an enormous moral difference between the democracies and the Soviet system, and I do very much want that system to change. The point I'm trying to make is that governments have to deal with other governments—they have to deal with situations which exist in the world. We often have to deal with governments of which we morally disapprove, and we have to try and arrange conditions in the world so that war does not break out. Our basic interest is to make sure that a reasonably peaceful world continues and that minimum relations between governments are carried out as best they can be. But I don't at all think that this means that we have in any way to give our moral blessing to regimes which we regard as detestable. I suppose ninety per cent of the inhabitants of this country, certainly of those who know anything about it, would consider the Soviet regime one of the worst that there has ever been in history. Yet we have to deal with it as it is; we cannot hope to change it by moral gestures—these would be as ineffective as if the oil producers would not sell us oil unless we all went on pilgrimage to Mecca.

Governments cannot be expected to take this kind of attitude to each other, and here we have to draw a strong distinction between what governments can and can't do and what public opinion and non-governmental people can and can't do. If I were still in government service I shouldn't find it easy to talk freely the way I'm talking now about what I really feel about the Soviet regime. But the fact that governments and their servants have to observe certain restraints does not mean of course that *public opinion* can't do everything by any action open to them to make plain the detestation they feel for the Soviet Government's treatment of dissidents, emigration, racial discrimination and so on.

But these are not issues governments can bring into their transactions at inter-governmental levels. The only way in which we can move forward in the direction of a more liberal Russia is, paradoxically enough, through détente. If we have a less tense relationship with the USSR a certain intercommunication of ideas might follow. You might get an internal relaxation—perhaps contrary to the will of the Soviet Government—within the Soviet Union itself, and this might lead to changes in the direction that people like Sakharov and Solzhenitsyn are working for. We would find it much easier to deal with the kind of Soviet government that eventually emerged.

URBAN: The dilemma facing us in pursuing détente with the Soviet Government is summed up in what has been called the Kremlin's first law of thermodynamics: the more conciliatory the Politburo is in its external policies the tougher it is in its domestic policies. From the Soviet point of view, this may well make sense. If Moscow can no longer justify some of its illiberal internal policies by pointing to the dangers of an aggressive American capitalism, German revanchism and the like, it must create an atmosphere of ideological siege to provide a substitute.

HAYTER: I have seen this suggested but I'm not sure what the evidence for it is; I can't see any correlation between the two. I agree with you that there has lately been a lot of pressure on dissident writers and intellectuals but I don't know whether the connection with détente is clear. It is conceivable that there is a connection. If so, it is rather encouraging because it shows that what the Soviet regime is afraid of is that détente may expose their country to a penetration by western ideas. But in fact I do not think the alleged Kremlin first law of thermodynamics exists. The Malenkov-Khrushchev period, after Stalin's death, was one both of relaxation of international tensions (ending the Korean War, settling Austria, etc.) and of the beginnings of substantial internal liberalization.

I notice that in your talk with Pittermann you quoted various East European sources to the effect that peaceful co-existence does not mean an armistice in the ideological confrontation and that the western world will not be spared communist propaganda. The curious thing is that communist propaganda is not in the least dreaded by the western nations. Between the two world wars western governments were always trying to get agreements with Russia that the Comintern would stop communist propaganda because it was thought very dangerous. Now there is very little inhibition on communist propaganda; it is going everywhere freely and nobody pays the least attention to it. On the other hand the trembling fear which the Soviet regime seems to have of western ideas reaching their people is a sign that their faith in the solidity of their system is far from being firm.

URBAN: I sometimes wonder whether we take Soviet spokesmen seriously enough when we hear them insist that there can be no suspension of hostilities in the ideological confrontation. There is a tendency to regard such talk as part of Soviet liturgy, or as a sop to the Party diehards, but remembering how totally we misjudged the intentions of Hitler because few of us bothered to read *Mein Kampf*, and those who did refused to take it seriously, it may be as well to remind ourselves that in Soviet thinking détente really is (as you have said) Cold War by another name.

Soviet ideological declarations have been endorsed by a number of bilateral talks and agreements between the Soviet Union and the East European countries. Their purpose is probably to immunize Eastern Europe ideologically and culturally. But while this apparently defensive action is being taken, Soviet spokesmen emphasize that America and her allies are being forced to the conference table. B. Svetlov wrote in *International Affairs* (February 1972): 'The Cold War-mongers have not laid down their arms.' However, 'having lost much of their room for manoeuvre, the US ruling circles were forced to reckon with the realities of the situation in international affairs, and in particular, had to take a more sober view of the prospects of Soviet-American relations.' Hence the American willingness to seek détente with the Soviet Union.

This kind of language is closely echoed in the East European states, even in relatively permissive Hungary. For example György Aczél, a Secretary of the Central Committee (as he then was) and a member of the Politburo of the Hungarian Communist Party, said in the autumn of 1973:

> Two world systems, capitalism and socialism, the working class and the bourgeoisie, social progress and reaction, the forces of peace and the forces of aggression are locked in battle in every sphere of life. We are passionately and unequivocally committed in this struggle. . . . Proletarian internationalism is our inexhaustible source of strength. . . . The goal of the class-struggle, which is being waged on an international scale, has not changed, nor has the aggressive nature of imperialism. Imperialism, however, is increasingly unsuccessful in its efforts to hold or regain its position by armed force. The historic victory of the international workers' movement, of socialism, and within it primarily of the Soviet Union, achieved and still achieves peaceful co-existence overcoming the resistance of aggressive imperialist forces. We are speaking of compulsion, that is, the compulsive force of realities, of the development of socialism.

Also, the non-reading of Soviet sources, or unfamiliarity with the ideological framework in which Soviet policy makers operate, can lead to dangerous misunderstandings. Walter Laqueur has pointed out that in the writings of Senator Fulbright, for instance, the concept of 'bridge-building' occurs frequently. For example, in *The Arrogance of Power*, Fulbright says: 'If, however, the US fails to lead the West in the building of bridges to the East then Western Europe will almost certainly continue to build bridges of its own.' In another instance: 'The building of economic and cultural bridges could pave the way for the reunification of Europe.'

The trouble with Fulbright's idea is that the Soviet leaders see 'bridge-building' in a totally different light. 'Bridge-building is the old poisonous brew now being poured into freshly labelled bottles', V. Kortunov wrote in *International Affairs* (August 1972): 'It is an "imperialist trick", designed to undermine the dictatorship of the proletariat and the Communist Party's leading role under the slogan of democratization'.

I am quoting these examples at some length because I know you have yourself written on the close relationship which exists between Soviet ideology, power politics and national interest.

HAYTER: I have indeed written extensively on this problem and my conclusion was that one can't separate the element of Soviet propaganda from that of old-fashioned Russian national interest. They coincide very closely, and I have often said and written that one must take Soviet pronouncements absolutely seriously. The Soviet leaders have been very consistent, since the time of Lenin, in their utterance on peaceful co-existence. More recently, at the time of the Prague Spring, those of us who read the Dresden communiqué, the five-party Warsaw letter addressed to the Czechoslovak Party, and Shelest's Kiev speech in July 1968 (to mention only the most obvious) had no excuse for not suspecting that the Soviet Union would countermand the Czechoslovak type of liberalization, with main force if necessary. Also, I very much agree that unfamiliarity with the Soviet ideological framework can be a great disadvantage. For example, the Czechoslovak reforms were denounced at the time in *Izvestia* (11 July 1968) as part of Washington's bridge-building activities. Of course they were being denounced on many other grounds too, but 'Building Bridges on Rotten Foundations' was the title of one authoritative warning.

Naturally, the Yugoslavs, Albanians and Chinese are perfectly aware of the importance of reading and digesting Soviet pronouncements. The Yugoslavs' anxiety to get an unambiguous statement of the non-applicability of the Brezhnev Doctrine to their own situation is therefore easy to understand and sympathize with.

That is why I am saying that, provided we understand that détente for the Russians does not mean a change of heart, provided we understand that it is an effort to get our cloak off us, provided we understand and accept all this—as I think we should—we ought to go ahead with détente. I don't think we are so weak or feeble-minded that we can't keep up a reasonable degree of caution in dealing with Moscow just because there isn't a high degree of international tension in the world.

We ought to be quite clear in our own minds that the Russians have not changed their policy, that they are basically hostile to us because of their ideology which is reinforced by Russian national interest; but ideology is the main constituent, as I tried to show in my book *Russia and the World*. With that said, however, I would repeat that an artificial maintenance of tension suits us as little as it suits the Russians and that it is worth-while working out a policy of détente provided we do it with our eyes open.

URBAN: One of the challenging ideas Pittermann put to us was an appeal to the Soviet leaders to humanize and liberalize the Soviet variety of socialism. He said: 'The West European socialist parties have more or less successfully injected socialism into a free society. It is now the turn of the communist parties in Eastern Europe to inject freedom into the fabric of Soviet socialism. I can assure you that when that has happened we shall have détente at the drop of a hat.'

This is really an appeal to the Kremlin to behave (in the words of former United States Ambassador Charles Bohlen) less like a cause and more like a country, and I gather you don't believe that the chances of this happening are very good.

HAYTER: I think it is very unlikely to happen; the chances of major changes occuring in the Soviet Union are slight. If they do happen, it will be perfectly splendid and I would agree with Pittermann that most of our international problems would rapidly cease.

But, as we have both said, we must take the Russians and what they say at face value, and it is clear from everything they have said and written over the past half century that a transformation of socialism on the lines Pittermann would like to see just isn't going to happen. This isn't the way Soviet minds are working. Therefore, the chances of the present regime being overthrown and replaced by another with a different set of policies are, we must all admit, very small indeed. So we are left with the fact that we are likely to be faced in the foreseeable future—that is to say, the only kind of future which it is worth making plans or models for—with the kind of regime that runs the Soviet Union now. And that is, as I have just said, a basically hostile regime, and we have got to work out some way of living with it. I don't think we shall find it easy to live with it if we say: 'We'll only deal with you if you yourselves behave in a way more like us', as Pittermann is suggesting. This does not seem to me to be practical policy in the modern world.

URBAN: One question that worries me rather more than most is whether a détente of the kind you have in mind isn't in fact going to make it easier for the Soviet leaders to avoid the liberalization of Soviet domestic policies than it might otherwise be. Let me explain what I mean by quoting the views of two students of Soviet affairs.

In an article in *Foreign Affairs* (October 1973) Wolfgang Leonhard says that the decisive problem for the Soviet Union since 1969 has been the Government's inability to solve the country's economic problems. The obvious conclusion—to make a fresh start and open new economic perspectives through a fundamental modernization of the outmoded, centralized bureaucratic system—was apparently rejected by the Soviet leaders because they feared that economic reforms might lead to demands for political change on the Czechoslovak pattern. The only realistic alternative was (says Leonhard) an 'opening to the West'—a policy of moderation coupled with long-term scientific, technological and economic co-operation. 'In other words, the Soviet leaders have consciously initiated a policy leading toward rapprochement in order to *avoid* a liberalization of domestic policies.'

The second view—that of the Soviet geneticist Zhores Medvedev—appears to be sounding a similar warning. Medvedev feels that the Soviet scientific and technological community is a considerable force for liberalization. It managed to prevent a great deal of re-Stalinization after the fall of Khrushchev and it was, and is, in a strong position to exact concessions from the regime in exchange for its co-operation. If—as a consequence of détente—technology, patents and know-how reach the Soviet Government ready-made from western sources, the Soviet scientific community's bargaining power is undermined and the Government's ability to resist reforms unwittingly supported.

I attach particular significance to this analysis because Medvedev—although now in involuntary exile in the United Kingdom—does not believe that détente could or should be tied to Soviet domestic liberalization. He feels that there is no realistic alternative to a slow process of democratization from within the existing system; nevertheless he is very conscious that Basket Two—technological and economic co-operation—might deprive Soviet scientists and technologists of the leverage they now enjoy as the brains behind the Government's economic plans.

HAYTER: Medvedev must know a lot more about this problem than I possibly can, but, for a number of reasons, I have always had slight doubts about this argument. First, I have never found the scientific community a great force for political change: they want to 'do their thing' and they tend to be rather non-political. Provided they get the liberty to pursue the kind of research or make the kind of gadgets they have set their hearts on and are not interfered with in their games, they tend to toe the line of the prevailing system. We saw this in the case of some of Hitler's best-known technologists and we can, I think, see it in Russia today. Of course, there have been exceptions, a notable one being Sakharov who is clearly one of the most politically motivated men in the country and a man of great courage. If he were Secretary-General of the Soviet Communist Party, all our problems would be over. But he is, alas, a voice crying in the wilderness. We know from Sakharov himself that the so-called Democratic Movement consists of a few dozen concerned individuals, and that, for a number of reasons, which we in the West may find it difficult to understand, the sympathies of the ordinary Russian are not with them.

The second reason for my doubt is that the pressure for internal reforms has to come from wider strata of Soviet society than that represented by scientists, and that this pressure has to be a continuous process. Now the best hope of widening the base of reform-minded Russians and injecting an element of continuity into the reform process is to extend rather than restrict contact with the western world at all possible levels. Appetite comes in eating—the wider the ground covered by an exchange of people and information, the more securely the habit of having and demanding such information will establish itself. And I firmly believe that men involved in co-operating with western scientists, technologists, economists and managers will, probably by a very slow process, eventually work for a political liberalization of Soviet society possibly through a pluralization of the single-party system. Keeping the Russians at arm's length may do them a certain amount of short-term damage in slowing down their economic progress, and it may even, as Medvedev suggests, take away some of the scientific community's bargaining power. But the long-term objectives of détente are better served by co-operation than non-co-operation.

Wolfgang Leonhard may be right in saying that the Soviet leadership decided on an 'opening to the West' as a substitute for internal reform, but I cannot see how such an opening can be effectively pursued without a significant extension of contacts between Soviet citizens and their western counterparts. This, at any rate, is one of the points we are trying to bring home to the Soviet Government when we talk of the need to incorporate Basket Three—the free flow of information and people—in any security arrangement we may sign with them. The Soviet scientists and technologists are certainly very conscious of the need to make these contacts a wide-ranging and continuous affair even though the Soviet leaders may be opposed to them.

URBAN: Parallels are sometimes drawn between the appeasement of Hitler by the British and French Governments in the 1930s, and the détente we are pursuing with the Soviet Union. They are drawn on both moral and practical grounds, the message being that by appeasing Hitler we lost both self-respect and a very good chance to stop him when he was still stoppable. I will readily admit that among those who see this analogy moral considerations predominate, but as such considerations come close to the bones of ordinary men and women, they will bear being looked at again. Goronwy Rees, a distinguished British writer and academic, formulated the point rather well (*Encounter*, November 1973):

> There were many people at the time who opposed Neville Chamberlain's policy of appeasement, not out of cool political calculation, for which most of them were not very well equipped, but out of a kind of moral instinct which told them that there could be no genuine basis for agreement between Britain and a state which, like National Socialist Germany, had deliberately abandoned any pretence of conforming to the normal rules and conventions which are the basis of civilized life; which indeed positively affirmed, and gloried in the affirmation, that in German eyes barbarism was preferable to civilization.
>
> In the same way, today, there are many people who cannot bring themselves to believe that any genuine basis of co-operation can be found with a state which, like the Soviet Union, systematically violates the constitutional rights of its own citizens, persecutes its writers, artists and intellectuals, uses terror and brutality as accepted instruments of state policy, condemns millions of people for trivial or non-existent offences to years of inhuman suffering and degredation, and recognizes none of those fundamental liberties which belong inalienably to all human beings. One might as well believe that it was possible for a human being to negotiate a meaningful agreement with a gorilla.

And Rees adds that so long as Kissinger's exclusive preoccupation with *raison d'état* is hedged around with uncertainties as to its outcome, who can blame anyone for 'having doubts, if not positive distaste, for the policy of détente and, even more, profound misgivings about what the position of the West may be if after all it meets with failure'?

HAYTER: There is a certain parallel, but of course the word appeasement can be used in two senses. Before the Munich period it used to have connotations such as 'trying to calm things down'—détente in reality. However, after Munich appeasement became a dirty word because it came to mean making concessions, generally at other people's expense, in order to assuage an aggressor who might otherwise go for you; you threw children over the sledge so that the wolves could eat them and not you. It is this kind of appeasement that is being rightly condemned by the world as a whole; so if one says détente is appeasement, one is perhaps giving it the wrong kind of categorization.

But if we mean by appeasement an attempt to remove or diminish the dangers of war—to make international tensions less menacing than they are—then appeasement is a perfectly desirable policy and one that anyone is entitled to pursue.

URBAN: But *aren't* we being asked to make concessions at the expense of others when we're invited to guarantee the status quo in Eastern Europe? It is true that the situation in Eastern Europe has been accepted and indeed scrupulously respected for the past twenty-five years, but in a very important sense Eastern Europe is culturally and historically part of us, which Russia has never been and is not now.

It was Raymond Aron who recently argued—and I very much agree with him—that at the moment political alignments cut across the cultural and spiritual affinities between the two parts of Europe. A strong element of confrontation will persist, he says, so long as certain freedoms and rights inherent in our shared civilization with the East European peoples have not been restored in Warsaw, Prague and Budapest.

If we look at détente from this point of view, aren't we under some tacit obligation to withhold our signatures from legitimating the de facto unelected governments of the East European states? This could and would obviously in no way change our continued respect of the status quo, but it would remove any misunderstanding that détente is, in fact, a first cousin of appeasement in the pejorative sense of that word.

HAYTER: There is some truth in this argument although of course there is a difference between accepting a status quo which you cannot alter, and altering the status quo in favour of an aggressive dictator, which was what was done in 1938. It is pretty clear that we cannot change the status quo—if we needed proof of that we only have to look at what happened in Hungary in 1956 and Czechoslovakia in 1968. Even that very modest degree of liberalization which the Czechoslovaks were pursuing was repressed with violence by the Soviet Government, and it was clear that we could not intervene. I don't think anyone *would* have wanted us to intervene—I don't think anyone suggested that any action taken by the western powers could have saved Czechoslovakia in 1968.

I myself was a little critical of the American Government for having made it too plain in advance that they were not going to intervene, but the fact is that when it came to the crunch, they could not have intervened and didn't. And if they didn't then, I can see no other occasion when they could. It is therefore perfectly clear to me that there is nothing the West can do to alter the status quo in Europe.

Now this isn't quite the same position as that of Munich, because there the status quo was the independence of Czechoslovakia, and on that occasion the British and French Governments put enormous pressure on Czechoslovakia to yield and, in fact, to surrender to Hitler. In 1968 the status quo was Czechoslovakia under Soviet hegemony from which the Czechoslovaks were trying to escape to some extent, and we could not intervene because by doing so we should most probably have caused a world war. So although there is an analogy between the two situations, it is far from being a complete analogy.

URBAN: Would you regard a drastic change in Finland's or Yugoslavia's present position in favour of the Soviet Union a breach of the status quo? The Soviet-Finnish Treaty of Friendship, Co-operation and Mutual Assistance could be invoked whenever the Soviet Union perceived a threat of military attack against her territory from Germany or countries allied with Germany. A Nato request for reconnaissance bases in northern Norway to replace the American base in Iceland—to mention one possibility—might bring Article II of the Treaty (which provides for joint military consultations) into effect with potentially far-reaching consequences for Finland's neutral position in the status quo.

HAYTER: Your question on Finland is a very difficult one to answer. My impression is that even if the Soviet Union suggested invoking Article II of the Treaty, Finland's internal position as an independent, sovereign state need not be affected so long as the peace were maintained. Any other action would not fit into our picture of what the Russians might do if my reading of their thinking is correct.

A more marginal and dangerous case would be that of Yugoslavia. Yugoslavia is always counted by the Russians in their pronouncements as part of the 'socialist commonwealth', and it is laid down in Soviet doctrine that relations between nations in the 'socialist commonwealth' are not governed by peaceful co-existence but by what is called a higher form of international relations: proletarian internationalism. This implies the right of the 'socialist commonwealth' to intervene in the internal affairs of one of its members if, in their judgement, the socialist regime there is in danger. And this confers the positive right—indeed the duty—on the 'socialist commonwealth', which really means the Soviet Union, to intervene to maintain communism inside Yugoslavia.

Now the Yugoslavs are (as I said earlier) very much aware of the reality of the danger of such an interference if, for instance, after President Tito's death, the present fabric of the Yugoslav state and society threatened to fall apart or could be so represented. Well, one is in very little doubt that if the Russians tried to invade Yugoslavia the Yugoslavs would resist, and this would lead to a situation open to very grave dangers. But if we had détente, if our relations with the Soviet Union were more relaxed, this kind of situation might not provoke a violent reaction in Moscow. In conditions of a real détente it should be possible to handle a Yugoslav crisis by direct, confidential, frank talks between Washington and Moscow. Similar situations can easily be envisaged elsewhere—Berlin, the Persian Gulf, and above all the Middle East. Direct contact under conditions of détente of this kind should prevent conflicts escalating owing to misconception of each other's intentions.

URBAN: Your position seems to me to be close to Kissinger's on most of the questions we have so far touched on: you seem to be principally concerned with power-relationships, and I understand very well that at a time when the alternatives are so daunting, this concern must, to some extent, override moral considerations.

Nevertheless, I wonder if *you* would go as far as Kissinger—and Brandt—did in maintaining that it is not realistic for foreign policy to try to influence the domestic affairs of the states you are dealing with. When questioned by the Senate Foreign Relations Committee shortly before his appointment, Kissinger said that the argument also applied to South Africa and that it would have applied to nazi Germany too. Brandt, on his part, said that he would have pursued his *Ostpolitik* even if Stalin were still at the helm in the Kremlin.

I find these statements slightly disconcerting, especially as Kissinger repeatedly says in his writings that power and diplomacy alone cannot comprise a sound policy—a nation must have higher purposes. What, one may ask, might these higher purposes be if—at a time when in *The Gulag Archipelago* Solzhenitsyn is revealing the unspeakable and unpunished horrors of the Soviet camp system— our efforts are concentrated on befriending the very men who were, in one way or another, responsible for those horrors? The American people in particular are very conscious of the need to be, and to be seen to be, moral beings in their policies. They are ashamed and almost incapacitated by the Watergate affair, and I would suggest that in the long run they may experience a similar loss of self-respect if détente were bought at too high a price. I must confess that this self-searching quality is the one I admire most in the American people, for their seemingly impractical and seemingly self-destructive moralism is also a self-correcting device—the backbone, in fact, of any democracy.

HAYTER: Well, it is difficult to answer the first part of your question as it deals with a hypothetical situation. The problem with nazi Germany was that its internal policies had a dynamism which inevitably extended to foreign affairs and forced, or seemed to force, it to expand in a way which endangered the rest of Europe if not the rest of the world. This has been true of the Soviet Union too at certain periods of its history, certainly in the later Stalinist period, although there was in Stalin's policies always an element of caution—a feeling that time was on his side and that his goals did not have to be achieved within the next decade. Hitler was in a hurry. The difficult problem we had to face with Hitler was the extreme hatred which he aroused by the persecution of the Jews. This became much less concealed and much more violent after we had gone to war with him, but even before 1939 it was clearly there, which made the acceptance of his regime, as one with which one could decently deal, always very doubtful. The same is true of the South African regime. It is very distasteful to practically everybody in the world, but South Africa, unlike nazi Germany and the Soviet Union, is no particular danger to anyone outside its own borders.

At the same time South Africa, the Soviet Union and nazi Germany are all countries with which one would not want to have close relations—even relations at all if one could help it. But in the case of major powers like Germany and Russia—they are there in the world; one has got somehow to limit the degree of harm they can do to the world, and this must be done by the means that seem most appropriate to the particular situation. If they are in a very aggressive mood, one must organize coalitions against them. If they seem to be in a less aggressive mood, one can perhaps work out ways of living in relative peace with them. But none of this implies any kind of approval of the manner in which they conduct their internal affairs.

I know that all this sounds like power-politics, and that power-politics are dirty words in the American vocabulary. I can only say that the Russians play power-politics all the time; I once heard Stalin with my own ears, at the Potsdam Conference, say 'policy should be based on the calculation of forces', and if that is not power-politics I do not know what is. I do not think his successors are all that different from him, in that respect at least. Now if someone is playing power-politics with you and you do not play it back, you are in a rather weak position; it is rather as if you tried to counter a rough football tackle with a chess move. Kissinger at least seems to be playing football, not chess.

URBAN: You say that the nazis' treatment of the Jews generated so much hatred abroad that it came to influence the western powers' attitude to nazi Germany. Have you any explanation why the West has always taken a much more lenient view of, or indeed refused to believe, the crimes and atrocities committed by the Soviet regime, and especially by Stalin?

I once talked to John Strachey about this and his explanation was that while the Germans' crimes were committed within the tribal culture of the West and were thus a terrible self-indictment and a warning of what could happen to us all, Soviet misdeeds never had this effect on us because we never felt Russia to be part of our political culture and so never expected Russians to behave like Europeans. Russian misdeeds did not reflect on our civilization—the German ones did.

HAYTER: I agree with Strachey. West Europeans tended in the past to regard Russians as semi-barbarous, and have therefore expected less of them than of the Germans. But there is another point. The Soviet Government could, with a superficial plausibility, represent their persecutions as politically justified, as suppression of elements hostile to socialism, and in this sense some people in the West, provided they were unaware, as they mostly are, of their extent and intensity, could feel some sympathy with the Soviet Government. But persecution of people simply because of their race is clearly wholly irrational and unjustifiable, and no one but the lunatic fringe could feel any sympathy with that.

URBAN: I have already briefly touched on the fact (if fact it is) that the Soviet Government's decision to see western capital, technology and expertise invested in Russia amounts to a request for what used to be known as development aid in less polite times. Let me assume for the purpose of this argument that the Jackson Amendment does constitute interference in Soviet domestic affairs and that no such thing could be tolerated by a sovereign state. But are *we*—the future donors of capital and technology—really so denuded of imagination and power that there is no incentive we can hold out to the Soviet leaders to induce them to change their internal policies to an extent that would at least make it possible for us to co-operate with them without being haunted by the idea that we are dealing with the men who ran and perhaps still run the Gulag Archipelago? If common sense demands that we should not overload the political processes on the Soviet side by making demands on the Russians which they cannot satisfy, haven't we a similar right to ask the Soviet leaders to show some consideration for the kind of thing that is domestically acceptable in a democratic society? I would have thought the Gulag Archipelago and the psychiatric asylums were certainly not acceptable to us in terms of our internal political processes, and are bound to tie the hands of any western government in its dealings with the USSR.

HAYTER: Of course 'Gulags' and the misuse of psychiatric asylums will always be unacceptable to opinion here, and we should never hesitate to say so. But nothing we *say* can change them, and I have argued throughout that to try to tie changes of this kind to détente would be self-defeating and counter-productive.

The implication of what you say is that détente is advantageous only to one side—the Soviet Union. As I indicated before, I don't think this need be so. Most people in the West would prefer a more peaceful world to repeated confrontations. If this can be achieved, we shall all of us prosper, including perhaps the Russians. But I do not believe that we could achieve this peaceful world if we imposed on it a price which no Russian Government would pay. There may be commercial advantages for western countries in trade with the Soviet Union, but it is no good trying, so to speak, to cash these advantages twice over, once in political and once in commercial currency. I do not believe that expecting political concessions in return for technology and investments would work. One may get a few gestures but little more, and one would run the risk of Russia reverting to a variety of Stalinism. Perhaps you would prefer that—you have argued yourself that this would keep people on their toes, keep them alert and so on. I'm not sure if that is how I would want to do it if I were in charge of things.

URBAN: I don't suppose, then, that Basket Three—the free flow of people and ideas—has any chance of genuine acceptance by the Soviet Government. Given the Russians' passion for secrecy, a really free flow would surely strike them as subversive.

But supposing Basket Three were accepted by the Soviet side under pressure from us under the slogan 'all exchange is indivisible'—that it is as unfair to exclude our radio broadcasts as our advanced technology—how could we make sure that such agreements were respected? How could we stop the KGB from buying up all copies of *Animal Farm, Le Monde* or *The Economist,* or tampering with western films as they are in fact already doing? And how would we react if Moscow simply told us that there were no Soviet scholars interested in eighteenth century English verse or American sociology, or that Soviet citizens had no wish to travel individually, or to see the capitalist world at all?

HAYTER: I am not really familiar with the contents of Basket Three. But I quite agree with you that a genuine acceptance by the Russians of the free flow of peoples and ideas is out of the question. In 1839 the Marquis de Custine wrote that 'the political regime in

Russia would not survive twenty years of free communication with Western Europe'. One might put the figure lower than twenty years now. The Soviet leaders know this as well as everyone else, and of course they will not permit 'free communication with Western Europe'. Nevertheless this is an area where perhaps something can be achieved. It is quite easy to put the Russians on the defensive on this particular battlefield. To save face, and also to maintain some reciprocal rights for their own activities, they may feel the necessity to make some kind of concessions here, to allow some movement of people to and fro, to let in a few western publications. It will not be much but we can probably get something. For instance, the circulation of *Anglia* and the corresponding American publication in the Soviet Union, enforced by insistence on them as reciprocity for allowing Soviet publications in our own countries, shows that we are not without bargaining counters. Of course the Russians will cheat on this, but something will get through and any penetration of the enclosed Russian scene is of real value. What they publish on our side makes little impact amid the multifarious confused voices of a free society; what gets published in Russia by anything but the stifling authority is altogether different in impact. We can and should press on this. It will not be merely a question of signing an agreement; continual vigilance over its enforcement will be necessary, and evasions will have to make an impact on other parts of the agreement more important to the Russians.

URBAN: It has been argued that Kissinger's rather cool *Realpolitik* lacks vision although he himself believes (as we have just seen) that a nation needs a purpose higher than that represented by a narrow interpretation of national interest.

Kissinger's attitude to détente leaves a lot of Americans and Europeans wondering what exactly it is we are supposed to be standing for. Averell Harrimann recently said: 'One hears that Kissinger believes basically in power. But the US must stick to its political ideals. When Roosevelt died, people in other countries wept in the streets; the same was true when Kennedy was shot. These men were as much realists as Kissinger. So was Churchill, and he thought the Bill of Rights the most noble document ever penned. Kissinger, I suspect, would not pay much attention to that sort of thing. But if the United States doesn't have political ideals, how else is she to have influence in the world?'

This brings us close to my original question: whether western foreign policy should be a more imaginative, universalistic, philosophical exercise than it is, in other words, whether we should act a little more like a cause and slightly less like a business. The Soviet idea that in matters of ideology no peaceful co-existence exists between the two systems is a game that can be played by two, and we are, I believe, by no means at a disadvantage if we do decide to play it.

HAYTER: I wonder whether leadership expressed in inspired rhetoric would be appropriate to our problems. Harrimann is, of course, quite right: both Churchill and Kennedy were *Realpolitiker*. They examined the problems facing them with an acute sense of pragmatism, but then they also had the special gift of putting their message with great oratorical force. They had a sense of style which can be all-important in certain situations. Kissinger hasn't got this flair, and it would not be very easy for Kissinger to take a great moral stance in foreign affairs when he looks over his shoulder at what is happening behind him in the White House.

But I don't think it would be fair to say that the line of his policies differs basically from that which Kennedy was pursuing. If it differs from that of Churchill it is perhaps more in the direction of accepting the facts as they are. Of course Churchill was dealing with a different situation: the Soviet Union was in an aggressive mood and he and Bevin were among the great organizers of the coalition—Nato—which stopped that aggressive mood from spilling over into action in Western Europe. Our situation today is different and different tactics are required.

Western policies vis-à-vis the Soviet Union have gone through three different phases since the end of the second world war. First, we had the immediate post-war period when Stalin was wrenching his people back from a sort of war-time all-nation coalition attitude into a mood of aggressive expansion, and this provoked us into organizing ourselves in Nato to resist this expansionism. Then, after the death of Stalin, we had a mood of uncertainty in Moscow; it wasn't clear where Russia was going and by whom she was going to be led. Unfortunately this phase coincided with the Dulles era in Washington, with 'roll-back' and other grand phrases about defeating communism occupying the stage without anything really being done about them. And now we have a phase in which both sides show a cautious acceptance of the existence and irremovability of the other, complicated by the presence of an important third factor, China, which was not a serious factor in the two earlier phases.

What all this means is that there is rather less room for rhetoric, a rather greater need for circumspection and a growing realization of the dangers that an endless expansion of armaments brings with it, not only in the sense that armaments have their own rationale and can lead to war, but also in that they undermine the economies of the countries involved. For all these reasons it seems worthwhile to both sides to explore the possibilities of limited agreements which may make life in a world which is half slave, half free, a little more tolerable for both halves. The concept of the idealization of leadership is very American. The Americans have this urge to love their partners, and if they can't love them, they hate them. They find it very difficult to accept the rather more pragmatic (and British) attitude that you have to live in the world with people as they are. You'd like them to change and you help them to change but you can't force them to change. And of course the fact is that Kissinger is not American basically and probably he does not have this impulse to highfalutin moral ideas, which sometimes we find agreeable when people like Churchill and Kennedy utter them, but not so charming when we hear them from the lips of John Foster Dulles. It is not the kind of thing the situation demands at the moment.

URBAN: What would we be losing in hard practical terms if we had not gone to the Security Conference? The Russians have been working for it, directly and through other countries, very assiduously since the Karlovy Vary meeting, and for quite a long time it wasn't at all certain whether the West would pick up the invitation. The British Government was especially reluctant to let itself in for a mammoth conference that promised to produce little more than a reaffirmation of time-honoured slogans about peace and the status quo.

The Soviet Government's aims were clear enough: the legitimation of Soviet hegemony in Eastern Europe, the modernization of the stagnant Soviet economy with western capital and know-how and—as a result of these—a beefing up of Soviet power vis-à-vis China, plus any grey areas where the West might be in retreat. As you have yourself said, the Chinese factor is the new element in the European security equation, and it is not to be wondered at that the Chinese are opposed to any security arrangement between the West and the USSR. What they dread most is that an American withdrawal as a result of détente, coupled with the failure of EEC to develop a united political and military arm, might lead to China finding herself isolated and facing Russian imperial power drawing support from the industries of a Finlandized Western Europe.

HAYTER: The gains of our participation at the Security Conference are tactical. I have always thought myself that it was a great mistake to refuse to talk to the Russians, if only to see if we could extract something from them. Dulles seemed to think it shocking to deal with the Russians at all. He thought that if you talked to them you would find yourself involved in unwanted situations. So he avoided talking to them, which gave him a reputation of being more dangerous and more aggressive than he really was.

I can only say once again: provided that you know what you

want, provided you know what you don't want to give away of any value and—very important—provided that you are prepared to be extremely patient, you may find that something will emerge from these talks which will be of benefit to both sides. I must stress my point about patience, for the Russians are very good at wearing us down by sheer obstinacy and their willingness to spend years, if necessary, at the conference table. But in this respect our short-comings are perfectly remediable. We—and especially the Americans—must learn not to be in such a terrible hurry. We *can* sit it out with the Russians, and we have done it before; we sat it out with them over Austria and it worked. On other occasions too we learnt to play their system at marathon conferences, refusing to give way on things that really mattered to us. As long as we know what we will and what we won't do, I am confident that the results of the security talks can make the world just that little less dangerous for all of us.

To sum up, then, we cannot hope for a regime in Russia that we can love. We cannot change the present regime, which is basically hostile to us, or even induce it to modify its policies or relax its grip on its satellites, though by insisting on reciprocity we may be able to infiltrate a few subversive ideas. But we can achieve a sensible re-lationship with it, involving a lowering of the temperature, the avoidance of confrontation and perhaps a deal on armaments. We should work hard on this, and never be afraid to talk to the Russians. We should carry on such trade as we find advantageous to our own economies. We must sit tight and keep our powder dry in this world which, as I said at the beginning, is going to remain half slave and half free for a long time to come.

FRANÇOIS BONDY

Cultural exchange and the prospects of change in the Soviet Union

URBAN: The idea of 'cultural exchange' makes me feel uneasy, for the linkage between 'culture' and 'exchange' conveys the impression that culture is some package of goods of known value which you barter away for other cultural commodities of the same value—and this isn't at all self-evident. 'Exchange' itself brings this analogy to mind, but we also talk of 'flows' of people and ideas; we insist that there has to be a 'balance' between the exchange of basketball teams and opera singers; and our cultural agreements are negotiated by state monopolies (ministries of education) with a fine sense for keeping a positive balance of payments between cultural 'exports' and 'imports'.*

I'm not sure if I know what exactly culture is, but I think I know what it isn't—it is not a commodity. Aren't we then betraying culture by forcing it into the Procrustean bed of intergovernmental barter?

BONDY: The question has been worrying me too a great deal lately. There is a lot of talk of making culture perform the kind of functions politics and economics do. This is, of course, nonsense. Culture is elusive; one cannot put it into any particular pigeon-hole, for it continuously crosses barriers. Culture, for an easy definition, is a flux, and fluxes aren't caught in baskets.

But coming to the specific case of having cultural exchange with the Soviet Union and the East European countries, my dilemma is that we betray culture if we have such relations but we also betray it if we refuse to have them. Those of us involved in seeing people from Eastern Europe and the Soviet Union and travelling to these countries are faced with the morally uncomfortable situation of having to entertain, meet and be kind to a lot of hacks and bureaucrats if we want to get through to the really valuable and independent-minded people, the creators, if you like, of culture. So one has to meet the apparatchiks, including often sinister people, and one has a tongue-in-cheek relationship with them. They will be very genial, they will

* Peter Wiles originated this analogy in his paper, 'On the principles of cultural exchange'.

49

joke with you and even give you subtly to understand that they, too, know perfectly well the nature of the game you are playing. There is double-talk on both sides.

This is clearly regrettable. But on the other hand, if—out of a sense of integrity and solidarity with the persecuted writers and intellectuals—you refuse to let yourself in for this game, then you may not reach these persecuted or isolated people at all. The amount of double-talk needed and the length of the detour varies, of course, from country to country, so one should not generalize, but it is true of all socialist countries that in order to reach the genuine people, you have to go through the functionaries.

I am therefore reluctant to accept the point implied in your question, namely that our attitude should be one of straightforward revulsion at this notion of cultural good. If, in order to preserve our integrity, we were to communicate with the genuine East European and Russian writers and scholars only through a clinically sterilized, narrow channel, then we might not be able to give them the feeling that they are in touch with us, which they so obviously need. I have seen it suggested before: walk on stilts through the excrement if you want to make any headway at all—but this amount of moral fastidiousness would be an easy way of evading the problem altogether and I am not for it. One might as well abandon any pretence that cultural exchange has anything to do with culture.

URBAN: The distaste one feels for the apparatchiks with whom one has to rub shoulders varies, I think, with the background of the apparatchiks. The standard opportunists are such an ageless type that I find them the least embarrassing to deal with—we know exactly where we are with them, and they are the vast majority. The hypocrites of the refined Tartuffian stamp are a more complicated case, but one's real difficulties start only with the hard core of true believers of whom there are, fortunately, not too many.

BONDY: Obviously we deal with people whose profession as bureaucrats is to oppress and silence a lot of people, to send them to gaol and asylums and—in Eastern Europe—to exert pressure and keep tabs on intellectuals in less visible ways, for example by preventing them from existing as intellectuals, preventing them from travelling, and so on.

For instance, in the coming days I shall be playing host to a leading cultural functionary of an East European state. The organization in my country which had invited him asked me if I would like to show him around, so I invited him to my house. Now I know that this man and many others like him have very little to do with culture, and the genuine writers of their country would be reluctant to have anything to do with them. However, if I refused to deal with functionaries of this sort while they were visiting us in the West, my chances of returning to the East European countries and of meeting the writers and scholars I really want to see would be much reduced. So I don't know how to avoid this kind of contact. There are, I know, writers in Russia and Eastern Europe who feel betrayed: 'You have wined and dined this or that monster and are making sure that the suppression of culture and censorship are here to stay.' But if you stand on your integrity and avoid the apparatchiks, aren't you punishing the people you are most anxious to help? It is an awful dilemma.

I was once invited to dinner at the house of a distinguished East European intellectual: I had marked the wrong day in my diary and turned up on the wrong night. There was some slight embarrassment—a government minister was there and a couple of other high officials. However, I was asked to stay and one of the topics we came to chat about was the films of a well-known director. 'It is a pity', I said, 'that we don't see enough of these films in the West and I'm told that some of them are heavily censored.' At this point one of the guests at the dinner table gave me a good-humoured look and told me with a broad smile on his face that he was the one who censored films and that he had unfortunately had to make a lot of cuts in the films of this director. Now it was my turn to be embarrassed. But the censor wasn't in the least put out; he said he understood my point perfectly and that he'd discuss the matter with the director.

You see, it is not a pleasant experience to be at dinner with a censor, but I am certainly prepared to be on good terms with anyone I can in Eastern Europe so long as this keeps my way open to the writers I want to stay in touch with.

URBAN: You are up against the oldest of dilemmas: do ends justify means? And, in this specific case, are the ends good enough to justify stretching one's conscience a little? I suppose in Eastern Europe the question is not being put very sharply at the moment for—with the exception of Czechoslovakia—the cultural commissars are not the unpalatable lot they are in Russia. But one has, of course, no assurance that this state of affairs will last, and it may well be that one day the means will become so heavily tainted again that they may nullify any good we may have hoped to serve by using them.

BONDY: Once you become professional about anything the means become your sole concern. In cultural exchange, too, we have reached a stage where we are beginning to feel that the means are self-sufficient—that keeping the channels open is an end in itself no matter what, if anything, flows through them. This is a great problem. I think we ought to subject the stuff that actually comes through these channels to very serious examination: whom have we actually helped? What publications, what translations can be directly ascribed to our interest? What films and plays owe their existence or staging to our encouragement? We have to draw a balance sheet to see whether we have in fact made any headway— whether we aren't under the illusion of having achieved something, whereas in reality we are just making excuses for some of our activities for the simple reason that they flatter our vanity. The lure of the red-carpet treatment has to be resisted.

It is under conditions of the latter kind that the medium of exchange becomes the message itself. It is then that the medium no longer transmits any message, or that the message is so garbled as to be meaningless. This can very easily happen.

URBAN: At what point would you refuse having apparatchiks sent over under cultural exchange agreements? As long as exchange is conducted through official channels, we aren't in a strong position.

BONDY: There are issues on which we cannot compromise. If, for example, the Russians propose to send us scientists who have condemned Sakharov in some open letter, we should flatly refuse to allow them in. People of this kind already enjoy too much western largesse and hospitality. We are, of course, caught in an ugly dilemma: we want cultural exchange, but cultural exchange may very well function against the people who create and represent culture.

There are issues on which we should even risk a complete breakdown of cultural exchange. Suppose a distinguished Russian mathematician is confined in a psychiatric asylum for his political views; then it is the duty of western mathematicians to stand up as a body and tell the Russians that they will see no *official* Russian mathematician until the one in the asylum is free to talk to them.

URBAN: But this solidarity is very hard to come by.

BONDY: It is, as we could see from the horrible example of the World Psychiatric Congress in Mexico where the assembled psychiatrists refused to protest to the Soviet Government against the committal of people to so-called psychiatric asylums on grounds of 'incurable reformist and utopian ideas'. *The Times* backed the refusal in an editorial, taking the line that psychiatrists throughout the world were in the same boat and that we in the West were in a poor position to rock it. The reason given was that in some western countries psychiatrists commit people at the request of their families, without being too squeamish about the patient's real state of mental health, and once committed, it is extremely hard to get them out again. The Russians (*The Times* was implying) do this sort of thing on government orders—we do it for different reasons, but we are in the same boat.

Our answer to this argument should be that this is the kind of boat we don't want to share with the Russians, and if it is true that we are sharing it, we must indeed rock it.

Eventually, but only under public pressure, the psychiatrists decided to make a token move at their Moscow Congress and saw General Grigorenko—but this didn't lead to anything. Indeed, the Secretary-General of the World Psychiatric Association came out with a statement saying that none of this was their business—psychiatrists were serious scientists and they *would* not meddle in politics.

I am scandalized by this attitude, for psychiatry goes to the heart of the most important questions we can ask about man: 'what is a human being?', 'what are human values?', 'what is normal behaviour?' and so on. We cannot permit psychiatry to become a technology, for if we concede that it is a value-free activity, we are in fact throwing the gates open to brainwashing and menticide.

So here we have a really frightening example of how cultural relations must not be conducted.

URBAN: At the 1973 Salzburg conference on détente, which we both attended. Thoreau's classic question was reformulated and put to us by Robert Byrnes: if our message to the Soviet intellectuals were to be summarized on a postcard, what would we be saying to them? I should like you to answer that question for I have my personal doubts whether we *have* the kind of message a man like Sakharov (or previously Solzhenitsyn) would expect from us—a message transcending complacent statistics about living standards, the permissiveness of our society and the pluralism of our political institutions.

BONDY: Well, postcards with a maximum of five words on them go at a reduced rate, so I would make our message very brief and simply say 'we are concerned', for the one thing our friends in Russia and Eastern Europe need constantly to be reassured of is that they have not been forgotten, that we are concerned over their freedom and are listening to every word they utter. We must remember that the voices of many Russian and East European writers, artists and intellectuals are not as loud as were Solzhenitsyn's —yet they have important experiences to convey to us, they have thoughts they want to communicate and wishes we would want to be aware of and satisfy. This does not mean that we have to accept everything they say uncritically, but we must keep our ears open and give their message the most careful consideration. And I know how crucially important it is for their morale to know that we are informed of what is happening around them—that we know who can and who cannot publish, who is free and who isn't, what pressures are being brought to bear on this or that writer, scholar or publishing house. This, I am sure, is the most important thing we can do.

What we write is in one way or another already conveyed to the unofficial intellectuals, and even if it isn't, they have a shrewd sense of discovering it for themselves; it does not have to be specially channelled to them. But the knowledge—and especially the well-publicized knowledge—of our concern is a great reassurance to them and it helps them with their establishments. A man who is in the focus of western attention is much more difficult to silence or to arrest than one who is not. I say difficult—not impossible—for the deportation of Solzhenitsyn shows that the Soviet Government has many illegal means at its disposal for putting (as it hopes) a man out of action without actually killing or physically silencing him on Russian soil.

Moreover, it is also in our own best interest to keep in touch with these people, for we have so much to learn from them.

URBAN: But do we? When we in the West talk of cultural exchange we silently—and I think rightly—assume that by and large we are the ones who have something to impart and people in the East the ones who have something to learn. This may sound patronizing, but is it all that unjustified? I remember a meeting I had with Kuznetsov some time after his defection from the Soviet Union: this once celebrated Russian writer, who is nobody's fool, was a babe in the woods as far as western literature of the last hundred years was concerned. Yeats, Proust, Eliot, Rilke were all news to him, and he made no secret of his bewilderment. One would rarely come across this kind of ignorance in an East European writer, but I don't think Kuznetsov is untypical of Soviet writers and intellectuals. So what exactly do you mean when you say 'we have so much to learn from them'?

BONDY: One of the two stereotypes we have about Russia is either that she is much more eastern than western or that she is a halfway house between Asia and Europe. But then suddenly along come people like Solzhenitsyn and Sakharov—and when I use these two names I also mean all those many, gifted samizdat writers whose voices are not reaching us—and they have a message for the world which we have always thought was typically western: the dignity of the individual, the inviolability of his conscience, his right to refuse to be submerged in race, class or nation. Here in the West such ideas are being very sparingly used these days—the clear sound of the trumpet comes from Moscow. This gives us much food for thought; perhaps we ought to revise our ideas about what is typically eastern and typically western.

URBAN: I would have thought this was the reaction of a few sensitive minds to fifty years of collectivism. I can see no sign that the ordinary Russian is any more inclined to assert his individuality than he was under the Tsars.

BONDY: This may well be so, but the culture we are now talking about is 'high culture' where the keynote is struck by people like Solzhenitsyn.

URBAN: Let me try and turn Solzhenitsyn and Sakharov against your principal position. It is quite clear from their many warnings that they regard détente on Soviet terms as a gigantic confidence trick. Buttering up a commissar every time you want to talk to a genuine writer is not the sort of thing these two men approve of. They firmly believe that if you accept Brezhnev's rules of the game, you'll be beaten by the Soviet system and you'll end up making Russia more powerful and more dangerous. So while we know from their own statements that Solzhenitsyn and Sakharov are extremely conscious of the benefits of western publicity, they are on record as disapproving of any move that might lend the Soviet system an aura of respectability. They feel, in fact, that our connivance at Soviet double-talk has already gone too far.

BONDY: Yes, they feel that. I suppose one of the tests may be when the Soviet Union first tries to enforce its interpretation of the Universal Copyright Convention signed in May 1973. Boris Pankin* made it clear that the Soviet Government would not permit Russian authors to be published abroad except through approved channels which would, of course, mean gagging the whole of unofficial Russia.

Solzhenitsyn promptly threw down the gauntlet by having *The Gulag Archipelago* released for publication in the West, not, I think, directly to challenge the Soviet gloss on the Convention, but challenge it he did all the same. However, with Solzhenitsyn's expulsion the question is unlikely to arise. Some other book may become the test case.

The Soviet Government ostensibly signed the Convention as an act of 'normalizing' a long-standing anomaly. The problem is that the Soviet leaders and the western world do not always agree on what 'normalcy' is. To official Russia the present relationship between rulers and ruled is normal. To us it seems highly abnormal and abhorrent. A 'normalization' of the copyright situation *à la Russe* may well result—in fact we know it will result—in the silencing of the voices that are trying to reach us. So when the Soviets talk of 'normalization', we ought at once to remember how that concept

* Boris Pankin is head of the Soviet Copyright Agency.

was used in Czechoslovakia and be on our guard. We reject this interpretation of 'normalcy', and if 'normalcy' threatens to cut the channels of communication between unofficial Russia and the West, we shall have to use unconventional means to keep those channels open.

URBAN: This touches on the question of Soviet 'laws, customs and traditions'. The Soviet premise for any security treaty is that we must respect 'Soviet laws, customs and traditions'. We are, rightly, I think, reluctant to go along with this formula for we find some of the Soviet laws and most of the customs and traditions detestable. The death penalty for the theft of state property, the internal passport system, which is a hangover from serfdom, and the arbitrary and inhuman treatment of ordinary people at every turn are normal things in the Soviet Union, but we can surely never agree that they are.

BONDY: Perhaps we ought to make a distinction here between Soviet laws, most of which are, on paper, civilized and acceptable, and Soviet customs and traditions, most of which are not. We ought to tell the Russians: 'We don't want you to respect our laws, but you don't even respect *your* laws. Your 'customs and traditions' run slap in the face of your own constitution. Why on earth should *we* help you to defy your own laws and permit you to get away with illegality?' After all, there is nothing in Soviet law to prevent citizens from gathering together in small groups and shouting 'Freedom to Czechoslovakia', or from publishing books abroad, and when they get arrested for these things, no law is quoted against them.

URBAN: The Soviet leaders' record of complying with this kind of point is not a very good one. While they may, so long as they have a stake in détente, refrain from doing certain outrageous things such as imprisoning or killing Solzhenitsyn—they are most unlikely to say to us: 'Give us your interest-free loan, help us to build a steelworks at Kursk, and we'll mend our ways on civil liberties.' They will want to keep their 'customs and traditions' intact *and* get the steel-works and fibre plants too. And by all the indications we can see at the present, the western world—and especially the Federal Republic which wants to get its *Ostpolitik* moving again—will quietly assist the Russians in having their way.

BONDY: One could argue that by speeding up the sophistication of the system in Russia you are also speeding up its demise, for highly-trained Russians will not (so it is claimed) put up with totalitarianism. I am not at all convinced that this is so. The simple and sobering fact is that our relationship with Russia is unlike that with any other country, and this is due to the historic, cultural and political 'otherness' of the Soviet Union. Pierre Courtade, former editor of the French communist daily, *l'Humanité*, described the Soviet Union after a recent visit as 'a Congo equipped with rockets', echoing Alexander Herzen's fear of 'Genghis Khan with the telegraph'. We have, frankly, no answer to this problem. The best we can hope to do is to encourage the custodians of the rockets to keep the rockets at bay and put a premium on any move the system may make to work its way out of its Congo. On the practical plane this means that, so long as the cost of keeping the channels of communication free is not unacceptably high, we should go on exploring any opening we may find—whether it is through radio, cultural exchange, scientific co-operation or whatever. But we must do this with our eyes open and be fully conscious that, certainly in the short run, the Soviet system is unlikely to change.

URBAN: One important point is whether the free flow of people and ideas—Basket Three—would really undermine the Soviet system and thereby fundamentally change the status quo. Do you feel that the Soviet leaders' fear is real, and if so, is it justified?

BONDY: I can't attempt to answer this question before first looking at the character of the personalities involved—a very un-Marxist approach foisted on us by the un-Marxist manner in which Soviet leaders come to power and exercise power.

Khrushchev did not have this fear very strongly, Brezhnev does. Khrushchev was an adventurous man, perhaps the last Soviet leader to believe quite sincerely that the Soviet system could stand up to competition with the United States, for it had, through its ideology, the key to a morally, politically and economically superior social order. Brezhnev appears to have no such faith whatsoever; he behaves like the head of a country that needs development aid to fend off the consequences of a bad harvest—a country that is economically unable to pull itself up by its own bootstraps and is openly acknowledging the economic superiority of the West. Khrushchev was storming around the world challenging everyone to tackle him on the rival merits of the socialist and capitalist systems, and he really *was* convinced that he would 'bury us'. Brezhnev knows that in 1974 the Soviet Union has no charisma—that a recipient of development aid cannot expect fanatical commitments at home or abroad, and that the 'God' has not only 'failed', but that its only chance to avoid being toppled is to exact the passive obedience of its citizens. The fall, when you think of it, from *The God that Failed* of the 1930s to a poorly functioning society that cannot afford to pay a modest *interest* on the loans it is trying to borrow from us, is truly remarkable.

All this prompts me to believe that the Soviet leaders of our day are genuinely worried that a free flow of people and ideas might upset the apple-cart.

On the other hand we have the example of Yugoslavia to show that a communist government can happily survive intense and continuous contact with the West. The Yugoslavs have hundreds of thousands of their citizens temporarily domiciled in Western Europe. They travel backwards and forwards, they enjoy western living standards and civil freedoms and carry the 'infections' of the West with them; yet the roof in Yugoslavia hasn't fallen in (and if it does fall in it will be for different reasons). So what we can learn from Yugoslavia is that the communist system—the one-party state—can co-exist with a much larger degree of openness, with a much freer movement of people and information than the Soviet leaders would allow.

URBAN: But what are the reasons for Yugoslavia's immunity? Of all the communist regimes in Eastern Europe, only two—the Russian and the Yugoslav—are indigenous. This entirely home-based, nationalistic nature of Yugoslav communism would partly explain its relative invulnerability. Moreover, one has to remember that the great migration of Yugoslav workers to the Federal Republic and other western countries did not start until after the Yugoslav Party had been thrown out of Cominform and the regime had considerably mellowed. There is, in addition, the cultural westernness of the Slovenes and Croats and their tradition, going back to the Habsburg Empire, of free communication with Austrians, Hungarians and Italians.

Of these conditions only the first—the indigenous nature of the communist regime—applies, and only partly applies, to Soviet communism. In all other respects the Soviet regime inherited a wholly different set of traditions—secretiveness, xenophobia, and centuries of isolation from the West. So my impression is that the Yugoslav regime's ability to resist western infections does not really allow us to infer that the Soviet regime would prove equally immune.

BONDY: Yes, there are these differences. It is, in history, always very difficult to make valid comparisons. What would communism be like in Poland, Hungary and Czechoslovakia if the Soviet Union had not interfered? Would there be any? Today Hungary, for instance, is much more accessible to western people and ideas (and vice versa) than any other communist state outside Yugoslavia, and Poland seems, to some extent, to be following suit. Yet communism in these countries is not collapsing. And my explanation of the survival of the system in these countries would be that the local regimes can afford a certain liberalization precisely because they know that the ultimate sanction—occupation by a tough and strong Russia on the pattern of 1956 and 1968—is there in the background to punish those who go too far. In other words, we can deduce no political laws about communism in Eastern Europe. We can only say that the geographic position of this or that country has made it inevitable that she should be under a specific form of communism.

But the position of Eastern Europe is *totally* different from Russia. Most of Eastern Europe is part of the West which happens to be under Soviet control—and I include, of course, in this notion of Eastern Europe Latvia, Lithuania and Estonia. Ninety per cent of what is written and thought there is western. Even under Stalin Eastern Europe was less hermetically sealed off than Russia. The inhibiting vicinity of the Soviet Union has never really eradicated the cultural westernness of these countries and it is most unlikely to do so in the future.

URBAN: Cultural exchange, then, with the East European countries is a very different proposition from what it is with Russia.

BONDY: Very different indeed, it is like talking to like. When you visit Poland, Hungary or Czechoslovakia, you are over-whelmed by a feeling that you are among western people with west-ern values—sometimes more western than our own values precisely because so many East European intellectuals feel cut off and frus-trated. And it is not just a minority—a small band of brave intel-lectuals, who carry this tradition of belonging to the West—but the broad mass of the people. It breaks surface now in this, now in that form and it is quite irrepressible. The paintings painted, the books written, the films made in Eastern Europe are so close to our own and so distant from the Soviet traditions that, seen from the Soviet point of view, they must surely seem even more squarely western than they seem to us. I am pretty certain that a good deal of the Russian apprehension about Eastern Europe has to do with this great cultural gap. The Russians can see that the East European countries aren't really part of themselves, that they are merely under temporary Soviet management, that they may explode in their hands again and that they can, therefore, never be regarded as permanent building stones of the communist world.

URBAN: You mentioned the culture of the Baltic republics as being part of the western tradition.

BONDY: Yes, recently I attended a writers' conference with participants drawn from both parts of Europe. Well, one remark-able thing I noticed was the behaviour of the Estonians: they sided in virtually all questions with the West Europeans and East Euro-peans and practically never talked to the Russians—not, mind you, out of any racial or nationalistic prejudice, but simply be-cause the Estonians were genuine writers while the Russians were bureaucrats—they had nothing to say to each other. And I suspect—in fact I know—that Estonian literature is much freer than Russian literature; it is much closer to Finland and Poland than to Russia. So it may be a useful mental exercise to carry the notion of a 'western' Eastern Europe further back into the multinational Soviet state itself, for it may well be that the dividing line runs deeper than we normally think.

At the same time it is perfectly true that in the Soviet Union—unlike Eastern Europe—the struggle for civil rights is entirely in the hands of a very small number of individuals. If you look at the background of the people who participate in the protests you will find that the girl talking to some American professor in Moscow is Tvardovsky's daughter, that the protest in Red Square is led by the grandson of Litvinov and so on. Wherever you go the dissident movement is largely carried by family traditions, some Christian sect, Jewish and other minority cultures. You can, unfortunately, too often identify the source of protest as being untypical of the Russian people as a whole. You could not do that in Poland or Czechoslovakia where the protesters are simply *Jedermann*.

URBAN: In an earlier part of this conversation you corrected a patronizing misjudgement we are only too apt to make—that in cultural exchange we in the West are the natural donors and the Russians and East Europeans the natural recipients and beneficiaries. If we think of culture in the broad sense and include in it, as we should, the political culture of a society, I can see a very real possibility that a two-way traffic in people and ideas may make *us* into the recipients in ways we may not find beneficial.

Take the increasingly complex relationship between the Federal Republic and the GDR. As more and more West Germans come to know East Germany at first hand, they find an emotional chord being struck by certain aspects of East German life. They discover that East Germany is a less rushed Germany, a land of simpler values and more innocence than pulsating, chaotic, over-saturated, materialistic West Germany which is open to every influence. The West German finds a purposefulness, a single-mindedness to life in East Germany that he misses in the West. My impression is that the more we are exposed to the perturbing complexities of our civilization, the more people will hanker after order, ground-rules and unchanging values, and for many of them an ideological framework is perhaps the next best thing to living in a state of grace, which, in a sense, it is.

BONDY: The lure of possessing a single key to the world's problems has always been very strong, and the knowledge that a power exists which is using that key in its daily policies can add to the attraction, especially if one is in a position to form judgements about it from a safe distance.

Stalinist Russia with its unspeakable crimes has had an immense attraction for western scientists, writers and scholars. In 1935 I was myself present, as a student, at the first communist-inspired Congress for Cultural Freedom—Gide was there, Malraux was there, even Musil was there, quite apart from people like Ehrenburg. This was the time when Soviet Russia had a magnetic attraction for western intellectuals and one overlooked the realities, and those people who did travel to Russia chose to shut their eyes to the facts. Koestler has brilliantly described this in his own case and so have others. Stalinist Russia, of which one normally knew only from a distance, was admired—the Russia which in our view has become a little more civilized, the Russia to which one can take package tours, has lost all magic.

Sartre, for instance, who backed Stalin, never backed Khrushchev—he felt that a dictatorial state should not expose its ills to the wide world. Distance increases the mystery—familiarity (as the saying goes) breeds contempt. Diderot, philosophizing from Paris, was profoundly attracted by Catherine's Russia, but when he *did* see Russia (he was conducting a series of philosophical discussions with Catherine at the time of Pugachev's uprising) his feelings cooled very quickly. Pugachev was publicly quartered and decapitated, and Catherine had the guerilla's limbs exhibited on wheels in four suburbs of St Petersburg.

Now the case of the West Germans is a peculiar one. The majority of young students of the New Left are no longer anarchists: many have moved over to the Communist Spartakus League and support the GDR. Even people like Martin Walser give their vote to the Communist Party. He, too, is for the GDR and so, to some extent, is Peter Weiss. Quite a few of the better writers have become communists not, of course, because they have been exposed to cultural exchange. It is much more because they want to shock their society by showing it that they mean business. And how do you do that? Not by talking in the name of some utopia that will obviously never be, but by being on the side of the big battalions which may one day really take over. And, in fact, when you stop being a talking shop and support a regime which has existed for twenty-five years and has now exacted recognition and can be held up as a practical model of society, people will sit up and listen to you because they are afraid that what you're preaching may come true. And what can give an intellectual greater satisfaction than the thought that he is capable of frightening people?

URBAN: I wasn't thinking so much of the back-room intellectual's admiration for power (though this is clearly as important as it is psychologically intriguing) as of a more and more bewildered western public's demand for a cohesive social and moral framework in which right is right and wrong is wrong. Our senses are battered by an information explosion we cannot assimilate; we are being assaulted by environmental crises, news of the exhaustion of energy resources with its awesome consequences, the collapse of governmental and presidential authorities, strikes, chaos in industrial relations, terrorism, technological innovations with which we cannot catch up and so forth.

When a society's bewilderment has reached that stage, almost any alternative may seem preferable—people will not only not shy away from a black and white answer to their problems, but they may be positively looking for one.

So I would not be too surprised if a lot of ordinary people would have this kind of reaction: 'Our institutions aren't working too well; our money is being eroded by inflation. Perhaps we ought to try something else. Why democracy? Why pluralism? Why a free for all in moral values? Wouldn't it be safer to have a narrower band of options and a stricter discipline? Hasn't the communist world got at least part of the answer—badly applied, to be sure, but couldn't we improve on it?' I would have thought the Germans might be especially prone to say (as some East Germans already do): 'These inefficient Muscovites have botched Marxism which is, after all, a German invention. *We* would know how to make it work.' Nor would this be a new departure in modern German history. Ricarda Huch wrote from Munich in February 1919: 'The opinion that the Germans are called upon to carry through what Russian Bolshevism would like to do, but cannot do, appears to me correct.'

Then there is also the fact that no country which has sustained a rate of inflation of over twenty per cent for long has been, or has remained, a democracy. To take one very pertinent example: between 1970 and 1973, inflation in the United Kingdom was running at an annual rate of about ten per cent, and the British shopping basket between December 1972 and December 1973 alone went up by twenty-three per cent, with a forty-six per cent increase in the price of all basic materials and fuels. In February 1974 the *Financial Times* commodity index was 225·58 compared with 114·63 a year before. In 1975 inflation reached 26%.

It is not a happy package.

BONDY: Well—to skip from young men to old men—Martin Heidegger, who still comes to Switzerland from time to time to attend seminars in private groups, said on one recent occasion that the GDR managed its university problems rather better than the Federal Republic. East Germany, he said, maintained at least some respect, some order and some authority. In 1933 Heidegger had very similar feelings about the nazis—now he admires the East German interpretation of Marxism as a social technology which has produced results. You can have this transfer of values if you are a psychological type that needs order in preference to all other things.

Of course, if you are looking for a radical alternative to a bourgeois industrialized society like ours, you are trying to find one that offers a complete contrast to it and is not just another—and poorly ordered—example of industrial society on the way to embourgeoisement, such as the USSR.

You mentioned the environmental package of problems: well, the Soviet Union faces pollution problems which are much graver than its development would warrant. The Soviets are very backward in this area—they are just beginning to be aware of what is at stake, and the piquancy of their backwardness is that it is grounded in Marxist theory, for in the labour theory of value, all value is ascribed to human work and none to natural resources—the value of these is rated zero; so it is, for a Marxist, extremely difficult to quantify pure air, clean water, energy resources, etc. and treat them as goods we may lose. To fight pollution from a Marxist platform is therefore much more difficult than it is for us because bourgeois theory—in so far as there is such—is at least entirely open-minded on this matter. Those who have been to Russia to look at Soviet pollution problems tell us that the damage done to the Volga and the Caspian Sea is quite horrendous and that there has been deforestation on a gigantic scale.

Coming back to the question of what kind of society offers a complete contrast to ours, it is obviously China, not the USSR, and China is in fact becoming the object of admiration of many intelligent and sensitive people. I know one of Europe's leading paediatricians—a researcher in premature birth—who believes that China is way ahead of us in social medicine. The 'barefoot doctors' (he says) practice a simple form of preventive medicine which is highly effective.

This kind of admiration for some particular achievement of a distant and mysterious dictatorship is familiar to us from the 1920s and 1930s when the Soviet Union was the object of admiration, only in the case of China the mystery is excitingly deepened by the unfamiliarity of the language, and ignorance or near-ignorance of Chinese history and culture, all of which makes it simpler still to visit China and come back convinced of the same sort of things western intellectuals—the Webbs, Shaw, Kingsley Martin, Gide, Feuchtwanger,

Romain Rolland and many others—used to be convinced of about Stalin's Russia.

The Soviet Union is (as I have just said) a poor man's version of the United States. It has no ethos of its own. It is trying to catch up with the United States, borrowing techniques from it and copying some of its values. These are the standards the Soviet leaders have set themselves. China is, so far at least, genuinely different or can easily be so represented.

URBAN: The anti-Americanism of many European intellectuals is probably an additional incentive to see China rather than the Soviet Union as the valid alternative to western bourgeois society.

BONDY: Yes, and this is affecting the European Left's whole attitude to cultural exchange with Russia. Anti-American feeling has always run high among European intellectuals, and the war in Vietnam has done nothing to lessen it. For example, Heinrich Böll recently turned against official Russia with the argument: 'If Brezhnev has lowered himself to talking and making pacts with a detestable man like Nixon, then I can have no respect for Brezhnev or the regime he heads.' The mere fact that détente has opened the channels between the leaders of the Soviet Union and the American leaders has turned many European intellectuals against Russia: how (they ask) can you compromise or even talk to evil people like Nixon? The European Left is looking for some embodiment of an uncompromising counter-force to the hated western establishment. As Russia does not look like being that any more, she becomes unattractive and the whole idea of having cultural exchange with Russia loses its fascination. And this is where China again comes into the picture—

URBAN: —except, of course, that the Chinese are also on their way to hobnobbing with the American leaders, in which case the European intellectual Left may soon run out of worthy targets of admiration.

BONDY: What can I add to your point about the accident-proneness of Germany? My impression is that what the West Germans like about the GDR is precisely that it has not caught up with modernity—that it is a more quiet, car-less place with many of the virtues of the older Germany still preserved intact. So if it is seen as a model, it is certainly not seen as a model of progress but rather of nostalgia.

URBAN: The German case has many peculiarities. Whereas in the United States and Britain 'culture' is never spoken of in the context of power, in Germany, and especially in France, it is. There seems to be a difference here between the Anglo-American and the continental traditions.

BONDY: Let me go into this in some detail. When the Americans talk to the Russians about cultural exchange, it is quite clear that they speak from a position of strength and with enormous self-confidence. Western Europe has no comparable power and we are much more likely to want to appease. This is not obvious to the naked eye, but the Europeans' tacit fear of the Soviet Union, their unwillingness to drive an issue home, is never far under the surface.

URBAN: I'm not sure that I agree with that. In the preparation of the Security Conference, for instance, America seemed much more pliable than most of Western Europe, and on Basket Three Europe is really carrying the ball. If you compare the American Secretary of State's speech at the (1973) Helsinki meeting with that of the British Foreign Secretary, the differences strike me at least as more than differences in style; I had a distinct feeling that the two men were reading from different scores.

BONDY: Western Europe is too large a word, for there is no such thing as a West European or EEC attitude to détente. The European attitudes vary according to tradition. The British looked upon the Security Conference as a straightforward exercise in foreign policy and could, for a long time, see no virtue in it. So they were, and are, quite tough. The French have, as always, played their own game. The French tradition of *rayonnement*—of looking on culture as a weapon in your political arsenal which you deploy the way you deploy your diplomacy—is a very old one and is being pursued with great vigour. A visit by the Comedie Française to the Soviet capital is regarded in Paris as an event of national importance—something the British would find mildly funny and quite incomprehensible. It is this cultural 'imperialism' that makes it rather easy for France to co-operate with the Soviet Union whose attitude to culture is, mutatis mutandis, rather similar—

URBAN: —which is not surprising as the Russian attitude to culture as a means of political policy is largely French in origin.

BONDY: Quite; in Russia, as in France, 'high culture' means prestige, it touches on politics, it has to do with the image of the country and so on.

The German case is different again in the sense that the attitudes of the people who make and condone policies suffer from a peculiar weakness: the Germans have always felt a great urge to be *Musterschüler*. They stood out as *Musterschüler* in the Cold War and are now models of tact in pursuing détente. Their inclination always to do a little more than what is required of them—to indulge in *Fleissaufgaben*—makes me feel uncomfortable. When German officials believe that *Ostpolitik* demands certain policies to be adopted in their diplomacy, they do not hesitate to apply them to culture, expecting German artists, writers and scientists to fall into line with them. This is where Germany's much-vaunted pluralism—codetermination—should come in but apparently does not come into the picture. Culture cannot be harnessed to diplomacy without utterly betraying itself.

Let me give you a recent, and by now famous, example. In the summer of 1973 Günther Grass was due to give a private reading from his works in Moscow in the house of Ulrich Sahm, the German Ambassador, who had also invited Grass to stay with him. Grass made his preparations—he had got indirectly in touch with both Sakharov and Solzhenitsyn, and Solzhenitsyn was prepared to give him a manuscript to take back. In the meantime Sakharov and Solzhenitsyn came out with their statements about the risks of détente. Grass received a private letter from Sahm in which he was told that in view of the new situation it would be better if he called off his visit, and Sahm withdrew his invitation. Sahm thought he was acting as a private person cancelling a private arrangement. However, Grass took the matter in a different spirit; he had the letter published, made two television appearances about it and discussed the issues raised by the cancellation in the press. He argued that if *Ostpolitik* meant that people who had travelled to Russia before could travel there no longer, because, for diplomatic reasons, culture had become too dangerous, then he, who had always stood up for *Ostpolitik*, must turn against it. *Ostpolitik* (he said) then becomes the betrayal of culture and of the Russian writers.

You might say Sahm's letter was a faux pas on the part of one German diplomat acting in his private capacity and over-zealous in his interpretation of détente, and that the German Government had nothing to do with the whole business. However, Grass's publication of the letter earned him a public rebuke from a spokesman of the Ministry of Foreign Affairs, who thought the case called for an exercise of official humour and punned the following sentence: *Das wollen wir nicht gleich an die grosse Blechtrommel hängen sonst kommen wir in die Hundejahre*. The spokesman wanted to be witty at the expense of a committed writer and at the expense of an issue which Grass took very seriously. This was really despicable.

Well, you know how governments—all governments, I think—tacitly sponsor research institutes, books and periodicals. Ten years ago the German Government sponsored rather hawkish Cold War type of books. Now they will not sponsor anything that puts across a truthfully critical view of the USSR because they think it goes against *Ostpolitik*. They are once again caught in the spirit of *Fleis-saufgaben*.

Then there was the case of the Russian poet Brodsky who had been invited to give a poetry reading in Munich. This was going to be subsidized, as all occasions of this kind are, by the Government-sponsored organization, *Internationes*. However, Brodsky is out of favour in Russia, and *Internationes* opined that an official subsidy would displease the Russians and refused to pay. Hans Maier, the Bavarian Minister of Education, eventually found the money; Brodsky came and his reading was a great success. But, mark you, the Soviets showed no concern either before or after the reading. There is no proof that they were in any way interested. Some over-zealous officials were simply anticipating Soviet displeasure.

URBAN: I should like you to give me an easy answer to my last question, which is a difficult one: is there likely to be any connection between détente and the domestic climate in the Soviet Union? In other words: do all our careful deliberations about cultural exchange, Basket Three and so on refer to the real world or are they nonsense?

BONDY: I must frankly say that I find a correlation very hard to establish. One should, of course, always be for an open-doors policy, free travel, the unimpeded exchange of people and ideas with all nations. However, in the specific case of the Soviet Union I can see no evidence that general trends in Soviet domestic policies have ever responded to particular acts of western policy. Whether the Soviet Government had an open-doors or closed-doors policy in its cultural relations with the West in the past fifty years was almost entirely due to internal reasons, not western influence.

I am speaking of general trends—of course it is true that Professor Barghoorn was set free and sent home under Kennedy's personal pressure, and that Solzhenitsyn was forcibly expelled rather than tried and convicted because the Soviet Government feared that the subsequent outcry in the world would damage the already tenuous fabric of détente.

But if you look at the 1920s and the 1930s, in the worst days of Stalinism writers and scholars and artists and musicians could travel much more freely to and from Russia than they can today although (and probably because) there were no exchange programmes. So I don't think we should delude ourselves into believing that détente and cultural exchange can have a fundamental impact on either making the Soviet Union more or less liberal than it is. Change in the Soviet Union is very largely the outcome of pressures within the Soviet leadership, and no one has, to my knowledge, yet found a recipe for wielding influence over the wielders of Soviet power. I'm not saying that it cannot be done; what I'm saying is that

we don't know how to do it. Nor do we know whether we have unwittingly ever done it on any scale that mattered. None of which
relieves us of the duty to go on trying.

ROBERT F. BYRNES

Can culture survive cultural agreements?

URBAN: The Conference on Security and Co-operation in Europe, and especially the third item on its agenda—Basket Three—has made the question of cultural exchange one of topical interest.

Do cultural contacts have a real influence on the course of political relations, or does an improvement in the political climate have to precede any thaw in the exchange of people and ideas? In what way can academic exchanges most profitably contribute to détente in the broadest sense of that word? Aren't 'cultural relations' almost by definition another way of saying that each side is hoping to have some impact on the thinking, values, tastes and priorities—that is to say, on the domestic status quo—of the other? And shouldn't this be welcome both to the communist side, because it is in perfect accord with their frequently proclaimed doctrine that in ideological matters there can be no suspension of hostilities with the bourgeois countries, and to us in the West, because free democracies are natural cultural exporters? And how should we react to the communist assertion that in the cultural field peaceful co-existence is ruled out between us? Should we follow suit and look upon culture as an instrument in political warfare rather than an agent that might help us to cement over our differences?

And what if a better understanding of the other side leads us, or them, or both to conclude that our differences are indeed insoluble?

One of the silent assumptions of the Cold War has been that Soviet Russian culture, as well as Soviet Russian society, are very different from our own. Was this a concomitant of the Cold War or is it still true that there are two different cultures facing each other—one closed, the other open?

BYRNES: My answer will be entirely negative. I don't think the Soviet cultural milieu has fundamentally changed in the past fifteen years. The changes we have seen are entirely on the surface. The authoritarianism of the system has not gone away, the bureaucracy has not gone away, centralization has not gone away and the secretiveness of the apparat—and the vast majority's willingness to go along with it—are just as predominant as they have ever been. For the American exchange scholar the difficulties are the same. If anything, the first signs of détente have induced an apprehensive establishment to tighten down the screws on the cultural and intellectual life of the country, possibly to pre-empt any contamination, possibly as a concession to the die-hards in the Politburo, and probably both. Eastern Europe is a different matter. It has a different history and different traditions. If one takes the same fifteen-year period, one cannot say—with the natural exception of Czechoslovakia—that Russia's cultural grip has tightened on the client states. Some of these countries have been able to come culturally closer to us, but then, as I say, they started from a wholly different base which makes any comparison with the Soviet Union extremely tenuous.

Our principal problem with the Soviet Union is that the Soviet Government, and to some extent the Russian people, have a different attitude towards culture and intellectual life than the governments and people of the United States and Western Europe. The role which the communist party plays in Russia and Eastern Europe is not duplicated in the United States and the West European countries. The role of politics in culture is one that Americans do not accept and will not accept and that most Europeans (one has to make some exception here for the French who have always had a politically coloured attitude to culture) would also reject.

Of course this makes cultural co-operation slightly difficult because, on the one side, culture is seen as an aspect of a totalitarian political programme, while on the other, at least ideally, we should like to restrict the authority of political forces in the state and to have a completely free cultural life.

URBAN: How, then, are these differences overcome in practice? I suppose there is no way of getting round formal agreements if you want to cultivate relations with the Soviet Union, and culture conducted in a bureaucratic framework is almost a contradiction in terms.

BYRNES: Cultural agreements are an evil but they are perhaps a necessary evil. American and other western scholars would much prefer that there be no exchange agreements and that scholars be able to travel and work freely in the Soviet Union as they do within the West. The Soviet Union, however, will not allow western scholars or western artists or westerners in general into the Soviet Union unless the Soviets receive some reciprocal advantage which they deeply desire. So the formal cultural exchange programmes are the only way in which western scholars can study for any period of time in Russia. We regret this and we are trapped by it. Moreover, we may be on the way towards taking this system for granted, allowing it even to spread to our relations with other countries and within our own society, and thereby nullifying our belief that men and women of all kinds should be able to travel freely and to have free access to information.

Culture conducted by bureaucrats is a monstrosity. The Soviet Government is one of the most conservative governments in the world: once you have an agreement which says that we will send one jazz group and receive one basketball team—once you get that fixed in writing in a two-year or three-year agreement—it becomes impossible to change it. These agreements tend to get cast in concrete and tend to become an albatross rather than an engine. Also, as an American, I dislike bureaucrats and I dislike the influence and control they may have over any kind of operation. I dislike in particular Soviet bureaucrats because they are even less efficient than our own. But exchange programmes tend to be controlled by bureaucrats who don't understand intellectual work, who have no knowledge of universities and will, therefore, spoil and hinder these programmes. Formal agreements are, as I say, an evil. We should drop them as quickly as possible, but my hopes are not very high that it will be possible to drop them.

URBAN: How do formal exchange agreements affect educational politics in the western countries?

BYRNES: Restricting myself to America for the moment, there is a disagreement—a perfectly candid one—between the American universities and American scholars on the one hand, and the American government on the other about the purpose of sending American scholars to the Soviet Union. Seen from the American scholars' point of view, the principal benefit derives to those men and women who are professionally interested in Soviet studies, particularly Soviet history, literature and government. It is of great advantage to them just to live in Russia briefly. Usually they also obtain access to materials and libraries which are not available in the western countries; sometimes they are able to get into archives and have important conversations with the people in whom they are particularly interested. They return to America better-informed, better teachers and scholars than they had been; their books presumably reflect their improved knowledge and there is, thus, public benefit from time spent in the Soviet Union by these scholars because they raise our general understanding of the Soviet Union.

The interest of the American Government in academic exchange programmes with the Soviet Union is different. Our Government is, of course, in favour of increased knowledge and understanding of any country and it certainly applauds what our scholars learn in the

Soviet Union. But that is a small part of its interest. The Government's main concern is to persuade the Soviet Government that we are peaceful people in America and to remove any misapprehensions which the Soviet leaders may have about American power and policy. In other words, we seek to inform them about us, believing that the more they understand us the less likely they will be to consider us to be aggressive, and the more likely they will be to accept peaceful positions.

The State Department sees the exchange programmes as a kind of barometer in its relations with the Soviet Union: when the Soviet Government gives Soviet scholars a little more freedom to travel in the United States or expands an exchange programme or even (to be quite frank about it) honours an exchange programme, the State Department concludes from this that it reflects a particular line in foreign policy. This is, of course, an imperfect barometer but it gives the State Department some indication of Soviet foreign policy, much of which is usually concealed.

URBAN: Is it reasonable to assume that a trickle of American Slavists and ballet dancers, for example, will in fact change the Soviet leaders' view of what American capitalism is about?

BYRNES: It requires, at best, a very long period of time for this kind of conception to filter through the minds of the Soviet leaders. Scholars are more likely than politicians or the general public to take seriously the influence of gestures and ideas—which is not surprising as scholars deal in and believe in the influence of ideas, especially their own. Most people are not much influenced in this fashion and I am sure you are right in hinting that of all people the Soviet leaders would be about the least likely to be so influenced, especially on a cardinal point in their philosophy. But America is an optimistic country and this is the best hope we have.

URBAN: If we look at the character of the exchange programmes, it strikes me that the benefits are somewhat unevenly divided. You have yourself shown in one of your lectures that eighty per cent of all Soviet exchange scholars are scientists and technologists, whereas eighty per cent of American scholars, and indeed of all western scholar-teachers who have visited the Soviet Union, have been specialists in 'soft' subjects such as Russian studies, history, literature and political science. In other words, the Russians come over to assimilate our industrial know-how while we study Old Slavonic syntax. Do you feel the advantages are more even-handed than would appear from this quick comparison?

BYRNES: That is a good question. The western countries have, of course, given this matter a great deal of thought and concluded

that these exchanges were to their advantage. Stupid as we sometimes are in negotiating with the Soviet Union, we would not be so
stupid as to go on with a programme from which the Soviets would
obviously benefit more than we do. The Soviets, on their part,
clearly believe that *they* are the main beneficiaries, otherwise *they*
would not continue these programmes.

URBAN: Both sides, then, regard themselves as winners, which
is as it should be in international relations.

BYRNES: We use different standards. The Soviets get scientific,
technical and economic information which enables them to
strengthen their system at our expense; we get an understanding of
their society and a number of opportunities to influence the future
of their system.

URBAN: How do we do that?

BYRNES: We have western scholars and teachers living in
Soviet hostels and dormitories. They meet and mingle with their
Russian peers very effectively as Soviet society is a highly élitist society, infinitely more class-ridden than anything we have in America. Thus our scholars are getting to know and presumably
influence many of the future leaders of the Soviet Union, and the
hope is that these young Russians will gain a better understanding
of the West, and that the biases which they have from their Marxist-
Leninist classes, from their general educational background, from
the denial of information and from misinformation, will gradually
fall away.

URBAN: Do the Russians reap any benefits at this social, open-
horizons level?

BYRNES: I think they do. Their understanding of the United
States is improving. In 1970 (the last time I made a count) ten
former Soviet exchange participants were at work in the United
States either at the Soviet Embassy in Washington, at the United
Nations or as correspondents of Tass or the Soviet radio and television services. It is a great advantage to them to have men who have
lived in the American university community for a year. It is also of
advantage to us because we would much prefer to have as their
representatives men who know America and can report back to
Moscow more accurately than they would otherwise.

URBAN: I would have thought that, given the technocratic
nature of Soviet society, even Soviet exchange participants drawn
from science and technology might act as a leaven. The Soviet
Government obviously favours maximum know-how with minimum exposure to ideas (and minimum expenditure of hard currency, which is an important factor). But even on the most single-
minded seeker of technological know-how a measure of ideas must

surely rub off during a year spent in America.

BYRNES: Well, it goes deeper than that. When our exchange people—linguists, historians, musicians—return from the Soviet Union their chances of carrying great political weight in the American political arena are, to say the least, very limited. But in Soviet Russia, where government and society are more and more controlled by technocrats and where scientists and technologists are greatly in demand to run the elaborate machinery of a planned and centralized economy, the exchange participants are coming to yield some influence, and it is quite possible that these men will judge the West as they found it and not as it is depicted in communist propaganda. Of course, we can't be sure.

URBAN: Do the American exchange visitors to the USSR return more kindly disposed to the Soviet system than they were before?

BYRNES: The great majority of even those who went to Russia with a favourable view of the system return anti-Soviet. The others usually arrive back white with rage—seldom red.

URBAN: What sort of numbers are we talking about in these academic exchanges?

BYRNES: The numbers are disappointingly low. In 1973 some 150,000 foreign students and scholars were studying in the USSR, but of these only a handful, about 200, were from the western countries. The Fulbright Act of 1947 and the Fulbright-Hays Mutual Education and Cultural Exchange Act of 1961 have together supported an exchange programme involving more than 100,000 students and scholars from over 100 countries. But of these less than 300 scholars from all western countries spent a semester or more in Soviet institutions throughout this period. So our bridge to Soviet society has been very narrow and the number of men and women each way has been little more than symbolic. Nevertheless, the hope is that an increased access to information by Soviet and western scholars will act as a liberalizing and moderating influence.

URBAN: I'm always surprised by the poor foundations on which this hope is built, for our very recent experiences with nazi Germany tell a different tale. (I am, you will notice, re-formulating a question I asked you before.) Here was a state slap in the middle of Europe. It had few, if any, restrictions on cultural exchanges, or indeed on exchanges of almost any kind. Ordinary people could travel in and out of the land as easily as orchestras, painters or clerics. Moreover, Germany was at the top of the world education league-table. It had the largest number of Ph.D.s per head of population and great traditions in almost every field of learning and the arts. Its industries were managed by highly trained scientists and technologists, with friends, colleagues and travel-experience throughout the world. Germany's basic cultural tradition was a western tradition, with the Reformation, of course, standing out as a landmark.

None of this made it particularly difficult for Hitler to enlist the support not only of a very large part of the German nation, but also of the technical—and (with many honourable exceptions) of the non-technical intelligentsia. Nazi Germany became a totalitarian state and the world's leading power under the managerial guidance of a western-educated, much travelled and sophisticated technocracy.

I realize the imperfections of historical analogies, but as the nazi experience is the only comparable experience we have, I want to risk indulging in it and ask you: what reason, then, have we to suppose that a trickle of archivists and pop groups is likely to make any lasting impact on a country like Russia which lacks the historical and educational advantages Germany inherited in 1933?

BYRNES: I share your doubts—everything in Russian history and the Russian character speaks against a liberalization of this kind. However, Americans are slightly naïve people. They have seen that education in the United States has brought about such fundamental changes that they can't help feeling that it will do the same in the Soviet Union. They are optimistic about education throughout the world. Also, Americans have very much less knowledge of the long-term nature of history than Europeans. History is not a fashionable subject in the United States; to the young, nazi Germany seems as distant and as irrelevant as the Thirty Years War or Napoleon. So I suspect most Americans have never considered the Hitlerian experience, relevant as it certainly is to many of our policies vis-à-vis the Soviet Union.

Then there is the American idea that wealth defuses ideology. Most Americans believe that if the Russians develop a 'middle class' and acquire a taste for the same great panoply of goods and services as we have in the West—a large house, a second car, a cottage in the country, opportunities to travel and so forth—they will moderate and mellow, to use George Kennan's phrase.

As you know, there is no evidence at all that this is likely to happen: 'Middle class manners do not a middle class make'. The Soviet Union, as it becomes more prosperous, is likely to become more aggressive, rather than less so. There is in social history no evidence that rich people are generally less vindictive than poor people.

URBAN: The American misconception is shared by quite a few well-informed people on this side of the water. It was Sir Alec

Douglas-Home who said some years ago that it was safer for us to have fat communists in Russia than lean communists.

BYRNES: This may be true in certain circumstances: if the fat communists did not have the same political philosophy as the lean communists, and if their military power were not increasing—and it is increasing enormously—Sir Alec might be right.

In the last five years, since our contacts with the Soviet Union have expanded and become more relaxed, the western press has seldom missed an opportunity to tell us that our forces might bear cutting. I have never seen any mention in the Soviet press or in the speeches of Soviet leaders of reducing the size of *their* armed power. Détente has not influenced Soviet military planning. While Nato is in disarray and the battle for decreasing stakes in our common defence continues, Russia is increasing her strength. What is her vast and cripplingly expensive force for? What are the Russians planning to do with it? At the very least, their superiority in conventional forces provides a means for putting political pressure on Europe at the time and place of their choosing. A hot peace of this kind might make a shooting war, or even any openly war-like threat, quite unnecessary: individual Nato countries would be drawing their own conclusions from the disparity of conventional power.

URBAN: Is the knowledge which Soviet scientists and technologists are gaining in the United States actually helping to boost Russia's economic and military potential?

BYRNES: The impact of the knowledge gathered by Soviet exchange visitors in the United States tends to be exaggerated. The numbers are very small: in the last fifteen years fewer than 3,000 Soviet scholars studied in all of the western countries put together. It is true that more than eighty per cent of these were from the sciences and technology and presumably they take back to the Soviet Union knowledge and techniques in chemistry, biology, business management and so on. But, by and large, the western countries have denied these Soviet scholars access to developments of a distinctly military kind and to areas of knowledge where our superiority is so manifest that it would be the ultimate folly to allow the Russian visitors to learn from them. So I don't think there has been a vast increment to their know-how.

I'm not sure whether Russia's formidable economic difficulties are fully understood in the West. The Soviet system basically does not work—economically, scientifically and technically. In fact the figures show that the Soviet economy is slowing down. In 1972, according to the best American estimates, the Soviet GNP grew by only two per cent and the Soviet productivity increase was practically zero. The Russians have no choice but to turn to the West for assistance to get their economy going.

From our point of view, of course, the situation could be a lot worse. Imagine the fears we would have today if Russian size and Russian natural resources were combined with German efficiency or Japanese ingenuity for adopting the discoveries of others and making their own! The Russians have shown up very poorly in all this, and they are especially backward in the sciences that have developed in the last twenty years. In electronics, for instance, they started more or less level with the Japanese, yet in the use of computers the Russians are only ninth in the world whereas they should be second by virtue of their size. Some day the Russian people are going to ask questions: 'How is it that the Japanese, just as badly destroyed as we were, have been able to achieve this miracle? Or the West Germans?'

URBAN: One interesting line of argument, much favoured by a section of the 'Sovietological' academic community in the United States, is in direct response to the fragility and backwardness of the Soviet system and strikes me as providing a highly original interpretation of détente. I shall quote Vernon Aspaturian's formulation of it for it is especially telling.

Aspaturian dismisses the Soviet view that no peaceful co-existence is possible in the realm of ideology as essentially defensive rather than aggressive in its function, and there is, he implies, no reason for us to worry about it. He then proceeds to show that the only way of reassuring the Soviet leaders of our own peaceful intentions is by actively supporting them to make the Soviet system work. We have, he says, already achieved nuclear parity—what is now required is to help the Soviet Union to achieve 'system parity':

There are too many glaring weaknesses ... in Soviet society for the Soviet leaders to risk the importation of competing ideas or to allow the expression of dissident and critical views on the part of its own citizens.

What is more likely to open up the Soviet system is a policy not of challenging the system, but of assisting in its efficient operation. This would require the United States to help the Soviet system to work within the parameters of its own goals and objectives. It would result to some degree in subsidizing the Soviet social order ... by providing help in such a way as to minimize the defects and malfunctioning of communism. Only when the Soviet leaders are convinced that the United States is not interested in undermining or weakening its domestic institutions will they give serious attention to the relaxation of ideological controls . . . The Soviet Union might eventually wish to reciprocate, thus providing a more profound sense of security than that provided by a nuclear stalemate and mutual exhaustion. The Soviet leaders would have less to fear from foreign ideas or the dissident views of their own citizens, and the system could adapt and adjust to accord more faithfully with its own values and goals as expressed in the Soviet Constitution. In this manner, the Soviet Union might achieve 'system parity' just as it has achieved nuclear parity, and thus provide a more durable basis for peace and co-operation (paper presented at Stanford University in 1973; *cf. Survey,* No. 87, 1973).

BYRNES: This seems to me the most utter nonsense one could possibly come up with, and it shows a complete inability to understand the various historical factors that have gone into the making of western and Soviet society. I'm afraid Aspaturian represents, mutatis mutandis, a rather typically American approach to social problems: many Americans used to believe—mercifully fewer now believe—that if we poured money over our slum-dwellings, our racial minorities, over illiteracy and so on, these problems would go away. For twenty years now we have been indulging this simple-minded, materialistic and sociologically quite unwarranted idea, and our problems have progressively got worse. We are discovering that the solution of certain problems just cannot be bought any more than a person's love can.

What the Soviets are suffering from is not just an economic problem (although it is, as I have said, that too) and not just some misunderstanding of American motives. I'm appalled by the naïvety of this suggestion. The Soviet sources of hostility are much more deeply rooted than that. Even if the Soviet Union were a capitalist country, with the same political and economic system as our own, the problem would still be a very serious one because these two large countries have different national interests which tend to collide regardless of internal structure and ideology.

There was no real ideological hostility between Britain and Imperial Germany or France and Prussia, yet their national interests collided on many crucial points. These could not be bought off any more than the conflict between Israel and the Arab states can be bought off today. The conflict between the USSR and China is, of course, an especially serious case, for there you have national interest *and* ideology mutually reinforcing each other, which does not bode well for the peaceful future of these two countries.

In a sense Aspaturian's suggestion is a tribute to the character of American society—its generosity, its willingness to go the extra mile and to make a sincere effort to persuade the other side that we mean no harm. But it is, to put it charitably, a little simple-minded: Aspaturian is acting like someone who is robbed at midnight offering to surrender to the robber, not only everything he has on him, but taking him back home to give him his house as well.

URBAN: But *is* there a collision of national interests between the Soviets and the United States? Those in Europe who look with apprehension at the present duopoly between the two super-powers have a special fear that the Soviet-American détente is on the point of turning into an entente of sorts precisely because Russia and America haven't, and never have had, an eye on each other's territories, raw materials or commercial interests and have therefore never gone to war with each other. This has not been the case between the European powers and Russia, so an inward-looking and entente-minded America might (so it is feared) leave a politically and militarily disunited Western Europe denuded and exposed to Soviet blackmail—all of which would make the irresponsible talk of a collusion between, rather than a collision of, Soviet and American policies less fanciful than it sounds at the moment.

BYRNES: The traditional conception of national interest as one consisting of territorial claims, access to raw materials, etc. is, I think, no longer valid. America and the Soviet Union are natural rivals because they alone possess the power to do irreparable damage, through their nuclear arsenal, to each other and the world. This prompts them to step into any power vacuum that may occur in the world. Soviet policy since the end of the war has been one of expansionism—defensive expansionism first, signified by the incorporation of Eastern Europe and the Baltic states in the Soviet sphere of hegemony, a more offensive expansionism now in the Mediterranean area, and a still more offensive expansionism to come, as I firmly believe it will come. For example, Gromyko's statement to the Supreme Soviet in June 1968, asserting the Soviet Union's right to intervene anywhere in the world, represents a very different concept from Stalin's land-based, continental conception. The Soviet Union, Gromyko said,

is a great power situated on two continents, Europe and Asia, but the range of our country's international interests is not determined by its geographical position alone ... The Soviet people do not plead with anybody to be allowed to have their say in the solution of any question involving the maintenance of international peace, concerning the freedom and independence of the peoples and our country's extensive interests. This is our right, due to the Soviet Union's position as a great power. During any acute situation, however far away it appears from our country, the Soviet Union's reaction is expected in all the capitals of the world.

This is spelling out Soviet intentions with great clarity. And if any doubt remained as to what exactly Gromyko had meant, I have here a statement by Admiral Gorshkov, Commander-in-Chief of the Soviet Navy, summarizing Russia's new policy quite unambiguously:

In the past our ships and naval aircraft have operated primarily near our coasts . . . concerned mainly with operations and tactical co-ordination with ground troops. Now we must be prepared through broad offensive operations to deliver crushing strikes against sea and ground targets of the imperialists on any point of the world's oceans and adjacent territories.

While we may all welcome détente as a step towards a calmer international climate, I don't think Europeans have reason to worry that American policy is conceived in less global terms than Russian policy and that Europe would therefore be sacrificed to a Soviet-American understanding. I do not doubt that this is one of Moscow's objectives, but there are formidable risks to be faced by the USSR between having such an objective and trying to achieve it, and I'm persuaded that Moscow is extremely conscious of these risks and anxious to avoid them.

URBAN: While we discussed the merits and de-merits of having formal cultural exchange agreements with the Soviet Union, you said that the habit of having such formal agreements tends to impose its restrictive logic on our own academic freedoms and our relations with other western countries. What exactly does this mean in practice?

BYRNES: Official cultural agreements hoist the state in the driver's seat on both sides. That the Soviet Government is in direct control over Soviet cultural policy is unfortunate but has long been accepted. Alas, official cultural agreements also give our own governments—in America, the State Department—control over our part of these programmes. In the United States, the State Department isn't very keen on having this control, but it does now wield some influence over scholars and universities and we resent that. We want to be free from the influence of any government.

Secondly, the American universities become involved in relationships with the Soviet Ministry of Education and, willy nilly, accept restrictions placed on them and their scholars working in the

Soviet Union. These have unfortunate repercussions on two fronts: they tend to undermine the United States universities' *Lehrfrei-heit*—as bad but bureaucratically tidy examples often do—and they also tend to be applied to relationships between American scholars and their colleagues in other countries.

URBAN: What you are implying is that American universities have to exercise a form of self-censorship in the choice of their subjects and the scholars they nominate so as not to offend Soviet sensitivities. Some subjects are obviously more exchange-worthy than others, so the latter would tend to be neglected.

BYRNES: Indeed, and the best illustration of that is the simple fact that for American scholars the most interesting subject of study in the Soviet Union is Soviet political history—for example Stalin and Trotsky, the history of the party, the relationship between party and government, the purges of the 1930s, Soviet foreign policy, Soviet economic policy and so forth. We have never been able to send a single American scholar to the Soviet Union to look at any of these problems.

When the exchange visits first started there were applications on our side for the study of these areas, but the Russians resolutely refused to allow our applicants into their country. Then, realizing how applications in these fields of study would be treated by the Russians, our young scholars shifted their applications to the study of less sensitive questions, such as local government, which hardly exists in the Soviet Union, or nineteenth century political history and problems of that kind. In other words, the Russians turned us away from the issues which are central to us, and we are now doing their job for them, because our professors tell their young students not to bother with subjects that would prejudice their chances of being allowed into the Soviet Union. So we censor ourselves even more effectively than the Russians do because, to be on the safe side, we tend to exclude a much larger area from our studies than even the Russians might. I regard this as a grave and refined threat to the freedom of scholarship.

URBAN: Doesn't the hope of an exchange visit immobilize some American scholars' moral sensibilities?

BYRNES: Yes, it often does, and this is an insidiously dangerous cost we are paying for the exchange programmes. Soviet control over opportunities for study in the USSR has so influenced some of our more timid colleagues interested in going or returning to Russia, that they will not join other intellectuals in protests against the Soviet treatment of dissidents, minorities, etc. and will even refuse to participate in conferences that may be distasteful to the Soviet Government. The Soviet Government has in fact acquired some influence both over the direction of western scholarship and over western political attitudes.

URBAN: How are these facts reflected in the number of exchange-visits paid to the USSR by American students of Russian affairs?

BYRNES: Very sadly; between 1952 and 1965 only twelve per cent of young United States scholars who had been given fellow-ships for study of the Soviet Union on a national competitive basis sought to study *in* the Soviet Union. In 1964 only twenty per cent of those Americans who received Ph.D. degrees in any field of Russian studies in the previous five years had even attempted to work in the Soviet Union. Our scholars have concluded that Soviet studies are infinitely more easily pursued in western archives and libraries than in Soviet Russia. And this is, incidentally, also the conclusion of many Soviet scholars. Hence our knowledge of Soviet affairs is gen-erally more thorough and sophisticated—and of course much more objective—than that of our opposite numbers in the USSR.

Even a Soviet scholar with a high security clearance, which gives him access to certain types of information in the Lenin Library, cannot obtain access to materials that are freely available at Har-vard or Chicago or Indiana. Early issues of *Pravda*, for instance, are denied to the Soviet scholar unless he obtains special permission, and vast areas of Soviet literature are entirely closed to him for obvious reasons.

But secretiveness and compartmentalization are continuous throughout Soviet society, and this is one of the Russians' fatal weaknesses. Soviet scholars are blindfolded by their government. More important still, there is no impact from scholarship of a high quality on the upper levels of opinion in the government.

URBAN: I would have thought this would be an almost auto-matic process in a technocratic society.

BYRNES: It isn't in the Soviet Union and the basic reason for it is very simple: the quality of Soviet scholarship is, by and large, poor. You can't deny a chemist access to all the information he needs for his work and then expect him to come up with first-rate research. The one single factor which gives us the greatest advant-age over the Russians in this field (as also in many others) is our openness—we have better information and we are better prepared to make reasoned judgments on it. And it is because the Soviet scientific system is like so many intellectual ghettos, each sur-rounded by barbed wire, that the Russians are turning to us for knowledge.

URBAN: But wouldn't it be reasonable to assume that Russia's spectacular achievements in space technology and the armaments industry are due to a fairly efficient flow of information between research and its application, at least in these privileged fields of technology?

BYRNES: It is true only in these highly restricted fields. Elsewhere the spread-effect is extremely limited. In western countries scientific information is published very quickly and it spreads all through the system. Our scholars are also teachers so that the time-lag between a discovery in the laboratory and the teaching of that discovery, first to graduate students and then to undergraduates, is short. Not so in Soviet Russia where the great majority of scholars work in research institutes and have no teaching functions. This means a big time-lag, made all the more serious by the Russians' traditional secretiveness about publication even within their own country. Where our time-lag may be a year, theirs may be twenty-five years. So the Russians cripple themselves through the unfreedoms which their leaders have foisted upon them and about which they appear to be able to do very little.

URBAN: I have been under the impression that the Russians have a first-rate system for translating western publications.

BYRNES: This is, as far as I know, perfectly true but, for the reasons I have just mentioned, the translated information doesn't flow freely. Or take the fashionable concept: 'transfer of technology' (cross-fertilization between sciences and technologies). Here, too, the Russians have their hands tied by secretiveness, compartmentalization and straightforward muddle. For instance, a significant discovery in some branch of Soviet chemistry is not even allowed to run freely through the rest of Soviet chemistry, let alone cross that thin barrier which separates chemistry from biology.

In the western countries there is today a very strong interdependence between chemistry and biology, from which both sciences benefit and so, of course, does the public in terms of new chemicals, medicines and treatments. The oneness of all things, which Heraclitus stressed more than 2,000 years ago, is practical policy in western science. So long as the Russians are caught in their pigeon-holes, the left hand never quite knowing what the right hand is doing, there will be no transfer of technologies in the Soviet Union, and Russian scientists will continue to have to come to us for extra knowledge.

A colleague of mine at Indiana University made a study of the transfer of Soviet military and space technologies to the consumer industries. In the United States and in Western Europe this kind of transfer is quick and efficient. In the United States we make a special effort to harness any technology we have invented, or any new materials we have manufactured for the space programme, to civilian industrial uses: for example, new kinds of rubber are immediately put into the manufacture of better umbrellas, etc. My colleague's findings show that in the Soviet Union there is no such transfer whatever, again because the Soviet military and space programmes are completely cut off from the rest of science and industry. So the Russians have blindfolded themselves in this field too, and it is, of course, the man in the street, footing as he must the bill, who is deprived of all practical benefits. He can't turn a lunar module into an apartment.

URBAN: Hasn't the Russians' interest in American management techniques improved their performance?

BYRNES: It may help them in the very long run, and their willingness to learn is one of the more interesting developments in the last five years. The Russians *are* coming over to study management, but my impression, based on long familiarity with Soviet institutions, is that these injections will never pass as freely into the Soviet system as they would in a western country.

URBAN: Let me take this problem on a wider ground: if the information-flows do not, in fact, flow in the Soviet system, if there is suspicion and a grave lack of communication throughout the system itself, can the West hope to engage the Soviet Union in free cultural intercourse? Culture has to do with a meeting of minds, mutual enlightenment and the free circulation of thought and information. Exchanging bits of machinery, picking up a technique or exchanging a bass for a tenor are at best substitutes.

We are, then, back where we started this discussion: can we open up the channels of communication with the Soviet Union without opening up the Soviet system itself?

Russian history does not encourage us to think that the Russian system can be opened, or closed in so far as it has ever been properly opened, without enormous suffering. Peter the Great murdered his intelligent but reactionary son because he feared that his westernizing policy might be reversed. Stalin used similar means, on a much larger scale, for fear that his Russocentric policies might be jeopardized in Eastern Europe.

BYRNES: Our experience in the last fifty years shows that we have, with minor ups and downs, made almost no progress in this field. Basket Three at the Geneva negotiations should give us a chance to make a dent in this situation. How large a dent it will be is another matter. But we should absolutely insist that the Soviet Union cease jamming western broadcasts, allow the completely free sale and reading of western books and newspapers, the free travel of Soviet citizens throughout the world and free contact between foreigners and Soviet citizens inside the Soviet Union, to say nothing, of course, of enforcing the Universal Declaration of Human Rights and various other United Nations documents which the Soviet Government has signed, but fails to respect.

My general view is that the Soviet Party and Government will simply have to make a vast effort to understand the West if our hope of arriving at any kind of a peaceful relationship is to be realized. We'll have to press very hard for this, pointing out to the Russians that both the United States and the USSR have immense military power, that rightly or wrongly the western nations believe that the Soviet Government is a dictatorial one, that for historical reasons we tend to be very suspicious of despotic governments with vast military power at their beck and call, and that until the Soviets reduce this suspicion by opening up their country and enabling their people to understand other peoples, we are inevitably going to remain suspicious, and the 'Cold War'—which has never really ceased between us—will remain at a very high level.

Of course, even this would not be getting at the real problem, which is Soviet military power combined with ideological aggressiveness. It is this that will have to be reduced before we can talk of a genuine détente. However, if we can press home our suggestions under Basket Three—and make sure that any agreement resulting from them is respected—we shall have made a step in the right direction.

URBAN: My hopes of getting the Soviets to agree to your suggestions are not very high. Wasn't the Soviet move against Czechoslovakia in 1968 a prophylactic move against Basket Three really—against the spectacle of civil liberties, a free press, free radio and television asserting themselves within the socialist commonwealth?

BYRNES: Very much so. The Soviet leaders regarded the Czechoslovak reform movement as an internal Soviet process. What disturbed them most was the abolition of censorship in the Spring of 1968, because in the Soviet view control of information is the core of dictatorship, as indeed it is. Worse, the Czechs began to allow what really amounted to a rudimentary, multi-party system to take root and that, too, was highly objectionable to the Soviet leaders. They could see that the Czech example was an infection threatening to spread to the whole body of communist society—to Hungary, Poland, East Germany and then, through a restive Ukraine and the Baltic republics, to the Soviet Union itself. So the infection was removed and the doctrine of the limited sovereignty of the socialist states laid down.

URBAN: If a Soviet and an American cynic got together to discuss academic exchange programmes with no holds barred, my guess is that they would be saying something like this to each other:

Exchange visits are intelligence work by another name—you're trying to get at our technology, we're trying to get at your system. We're both trying to let the other learn as little about what he wants to know most as we can decently get away with. Basket Three is padding. Why pretend that it can be otherwise?

BYRNES: This *is* taking a cynical view of cultural relations—it might correspond to what the Soviets have been thinking about it all the time but it certainly does not accord with our view. The point is, we're not expecting to have any intimate association with the Soviet Union. We needn't echo the warning of Demosthenes to the Athenians that 'close alliances with despots are never safe for free states', for we aren't thinking of having an alliance. At the same time we can be entirely pragmatic about Basket Three and say to the Soviet leaders:

If you want us to do certain things for you, we'd like to make sure that we are not being taken for a ride, but we cannot be convinced of this until you allow the two protagonists concerned in any genuine détente—your peoples and ours—the elementary freedom of talking to each other. This is surely reasonable.

What we must be very much on our guard against is any acceptance of the Soviet formula that any security declaration must rest on the 'strict observance of the laws, customs and traditions of each other'. This formula is already enshrined in the cultural exchange agreements (now, alas, extended by ex-President Nixon and Brezhnev to 1979), and that is where all our troubles started. The last thing we want to write into a security document is the acceptance of Soviet customs and traditions. If the western states accept Soviet definitions they will be endorsing censorship and other controls familiar in Soviet society but detestable to ourselves.

URBAN: We have noted that among the unwelcome side-effects of sending western scholars to the Soviet Union is the fact that the Soviet government acquires influence over sections of our scholarship by discouraging certain fields of study and penalizing those who insist on pursuing them.

Patronage, and the withholding of patronage, are, of course, openly practised in the Soviet Union where the Soviet authorities are sole arbiters in deciding who is going to get a trip to a western country and who is not. I should imagine this can lead to grave injustices, for the lure of the West is such that the vast majority of scholars and intellectuals will do their utmost to avoid earning a black mark against their names for fear of weakening their eligibility. This, in plain language, means that American institutions which finance some of these trips are indirectly helping the Soviet authorities to discourage support of the Russian civil rights movement.

BYRNES: The ordinary Russian's loyalty to the system is not in doubt. He accepted the official line on the suppression of Hungary and Czechoslovakia and he is now sharing his Government's anxiety about China. But the main internal concern of the Soviet Government has been the élite who have always been given special treatment, corrupted and bought off by a great variety of devices. To mention only one: the differentials in earnings between the Soviet intelligentsia and the workers are much greater than in any western country. But there are two things the Soviet élite do not normally have and covet above all others: foreign travel and access to information. The opportunity to travel abroad, or the hope of an opportunity to travel abroad some time in the future, are the greatest inducements the Russian Government can offer; it is therefore very much in the interest of the Soviet intelligentsia, the great majority of whom haven't the mettle of an Amalrik or a Sakharov, to conform and support the system. So, as you say, we are in fact destroying one of the roots of the dissident movement in the Soviet Union by enabling the Soviet Government to offer this bonus, at our expense, to its loyal citizens.

URBAN: To appreciate the human tragedy involved, one has to meet some of the people debarred from foreign travel. Take the case of a distinguished Czechoslovak university professor dismissed from his job after August 1968. His successor—a loyal hack—was put up, and duly selected, for an exchange visit to the United States. How does the new professor's now jobless, demoralized and impoverished (if indeed not imprisoned) predecessor feel about all this? Here is one reaction I've personally come across:

Not only have I been thrown out of my job, not only has my wife been stigmatized and deprived of her part-time earnings, not only has my apartment been taken away from me and my son expelled from the university, not only do I live on a pittance as a hospital porter, but I now see that my successor, whose only claim to his post is his Party-card and his support of the hard-liners in 1968, is going to spend a year in America, on American money.

This is the sort of thing that provokes gut-reactions in Eastern Europe, and I should imagine Russian scholars in a similar position wouldn't respond very differently. If détente is to mean anything, we must, I think, make sure that the right to take up foreign invitations, and to return home when they have expired is extended to the unapproved writers and intellectuals both within the exchange programmes and outside them.

BYRNES: The situation is quite scandalous, and the first thing we must do is to acquire a much greater role than we have now in choosing Soviet exchange scholars. But I doubt if we can redress the moral outrage perpetrated by the sort of case you have described.

URBAN: How are the selections made?

BYRNES: In a typical case, say that between the British Council and the Soviet Ministry of Higher Education, each side sends fifteen to twenty scholars every year. The British Council chooses the British scholars through the regular fellowship process, paying due attention to achievement, character and seniority, and the Soviets do the selection on their side. Now this system has the (I almost hesitate to use the word) advantage that the western countries at least retain the right to choose the men and women they want to send to the Soviet Union. True, this gives the Soviet Government a reciprocal right to choose *their* people, but western scholars believe this is the lesser of two evils, for the alternative would be to give the Soviet Ministry the additional right to choose the western scholars they want to have in the Soviet Union too—a right they would dearly like to have and do, in fact, have to some extent, as the Soviet authorities are even now in a position to say that a western scholar's suggested field of study does not promise to be profitable or that research facilities cannot be provided.

URBAN: This may be an even-handed arrangement but I would not like to offer it as an answer to my outraged Czechoslovak professor.

BYRNES: It is the better of the two options. If the Russians want to send us hacks, as they often do, the hacks get some personal pleasure out of their trip, but the Soviet Government does not get the advantage it would obtain if it sent us competent scholars.

However, the rules of acceptance are being stiffened in the United States precisely because we want to avoid giving unwitting support to the Soviet and East European patronage system. Our policy now is that if the Soviets won't take our scholars as they are being put forward by us, we won't take theirs. There is also the consideration that when, out of politeness, we accept Party hacks from the Soviet Union, we lower our scholarly standards and put up with a lot of nonsense as though it represented genuine scholarship. This too must end.

URBAN: You've said that our scholars have no access to subjects of primary interest to them in the Soviet Union—communist party history, population policy, nationalities policy, economic management and many others. I know that the Soviet censor works from a three-hundred page index of subjects which cannot be referred to without special permission. These include items like natural disasters and major accidents in the USSR, jamming of foreign broadcasts, incomes of party and government officials, price increases or food shortages, the purchasing power of average incomes, the existence of censorship (Glavlit) itself, etc. It is a fair inference that the limitations on foreign scholarship in Soviet-Russian subjects inside the USSR would be at least as debilitating as the limitations imposed on the Soviet public itself.

Are we in the West restricting the work of Soviet scholars in comparable fields? Can they investigate our administration of justice, can they examine the purchasing power of the average American, can they look at unemployment, crime, prostitution, racial tensions, slum dwellings, the treatment of Indians in the United States?

BYRNES: They can, of course, do all these things and much else. We treat the Soviet scholar precisely as we would any other scholar. The Soviet scholar can travel anywhere he wishes in the United States, and he gets the same access to libraries, archives and laboratories as an American or British scholar.

URBAN: Supposing a Soviet scholar wanted to probe into some really murky area of American life such as the Watergate affair or local government corruption—would he be allowed to do so?

BYRNES: In the last few years Soviet Scholars have studied the student riots at our universities and high schools, the role of the blacks and other minorities, the negro liberation movement, inflation, unemployment, urban squalor, crime—anything they wished. The only restrictions on them are those also applying to American scholars, that is to say, studies which have to do with military technology in the narrow sense of the word.

URBAN: The Soviet visitors are, in fact, allowed to look into the weaknesses and breakdowns of western society?

BYRNES: They are.

URBAN: And they go home writing up what they have seen in scholarly works of good quality?

BYRNES: Their works are neither scholarly nor of good quality. Most of them are straightforward propaganda of a rather primitive kind. The Russians are now publishing one book of essays each year on American history and there is also a new journal in the field of American studies plus some more general writing on the American scene. I have been closely following this Soviet scholarship in recent years, and I can only conclude from what I have seen that the level is very low. The work they do is not only propagandistic but also shows an inability to understand our culture. Some of this Soviet writing is not even malicious—it simply displays a total lack of comprehension. There is, of course, also a great deal of directly malicious propaganda but that, to my mind, is less surprising than the fact that even those Russians who have spent a year in America work on a mental frequency that will just not pick up American signals. This is both sad and extremely dangerous.

There was a conference recently in the Soviet Union which brought together all Soviet specialists in American affairs. The total number was 130 and of these only a handful had ever been in the United States. We in America have some 2,500 scholars and teachers dealing with Russian affairs at our universities and a great percentage of these have been to the Soviet Union, most of them a good number of times. We have, on our part, made an enormous effort to understand the Soviet system which was a closed book to us for many years, and I think we have made good progress. The contrast with the Soviet scholars' lack of understanding of what makes us tick is all the more striking, and I would assume that this low level of understanding pervades the whole system, including the very top.

URBAN: My impression is that what puzzles Soviet visitors most is the American willingness to show them America no matter what crises might be shaking Washington, San Francisco State College or the negro ghettos. I'm sure the American predilection for looking into every nook and cranny of American public life and baring the American soul to the wide world with a zeal that borders on masochism must strike the Soviets as utterly incomprehensible.

I can see Soviet visitors reacting to this spectacle in two different ways. Some might be enormously impressed by the strength of a society which can afford to tear itself to pieces every two or three decades in full view, and to the obvious *Schadenfreude,* of its adversaries. Others, closer to the spirit of Potemkin, might think that a system which is stupid enough to allow itself to be pushed to the brink of self-destruction and which thinks nothing of inviting a hostile world to cash in on its discomfiture, deserves everything that is coming to it.

BYRNES: I don't think we know the answer to this interesting question. It would, in fact, be one of the most important studies anyone could now make to find out how the Soviets see us—to depict the Soviet estimate of what is going to happen in the USA. If they have the same view I have, then our situation is even more desperate than most Americans realize.

I have come across cases of both reactions you have mentioned, but I would hesitate to generalize about them. Most Soviet historians I have met in the United States were extraordinarily impressed by what they saw; it was quite clear to them that, with all our penchant for self-denigration, our social problems and our other weaknesses, we are an enormously powerful country. They could see that we are a land of outstanding vitality, enthusiasm and practical expertise, and that we are making visible progress in giving equal opportunities to blacks, expanding education, helping the disadvantaged, undoing some of the environmental ravages of mindless industrialization, and in a thousand other ways. Soviet scholars realize that some of these problems are very much like their own, and I would assume that they return home with a better appreciation of our strength and our ability not only to plan for the solution of vast social and technical problems, but actually to do the job.

But there are also Soviet scholars who fit into your second category. A lot of Russians worship power. They like a man who knows his mind and acts upon it. Visiting scholars of that psychological type return to the Soviet Union with a certain scorn for the United States because we have been so free in exposing our weaknesses.

I remember talking to one Soviet economist just as he was leaving the United States; I asked him what his impressions had been. He said: 'Even worse than I thought they would be.'

URBAN: This brings us back to a point I made in my introductory statement: what if a better knowledge of the other side leads us, or them, to conclude that our problems are indeed beyond solution? I should imagine your Soviet economist went home with that sort of conclusion in mind, and your disenchanted American scholars returning from Russia 'white with rage but seldom red' may have arrived at a similar conclusion.

BYRNES: The mistake we often make—and American intellectuals make it more often than most—is to believe that cultural exchange is going to solve our problems. I don't think it will, for cultural exchange does not get at the basic issue which is (as I said earlier in this discussion) Soviet power combined with the political ambition of the Soviet Communist Party.

URBAN: How, then, would you go about working for a détente with the Soviet Union? Would you make the satisfaction of Basket Three a condition of Basket Two? In other words, would you withhold aid, trade and investment from the Soviet Union unless Russia opened herself up to us as envisaged in Basket Three?

Peter Wiles has made the point that the West has two great weapons: high techology and cultural freedom. Both are highly exportable. The communists want the first and fear the second. We should not give away our technological advantage for an unproven economic hope—we must barter it away for a sure cultural thing. And as (Wiles insists) in the long run our security depends on concessions in the field of cultural freedom, our economic concessions to the Soviet Union should be against cultural concessions —against an irreversible ideological détente.

BYRNES: I am in agreement with that view, only I would spell it out a little further.

First, we should point out to the Russians that in the modern world it is anachronistic to talk of the 'sovereignty' and 'independence' of states. Every state interferes with other states by whatever it does. The Soviet purchase of American grain sent the price of bread up in the United States and contributed to inflation. The oil sanctions in the Middle East have deeply affected the American housewife and motorist and are causing a serious recession in Europe and elsewhere. A poor harvest in the United States could cause starvation in India and other parts of the world, not excluding—if it coincided with a drought in the Ukraine—the Soviet Union, and so on.

I would also tell the Russians that we have no intention of separating Basket Two from Basket Three. The Soviet view is that détente—peaceful co-existence—is a higher form of the class struggle in the international arena and that our two societies are therefore locked in a political and ideological battle with each other. Fine—we should accept that; and precisely because we accept that interpretation of détente we should use our great economic, scientific and technological strength, and the strength of the spirit of free enquiry which is the source of all our other strengths, to exact those very modest concessions we have packed into Basket Three. This would be taking the Russians at their word and they could have no grounds for complaint.

URBAN: How would you monitor and police an agreement in which high technology were bartered away against cultural freedom? One danger I can foresee on our side of any barter is that we might, as individual countries, give the Soviet Union bilaterally what it may not be able to negotiate with us collectively.

Would you say, as Wiles suggests, that our computer sales, for example, should be kept down, as a threat, to an annually renewable minimum? If the cultural side of the agreement has been fully honoured in that period, the economic agreement is renewed. This means that culture would be openly and formally bargained against economics. Is this a practical proposition?

BYRNES: It is both a good and a practical idea. In fact the US-

Soviet cultural agreements now in force are made up in precisely that way. For instance: Section A provides for the exchange of sports teams, Section B deals with artists and ballet dancers and C with orchestras. A, B, and C are jointly negotiated (usually over a long and painful period), with Americans giving the Russians more in C than they would in A because they use A, B, and C to balance out each other. Bringing Basket Two and Basket Three into the same package would simply mean that the agreements would be more complicated, but also much more realistic.

As to your fear that we might grant the Soviets bilaterally what they cannot obtain under Basket Two, this is a possibility; but unenlightened as we often are in the pursuit of narrow national interests, I don't think we are unwise enough to pursue such a self-defeating policy.

URBAN: Coming back to the idea of bargaining Basket Two against Basket Three, would you, to take one example, check the export of western oil-drilling machinery against the cessation of the jamming of western broadcasts?

BYRNES: That is the sort of thing I have in mind. What we must remember is that we have very little, if anything, to lose by not having a cultural exchange agreement. In the field of Soviet-Russian studies (the only one where we have anything of importance to gain) we are in a very strong position. Our knowledge of all things Soviet is infinitely greater than it was even fifteen years ago. We have so many educated Americans well versed in the field that we could go on for ten years or more virtually without any loss if no more American scholars were admitted to the Soviet Union. We would, after a time, be simply back where we were during the first thirty-five to forty years of Soviet rule.

We are, therefore, well placed to say to the Russians: although we would very much like to continue with these cultural exchanges, we regard the present arrangements as being highly unfair. We propose terminating all cultural exchange agreements unless, as a first step, you end the jamming of all western broadcasts and allow our books and newspapers to circulate among those who wish to purchase them. We have never jammed your radios and we have never stopped your books and newspapers at our borders. There must be reciprocity, and if you can't provide reciprocity, let us forget this nonsense about cultural exchange programmes. Let me repeat: I regard the end of jamming of all Western broadcasts as the sine qua non of any barter arrangement between Basket Two and Basket Three as well as a barometer of Soviet intentions.

URBAN: One has to be aware that Basket Three, if it were to be fully put into effect, might undermine the whole Soviet system. That is certainly the view the Russians take of it.

BYRNES: I'm not at all convinced that this is so. Basket Three would certainly change the chemistry of the system, very probably to its long-term advantage. If the Soviet leaders want to avoid trouble in the near or more distant future, they must resolve the very serious economic and technical problems which are eating away at the foundations of everything they have built since 1917. If these difficulties are not removed, those members of the Soviet intelligentsia who are very privileged and largely support the system will become disillusioned and turn against the causes and perpetrators of their frustrations. Even the ordinary Russian, docile as he is, would be more and more unwilling to put up with the poverty, overcrowding, shortages and regimentation that would still be his lot sixty or seventy years after the October Revolution.

The Soviet leaders' choices are therefore very limited (if, that is, they want to exclude the possibility of going back to the double-edged weapon of a Stalin type of tyranny): in order to make their system work reasonably effectively they need a massive injection of capital and know-how from the West. So we should be simply saying to them: if you want to buy time for your system, you will have to pay a price for it. What the Soviets are now asking the West to provide is aid and very low-interest credits for which they would, in fact, not have to pay. If we are unreasonable enough to fall in with their wishes, we deserve whatever happens to us in the future.

URBAN: One may look at the Soviet-American conflict of interests as a conflict of two revolutionary traditions—that of the libertarian heritage of the French and American Revolutions and the tradition of 'popular' dictatorship of which the October Revolution is the prototype.

BYRNES: We can safely agree with the Chinese communists that the Soviet leaders are betraying the October Revolution because détente, involving as it does the recognition of western economic superiority, co-operation with capitalism, and the joint management of international crises, is a revisionist policy dictated, to be sure, by necessity, but revisionist all the same.

My great concern is that we should not betray *our* revolution: the spirit of 1776, the idea that all men are created equal, that they are endowed with equal rights and that these rights cannot be restricted by frontiers and ideologies.

If we accept the Soviet position in Eastern Europe as unalterable, if we cease to be concerned with human suffering because it is convenient for us to do so, if we put our names to cultural agreements that are manifestly inequitable, if we sell an oppressive power sensitive machinery in return for promises written in water—or for sheer commercial gain—we may or may not get a détente with the Soviet Union, but we will be most certainly betraying our revolution.

So let us not be fuddled by loose talk that the Russians alone have a revolutionary tradition. *We* have our own, but while the tradition of despotism is as old as man's history, the idea of individual freedom, equality and democracy is new, totally revolutionary and therefore as yet imperfectly realized. And because it is imperfectly realized, I hope that the conflict between the two will go on.

CLAUS D. KERNIG

Why world stability requires the stability of the Soviet system

URBAN: One profitable approach to testing the acoustics of cultural exchange is that of looking at the Soviet system as a society in the process of modernization. The spectacular preponderance of technologists and scientists among Soviet exchange scholars is proof enough that now, as in earlier centuries, Russia's principal problem is simply that of catching up with western technology. But while both Peter the Great and Stalin thought that the appropriate method of overcoming Russian backwardness was to use 'barbaric means to defeat barbarism', Russia's present leaders are more delicate in their choice of means. Yet their fear that modernization cannot be contained within science and technology is as real as was Stalin's, and their ultimate sanctions against any unwanted spin-off just as daunting.

KERNIG: The heavy Soviet emphasis on technology in all exchange programmes does indeed show the Soviet leaders' concern that modernization must be pushed ahead with all possible speed. But the Soviet conception of modernization is very different from ours. It is restricted to technology and is not felt to be in conflict with the manipulation of the political process, authoritarianism and one-party rule, whereas for us modernization means, broadly speaking, liberal democracy. The Soviet leaders believe, I'm sure quite sincerely, that they can have technological modernization without the habit of free enquiry bursting the bounds of technology. In fact one of the most fascinating topics of western research into Soviet conditions concerns itself with this problem, and we are far from having a clear answer. The Russians may or may not be able to modernize their technology without their society and culture being modernized along with it.

URBAN: Are we being too uncritical in our assumption that a spill-over from one into the other is a good thing? From Aneuran Bevan to Galbraith we have always assumed that the kind of rationality which a technological civilization demands from its operators is continuous and irresistible, that it makes for liberal democracy and that we all approve of the latter. But aren't we begging some of these questions?

KERNIG: One would, of course, not quarrel with the principle that individual freedom is a more desirable state to live in than despotism, a multi-party system more desirable than a one-party state, but that, to my mind, is not the question we are being asked to answer.

We have to conceive of all human activity on our planet as parts of one, closely meshed system. This is new. We tend to forget how very new it is, for even a hundred years ago, when power in the world was shared between six or seven nation-states of similar rank and influence, change or even an upheaval in one did not have an automatic effect on the others. Our system today is centred on two poles, the United States and Russia, and the stability we enjoy is entirely due to the interplay between these two principal powers. Change the power or nature of one and you have destabilized the world system. What I am therefore saying is that before we press harder for speedy liberalization inside the Soviet Union via Basket Three or any other form of politico-cultural influence, we should be fully conscious of the possible consequences of what we are doing.

At the moment the cry for liberalization as a necessary condition of détente is drowning the voices of those more cautious observers of the world scene who would not like to see the world's precarious stability disturbed for an unknown and unknowable quantity. So, coming back to the narrower question, we ought to ask ourselves whether the spread-effect of imported science and technology *will* act as a destabilizer in the Soviet Union, and if it will, is it wise of us to want it?

URBAN: What you are saying is that you would not swop a bad but stable peace for an uncertain future, for although a more liberal Russia is desirable, you do not want to have one at the risk of upsetting the world's power-equilibrium. 'Only fools exult when governments change', says a cynical Rumanian proverb.

KERNIG: I would put it differently. I am for the uninhibited flow of people and ideas throughout the world. Among the western nations free cultural exchange is well established. It works, it is wholly beneficial and there is no more to be said about it. We have no such free exchange with the Soviet Union.

Now Russia is industrially uncompetitive with us, but she is trying to become competitive, and this forces her to modernize. Modernization in turn means the importation of science and know-how, but this isn't all it might mean. The Soviet leaders are extremely nervous about the possibility that under the seal of technological and scientific imports, contraband materials of the kind that might upset the internal status quo might also reach Russia.

And because a bipolar system does not make sense unless both poles preserve their integrity, we have a real interest in doing nothing that might undermine the stability of the other pole—the Soviet Union.

I am, in fact, making the unorthodox assertion that we have, as members of a precariously balanced world system, an interest in the preservation of stability in the Soviet Union. To pose the question of cultural exchange in isolation from this overriding necessity is to divert our attention from the real issue. In so far as cultural exchange might undermine the stability of the Soviet system, or even destroy it, we have no interest in promoting cultural exchange, for we would, in fact, be promoting the destruction of the world balance of power. So we have a vested interest in the stabilization of the Soviet regime. This may strike you as outrageous—

URBAN: —no, I find it interesting—

KERNIG: —but let me spell out my reasons for making this assertion. A completely uninhibited form of cultural exchange would, of course, meet the wishes of many Soviet people, especially of the educated and highly educated sections of the community. However, it is an unfortunate fact that very few of these highly educated Russians have a broad, analytical understanding of the intricate connections which hold the world in balance—they are, quite understandably, solely concerned with their immediate circumstances: the state of civil liberties, of literature, and so on. I don't think we should always try to meet the wishes of these Soviet citizens and act as though their interests were ours.

URBAN: You are referring to the dissidents in the Soviet Union.

KERNIG: Yes, I am, and I would go a step further: we should bear in mind the interests of the Soviet leaders too. Whether we like the Soviet leaders or not is not our concern here. I am not speaking as a friend of the Soviet leadership when I say that our own security is intimately connected with the interests of the Soviet leaders, and that we would risk our own security if we tried to foist a completely unrestrained kind of cultural exchange on the Soviet Government.

URBAN: Your estimate, then, of the stability of Soviet institutions cannot be very high.

KERNIG: No, it isn't in our sense of the word, because these institutions are not self-supporting. They are, however, stable in the sense that a modern totalitarian system is internally all but invulnerable. Cultural exchange of the kind contemplated on our side would entail a form of modernization which would make it impossible for the Soviet Party and state to go on existing as they have done since 1917; it would in fact open a chink in Moscow's ideological armour—

URBAN: —which is what a lot of people are fervently hoping would happen—unmindful, I suppose, of the interdependence of the two systems.

KERNIG: I have a suspicion that when Khrushchev, at the end of his rule, divided the Party into an agricultural and industrial wing, he had a vague understanding of the fact that modernization demands at least a rudimentary form of political pluralism. But we know what happened to Khrushchev.

URBAN: Isn't your position open to attack at a rather basic level? Your assertion that the world's stability is a function of the continuing stability of the Soviet regime assumes that the Soviet regime *is* stable as it is. This is called in question by those who argue that a dictatorship is always inherently unstable, and doubly so if it is economically inefficient to boot.

There are two variants of this basically single critique, both of which I consider relevant. The 'weak' case has it that stability grows out of a much improved economic performance and higher living standards, and that this performance cannot be attained without giving the performers a good deal more freedom than they enjoy at present: despotism is not only unpleasant but also wasteful and inefficient. On this showing, the Soviet Union cannot be relied upon to maintain its end of the world's bipolarity (in so far as one really exists) unless Soviet stability is guaranteed by the democratization of Soviet government and institutions. The changes envisaged are endogenous.

The 'strong' case takes this argument a lot further. It holds that any regime that denies elementary freedoms to large sections of its population, failing even to enforce respect for its own laws and constitution, cannot be trusted—not because it is too strong, but because it is too weak. The Soviet Union fails to inspire confidence, first because it has shown itself crisis-prone in every one of its satellites (with the possible exception of Bulgaria), and second because the habit of domestic lawlessness and violence makes us wonder whether this or that team of unelected Soviet leaders might not be tempted to apply the same lawlessness to the conduct of foreign affairs. Hence (it may be argued) it is right and in the western interest to encourage the liberalization of the Soviet system even through outside incentives. Solzhenitsyn's deportation endorses this argument: a state as outwardly powerful as the Soviet Union, which can only deal with an author by exiling him, must be so unstable as to be highly dangerous.

There is undoubtedly a hypocritical element in this argument, for most people who use it do not want to see the Soviet system improved but destroyed. Nevertheless I happen to believe that a

liberalized variety of the Soviet regime—one that would not have
to keep down Czechs, Hungarians and Poles with force of arms, one
that could put up with dissent and dispense with internal pass-
ports—may well turn out to be a much strengthened system. The
Prague Spring began to point a way. Whether one would personally
like this to happen need not concern us here, but it seems to me a fair
assumption that an improved Soviet system would be much less
likely to be rocked by upheavals and much more likely to provide
the stability which, as you say, the bipolar international system
requires, than does the present system.

KERNIG: This is an attractive argument. If we want to answer
the problem it implies for cultural exchange, we must go back a step
and ask ourselves: do we have a reliable understanding of how the
Soviet system—in fact any social system—works? And our answer
must be that we don't. We have theories for small and homogeneous
systems, but the present state of our knowledge does not permit us
to make statements about anything as multivariant and complex as
a social system as a whole. If we had usable knowledge in this area,
the world would not be in the sorry mess it is—ecologically, socially
and politically.

Before one proceeds to recommend particular means for stabilizing the Soviet system on the basis of the argument you have just put
forward, I would say it is necessary to analyze the Soviet system with
great care, and having understood whatever we can understand
about it, we should then ask ourselves: can we risk confronting the
system with inputs such as free cultural exchange, the freedom of
information, etc. without risking the destabilization of the whole?
And if (as I suspect) we cannot, with the imperfect tools at our disposal, calculate the risks we would be running, we are better off if we
do not press the issue for we do not know where it may lead us.

Nor could we, if we accepted your analysis and induced, through
cultural liberalization, radical change in the Soviet system, suggest a
reliable social and economic alternative to the present system. In
order to say how Russia may be more efficiently and more democra-
tically governed without a one-party state, without centralization,
without a state-controlled economy, we would have to know infinitely more about how societies work, past and present, than we
now do. Our knowledge is restricted to national accounting, but
that is very far from being a reliable theory of society. In short: as we
are absolutely ignorant of how radical change in one area might
affect the Soviet regime as a whole, we should take no chances with
Russia's—and our own—security.

URBAN: You are, then, recommending a very cautious and
slow approach, which strikes me as being out of keeping with the

spirit of the 1970s. The Russians are in a hurry for economic assistance, and we presumably want them to be acceptable as recipients
of assistance before we give it to them; so a long wait for the systems'
analysts to hit upon a global theory of society which would make
the risks of move A or B neatly calculable, does not seem to me to be
a practical proposition. And I doubt if a theory of this kind would
ever be reliable enough to make the political, economic, and above
all the psychological spread-effects of any one input reasonably
predictable. How, then, do we make any headway?

KERNIG: We must involve both Soviet scholars and scientists
and our own in an urgent and co-operative learning process. They
must become aware that they are, individually and conjointly as
scholars and scientists, responsible for the stability and survival of
civilization. This, in its broadest sense, means responsibility for the
world's ecological stability through the realization that the world is
a single eco-system. Scientists must see to it that the food/popula-
tion collision does not occur in the 1980s as many fear it will, that
the birth-rate/death-rate imbalance is not restored by a nuclear
holocaust, and so on. But more particularly we should bring it home
to Soviet scholars and scientists that they are as heavily involved in
protecting the world's political stability as our own scientists are,
and that they have a responsibility for not interfering, without very
careful reflection, with the magnetic fields of either of the world's
two poles, especially their own. Cultural exchange and all that goes
with it should, therefore, be designed with these constraints in mind.

URBAN: Let me get this clear: you are in fact suggesting that
every package of technology we export to the Soviet Union should
carry a maker's warning: 'Not to be applied outside area specified
by importing authority', or words to that effect. Thus the scientific
co-operation you envisage would make it our responsibility to dis-
suade Soviet scholars and scientists from acting like free and questioning human beings outside their narrow specialisms. It would be
up to us—ecologically sophisticated and systems-trained people
that we are—to persuade them not to challenge the received truths
of the Soviet system.

KERNIG: This is the conclusion I should ultimately like to
arrive at if you insist on putting it in such simple terms, but my argument leading up to it is a little more complicated. If you look back
upon the history of the last thirty-five years, the most important
human utterance I have been able to discover was Einstein's advice
to President Roosevelt that it was feasible to build the atomic bomb
and that the Germans were in the process of making one themselves.
Now Einstein's second point was based on a fallacy which the
Americans ought to have been able to track down as the Manhattan

project was progressing, for Hitler never ordered a nuclear bomb to be built and no undertaking of that nature was pursued in nazi Germany. Nevertheless, Einstein, with his enormous prestige, stepping outside his field of competence, was able to persuade the President of the United States of the correctness of what was an entirely political judgement and so the American atom bomb was built and eventually used on Japan. The consequences of this single judgement of a famous physicist have had the most far-reaching influence on the future of the world.

I am mentioning this extreme case to illustrate my thesis that scientists must be made to be aware of the moral and political consequences of their activities, especially when they arrogate to themselves the right to speak with authority outside their fields of expertise. Of course, before we apply this principle to Soviet scholars and scientists, we should first apply it to our own, but the task of our dialogue with our Soviet colleagues must be to spread the awareness that scientists must never stop reflecting upon the implications of their scientific or scholarly work for the whole of humanity—

URBAN: —which is—according to your interpretation— another way of saying that Soviet scholars and scientists should do nothing that might damage the Soviet system.

KERNIG: I would put it differently. I would say that we must first get our own scholars and scientists to accept the idea that scholarship is socially and morally accountable. As a second step I would then try to win acceptance for this idea by Soviet scholars and scientists; but I would not confront the Soviet leaders with the stark proposition: if you take our technology you must also take the habit of critical enquiry, democracy and the freedom of dissent as parts of the package. I would envisage the spill-over effect to be a very gradual process. The feeling of fraternity between eastern and western scholars would evolve naturally from a shared concern for the eco-system and the bipolar interdependence of the world. Confrontation would gradually give way to co-operation and to a better husbandry of peace and the world's natural resources.

URBAN: I can't see how scientific accountability could restrict the spin-off for the Soviet system—for that is what you are implying it should do. Take the example of a Soviet doctor who runs into a large number of TB cases in his area. If he is more than a mere medical technician, he would ask himself whether the incidence of TB wasn't due to damp housing, overcrowding and undernourishment. He would then have to advise his patients to move to better homes, have a better diet, spend more time in the sun and so on. If he found that none of these conditions could be met, he would have to go on asking himself what social and political forces made it impossible to improve his patients' housing? Why was it that they could not earn a decent wage? Why was there a shortage of fresh vegetables in the shops? This in turn would lead him to ponder whether the single-party rule and an autocratic bureaucracy were responsive to the conflicting needs of society, and if he were satisfied that they were not, he would—as a scientist with a social conscience—have to ask himself whether a multi-party democracy wasn't more likely to do justice to the needs of society than a dictatorship.

What I am saying is that a scholar's or scientist's social responsibility is inherent in the ethic of his work and that this ethic does, or should, make him into a critic of every form of autocracy. It is unhappily the case in the Soviet Union that the Russian tradition of fear and conformism has blunted the edge of this ethic, but, as we know from recent examples, it is still there, acting as a pressure for change and not—as you suggest it ought to act—as a brake on change. So, if I understand you correctly, you are *for* the social responsibility of science in a global context but *not* for the social responsibility of scientists if it threatens to upset the status quo in Soviet Russia. This is an interlocking and logical position to take but I doubt if it carries conviction, for to advocate the social responsibility of science in a global context is expressing a fine sentiment which costs us nothing, but to *practise* social responsibility in the face of the KGB is a very different matter. Am I paraphrasing you unfairly?

KERNIG: You are a bit inaccurate in that I am not arguing against endogenous change in the Soviet system, and I am most certainly not arguing against slow, adaptive change even if the sources of that change were exogenous. I am simply saying that the world is ecologically and politically a very dangerous place, and as the world's political and military balance is bipolar, we must do nothing to upset this bipolarity. In other words: don't confront the Soviet leaders with the choice: we'll give you technology if you publish *The Gulag Archipelago* and rehabilitate Solzhenitsyn. What Solzhenitsyn says is true enough, but that, I'm afraid, is not the point.

The point is—and I have to take this question on a very wide ground—that, for a variety of reasons with which you are familiar (the depletion of natural resources, the population explosion, etc.), the world system may soon stop broadening out. The western countries can no longer expect to get richer and richer. We have probably reached the point of optimum welfare and soon we'll start on a downward curve which we will find very difficult to accept and which might push us into a series of grave crises. To give you one example, the distinguished American economist, Oscar Morgenstern, told me recently that if the world's per capita ownership of motor cars reached the current United States level, our planet's oxygen resources would last exactly fourteen days. At the end of those fourteen days we would have no further worries.

To cushion and possibly to avert such crises, we have to spell out the social responsibility of science and the moral responsibilities of individual scientists rather on the lines you have suggested. But we have to start doing all these things at home—preparing ourselves for a shrinking estate, the improved husbandry of what we are going to have left in terms of world resources, linking each step in technological innovation with a careful analysis of its social and moral impact on the world as a whole, and so on. Only when we have done all this with some measure of effectiveness should we turn to the Soviet Union and suggest change in the Soviet system.

URBAN: I have an ugly suspicion that your real (though perhaps unconscious) reason for not wanting the Soviet Union to catch up with us in terms of popular freedoms and consumer democracy is your fear that if 250 million Russians, Ukrainians, Georgians, Khazaks, etc. were to attain anything like the living standards we enjoy, our welfare would take an even heavier tumble than it would otherwise. The Soviet regime, you might argue, is of course a deplorable regime, but it is an ecological asset which we don't want to throw away in a fit of liberalization: Russia is a developing system with low expectations and a low standard of living. It is not devastating the world's resources with anything like the speed we are—hence it is a world-interest not to push up Soviet living standards. And as internal liberalization would undoubtedly end up doing exactly that, we should either not press for liberalization at all, or approach it with very great caution. You would then have two cogent reasons for holding back on any speedy reform inside the Soviet Union: the military bipolarity of the world and the approaching exhaustion of our planet.

KERNIG: I would formulate the problem differently: is it more important for the survival of humanity to accelerate political change in Russia and Eastern Europe than to maintain the equilibrium of the world eco-system and the world's present balance of power?

I think there can be no doubt about the answer. I do not want to keep Russians and East Europeans poor so that we in the West can prolong the enjoyment of our privileges. I am interested in improving the quality of life throughout the world, including the USSR and Eastern Europe; and the only way in which an equitable standard of living can be provided for all is to break down the present divisions between East and West, North and South, and integrate the population of the world in one single socio-economic system. Keeping the rich rich and the poor poor is a prescription for world catastrophe, and I do not for a moment advocate it either in relation to the Soviet Union or the Third World.

URBAN: But human beings being what they are I cannot see rich Americans or West Germans giving up, say, thirty million of their motor cars to allow Russians or Peruvians to have thirty million of their own—not, that is, without a world war or an eco-catastrophe. The French will not even lend their support to planning the husbandry of the world's fast diminishing oil resources in a crisis situation that is already upon us. How much more can we expect the 'world', with its countless, disparate, centrifugal, egocentric interests to co-operate on the scale that its ecological situation undoubtedly requires? Foresight is not one of the virtues in which governments excel, otherwise the energy and food crises—predicted day in and day out for many years by the world's scientists—would not have come as so rude a shock to us. All the warnings and planning notwithstanding, the world system is spinning out of control.

KERNIG: The dangers are very real but I would argue that we can check pollution, defuse the arms race, keep the bipolarity of the world reasonably intact only if decisions of earth-jolting importance aren't taken heedlessly and planlessly. There are forms of planning more humane, more democratic and more far-sighted than any we have so far seen used. These must be applied and applied quickly if mankind does not want to commit collective suicide. The East-West confrontation, détente, cultural exchange are very small spots on the global map, and it is the *global* map on which we must now focus all our attention.

But looking at the advantages and disadvantages of change in the Soviet Union from the political scientist's point of view is not the only profitable approach. The historical perspective is just as important for it may well explain certain features of Soviet behaviour which a political scientist would not readily perceive. Let me suggest one such historical approach.

If we conceive of cultural exchange in the broad sense—in the sense in which cultures keep in touch and have an impact on one another—we can see two periods in European history when cultural exchange was free and fruitful. The first such period was (if I may use a coarse framework) from the Middle Ages through the Renaissance up to the French Revolution—a very long time in which theology, music, literature, architecture, classical studies, philosophy travelled freely from Paris to Bologna and from Oxford to Prague.

There were no frontiers to the thoughts and artefacts of men or to the free movement of men themselves. This was the age of internationalism based on Christian values and a shared language.

The second period of cultural internationalism is our own time with its electronic signal traversing the globe in a fraction of a second. Western technology has spread to the far corners of the earth, spawning common moulds of thought and feeling which we may loosely identify as culture. Things and people have become interchangeable. One can study in the United States, take a higher degree in Germany and hold down a job in Italy in a great variety of occupations without having to re-learn one's basic skills. The literature, poetry, architecture, music and life-styles of our age travel just as well and just as freely.

Between these two periods we have a century and a half of the culture of nation-states—of isolationism, chauvinism, national aggrandizement and national wars—but this is also the period of the industrial revolution and democratization, the period of transition from autocracy and paternalism to the rights and freedoms of the individual. Copyright, patent, specialization and modernization all have their roots in this age of romantic national self-consciousness.

I am using a very large and crude canvas to make my point: the Soviet Union, carrying as it is the ballast of Russia's authoritarian heritage, has never managed to shed the nationalism and paternalism of this transitional period. Its culture, mores, intellectual climate and vindictive nationalism are still those of the 1890s by West European standards, while in the fields of science and technology it has, since the 1950s, made a great leap forward and more or less caught up with the West. The reason for this jump was—as so often in Russian history—the Russian Government's fear of being left behind in weapons technology. But while, at enormous sacrifice to the living standards of the people, the USSR has now drawn level with America in this particular field, its state as a nation in terms of all the other indicators of modernity is (as I say) that of the late nineteenth century.

Therefore the Soviet system suffers, and is likely to go on suffering, from a split personality. This explains why Stalin's terror could go hand in hand with a rapid pace of industrialization and why, in our own day, the Soviet leaders—and I suspect the rank and file Russians too—see nothing incompatible between sending a rocket to Mars and sending Solzhenitsyn into exile.

Now this is, needless to say, not the kind of periodization Soviet historians would accept, but it does help us to understand that when we deal with the Soviet Union we are not really dealing with a modern state in the western sense of the word, and that we have to shape our policies accordingly.

URBAN: Whichever strand of your argument we follow to its logical conclusion, we come up against the warning 'don't rock the boat': don't rock the boat (a) because you might disturb the world's ecological balance, (b) because you might disturb the bipolar politi- co-military balance, and (c) because the Russians are really cultu- rally backward animals who wouldn't quite understand what we are on about. Our safest bet, then, is to do nothing beyond drawing Soviet scholars into our councils and helping them to understand that we are all fellow-travellers on the spaceship Earth and would share a fate in any nuclear holocaust.

KERNIG: Our efforts would be amply rewarded if we could make *them* understand the precariousness of our interdependence, for I am far from being sure that we ourselves understand it.

URBAN: I would find it easier to agree with your historical point if, in this age of universal techno-culture, old fashioned nationalism *were* confined to the Soviet Union. But it isn't. Nationalism is asserting or reasserting itself, side by side with great technological sophistication, all over the world including Western Europe, where from time to time France presents us with a sinister model. If we compare our situation with 1939 when the world was only marginally less of a global village than it is today—has our situ- ation undergone a qualitative change? In 1939 we used to think that the aerial bombardment of population centres would make any war very short or indeed impossible. Today the threat of nuclear an- nihilation has allegedly made war unthinkable. Perhaps it *is* unthinkable—but is it un-doable?

KERNIG: Nothing is un-doable if the myopia and wishful thinking of the human race remain uncorrected. But because we must, as rational agents, rule out the possibility that mankind is bent on self-destruction, we have no choice in the matter: we must deal with the world as a single system and subordinate to it all par- ochial considerations of power, nation, ideology, race, class and religion.

URBAN: I should like to have Brezhnev's views on this. We do have Ponomarev's. On 18 January 1974, at a Moscow conference marking the fiftieth anniversary of Lenin's death, B. N. Ponoma- rev, Secretary of the CPSU, said:

The acuteness of class contradictions in the capitalist system as a whole . . . the instability of the situation and the dissatisfaction of the masses in many bourgeois states has today reached such a pitch that at any moment, in one link or another of this system, a situation may arise which will open the way to radical revolutionary transformations. In this situation the role of the subjective factor, of the correct and effective policy of the Marxist-Leninist Party, grows immeasurably. Correctness of policy, resoluteness, the revolutionary preparedness and activeness of the vanguard of the working class . . . are the first condition of the realization of existing possibilities.

Well, it takes two to play bipolarity, and it seems to me that Ponomarev's words do not exactly betoken a Soviet wish to uphold our end of the system.

Earlier in this discussion you urged us to bear in mind that we had a vested interest in preserving the stability of the Soviet system. The Soviet leaders do not appear to have any corresponding desire to preserve our stability. We are being asked to see the world as bipolar—the Soviets are doing their best to make it monopolar.

KERNIG: This is a good point. However, we would be ill-advised to take everything the Soviets say at face value. I can think of quite a few recent developments that cannot have been to the liking of the Soviet leadership. The Soviet leaders were against cybernetics—today Russia has it. Soviet science rejected modern biology and especially modern genetics—today both are well established. There was objection to certain forms of mathematical economics—today mathematical economics is widely practised in Soviet Russia. Things change in the USSR, too, but—I repeat—it is in our interest to see that these changes do not throw the Soviet leadership off balance, for if the Soviet leaders were made to fight for their lives, they would make us fight for ours.

What we have to try to do is to negotiate a narrow channel between two unacceptable alternatives: on one side we have the unconditional acceptance of Soviet hegemony; on the other we have the dangers flowing from the unconditional support of liberalization in the Soviet Union. We must pick our way in the middle.

JOHAN JØRGEN HOLST

Security as mutual education

URBAN: In September 1972 Norway voted against membership of the European Community. How does this affect her relationship with her Nato allies and her attitude to European security?

HOLST: The vote has no material effect on Norway's attitude to either. Our non-membership of the European Community poses a procedural problem for Norway's policy-makers and diplomatic representatives in that it deprives us of assured access to the forums where decisions are made. One could see this at the security talks in Helsinki and Geneva where we were confronted with a caucus of the Nine and found ourselves somewhat isolated.

While it is true that the energy crisis, tension between the United States and the Nine and uncertainties about Britain's will to pull its weight in the European Community are threatening to slow down, or even to stop, European integration, we are faced with the paradoxical situation that on the question of European security the Nine countries have closed ranks rather impressively, so, in spite of the negative factors I have just mentioned, I am prepared to predict that the whole business of community-building will be furthered by the very process of East-West negotiations. This consolidating impact of the security talks on the unification of the Nine does worry us, not because we are against European integration, but because we don't like being left unconsulted.

URBAN: Surely any fear that the European Community will, in the foreseeable future, possess anything like a common foreign policy, let alone a common defence policy, has now become—sadly, as I think—unrealistic. Europe can count itself lucky if it manages to run fast enough to stand still.

HOLST: This is so at the moment, but it need not be so in the long term. We are worried that the European Community might develop a certain continental propensity. One of our concerns about détente is precisely that it may become a mechanism for breaking down the continuity of the security arrangements in Europe, limiting them to Central Europe and weakening their already tenuous links with the peripheral areas of Europe such as Norway.

URBAN: This drawing together of the Nine is rather paradoxical if you look at it from the Soviet point of view or set it against our own conventional political wisdom: when the Russians were openly hostile to us under Stalin, we put up the European Communities (as they then were); now that the Russians are smiling at us, we are—according to your analysis—drawing *further* together. So whatever these hard-working Soviet leaders do, the result is the consolidation of European unity. This is surely not their idea of what détente should bring about, and I am not at all sure that this is what is, in fact, happening. European unity is in a parlous state, not because the Russians have successfully manipulated us into a position of weakness, but because we are—for various reasons which we need not go into—unable to turn our great economic strength into the hard, palpable facts of power.

HOLST: The consolidation of the unity of the Nine as far at least as their attitude to Soviet détente policies is concerned is, of course, unlikely to be popular with the Russians, but they probably argue that, dialectically speaking, this tends to be an early reaction to a relaxation of tensions, and that it will go away as détente gets more firmly established—

URBAN: —a symmetrical case being the affirmation of ideological orthodoxy in Eastern Europe as a prophylactic against the disintegrating effects of détente—

HOLST: —yes, one may see a certain parallel there.

One interesting fact we have to note about the European Community is that the *Marxisant* assumption on which it was built—that economic integration would more or less automatically generate political unification—has not been borne out by facts. The Community has always responded to outside stimuli much more robustly than to the rationale of economic integration. Indeed it owes its existence to outside pressure.

URBAN: But—as you have yourself just said—the EEC governments' panicky reaction to the oil crisis damaged rather than enhanced European unity.

HOLST: Without wanting to belittle the short-term effects of the affair I would say that the long-range result of Europe's disarray may well be more unity rather than less. The main sufferer of Europe's unco-ordinated reaction to the cut-back in oil production has been the Atlantic relationship. The damage is very real but not irreparable. I would stand by my thesis that in terms of foreign policy co-ordination external pressures have—over a long period of time—a beneficial effect on European unity. The Security Conference, the oil crisis and the American Government's subsequent moves have forced the Nine into a situation where they have to take a very long-term view of their relations with both the Soviet Union and the United States. This concentrates their minds wonderfully.

URBAN: One of the Soviet objectives of détente is to pick off the European countries one by one so that the patchwork quality of Western Europe as it now is gets no chance of being worked into a solid fabric. If what you are saying is correct, the Russians have dismally failed to achieve that objective. But have they?

HOLST: The Soviet leaders find it very hard to put détente into practice. They have ideological difficulties, problems of communication with the West, difficulties anchored in the Soviet power structure, in communist rhetoric and so forth. If détente is aimed at destroying or basically weakening the European Community—and we have no conclusive evidence that it is—then the Russians are going about it in a clumsy and rather self-defeating way. But one of the things the Russians *can* achieve with détente is to rule out certain forms of military co-operation among the Nine, more specifically any thought of giving the European Community nuclear teeth.

I don't think this is a bad thing. It might, in fact, benefit everyone if the Soviet leaders came to see that the *sine qua non* of preventing a new and directly hostile military power from arising in Western Europe is for themselves to advance the first acts of relaxation. This might then lead to a conception of Soviet security in terms of interdependence with Western Europe, and not as a linear pursuit of national interest, which is the traditional Soviet conception.

URBAN: This is assuming that the Russian leaders are negotiating in good faith—that their friendly noises towards us convey their real meaning, whereas their spirited repudiations of détente in the ideological and political fields are window-dressing for the benefit of the party faithful. And this is, in the light of Soviet history, a large assumption to make. In any case, if one accepted your reasoning Western Europe would be signing away its right to possess a nuclear deterrent now or at any time in the future. Wouldn't this leave us at Moscow's mercy?

HOLST: I'm not so sure. There has for years been an American deterrent, yet we can never be absolutely certain that the Americans would, in fact, use it to defend Europe. We can't even be sure that they would use it to defend the United States, and I can think of a lot of good reasons why, if the deterrent should fail, the Americans might not want to use nuclear weapons for directly hitting Russia. But the important point is that the Russians can't be sure either. It is this residual uncertainty, and the enormity of the catastrophe should the calculations go wrong, that makes the deterrent work.

The point is: we must learn to think of security in a new conceptual framework. The old, nationalistic idea that when the chips are down you can only rely on yourself and must, therefore, remain master of your options—and this is the essence of the French attitude to European defence—no longer carries conviction. The possession of the nuclear bomb is fast becoming a rich man's burden—something the super-powers will find it increasingly difficult to translate into politically useful terms. The fact that Western Europe lives off its drawing rights on the American deterrent may, paradoxically, make it feasible for the European governments to derive a certain political freedom from their dependence, whereas the nominally independent Americans—owners and controllers of nuclear weapons—have not the same liberty because they are locked in nuclear stalemate with the Russians. Should the Europeans, by some misfortune, tumble into the possession of nuclear arms, they may soon come to feel that a nuclear arsenal constrains them rather than increases their freedom of action. Of course, whether this *would* be the experience of the West European governments depends on Russian behaviour—whether, and if so in what form, the Europeans would see themselves threatened by Russia.

URBAN: One experience that comes to mind in this genre of political behaviour is the 1973 unguided war between Arabs and Israelis. Each side had drawing rights on the conventional arsenal—and one assumes ultimately on the nuclear deterrent—of one of the super-powers, but I cannot see that their non-possession of nuclear weapons has benefited them greatly. It has, as you say, made them freer to act than the nuclear powers would have been in their position, but the results of this relative freedom can hold no attractions for Europe.

HOLST: I'm not suggesting that the Europeans should or would use their freedom in anything like a similar manner. The fact that you have the ability to pursue a certain course of action does not mean that you want to pursue it. But I certainly feel that the Europeans will be in a position to use their economic power to make their influence felt in any international economic bargaining, and I would hope that they would not set themselves global objectives. I get very suspicious when Britons and Frenchmen lecture the rest of the Nine on the desirability of giving the Community a world-identity, when what they may have in mind is a desire to smuggle British imperialism and French imperialism of the last century into our own through the back door of the European Community. Europe is better off without this kind of a global role.

URBAN: I would find your argument easier to accept if the nine European countries had not demonstrated their inability to assert themselves even as a purely European, let alone a world, power. We have been nearly outflanked in the south, and our vital energy supplies have been threatened and partly disrupted. In less dangerous times the 1973/74 Arab action would have been enough to spark off a very large war; in the circumstances it has reduced those once mighty nations—the British, the French and the Germans—to courting the favours of the feudal nabobs of their former protectorates. Europe had no say in the conduct or settlement (such as it is) of the Arab-Israeli war. Europe is not even represented at the Geneva peace conference although this war was fought on her doorstep. An American nuclear alert was called without Europe knowing why. The United States and Russia are talking about the limitations of strategic weapons—many of which are, on the Russian side, targeted on European cities—but no European country has been invited to the conference table.

I would therefore argue that when the French and British want Europe to assume a political and perhaps military personality of her own (and the British don't even want that), they are simply expressing the broadly held view that 270 million of some of the world's economically and culturally most sophisticated people cannot be expected to be satisfied indefinitely with second-class citizenship. To this one may, of course, plausibly answer that if 270 million rich Europeans are unwilling to match the conventional power of 230 million relatively poor and technologically stagnant Soviet citizens, they deserve nothing better than a second-class status.

HOLST: I'm not arguing against a united Europe—on the contrary, I'm for it, but, to stick to the present example, I remain unconvinced that the European possession of nuclear arms at the time of the 1973 Arab-Israeli war would have given the Nine any extra leverage. But it is certainly true that if Europe had been politically more united than she was in the autumn of 1973, the Americans could just not have afforded not to consult her.

Then, there is the pedestrian problem of sheer practicality: if there is an identifiable centre that can speak for the Nine, consultation is much more likely than it is now. In an international emergency it is extremely difficult to address yourself to nine (in the case of Nato fifteen) governments. But a Europe of the Nine, unburdened by the concerns of nuclear power, has the potential of making her weight felt *if* the political will is there.

URBAN: Would this 'potential of making her weight felt' encompass the East European part of Europe?

HOLST: It certainly would. I strongly believe that the current division of Europe is intolerable. I'm not arguing for a 'roll-back', but I do think that some sort of an opening up (even 'liberalization' might be the wrong word) is an essential precondition of any notion of a shared European security. It is not a question of wanting to change the Soviet or the Czech or the Bulgarian Government in the image of Westminster—we simply want to be able to see what is going on in the East European countries. A shared security concept presupposes that we know how decisions are made in Russia and Eastern Europe, what kind of information they are based on, how public reaction is fed back to the decision makers and so forth. We must be able to monitor Soviet and East European political processes with the same freedom as the Russians are monitoring ours. Security arrangements are built on sand unless one has reason to trust the predictability of one's partner's reactions. At the moment we have no such assurance.

The Russians seem to want to play détente à la carte—we, on the other hand, believe that détente is a set menu where you have to take the third course ('basket' to be precise) together with the first and second. The Russians apparently want to control all the, for them, uncomfortable aspects of interaction with the West, reaping at the same time the benefits of economic and technological co-operation. I fear they will have to face up to some difficult choices: can they risk trading off their concern about the stability of their system against the benefits of economic co-operation with the West?

URBAN: The answer, as they see it, is 'no', but I am not sure that they conceive of their position in terms of these options. If we in the West really insist that security is a set menu, the Russians will have to be informed of this in very plain language.

HOLST: The choice has to be presented to them, and that was, for example, what the Jackson Amendment was trying to do. Of course the Russians resent this enormously, but the exercise is nevertheless worthwhile.

URBAN: *Is* it an exercise or do we mean business?

HOLST: There are three points to be made here. First, we must make the Russians understand that in the democratic countries public opinion matters. Extrapolating as they are from their own uniformly undemocratic traditions, the Russians have always had great difficulty in assimilating this fact. The moment we start mobilizing the public in favour of a more relaxed relationship with the East, the public will start asking questions about the whole of Europe—their scrutiny will respect neither national frontiers, nor the status quo, nor the accoutrements of ideology on this or that side of the East-West divide. They will, rightly, want to know what sort of a system it is we want to have détente with—whether it represents a humane and just order—and whether we are not being taken for a ride. In a dictatorship you need not worry too much about this kind of scrutiny, but under a democratic form of government you do.

But—and this is my second point—the Russian leadership is not altogether unaware of this factor. That Brezhnev subjected himself (in the summer of 1973) to questioning by a United States Congressional Committee is an indication that he at least knew that the American Government's détente policies were very much subject to public approval.

My third point is that the political concept behind the Jackson Amendment goes beyond the issue of tying in most-favoured-nation status with Soviet emigration—on which it has failed. What the Jackson Amendment was really saying was that the Russians will not respect us unless we put a reasonably high price on our co-operation, not only in the context of trade, investment and arms control, but any issue. There is a great deal of economic realism as well as psychological truth about this assumption: (a) If capitalism has made America rich and the Soviet Union wants American help, the Soviet Union must pay a price for it—a price which is politically acceptable to capitalist Americans as well as the Soviet Government. (b) It would be wrong to give the Soviet leaders any impression that America is 'soft' in certain areas, for the Russians can no more compartmentalize in their judgements than most of us: if America is seen to be firm on any question raised in the East-West relationship, perhaps the Soviet leaders will take American policies more seriously than they do now—perhaps they will develop some respect for what America can give and withhold, and this may ultimately have a useful influence on the Soviet perception of the American nuclear deterrent too.

After Watergate and Indochina the Americans are not negotiating from a position of strength. Also, the greed with which American business interests are reaching for the Soviet markets, unconcerned with any factor other than profit, bears out Lenin's reading of the suicidal rapacity of capitalism and is unlikely to increase Soviet respect for the United States. You have to drive a hard bargain with the Soviet leaders.

URBAN: Your short answer to my question would then be: we want to be seen to be meaning business and, hopefully, we do mean business.

HOLST: Yes, in the sense that it is precisely business that we do not mean in the narrow interpretation of the word: we *mean* business because we do not mean *business*, or at any rate not business alone.

URBAN: Shall we say you stand for a gradual evolution of the Soviet system, gently goaded by western pressure?

HOLST: Yes, there is a case for thinking that even though measures such as the Jackson Amendment may not always achieve their

purpose—and the Jackson Amendment has not achieved its purpose—they may generate slow and gradual change. One may
eventually even achieve a redefinition of what in Soviet eyes are vital
interests of the Soviet system. This incremental approach may take
us a long way if we exploit every rung of the ladder for pushing just a
little further—

URBAN: —a Norwegian version of 'salami tactics' with the
signs reversed—

HOLST: —quite.

As far as Basket Three is concerned, we should stand firm on our
suggestions. The free flow of people and ideas is a basic human right
which we cannot compromise. Western governments have always
been curiously reluctant to present the suppression of human rights
in Russia and Eastern Europe in straightforward moral terms. This
is a pity, for if the freedom of information, the freedom of communication and the like cannot be put before our public as moral
issues, what can?

We suffer from a sense of double vision in these matters: we have
one standard of justice for right-wing governments and another for
the communist regimes. If any Nato country treated its intellectuals
and minorities in anything like the shameless fashion in which the
Soviets are treating theirs, our media and our parliaments would
resound with the opprobrium of the liberal conscience.

Our double vision is not only fraudulent but it also undermines
any idea that moral values have a place in political discussion. And
this is extremely dangerous, for if democracy is not about the
morally equitable co-existence of man with man, then it is about
nothing. I want to see our governments put the issues raised by
Basket Three firmly before the people. I want them to be quite explicit about what is going on in Soviet asylums, why the Soviet regime
could not tolerate Solzhenitsyn, why it is preventing Russian wives
from joining their non-Russian husbands, why there is an internal
passport system in Russia and so forth. The western proposals in
Basket Three are strictly in accord with the Universal Declaration
of Human Rights, which the Soviet Government has signed, and
indeed with the Soviet Constitution. They are non-negotiable.

URBAN: Is this a widely-held view in Scandinavia or are you
speaking for yourself?

HOLST: We probably have the same division of opinions on this
issue as other West European countries. I believe my views are not
too far from what ordinary people in Scandinavia feel about Basket
Three. By contrast, our foreign policy establishments have to some
extent developed their own, closed way of thinking, and their attitude to the free flow of people and ideas is much more legalistic than

mine is. You will find that, for them, foreign policy is what is transacted between governments—it must never concern itself with the internal affairs of foreign countries; more specifically it must never sit in judgement on the morality of a foreign country's domestic policies, let alone apply pressure to make them conform with your own moral values (unless, of course, you are talking to an allied country).

URBAN: That puts paid to the Rights of Man and the Sermon on the Mount, among other things.

HOLST: It does, but even if one takes a narrower view—in a rapidly shrinking world the bureaucratic distinction between foreign affairs and domestic policies is entirely anachronistic. Not that it has—historically speaking—ever been possible fully to divorce one from the other, but today it is even less possible than it has been before. I don't suppose I need rehearse the reasons.

URBAN: 'The Norwegian posture on Nato', you write in *Five Roads to Nordic Security* (1973), 'has . . . focused on critiques of the undemocratic regimes within the Nato alliance (Greece and Portugal), colonial oppression (Portugal, France), and of the policies of the major powers of the alliance outside the Nato area (e.g. the United States in South-east Asia). There is undoubtedly a moralistic streak in Norwegian foreign policy. . . .'

In the light of what you have just said about the necessity of having a single moral yardstick for Left and Right, I suppose you would agree that there is no good reason why the criteria of Norway's critique of the domestic policies of the former right-wing regimes of Greece and Portugal should not be applied to Czechoslovakia and the USSR too?

HOLST: I don't care whether human rights are violated in the name of nationalism, anti-communism or Marxism-Leninism. Persecution and discrimination are no less reprehensible when they come from one end of the political spectrum than from the other. If we don't stand up for human rights, what justifies our claim that we *are* liberal democracies—that our own system isn't, in fact, also built on a lie?

URBAN: 'Fighting a lie in the name of a half-truth' as Koestler complained during the war.

HOLST: Yes, and Scandinavians have always found this a difficult and undignified position to fight from.

URBAN: Watergate, I suppose, did not help.

HOLST: It did not. It is not for us in Scandinavia to pass judgement on Nixon's handling of the Watergate affair, but Watergate has certainly not boosted our moral authority at the security talks or elsewhere.

But let me round off the picture by appending an explanation to what we have said about the Norwegian perception of ideal standards in foreign policy. I have already remarked that, in the 1970s, foreign affairs and internal affairs can no longer be sorted into separate compartments. International relations have become inter-societal relations. Governments cannot interact with other governments on the basis of value-indifference. Foreign policy requires the support of the broad masses of the population, and it is realized that if the Norwegian Government failed to criticize the violations by, say, Greece and Portugal, of 'the principles of democracy, individual liberty and the rule of law', as laid down in the preamble of the North Atlantic Treaty, popular support of our Nato membership, which is very high, might rapidly disappear. This was the spring of our criticism of some of our allies when they were ruled by regimes of the extreme Right. Basket Three is trying to match it with a type of action that might—if it received Soviet approval and practical support—convince our public that détente with the Warsaw Pact countries was something civilized societies and freely elected governments might countenance without undue hypocrisy.

URBAN: I appreciate the significance of 'if' in your last sentence.

URBAN: I am a little bothered by the fact that Norway and Denmark appear to be sharing a platform with Russia in opposing any idea of a European nuclear capability, or even any tightly organized European defence community as a third force between the United States and the USSR. Are Scandinavian interests in fact coinciding in this matter with Soviet interests?

HOLST: There may be a certain coincidence on the particular and limited issue of nuclear weapons, but the Norwegian and Soviet reasons for opposing a European nuclear capability are entirely different. The Russians dislike the idea because a European nuclear force—even a relatively small one—would introduce a modicum of uncertainty into the nuclear equations they are working on with the United States. Our own concern must be seen against a wider horizon. We feel that should the Europeans make the possession of nuclear weapons a central issue in the current phase of EEC integration, the result may well turn out to be political fission rather than fusion. As I have earlier indicated, nuclear weapons make very poor political cement. We could see this at the time when Nato was trying to put up a multilateral nuclear force. I can't remember a more divisive set of negotiations: mixed manning brought out latent national jealousies; military tradition clashed with military tradition; 'who takes orders from whom' reared its ugly head, until the whole idea had to be abandoned.

Here at least I must concede that the French are essentially right in their insistence that you cannot have five or ten fingers on the nuclear trigger; you cannot share decisions about when and how to use nuclear weapons, and there is absolutely no way of giving iron-clad guarantees that the trigger will be used only in this or that set of conditions. The more you try to build political co-operation around shared nuclear weapons the more the participating nations will come to understand that they are trying to tackle an impossible problem: the more the European nations get interested in putting up a joint nuclear force, the greater the likelihood that they will end up having a number of small European nuclear forces, which would be obviously detrimental to the unity of Western Europe.

So my concern is that a European attempt to build up a nuclear capability would, in fact, hinder rather than help European unity. This is, of course, the reverse of the Soviet motivation. The Russians want no West European unity in any shape or form if they can help it.

Then we have the wider concern about the proliferation of nuclear arms throughout the world. This is a serious problem now and is going to be increasingly serious in future as the cost of running large conventional forces goes up and that of building a small but creditable nuclear arsenal goes down. Our problem is already not that of denying various countries the technological information or the hardware to build nuclear weapons, for there isn't a single technologically developed country that could not, if it so decided, manufacture nuclear weapons. It has, indeed, become the cheap and quick way of acquiring prestige and a military arm. Our problem is rather a psychological one—that of educating people in the political utilities, and especially the disutilities, of the possession of nuclear arms. The examples given by the rich countries are therefore extremely important. It is going to be very hard to convince Pakistanis and Indonesians that they should forego having these weapons if the French, the British, the Italians—and now even the Indians—all seem to think that you don't count in the world unless you are decked out with these rather infantile symbols of statehood.

URBAN: My fear is that your fear is premature—we can, alas, rely on the centrifugal pull of French Gaullism and British 'national' socialism, as spelled out in the Labour Party Manifesto of 1973, to wreck or to hold up, for at least many years to come, any advance of the Nine from customs' union to political and military integration. This setback to European unity is not in the Scandinavian interest and it is certainly not in the West European interest. But we have to be philosophical about it: after the enlightened

Europeanism of the 1950s and early 1960s, we are, once again, entering a phase of historical amnesia. However, with some help from the Soviet Union—and the Soviet leaders have seldom let us down in the past—this loss of the memory of recent history need not be lasting.

URBAN: The more I study the ways and means of Soviet détente policy, the more I am persuaded of the truth of one of Kissinger's remarks that (to paraphrase him rather freely) our position at the East-West conference table is that of a bunch of volatile amateurs tilting lances at unflappable, stone-bottomed Soviet professionals.

Let me illustrate the point by looking back for a minute to a seemingly distant and obscure meeting, the International Economic Conference at Genoa, on 10 April 1922, called at the suggestion of Lloyd George.

This was the first big gathering of the European nations after the first world war and it was aimed at restoring the shattered economies of the continent. For the young Soviet state Lenin himself was to attend, but his failing health, pressure of work in Moscow and concern for his security made it undesirable for him to leave Russia. In the event Chicherin was despatched, but Lenin retained the chairmanship of the Russian delegation and directed its activity.

Chicherin's speech had been carefully prepared. This was the first appearance of a leading Soviet representative at a major international conference; Lenin had approved the text, having weighed every word and nuance. What Chicherin said was in fact the first considered presentation of the policy of 'peaceful co-existence'.

Chicherin expressed Soviet readiness 'to release for cultivation millions of acres of the most fertile land in the world and to grant forest and mining concessions, particularly in Siberia'. He urged that collaboration should be established between industry in the West on the one hand, and agriculture and industry in Siberia on the other, so as to enlarge the raw materials, grain and fuel basis of European industry. He suggested long-term loans as a means of overcoming the world's and especially Russia's economic crisis. 'The Russian delegation' he said 'recognizes that in the actual period of history which permits the parallel existence of the ancient social order and of the new order now being born, economic collaboration between states representing the two systems of property is imperatively necessary. . . . The economic reconstruction of Russia appears as an indispensable condition of world-wide economic reconstruction.'

But the most interesting feature of Chicherin's speech was the discussion that preceded it and the things he was not permitted to say. On 23 March 1922 Lenin had an internal note sent to Chicherin which is a highly interesting precursor of Brezhnev's détente diplomacy. In it Lenin suggested important changes in Chicherin's draft of the Genoa speech:

1 'Definitely throw out' any reference to 'inevitable forcible revolution and the use of sanguinary struggle'. On the contrary, stress that 'we communists . . . having come (to Genoa) as merchants . . . positively consider it our duty to give the fullest support to any attempt at a peaceful settlement of outstanding problems'.
2 'Definitely to delete' the words 'our historic conception includes the use of forcible measures'.
3 'Definitely to delete' the words 'our historic conception being definitely based on the inevitability of new world wars'. To use such 'frightening words' would be tantamount to playing into the hands of one's opponents.

Clearly Lenin insisted on the deletion of these phrases not because he had changed his mind about the aims of the Bolshevik revolution, but because he knew the audience he was addressing and the desperate economic situation of the Soviet state. Chicherin himself said at the time of Genoa, although not *at* Genoa: 'It is necessary to create confidence. Without it the capitalists will not open their purses.'

It was Lenin's idea that Chicherin should present himself and his delegation as 'merchants', and that they should support all 'pacifist' trends in the bourgeois camp. But earlier, in the first enactment of the Soviet Union, Lenin linked peaceful co-existence with 'ideological contest and rivalry' which will be 'an inescapable element of the inter-relationship (of capitalism and communism), whilst the inherent contradictions of capitalism will tend to generate revolutionary situations'.

There are, to my mind, three lessons to be learned from this episode: first, that the Soviet Union is in almost the same need of western economic assistance as she was half a century ago although the reasons are different; second, that the present Soviet leaders are, therefore, using the same double-talk to disarm the West and persuade us to 'open our purses' as Lenin and Chicherin were using in 1922; and, third, that there is—for these two reasons—a very unremarkable consistency about Soviet détente policy stretching over the whole existence of the Soviet state.

To compound the piquancy of the analogy I might add that the Soviet delegation's journey to Genoa was interrupted by a stop-over in Berlin where Chicherin met Wirth, the German Chancellor, and Rathenau, the Foreign Minister. During their talks the ground was prepared for what was to become known as the Treaty of Rapallo, concluded on 16 April 1922. 'Genoa and the Treaty of Rapallo', wrote the Soviet scholar E. Chossudovsky, 'formed from the outset integral parts of Soviet diplomatic strategy'.

HOLST: We certainly cannot accuse the Russians of undue sophistication. The double talk was as transparent in 1922 as it is today. However, while in the 1920s no-one was in the mood, and perhaps in the position, to give Russia the aid and co-operation she needed, today the western response may be different—Russia has grown into a super-power and the world situation bears no resemblance to what it was in 1922. The consistency of Soviet foreign policy is, of course, a strength, but it is something every totalitarian system has and no democracy can match. You may look upon it as the more rewarding side of the Soviet system's innate orthodoxy—outweighed, to my mind, by Russia's catastrophic inability to reform her economy and to liberate herself from that strange mixture of westernizing Marxism and Russophile orthodoxy which has always been the essence of Stalinism and from which the Soviet regime has, basically, never departed.

Democracy can seldom pursue long-term goals. Once a democratic government has adopted détente as a policy objective, it has a vested interest in making that policy work and work quickly, for the next elections are around the corner and you have to show something for your efforts or face defeat at the polls. This is a short-term weakness but also a long-term strength, for it makes it possible for us to change course and respond to new situations quickly and without any need to justify our actions in terms of dogma. In his letter to the Soviet leaders Solzhenitsyn says: 'If the man at the head of the column cries "I have lost my way", do we have to plough right on to the spot where he realized his mistake and only then turn back? Why not turn back and start on the right course from wherever we happen to be?' Well, this is exactly what democracy *can* do and a dictatorship can't.

But to return to the springs of Soviet action in the current phase of détente—the Russians remain basically hostile to the ideas and values of western democracy. It is quite possible that they regard détente as a practical ploy to buy time—one could certainly read such an intention into the evidence. I do not myself suspect that the Russians are working to a master plan to conquer the world (there are, however, many students of Soviet affairs who do), but it is obvious enough that they regard themselves as being engaged in permanent conflict with the western world; therefore, from time to time, they review their tactics and choose the most profitable method of pursuing the conflict. My impression is that the principal aim of Soviet détente policy is to overcome the structural weaknesses of the Soviet economy. One can do that by re-thinking the whole rationale of the Soviet system—which is what the Soviet leaders have chosen not to do—or one can import western investment and technology, hoping that intercourse with the West may be limited to trade and know-how.

But as the economic and technological co-operation envisaged is to be a very long-term affair and quite unlike any run-of-the-mill commercial transactions between ideologically non-antagonistic partners, the Russians cannot be quite sure where exactly this co-operation might take them in human, social and cultural terms. If they feel, as they do, that the uncertainty is worth the risk, then they want at least to make sure that the risk is not aggravated by adding to it incendiaries such as we are supposed to want to export to them in Basket Three.

The Russians do fear that we want to barter off Basket Two for Basket Three, but they also realize that the will on our part to do so is not very firm and that our counsels are divided. So they are playing both on our differences and on our indifference, and I am rather apprehensive that we may let Basket Three go by default, allowing the Russians to get away with some watered-down declaration on cultural exchange. I am all for bigger and better guided tours and the accelerated exchange of dental technicians and folk singers, but I am not sure what any of this would have to do with the ideas we have attempted to put into Basket Three.

URBAN: The Russians seem to be putting an amount of energy into the policies surrounding European security which strikes me, for one, as being quite out of proportion with any results these policies are likely to achieve. What practical reasons would they have—apart from wanting capital and technology (which may be bought in simpler ways)—for deploying their men and propaganda on so spectacular a scale?

HOLST: One of the things the Russians have been after for a long time is security of tenure in Eastern Europe—they see a European security document as a means of getting the United States and Western Europe to guarantee the legitimacy of their hegemony. But the Russians must be aware that, to some extent, they may be playing with fire, for while their insistence on the non-violability of existing frontiers and non-interference in internal affairs may protect the Soviet hegemony vis-à-vis the West, it may also give the Rumanians, Poles and Hungarians a certain immunity from *Soviet* interference. The very fact that these matters have been openly discussed at an international conference weakens the Soviet hand, for it makes us, and the East Europeans, aware of the fact that the Russians are not, after all, as confident of their tenure of Eastern Europe as we thought they were, and that the Helsinki-Geneva affair was, in effect, their *in*security conference.

For the states in Eastern Europe the fact that the security and force reductions talks and their aftermath promise to be open-ended, is probably more important than the substance of the negotiations. A standing conference would give them breathing space, room for manoeuvre and some assurance that any Soviet intention to violate the rules would be inhibited.

URBAN: The rules being the United Nations Charter, international law governing aggression and so forth?

HOLST: Yes.

URBAN: In which case you do not expect the Russians would enforce the Brezhnev Doctrine if, for example, the Rumanians continued to obstruct the calling of an anti-Chinese world communist conference, or if the Poles or Hungarians got out of step for any reason the Russians would judge culpable?

HOLST: They might enforce it—at a price. Although political memories are notoriously short, I don't think the invasion of another fraternal state would go unnoticed or bring the Russians great benefits.

URBAN: The occupation of Czechoslovakia was, you will recall, preceded by an earlier wave of détente—and earlier still, we had the 'spirit of Geneva' in 1955, the 'spirit of Camp David' in 1960, and other false alarms of impending peace—

HOLST: —and, as we now know from the second volume of Khrushchev's memoirs, there *was* no 'spirit of Camp David' except in Soviet and western propaganda. 'Our negotiations were coming to an end', Khrushchev notes of his last day at Camp David with President Eisenhower. 'We had lost all hope of finding a realistic exit from the impasse. . . . Lunchtime came, it was more like a funeral than a wedding feast. Well, maybe that's going too far: . . . it was like a meal served at the bedside of a critically ill patient', and so on and so forth.

URBAN: When the blow fell in Czechoslovakia we mourned, rather hypocritically, for about six months, but then détente diplomacy was quietly resumed and any further western concern for Czechoslovakia was conspicuous by its absence. We went on protesting about Greece, Portugal and Uganda, but to rake up the memories of Czechoslovakia wasn't thought to be in good taste.

I am wondering, therefore, whether the kind of independence the East European countries now enjoy would be really protected either by the results of the Security Conference or even by a standing conference or secretariat?

HOLST: I'm not suggesting that any East European state is sovereign in the sense in which Belgium is for instance. Very far from it; what I'm saying is that the likelihood of their being pushed around by Russia is going to be marginally reduced. The whole notion of East European 'independence' is extremely fragile in so far as it is not altogether imaginary (there are, one supposes, gradations between, say, Bulgaria and Hungary), and all an on-going security conference, or some permanent body spawned by it, could do is to erect additional paper-barriers. These would not repel tanks, but they might influence the Soviet decision-makers. They would make it just that more difficult for the Russians to send in their troops to occupy another socialist country under the pretext of 'proletarian internationalism'—

URBAN: —a situation rich in irony, for it would then be the Soviet policy of 'peaceful co-existence' with ideologically antagonistic states that would protect the East European members of the socialist family against the fraternal attentions of 'proletarian internationalism'.

HOLST: Quite; but we cannot, and in my view should not, try to obtain a formal renunciation of the Brezhnev Doctrine. The Russians have, as you know, never conceded its existence in these terms. The challenge we face is to provide incentives and penalties to render the Doctrine inoperative. We should, to borrow a Marxist phrase, try to make it wither away. We should exploit the Soviet material interest in détente to create stakes for its continuation and stabilization, stakes that would argue against breaking the rules. A more co-operative atmosphere across the old lines of division in Europe might, then, reduce the need, as the Russians see it, to assert their hegemony in Eastern Europe by recourse to armed force.

URBAN: We have, in this symposium, repeatedly asked ourselves whether the Russians' anxiety to reduce their insecurity in the West is an expression of their grave sense of insecurity vis-à-vis China. Is the Soviet fear justified, or are we being conned by the Soviet leaders in the hope that, by holding out to us the prospect of a Sino-Soviet showdown, we might be moved to guarantee the status quo in Europe at a much reduced price?

HOLST: It is difficult for us to tell whether China really poses a threat to the Soviet Union or whether the Russians simply think she does. My impression is (and here I'm talking from imperfect experience) that the Russians' fear of China is deeply imbedded in the national psyche, that it is irrational and vastly exaggerated, if indeed not chimerical. The Russians are certainly more 'hung-up' on China than the Americans were at any time since Mao took power; the incalculable element in the Russian reaction to the yellow races makes it almost impossible to look at the Sino-Soviet dispute in the framework of cool facts alone. You have to be Russian, and as fully conscious as Russians still are of their defeat by Japan in 1905, to provide a convincing answer to your question.

URBAN: The sense of Russia's defeat by the yellow races is strong and totally unsocialist. I am reminded of Stalin's astonishing broadcast after the Soviet Union's quick victory over Japan in 1945, in which he said: 'The defeat of Russian troops in 1904 in the period of the Russo-Japanese war left grave memories in the minds of our people. It was a dark stain on our country. Our people trusted and awaited the day when Japan would be routed and the stain wiped out. For forty years have we, men of the older generation, waited for this day. And now this day has come.'

This extraordinary declaration was a complete reversal of the official attitude of the Russian socialists in 1905 as represented inter alia by Stalin himself—an attitude still enshrined in secondary school text books published by the Soviet authorities in 1941: 'Lenin and the Bolsheviks worked for the defeat of the Tsarist government in this predatory and shameful war . . . because the defeat facilitated the victory of the revolution over Tsarism. . . . Comrade Stalin wrote about the necessity of defeat: "Let us wish that this war will become a still greater disaster for the Tsarist regime than was the Crimean War."'

Stalin's words in 1945 were the voice of Russian nationalism, and I am sure you are right in suspecting that it colours the present Soviet leaders' view of China as heavily as it did Stalin's of Japan. Stalin's attack on Japan in August 1945 was, incidentally, in breach of his pact of friendship and non-aggression of 1941 with Japan. What Hitler had done treacherously to Russia, Stalin now did to Japan.

The continuity of Russian fears of the yellow peril emerges with equal clarity from the second volume of Khrushchev's memoirs. In the 1950s, he tells us (i.e. well before the Sino-Soviet dispute came out into the open), Mao agreed, at Soviet request, to send 200,000 Chinese workers to Siberia to fell timber. But, says Khrushchev, the experiment was not repeated. 'What had the Chinese been up to?' he asks. 'I'll tell you: they wanted to occupy Siberia without war. . . . It was a clever manoeuvre but it didn't work.'

Khrushchev's charge is so wildly unlikely that one can only explain it in terms of a Slavophile's atavistic obsession with Huns, Tatars and their supposed reincarnations in the twentieth century.

HOLST: I find it very hard to conceive of a Chinese military attack on Russia, or even a military type of threat being mounted by the Chinese against Russia. The effort would have to be stupendous and the Soviet answer would be devastating. The Chinese could have no political or military interest in violating the Soviet Union.

I find the idea of a Russian pre-emptive strike against China's nuclear establishment easier to follow. Why do I say that? There is a close relationship between military muscle and military enterprise, especially in a dictatorship. The Russians have so far been fairly cautious in using their military power, and I would ascribe their caution in part to the fact that, until quite recently, they did not have enough of the type of force one can translate into political influence. For example, the Russians have for long been terribly frustrated by their inability to project themselves into the Mediterranean. They could see American marines landing in Lebanon and the Sixth Fleet making the Mediterranean an American lake for all practical purposes. The Russians could do nothing about it for they lacked the means. Nor did they have a global outlook of their role as a military power.

But in recent years all this has been changed: the Russians have acquired a vast navy and built up a strong amphibious and air-born capability. Once you have such instruments of power, they generate their own dynamics, and there soon comes a time when you have to justify to yourself the continuing possession of these particular capabilities, and you start looking for roles. You have the gadgets, so you want to put them to use.

When the Americans ordered a grade three nuclear alert during the 1973 Middle East war because they saw that the Russians were at least going through the motions of preparing to put their air-born divisions into the war theatre, this American move may, ironically, have made a lot of the Russian middle-brass suddenly realize: 'Well, perhaps we *could* do something with all these highly trained troops if only the men at the top gave us the signal.'*

This learning process can be very rapid and dangerous. When I hinted a minute ago that I would not rule out the possibility of a pre-emptive Soviet strike against China, this kind of pressure by the

---

* The Soviet threat appears to have been real. According to Admiral Elmo Zumwalt (Chief of United States Naval Operations, 1970–74), the Soviet Union threatened to send troops into the Middle East war unless the United States stopped Israel from destroying the Egyptian Third Army which the Israeli forces had encircled. In his letter to Nixon (24 October 1973) Brezhnev 'made it clear that unless the Israelis were forced to end their encirclement of the Third Army, the Soviets would go in and free them'. On 25 October, Nixon ordered a grade three alert of American forces. Nixon accepted the Soviet ultimatum because the Soviet Navy outnumbered the Sixth Fleet by three to two. ('Admiral Zumwalt: In spite of détente talk "trends are going against America"', *Washington Post*, 28 July 1975)

military was at the back of my mind.

URBAN: In 1974 I visited the northern parts of Norway including the Norwegian-Soviet border area, and while I was most favourably impressed by the meticulous organization and high morale of the Norwegian forces, I was equally impressed by what I learned from your military commanders about the size and sophistication of the Soviet forces facing them in Murmansk and the Kola peninsula.

HOLST: Norway borders on a section of the Soviet Union in which the Russians have concentrated more troops and military hardware per square metre than there are in any other part of the world. To give you some feel of the barest essentials: there are two motorized infantry divisions (24,000 men) on the Kola peninsula. The two Soviet divisions are part of the Leningrad military district with a total force of ten divisions, two of which are of category II and four of category III readiness. They are reinforced by about 10,000 border troops under the Ministry of the Interior. There are two medium range ballistic missile bases south of Murmansk. The infrastructure on the Kola peninsula includes perimeter radar installations for the Moscow anti-ballistic missile system. There are some 40 airfields in the peninsula with a normal deployment of 300–500 aircraft.

The major military instrument, however, is the Northern Fleet with 465 vessels and about 100,000 men. The fleet includes a staggering total of 188 submarines of which 85 are nuclear-powered.

They include some of Russia's most modern, missile firing submarines with targeting ranges up to 4,000 nautical miles. The surface fleet consists of some 30 cruisers and destroyers, 35 ocean-going escorts, 33 landing ships, 25 missile-carrying patrol boats and 150–200 smaller vessels.

Clearly this enormous concentration of power is not directed against Norway as such—it is one element in the global race with America. But we are in the suffocating vicinity of this power and we, like the Chinese, have to be very much aware that power has its own imperatives. We just do not know how the Soviet leaders are going to see the security of their northern forces best served. Do they regard Northern Norway—Troms and Finnmark—as part of their forward defence theatre? Under what circumstances would they come to be so regarded?

Our attitude to détente hinges on these questions, and our attitude is twofold: first we are in favour of détente because we are a small country in a most vulnerable geographic position: every disturbance in the American-Soviet relationship crystallizes in increased military activity around our shores and our border with the

Soviet Union. So if tension is reduced between East and West, we are (or so we hope) bound to enjoy a more relaxed atmosphere in our immediate environment. This, in turn, increases our freedom of action in our political policies.

The second element in our attitude to détente—and I have already referred to this in the context of European unification—expresses the fear that détente through force reductions may become a purely Central-European regional phenomenon and that, even though Norway is located in a part of Europe where Soviet power is absolutely predominant, we may be left out on a limb despite our membership of Nato.

URBAN: Why, then, is Norway insisting on her self-imposed and entirely unilateral decision not to allow foreign military bases on her territory?

HOLST: This decision goes back to February 1949 when, prior to Norway's accession to Nato, the Norwegian Government sought to reassure Moscow that the Norwegian step would not threaten Soviet security. But, although it would be politically very difficult to change this base-reservation policy, the Norwegian reservation is conditional in the sense that it applies only 'as long as Norway is not attacked or subject to threats of attack'. 'Threats of attack' is an ambiguous phrase and throughout the 'fifties and 'sixties the Soviet leaders were trying to increase the constraints on Norwegian decision-makers and to acquire for themselves the right to decide how this base-reservation policy should be interpreted. The Russians, in fact, claimed the right of umpireship.

Today we are fully honouring our self-imposed undertaking on base policy vis-à-vis the Soviet Union, but at the same time we are also doing everything we politically can to be reliable and constructive members of Nato. We have agreed to the transfer of allied forces to Norway in war or in a situation of threat, we have constructed military installations large enough to receive allied forces in such a situation, we have agreed to hold allied joint exercises in Norway, barring some of the northernmost areas, and to permit allied air and naval forces to pay short visits in peacetime. Also, we participate in the Nato infrastructure programme, Nato's northern command (AFNORTH) has its headquarters outside Oslo, we participate in manoeuvres with the ACE mobile force, and we have constructed and maintained electronic warning, navigational and communications installations.

URBAN: Does this dual policy enjoy broad support among the Norwegian political parties?

HOLST: It does; by the end of the 1960s the credibility and predictability of our base policy was accepted by the world and especially the Soviet Union. At the same time, base-reservation has been established as the cornerstone of our security policy commanding the support of all political parties, so that any threat against the country must be explicit and immediate before we could, from the domestic point of view, eliminate base-reservation. This factor is one important reason why there has been so little dispute over the credibility of our base policy in Soviet-Norwegian relations in the 1970s.

Let me emphasize that Norway adopted base-reservation because it serves our *own* security interests. It was never a concession we would have preferred not to make. The point is that in the strategically sensitive area in the north of Norway our efforts to protect ourselves are entirely our own, thus not causing the Soviet Union to take offensive action in an emergency for fear of an immediate outside threat. The exclusion of foreign bases promotes our security also in the sense that our efforts reassure the Russians about the essentially defensive character of our interests. Our whole notion of security is based on interdependence, and it is my impression that we have managed to establish an acceptable balance between insurance and reassurance in our relationship with the Soviet Union. There are no perfect solutions in situations of this kind, but we have tried to establish and adhere to reasonable rules.

In the context of negotiations about European security and force reductions, we hope that the Soviet Union will—in the interest of equal and undiminished security for all—agree to certain constraints which will introduce a greater degree of reciprocity in Europe in general, and in Northern Europe in particular, than is the case now. I strongly believe that one cannot build a stable, viable and just order in Europe on the premise that Soviet territory and Soviet military dispositions are outside the rules of the game. We cannot treat Soviet territory as a sanctuary, outside the limits of mutual reassurance and restraint.

URBAN: What about Norway's self-imposed refusal to have nuclear weapons on her territory?

HOLST: Here the Norwegian stance is less flexible than it is on general base-reservation. Our self-denying ordinance in this matter has become a permanent feature of our domestic life which it would be extremely difficult to change. In any case, we believe that the emplacement of nuclear weapons in Norway would have a destabilizing impact on any crisis in the area. We have, therefore, excluded any possibility of reversing our present reservation on nuclear weapons. We have concluded no nuclear information-sharing agreement with the United States—information which would be necessary for the training of Norwegian forces in the potential use of nuclear arms. Any use of nuclear weapons in the defence of Norway would have to be made by American, British or Canadian forces. Nor has Norway concluded any stockpiling agreement with the United States for the preparation of the possible transfer of nuclear weapons under the dual key arrangement.

URBAN: It seems to me Norway is rather in two minds about her status in the western alliance. She wants to be defended, yet she cannot bring herself to do what it takes to make her—and the northern flank of Nato—capable of being defended with any chance of success. At the moment even the pre-stocking of conventional allied equipment is ruled out by the Norwegian Government, although the definition of base-reservation is probably flexible enough to make this possible. During my visit to Norway I noticed a definite reluctance to enter into any discussion of the matter.

With all due respect to Norway's small but impressive military capability, isn't this one sign that a slow Finlandization has, in fact, set in?

Moscow has claimed the right of umpireship which is as flagrant an interference in a non-socialist country's internal affairs as I can readily recall. A military constraint which Norway and Denmark had unilaterally imposed on themselves as a good-will gesture in 1949 (when the Russians had no atomic weapons but the Americans had) was abused by the Russians in an attempt to turn this gesture into a binding bilateral commitment.

Russia's ambition to exploit the 1949 opening revealed itself clearly in the Soviet, Danish and Norwegian Governments' joint communiqué after Khrushchev's visit to Scandinavia in July 1964.

This is a remarkable document; in it the Soviet Government expressed its appreciation of the refusal (sic) of Denmark and Norway to permit the stationing of nuclear weapons on their territories. The Danish-Norwegian reservation that this applied only in peace-time, and that it was voluntary and non-binding, was omitted. Thus the communiqué did in fact very nearly achieve what President Kekkonen had failed to achieve in 1963, when he suggested that the nuclear-free status of Scandinavia be confirmed by mutual undertakings, changing the unilateral and conditional declarations of the Nordic states into a multilateral and binding instrument. Kekkonen was, at the time, widely accused of promoting the Soviet cause at the expense of the security of Finland's western neighbours.

The purpose of the Soviet move was to induce Denmark and Norway tacitly to accept the Soviet interpretation of base-reservation or at the very least to make any reversal of this self-imposed restraint entirely unthinkable. And this, I think, has been achieved.

When you put all these pieces together—and one might add others such as Norway's reluctance to start exploiting oil off the continental shelf of Finmark for fear of touching off Soviet territorial and naval sensibilities; or Soviet opposition to the construction (and then to the length of the runway) of a civilian airport near Ny Alesund in the Spitzbergen—the pattern that emerges is a creeping loss of Norway's freedom to pursue an independent foreign policy. Some of this is undoubtedly due to an entirely realistic appraisal of Norway's geo-political vulnerability, but some must be surely ascribed to the Norwegian public's inability to judge whether there is much to choose between the kind of socio-moral order Norway stands for and the one she opposes. This is a crisis of self-confidence which besets us all in the West at the moment, but perhaps it is more in evidence in the self-searching, puritanic climate of Scandinavia than it is elsewhere.

HOLST: Your own omissions are as significant as were those of the 1964 communiqué, for what you did not mention was that, try as they did, the Russians never actually succeeded in interfering with our freedom to define base-reservation; that we refused to consider the 1963 Kekkonen Plan for a nuclear-free zone in Scandinavia, and that we also declined formally to commit ourselves to any unilateral renunciation of nuclear weapons on Norwegian soil because this might have carried the undesirable implication that we were succumbing to the geo-political diktat of the Soviet Union.

On the Spitzbergen affair—we did, after a dispute lasting fifteen years, reject the Soviet protest against building an airfield at Longyearbyen. The airfield is now under construction. The whole installation is essentially under Norwegian operational control and will not, as the Russians suggested, have a strong Soviet representation on it. What you have to bear in mind is that Spitzbergen is a legally complicated case, for although all the Svalbard islands (of which Spitzbergen is one) are under Norwegian sovereignty, an international treaty of 1920 granted some thirty odd signatories, including—in absentia—the Soviet state, the right to exploit the natural resources of these islands and to trade in the area on the basis of equal rights. Of these signatories only Norway and the Soviet Union are permanently present on the archipelago. The Soviet claim to share in the operation of the new airfield has to be seen in the light of these circumstances.

It doesn't therefore make sense to speak of Norway's Finlandization. We are, I can assure you, extremely conscious of the need to avoid satellitization, and our decision-makers are quite aware of the fact that we could not maintain our independence without our drawing rights on the American forces in Germany and Iceland. Indeed the negative result of our referendum on EEC membership has increased our dependence on the United States, for we are now the only developed and democratic European country in Nato which is outside the European Community. The discussion of Norwegian Nato-policy is no longer focused on the pros and cons of continued membership—that is now taken for granted by the great majority—but rather on adjusting to the evolution of Nato in the context of East-West negotiations.

URBAN: Yet Norway cannot bring herself to give her allies the kind of facilities which alone would guarantee her security. I find it a little disconcerting that while you predicate your security on the American presence, you are not prepared to help the United States to make her presence possible. When, in the early 1970s, it looked as though the United States might be forced out of her Icelandic base at Keflavik, Norway offered no alternative although a Norwegian base would have been the only suitable substitute. I am not sure how this curious and probably self-defeating attitude to national defence accords with the high moral principles which Norway has set herself in all other spheres of her foreign policy.

HOLST: When you are a small country thrust into the vortex of competition between the super-powers, you must adapt to your circumstances as best you can. We have chosen to obey certain self-denying rules in the hope of constraining the super-powers in their relations with ourselves. It is a fact of political life that, after a period of time, freely chosen and conditional decisions such as the one to deny ourselves foreign bases and nuclear weapons, become internalized in the domestic political process. They become permanent factors in one's arsenal of national assumptions and taboos. That the Russians play on these taboos does, of course, reinforce their power.

The Soviet-Norwegian military 'confrontation' is hopelessly asymmetrical, and there is no prospect at all of redressing the local balance by any mobilization of Norwegian resources. Redressing the balance by the stationing of United States forces in Norway would carry the risk—indeed the certainty—of imposing the super-power confrontation on the politics of the Nordic countries, and especially Norway, much more firmly than it has already been imposed on them.

Given these limited and uncomfortable options, Norwegian security reflects a deliberate balance between deterrence and reassurance vis-à-vis the Soviet Union. You have to remember that Norway's key position in the American-Soviet global competition is very new, and one of our ways of coping with it is to occupy a con-

sistently 'left-wing' position in favour of détente and arms control—
not because small countries are *ab ovo* 'soft', but because we feel that
a Russian stake in global security would be an impediment to the
demonstration of Soviet military power in northern Europe as well.

URBAN: You argued a minute ago that the possession of large
military power tends to create its own opportunities for the use of
that power—a reversal, incidentally, of the traditional wisdom *si vis
pacem, para bellum*.

At what point might the Soviet perception of the imperatives of
Soviet power in the Far East make a surgical operation against
China a serious possibility?

HOLST: If the Russians manage to secure their front in Western
Europe, and if the Chinese continue making the rapid progress they
are currently making with their nuclear weapons and missiles, the
Soviet Government might, under the marshals' pressure, decide not
to wait for the Maoist leadership to die, but opt for a surgical operation. The Soviet commanders are aware of the dangers of indeci-
sion: the longer they wait, the fewer options they will have left. This
may force their hand. The most dangerous time for the Chinese is
1975-76. By 1977 they may have an offensive nuclear arsenal of their
own which the Russians could not destroy without risking nuclear
retaliation. Here is a problem for American diplomacy.

URBAN: Is it in our interest to secure the Russians' back in
Europe?

HOLST: That depends on our estimate of how the Russians
would behave in a certain set of conditions. There is a case for
saying that it is easier to deal with a secure adversary than a frightened one. If the Soviet leaders feel insecure in Europe as well as in
the Far East, their entire global policy may become unpredictable
and even destructive. On the other hand, if we help them to feel
secure on their western front, they may be tempted to try for a quick
surgical intervention against China, and I do not believe that would
be in our interest.

URBAN: Why should that not be in our interest? When Chou
En-lai says that the Russians 'are making a feint in the East while
attacking in the West', he is implying the hope that a showdown
between Russia and the West would deflect the danger of Soviet
attack from China. By the same token, I would say that a showdown between Russia and China would lighten the pressure on the
West and increase our room for manoeuvre.

HOLST: This sounds neat and logical but nuclear war would be
a messy and incalculable affair quite apart from the colossal destruction and human suffering it would involve. A Soviet attack on
China's nuclear establishment would make the world situation at

once entirely unpredictable. The chances of miscalculation would be so great that our whole civilization would be put at risk. Kissinger is, I think, very conscious both of the possibility of an early pre-emptive Soviet move against China, and of the need not to let it happen. But, of course, he is far from having all the cards in his hands.

URBAN: However this may be, we are certainly in a strong position to impress on the Russians that the mild conditions we are attaching to détente must be met, for it is clear enough that the Russians badly want peace and security in Europe.

HOLST: That is so, and we have already discussed why we could, and should, insist on the Soviet acceptance of Basket Three.

The Soviet leaders perceive their position in the world in competitive terms. This is the combined legacy of Tsarist power-politics and the universalistic claims of Marxism-Leninism.

URBAN: Your point is well illustrated in the second volume of Khrushchev's memoirs where Khrushchev lectures and reprimands Academician Kapitsa for having refused to work on military research: 'What choice do we have? . . . As long as there are antagonistic classes and antagonistic states with armies, we simply must push ahead with defence research. Otherwise we'll be choked to death, smashed to pieces, trampled in the dirt.'

HOLST: I am certain that the thinking of the present Soviet leadership runs on similar lines. This is the sort of perception we must try to correct.

I regard the security and force reductions talks as a long exercise in education: we must try to make the Russians understand that security is not competitive. It is a shared value which the Russians will only have the moment we have it; our loss of security is not Russia's gain of security and vice versa. The moment Germans, Norwegians, Finns and Poles feel more secure, the chances of Soviet insecurity too are greatly reduced.

To effect change of this kind in the perception of Soviet security is especially important for the small West European countries, for as long as the Soviet leaders go on thinking in competitive terms, they *will* insist on trading off security concession for security concession; but a country like Norway has very little to concede: we are doing so little that there is hardly anything we can refrain from doing. Hence our emphasis on the reciprocal and interdependent nature of security, which I personally regard as being much more important than any technical clauses we may write into an East-West security declaration.

Sooner or later the Russians will come to understand that their traditional penchant for secrecy works against their own interests.

Take one example: the Soviet defence budget is not a public document; we do not know the exact amounts the Soviet state spends on defence; we do not know *how* what is spent is spent. We can see the missiles when they are put into their silos, but the finished product reflects decisions taken seven years ago.

What will the Russians be showing at their military parades seven years from now? That information cannot be obtained from satellites. Hence the western, and especially the American, defence effort has to be based on estimates, and there will, of course, always be those who will, for one reason or another, want to sell us high estimates. But can the United States Government, for example, really be blamed for hedging against uncertainties when the consequences of being wrong may be catastrophic?

The Soviet defence planners, on their part, may undoubtedly find arguments for a massive Soviet military effort by referring to the— openly conducted—United States defence debate. But that debate itself is due to the American fear that there is no certain knowledge of what the Russians might be planning. Thus the spiral of inflated threats, set in motion by the secretive operational code of the Soviet Union, is a major source of international tension; it produces an outsize security problem for the Soviet leadership which it can economically ill afford.

URBAN: You were saying that you would regard the security and force reductions talks as exercises in education. Weren't the SALT negotiations conceived with a similar purpose in mind?

HOLST: They were. These, too, were in reality confidence-building measures between the two super-powers, and I would regard this aspect of SALT I and II as much more important than the actual substance of the agreements reached, for these do not cut deeply into the programmes of the two powers in the strategic weapons field. Over a period of time the educational lessons of SALT should make both the American and Soviet decision-makers more sensitive to each other's concerns—and that would be a gain.

But, as far as SALT is concerned, we should be aware also of the need to generate the right kind of learning. I do not believe it to be conducive to détente, and an interdependent perspective on security, to grant the Soviet Union significant disparities such as the ones written into the Interim Agreement on offensive forces. According to the Vladivostok guidelines, these disparities will be made permanent in the follow-on agreement to SALT I and II. It may well be that the disparities are more optical than real, but perceptions are important.

URBAN: I do not doubt the desirability of re-educating the Soviet leaders in the facts of the modern world, but I doubt whether they *will* be re-educated. For one thing, the drag of power-politics and ideology is severe. For another, having success-fully pursued a militant foreign policy for half a century, why should the Soviet leaders change course now, at the peak of their fortunes?

For Americans, détente is an end in itself—it heralds an era of world order based on mutual confidence and negotiations. For the Russians, détente is synonymous with the struggle between two irreconcilably antagonistic forms of society—war without a shoot-ing war, but one in which the Soviet leaders never lose sight of vic-tory as the consummation of détente. Can our educational exercises at the conference table leaven this lump of ideological commitment and power interests?

HOLST: It will be difficult. The Marxist-Leninist view of inter-national relations is a latter-day version of the drama between good and evil, proletarians and capitalists. It has no room for any bal-ance-of-power concept of the kind Kissinger is trying to promote in the footsteps of Metternich; nor does it allow for any community of interests or any sharing of values by a large number of ideologically unaligned but globally interdependent nations. We cannot even fall back on Russian historical thinking for a precedent, because that, too, has always been articulated in the language of conflict and con-quest. The way ahead is, as you say, inauspicious.

Nevertheless, the effort has to be made. Nuclear weapons have introduced a new and revolutionary quality into international and—more important—inter-societal relations. After an exchange of nuclear blows there will be no victors. One in the eye for the bour-geoisie will not hoist the red flag in new places.

These are, by now, platitudes for the student of international affairs, but they remain to be internalized by the Soviet policy estab-lishment. It is here that a thorough reconsideration of received truths is clearly called for. Open-ended talks with the Soviet Union conceived as an exercise in reciprocal education need not be a hope-less enterprise provided that we can detach ourselves from the inhibiting tradition of the gain/loss, victory/defeat mentality. These are yesterday's metaphors. Even the Soviet system has become too sophisticated and too closely interwoven with our own to go on pursuing its interests in the framework of such dated simplicities.

WOLF H. HALSTI

Finlandization

URBAN: Finlandization is a loaded term, and Finnish politicians object to it, for it implies, wrongly they insist, that Finland's sovereignty is limited—that while the country is outwardly free to act as it pleases, it does so under licence from a superior neighbour which retains the right to intervene. The Finns deny the accuracy of this appraisal, but whether or not the appraisal is correct, Finlandization for the West European countries expresses the fear that unless they reaffirm their unity in Nato and the European Community, they may themselves forfeit the independence of their foreign policy and, with it, their ability to resist encroachments by the Soviet Union upon their domestic affairs.

To East European ears Finlandization has a totally different ring. Czechs, Poles and Hungarians would, if they could, happily settle for Finlandization because to them the amount of sovereignty Finland has had to abdicate seems enviably small in comparison with their own total loss of independence, and Finland's ability to emerge from the war with her democratic institutions intact bordering on the miraculous.

The West European fear is aggravated by Finland's apparent shift in recent years from neutrality to 'neutralism', that is to say, to a position of subservience to Soviet policies hiding behind a mask of independence.

The Finns do, of course, have a semantic problem with the Soviet Union, for in communist terminology to be neutral simply means to be indifferent. Neutrality (as one student of Nordic affairs has observed) does not fit into the Marxist world of black and white and must therefore be given a more positive meaning. But, say the Finns, whatever the semantics of neutrality, Finland enjoys the best of all possible worlds, for her actual position is positive for the Russians, acceptable to the Finns themselves and not harmful to anyone.

However this may be, for us in Western Europe Finlandization stands for all the things we do not want to see happen in our part of the world.

138

Is Finland, in fact, Finlandized? If so, is Finlandization in the national interest?

HALSTI: Freedom and independence are relative concepts. Every country in the world, including the largest ones, must adjust to the realities of its situation, the small ones more so than the powerful nations. The current use of the word Finlandization is misleading for it is being used to denote an erosion of Finnish independence, and this is patently not the case. If you compare Finland's freedom of manoeuvre today with what it was in 1945, the increase in Finnish sovereignty is striking. For some years after the war—and here I'm talking from personal experience—we had in our foreign policy no elbow room at all. Today we have a good deal of freedom within recognized limits. Our West European critics have gone wrong in their judgement of our situation because they have misread our search for the outer limits of our independence as a curtailment of our independence. The limits have not been drawn closer—what has happened is that we tried to break through the constraints and ran into overwhelming odds.

Our first attempt to demolish the wall surrounding us was soon after the death of Stalin. We thought, wrongly as we were soon to discover, that the disappearance of Stalin would change Soviet foreign policy. It didn't. Stalin's followers made many domestic changes, but the continuity in Russian foreign affairs was maintained. Russia did not want to give up anything she had obtained under Stalin.

Our Social Democrats were especially blind to the realities of the situation. In 1957 the Party elected as its chairman Väinö Tanner—a bête noire in Soviet eyes—

URBAN: —and in those of Kekkonen too—

HALSTI: yes, Tanner was one of Kekkonen's bitter opponents, but what mattered much more was that Tanner had been the undisputed leader of the Social Democratic Party until the end of the war and was then sentenced to imprisonment as one of the politicians responsible for getting Finland into the war against the Soviet Union. In other words, Tanner was highly unacceptable to the Russians and the Russians missed no opportunity of telling the Finnish side that they took a very dim view of Tanner occupying any leading official position in the Finnish Government. Well, when you are dealing with a mighty neighbour you can't shirk the responsibility of taking this kind of sentiment into account, whether it is based on fact, bias, a misreading of history or whatever. After the July 1958 elections Fagerholm, another Social Democrat, was appointed head of the new government, and Moscow reacted with deep distrust. The Soviet Ambassador was withdrawn, all trade negotiations were put off and a freeze set in affecting all aspects of Soviet-Finnish relations. Eventually, at the time of the 1961 Berlin crisis, the coalition which Fagerholm headed collapsed from within. An all-Agrarian minority government was appointed and the Social Democrats went into opposition. Relations with the Soviet Union were restored to normal.

My point is that there was nothing in the Russian attitude that had not been there before. The Russians did not escalate their concern with the composition of the Finnish Government—it had always been there. The blame for the Tanner-Fagerholm crisis rests with those who turned a blind eye to the limitations that we had accepted after the war and challenged the Russians to behave the way they did. In 1947 Paasikivi said: 'However well our foreign policy declarations may sound, the eyes of our neighbour follow what occurs at home.' This continues to be true and it clearly imposes constraints on us.

URBAN: We are not, then, disagreeing that Finland's position is one of limited sovereignty; the question is: how limited is limited sovereignty and is it the sort of thing a now sovereign West European country could, under certain circumstances, contemplate as an acceptable alternative?

We know from Ambassador Max Jacobson's book, *Finnish Neutrality*, that the Fagerholm Government was made to collapse by the resignation of its Agrarian members—a resignation controlled by President Kekkonen who considered it 'more important to regain Soviet confidence in Finnish neutrality' than to assert Finland's right to order her internal affairs without outside interference, come what may.

As Khrushchev later explained, the Russians suspected that a government led by Social Democrats might change the course of Finnish foreign policy, and made no bones about telling the Finns of their apprehension. 'What I am now going to say is not a demand, it is a friendly word and do not let it hurt you', Khrushchev told President Kekkonen on 22 November 1960. 'I speak because some elements in your community do not understand the importance of peace and friendly relations between our countries. For example, there is the policy of Tanner and Leskinen. I speak because this has made us anxious. We fear it will damage the relations between our countries.' And on an earlier occasion (3 August 1959) Khrushchev said to a Finnish Parliamentary delegation, in the words of President Kekkonen: 'The Soviet Union would feel concern if Tanner and Leskinen were to hold office.'

I would have thought these were gross forms of interference with the domestic affairs of a nominally sovereign country, and the

Finnish 'reaction' to them was classically neutralist in that President Kekkonen *anticipated* Soviet displeasure and moved against the Social Democrats, presumably to forestall worse to come from Moscow. I cannot judge the merit of the subsequent Social Democratic accusation that Kekkonen provoked, or even invited, the Soviet reaction to monopolize power for himself and his party. It is surely enough to note that the Soviet Government looked, and still looks, upon Kekkonen as the guarantor of Finland's postwar course. In November 1960 Khrushchev told a group of Finnish politicians representing all political parties: 'Whoever is for Kekkonen is for friendship with the Soviet Union and whoever is against Kekkonen is against friendship with the Soviet Union.'

Short of appointing a Finnish president direct from the Kremlin, this is about as explicit as a Soviet politician can be.

HALSTI: It is perfectly clear that when a small state lives cheek by jowl with a super-power, it has to observe a certain threshold of tolerance; the small state is (to change my metaphor) within the gravitational pull of a mass much larger than itself which limits its freedom of action. There is nothing very new about this or unique to Finland's position vis-à-vis Russia; at the time of the Cuban crisis President Kennedy marked out certain limits beyond which the United States would not stretch *its* tolerance, and the Soviet leaders, in their wisdom, decided to respect those limits. Of course, a totalitarian state has a much lower threshold of tolerance than a democracy, but one has to take that into account from the start and not push beyond it unless one is prepared to get hurt. I do not think the Finnish people are incarcerated in a cage—as western critics of Finlandization often intimate that they are. I would, rather, liken our position to that of a herd of horses which has a large field to graze in but must not stray beyond the boundary.

Take the example of EFTA: the Russians told our people under what conditions they would approve of Finnish membership. We complied with these Soviet wishes and joined EFTA. Our recent agreement with EEC has gone through similar stages of Soviet objection, hesitation and finally approval. Clearly the Soviet Government would not permit us to become full members of the European Community for that would run counter to the security of the Soviet state as Moscow sees it. However, by the same token, I do not think the United States Government is happy with the idea that there is a communist government off the shores of the American mainland, but it is prepared to put up with it so long as requirements of American security are respected. The important thing to remember is that Finlandization has not been suddenly sprung upon us; it has been there continuously since the second world war.

URBAN: The Soviet view of Scandinavia has certainly always been dominated by security considerations. Take the example of the NORDEK project: launched in 1968 as a customs union of the four Scandinavian countries with far-reaching features of integration, it came to a sudden halt and then collapsed on political grounds early in 1970. Why did it collapse? It collapsed because the December 1969 summit meeting of EEC countries in the Hague rekindled hopes of the enlargement of the European Community. Russia feared that through NORDEK all Scandinavian countries would drift into EEC which, for them, was synonymous with Nato. So the Finns withdrew abruptly under Soviet pressure. Similarly, it was the Soviet 'no' which blocked Ambassador Max Jacobson as Secretary-General of the United Nations after his election had become an objective of Finnish policy.

All these examples cast doubt on the credibility of Finnish neutrality as well as Finnish sovereignty. The confidence-inspiring posture which Stalin, Khrushchev and Brezhnev have all expectèd from Finland demands an unceasing display of self-effacement and self-censorship.

HALSTI: We are in a very difficult position. The Soviet Union is a totalitarian, centralized state where leadership is traditionally personalized and often capricious. The men in charge of this state are not accountable to parliament, they cannot be dismissed by election or referendum and they can fall back on nothing in the Russian national tradition to cool the passions of self-righteous commitment. Finland, by contrast, is a liberal democracy, and I can quite see why, from a West European point of view, our piecemeal, fence-mending, tinkering relationship with the Soviet Union must seem bizarre and even treacherous. But the relationship works. It would tax the patience of angels and the ingenuity of a Machiavelli to hit upon a formula better suited to serve the symbiosis of a vast despotism and a tiny democracy contiguous with it, than the one we have worked out by trial and error between the Finnish tradition of parliamentary democracy and Soviet dictatorship. We must, as you say, exercise a great deal of self-control and even self-censorship if we do not want to bang our heads against the wall, but we *have* come to possess a special sense for all this, we know how far we can press an issue with Moscow and where our insistence might prove futile or self-defeating. This is not the most dignified position to be in, but it is vital to our survival.

URBAN: I have great respect for Finnish skill and diplomacy, but when you say that Finland is a liberal democracy my first reaction is: yes, so she is; my second reaction, however, is to qualify that statement by adding: a liberal democracy within the bounds of the possible, for Finland's self-denying ordinance in her foreign policy has spun off into her domestic affairs.

We have already seen that Khrushchev's disapproval of Tanner and Leskinen, and of the Social Democratic Party in general, led to the collapse of an elected government. I find it equally telling—and perhaps even more important, for it strikes at the roots of democracy—that from time to time President Kekkonen should find it necessary to warn the Finnish press and writers not to say certain things that might upset Moscow.

In 1958, for instance, Kekkonen complained that after the return of the Porkkala enclave to Finland the Finnish papers published a large number of studies and memoirs which were 'tendentious towards the Soviet Union'. He said: 'Responsible leaders cannot pursue the foreign policy postulated in the 1948 agreement unless it is backed by public opinion.'

This is a very curious statement to make in a democracy. Does the President mean to say that 'public opinion' ought to support the agreement even if it disagrees with it? What if the public, or part of the public, or opinion-making writers in the press or academia, had changed their minds in the ten years that had elapsed since its signature? Or if they feel that the agreement, or some aspect of it, should be re-negotiated? Aren't they allowed to say so for fear of offending the Soviet Union? Later in the same speech President Kekkonen said: 'I have followed these phenomena with considerable disquiet. The open expressions of animosity towards the Soviet Union . . . taken together . . . constitute a heavy strain on our foreign policy.'

It is, of course, perfectly true that the Soviet leaders have never been able to understand how the free press works in the West. Lacking precedent in their own history, the Russians believe that there is some confidential mechanism between the government and the press whereby what the government thinks right is printed and what is antipathetic to government policy is withheld. 'Mr Khrushchev in his luncheon speech dealt with this matter [of the Finnish press] at great length', President Kekkonen said in a broadcast in January 1959. 'In our private discussions, Foreign Minister Gromyko pointed out that he had a large collection of extracts from the Finnish press in which the Soviet Union was criticized or ridiculed. . . . I believe it to be certain that without restraint and responsibility on the part of the press, relations between our countries will never attain the degree of confidence that our own interest requires. This is a sensitive point for the Soviet Union because unfriendly articles are regarded as reflections of public opinion.'

My impression is that this is an even more sensitive point for Finnish democracy: the Finnish press is put under pressure not to voice opinions that are unpleasing to Russian ears. The Russians correctly identify the Finnish press with public opinion, but they do not like what they see. Nor does President Kekkonen who is certain in his own mind that it is more important for Finland to survive in her present state than to be a faultless model of liberal democracy. Conclusion: the press must cease to reflect public opinion in certain areas or else Finland must face the consequences. But as Finland, represented by the conscience of her President, does not want to face the consequences, the press is, in fact, politely advised to say things that are not true, or at least to refrain from saying those that are true.

All this raises the question in my mind: how much tampering with its basic institutions can a democracy take before it ceases to be a democracy?

HALSTI: The Finnish press may be warned, but it does not follow that the Finnish press does as it is told. It mostly doesn't, and I can therefore see no reason why you should feel that democracy is threatened. You mentioned that the Russians were offended by the Finnish press-reaction to Porkkala. Frankly, I was not surprised. When the Russians left, our journalists took a very close look at what the Russians had left behind and they were rather appalled by what they saw. They then mounted a campaign criticising and ridiculing the way the Russians had lived in Porkkala—their primitive housing conditions, building techniques, architectural taste and so on. What they forgot to consider was that Porkkala was a military base which had not been put up by a fashionable body of Scandinavian builders and designers. It was a military area where troops did all the digging and building; there was no call for refined taste or any display of a higher standard of living than the situation of the Russians warranted. The environmental mess they left behind was in no way worse than what the Russians inherited from us after we had occupied some of their territory during the war.

If the press had taken all this into consideration their attitude to Porkkala might have been, and certainly ought to have been, very different. In our kind of situation the press, like everybody else, has to show restraint. We cannot force journalists to violate their conscience but we can try to educate them by showing them that in certain areas the Russians are extremely sensitive and that it is not in the national interest to arouse Russian hostility, especially when the issues in hand are non-issues such as the state of Porkkala at the end of the Soviet presence there. Now if you want to be absolutely categorical about the freedom of the Finnish press, perhaps it is true that reason and self-restraint do (or ought to) put a damper on some of its articulations but—and I must come back to this point again for it is essential—our freedoms today are incomparably greater than they were twenty years ago. Far from there having been a regression, as it is often assumed in the West, our room for manoeuvre has increased in a way which would have been inconceivable after the war. It does not, therefore, make much sense to talk of Finlandization. If you want an easy aperçu of our relationship with the Soviet Union, I would put it like this: a very small country carefully watched by a very large neighbour which believes that it has a legitimate right to do so.

URBAN: My impression is that Finland, in the person of President Kekkonen, is not quite content with saying 'this is the best we can make of an unsatisfactory situation', but that she is every now and then putting out a claim that the world might be a better place if other countries followed Finland's example. There is a certain proselytizing element in some of Kekkonen's utterances. For example, at a luncheon given in honour of Khrushchev in September 1960, the President said: 'We Finns are convinced that if other countries in the world were to arrange their relations upon the same principles as ours, the whole world would turn to that blessed state of lasting peace that all people so earnestly desire. Trust would supersede suspicion, goodwill bad.'

HALSTI: Well, banquet speeches given in honour of sensitive visitors ought to be taken with a pinch of salt. In any case, Kekkonen was putting his visitors on their best behaviour. This is clear from the preliminaries to the passage you have quoted, where he says: 'The Soviet Union has not coerced us, and does not coerce us, to adopt its own system. . . . The leaders of the Soviet Union know that we shall defend our own system under all circumstances. . . . And as the leaders of the Soviet Union pursue a peaceful and understanding policy towards Finland, they naturally will not force our people into anything that would be against the nature of our people.'

I don't think we are holding up Finland as a model. We realize only too well that each country has to adjust to the problems it faces and that it is up to the sovereign will of each nation to decide how it wishes to order its domestic affairs. No-one in Finland is saying that we should love the situation we are in; but we've got to live with it as best we can. Given the constraints, I think we have not done too badly.

It is, of course, true that Kekkonen is a powerful, and with the passing of years an increasingly self-centred, politician. I know the President well and my impression is that his long tenure of office has given him a rather inflated idea of his own importance. But then he believes he has a mission, and one cannot but admire the sacrifices he has made in order to fulfil that mission and the skill with which he has conducted his country's foreign affairs.

URBAN: Another case where Soviet pressure seems to me at least to have had a decisive influence on Finnish domestic policy was the withdrawal of Olavi Honka from the 1962 presidential elections. The background to this episode may be told very briefly: in the Spring of 1961 the Social Democrats allied themselves with the Conservatives and other non-socialist parties to prevent Kekkonen's re-election. They nominated Olavi Honka for President. In the meantime, parallel with the Berlin crisis of 1961, the Soviet Government sought 'consultations' with the Finns in accordance with the Soviet-Finnish Treaty 'on measures for the defence of the borders of the two countries against the threat of armed aggression on the part of West Germany and states allied with it'. The note caused alarm in Finland. As the German threat was not taken seriously in Finland or anywhere else in the western world, the idea that the Russians wanted to consult the Finns on defence was looked upon as a pretext for putting pressure on Finland. President Kekkonen, determined to avert a Soviet-Finnish confrontation, decided, after some hesitation, to see Khrushchev personally. On 23 November 1962 he flew to Novosibirsk where Khrushchev was on an inspection tour of Siberia. On the second day of their talks a message arrived from Helsinki that (in the words of Max Jacobson) 'Honka had given up his candidacy in the national interest'. Next day it was announced that Khrushchev and Kekkonen had reached agreement: the Soviet Government withdrew its proposal for military consultations, leaving it to Finland—now once again securely under the Presidency of Kekkonen—to let the Soviet Government know what steps *she* thought should be taken if the situation in Northern Europe gave cause for concern.

I discussed this matter with Ambassador Jacobson in Stockholm, and I raised with him the question I'm raising with you now: was Honka's withdrawal and the resolution, on the same day, of the Soviet-Finnish crisis a pure coincidence? Jacobson said that Honka and the parties which had nominated him withdrew his candidacy entirely off their own bat. There was no pressure; he bowed out in the national interest as it was clear that the Russians would not have him. (I hope I am summarizing Ambassador Jacobson's words accurately.) It is the last clause of Jacobson's last sentence that conveys to us the notion of Finlandization: he bowed out in the national interest as it was clear that the Russians would not have him.

HALSTI: We are now on dangerous ground. The trouble with Honka's candidacy was not that he ran for the Presidency—he had every right to do so—but that he ran for it with the support and, as it were, in the name of Tanner. Everyone with his political wits about him knew at the time that Honka stood for Tanner and that his candidacy was worse than madness—it was a mistake. One did not have to be particularly keen-eyed to see that Honka was going to come up against a brick wall. The whole idea of putting him up was absurd from the start. If our Social Democrats and their allies on the Right were determined to get rid of Kekkonen they ought to have thought of more sophisticated ways of doing it. All they did achieve by nominating Honka and providing no realistic alternative was to make Kekkonen quite indispensable: Kekkonen became twice as important as he had been before the 1962 election. I was, at the time, president of the Paasikivi Society. When I heard that the Social Democrats and the Right were really putting up Honka for President, I was very angry indeed, for I could see that this was a mad, hopeless and self-defeating move, and when you are in politics irresponsible moves are out of order. If you can't respect the limits within which you must work as a politician you should choose a less dangerous occupation.

URBAN: Honka was, in fact, a figurehead, no more.

HALSTI: Yes, he had no party ties at all. He was a retired high-court judge. I do not claim to be the wisest man in the land, but if the Socialist-Conservative coalition had come to me with the suggestion that Tanner would like me to run for the Presidency, assuring me that I would enjoy the support of his party, I would have screamed 'Never!', and run as fast as my legs would carry me.

URBAN: We saw a minute ago why Tanner was unpopular with Moscow, but when he *was*, once again, leading a strong Social Democratic Party, could the Russians not be persuaded to tolerate him?

HALSTI: Well, Paasikivi used to say that authoritarian powers are extremely set in their ways: once committed to a line of policy it becomes a matter of prestige for them to stick to it; their elasticity is nil. The Russians developed a visceral aversion to Tanner back in 1939 for the reasons I have already mentioned, and they have never been able to overcome it. Every child in Finland knew that Tanner was persona non grata with Moscow. The day he was re-elected to the leadership of the Social Democratic Party I remember telling my wife: 'The socialists have gone out of their minds. They are running to their destruction with their eyes wide open.'

URBAN: Soviet communists, and especially Khrushchev, have always reacted more strongly to Social Democrats than to any other party. Was the objection to Tanner coloured by Moscow's 'Menshevik-complex'?

HALSTI: To some extent it was, of course, but there are two

things here we must keep separate: Soviet power-politics and ideology. The Russians have always been cautious *Realpolitiker*. Faced with a choice between ideological commitment and power-interests, they have never hesitated to jettison ideology. Stalin signed a pact with Hitler because it was in the national interest. His communism was not allowed to interfere with his realism as head of the Soviet Party and Government. So I don't think the fact that Tanner was a Social Democrat had a decisive influence on Moscow's objection to Tanner. It was, I believe, Tanner's record during the war that made him unacceptable. Whatever the precise reasons, it was clear to us that the Russians would not touch him with the longest barge-pole on the Volga.

URBAN: What is the inside story of Honka's withdrawal? *Did* he leave the field to Kekkonen out of his own free will?

HALSTI: I cannot answer that question. I know Honka personally and I know him to be a good patriot. He is not the sort of person who would elbow his way through to power; he suffers from no delusions of grandeur, so I assume that his decision to retire from the race was entirely his own. I don't think he had been put under pressure.

URBAN: You mean that when Honka saw that there was a grave crisis in Soviet-Finnish relations, he took back his nomination.

HALSTI: That is what I think happened.

URBAN: But this happened under rather dramatic conditions didn't it: Khrushchev and Kekkonen are talking through the night in Novosibirsk when suddenly a wire arrives from Helsinki: Honka is out of the race.

HALSTI: Right.

URBAN: And within twenty-four hours a solution is found to a long drawn-out and ominous crisis.

HALSTI: True.

URBAN: I would infer from this that there was some inner compulsion in Helsinki—to put it no higher—some psychological pressure to get Honka out of the way.

HALSTI: Of course there was psychological pressure. The Russians never cease cautioning us: 'You Finns can do as you like—that is your business—but we draw our conclusions from what you do and act accordingly, and that is our business.' Well, when you have 230 million people on one side of the border and 4½ million on the other, this kind of warning carries its own momentum.

URBAN: In 1972 Kekkonen's term was up. However, no elections were held. Parliament passed a special law with a five-sixths

majority required by the Finnish constitution, which gave Kekkonen another term of office until 1978. One interpretation of this
unusual step was that Kekkonen was trying to spare Finland
another crisis with the Soviet Union which an ugly contest between
himself and his 'Poujadist' opponent, Vennamo, might have
sparked off. Other interpretations ascribe to Kekkonen's rather
heavy-handed action more personal motives such as his contempt
for his opponent and an unwillingness to leave office after sixteen
years in power.

HALSTI: I did not agree with the 1972 special legislation and I
said so at the time. However I am very conscious that we will go on
needing Kekkonen for some years to come, for the trust he inspires
in the Soviet Union is a great asset for Finland. Let me explain.

The whole post-war order of Europe is in a state of ferment, and I
expect a first-class crisis to rock us towards the end of the 1970s. By
then the Soviet Union must have its back covered in Europe. If this
can be done through *Ostpolitik* and détente, well and good. But if it
can't, Russia will have to find other ways of securing her European
perimeter for, in the Soviet perception, Russia must, by the end of
the decade, be completely free to devote her attention to China. The
time for a European settlement is therefore very limited and the
uncertainties ahead of us numerous and daunting. So it is as well for
Finland to have a man like Kekkonen in the driver's seat.

But while I agree that from our national point of view
Kekkonen's continued Presidency is an asset, I do not agree with the
way in which he has been kept in office.

URBAN: But if he has been kept in office by *raison d'état*—to
maintain Finland's present, unruffled relations with the Soviet
Union—would that not justify the methods used?

HALSTI: I do not know whether Russian influence, or the an-
ticipation of Russian influence, played any part in the special legislation. What I cannot understand—and what the Finnish people
cannot understand—is why the rules of democracy had to be violated to secure the extension of the President's office. This has set a
dangerous precedent.

URBAN: How did the various parties react to Kekkonen's re-
election?

HALSTI: The parties of the Left were for it. Some Social Democrats opposed the bill, but the whips were put on and the Party as a
whole voted for it. The Right virtually fell apart as a result of the
special legislation. In the political centre, in Kekkonen's own Agrarian Party, support was more readily forthcoming, and the Liberal
votes too were lined up by enforcing party discipline.

URBAN: It does not sound to me like a democratic decision

freely arrived at. Are you implying that the political parties accepted—although grudgingly—that Soviet-Finnish relations must take
precedence over domestic politics and behaved accordingly?

HALSTI: It is difficult to answer that question. One must differ-
entiate between Kekkonen in his role as a maker of foreign policy
and Kekkonen the domestic politician. While Kekkonen is
respected for his conduct of foreign affairs, his internal policies have
earned him many articulate enemies. Paasikivi always said—and he
has found a ready echo in Kekkonen—that in Finland's particular
situation foreign policy must always take precedence over domestic
policy, and I would myself agree with that. But it is not possible to
enforce such a rule in a democracy. There are people in Finnish politics who want to get rid of Kekkonen for internal political reasons.
They provide, of course, an easy target for the Finnish communists
who accuse any and all of Kekkonen's opponents of wanting to
bring him down because he is friendly to the Soviet Union. On that
showing any opposition to Kekkonen is, directly or indirectly, an
act of defying Finland's established course of foreign policy. But
this is simply not so: as I say, most of the President's opponents
want to see him go for entirely domestic reasons.

Naturally, his foreign policy has not completely escaped censure.
There are those among his critics who say that Kekkonen is too pliable in his relations with Moscow, that he ought to be more unbend-
ing and learn how to say 'no'. The best case I can make for these
critics is that they simply do not realize under what pressure Kekkonen has to work and with what consummate skill he has negotiated Finland's difficulties.

URBAN: Kekkonen has repeatedly underlined in his speeches
the great courtesy and good will with which he has been treated by
the Soviet leaders. He tells us that, far from having had to make concessions to Moscow, he has always been able to bring back something from the Soviet Union. I am reminded of a speech he delivered
at the Paasikivi Society in 1964 at the time when, I believe, you were
its president. He said:

> I was once about to go on holiday in the Soviet Union. A right-
> wing minister called on me. . . . He said that there was uneasiness
> in his party concerning my journey, it was feared that during it I
> would have to give way to Soviet demands. Perhaps I cheered him
> up a little with my reply: 'I have been in the fortunate position of
> never having had to travel to Moscow to give something, but have
> always received something from them. And I have so much polit-
> ical sense that if I suspected that Finland had to give something to
> Moscow I would certainly not go myself but would send you

instead.'

Whether or not one ought to take the President's assurance that he has never given but always received things from Moscow to be the whole truth, it is certainly the case that measured by the yardstick of East European politics Kekkonen, and Finnish sovereignty, have been treated with considerable respect. Nevertheless, isn't the President's claim slightly exaggerated?

HALSTI: In the twenty-five years that have now passed since we signed our treaty with the Soviet Union I can recall no instance in which the Soviet leaders' attitude to us was anything but entirely correct. Naturally I would not be so foolish as to imagine that this correctness was due to some personal sympathy between the Kremlin leaders and Kekkonen. I am persuaded that it was, and is, due to Russia's defensive military posture in Scandinavia. The Swedes have often told the world that Finland is Sweden's alarm bell—if Finland were Sovietized, Sweden would have to abandon her neutrality, and I am certain that this would in fact happen. Here we have the key to Russia's self-restraint in the whole Nordic area. The political and military watershed between Russia and the West now ends at Lübeck—why, I ask you, should the Soviet Union want to lengthen that line and involve the whole of Scandinavia? An extension of the present East-West boundary to include the Swedish-Finnish border would require pumping an extra million Soviet troops and untold amounts of military hardware into a region that has no primary military importance.

This, more than anything, explains to me why we have been able to preserve our democratic institutions and, within the limits of the possible, our sovereignty. The Soviet posture in Scandinavia has never been offensive. The military ventures the Russians undertook in Hungary and Czechoslovakia would simply not have been politic in the case of Finland. It is, of course, an open question whether the occupation of Hungary and Czechoslovakia was politic, and I have heard doubts expressed on that point by important Soviet sources. 'Do you think we liked doing what we did in those two countries?' one Soviet diplomat told me: 'We didn't, but we had no choice.'

It would be unprofitable for us to go into the controversial history of the Hungarian and Czechoslovak upheavals, but it is clear to me from all the evidence that the Russians moved into these countries not because they were bellicose but because in their perception of the Soviet position vis-à-vis the West, Hungary and Czechoslovakia were not expendable. Whether this view was right or wrong, it is difficult to argue with it.

In 1944 the Russians could have taken the whole of Finland

within a fortnight. They did not take her because even then, under Stalin, Russia's posture in Scandinavia was essentially defensive—Moscow was, as I say, anxious not to turn Sweden into an enemy. Whether this cautious policy towards Sweden will continue is anybody's guess. We have no assurance that it will.

URBAN: Aren't the Russians also inspired by a healthy respect for Finland's military record in the second world war? Stalin is said to have remarked after the war that he would not take Finland because 'Finland is a hedgehog, and hedgehogs are uncomfortable to swallow'.

HALSTI: Stalin may have said it—I heard it attributed to the last Tsar and Stalin may have plagiarized Nicholas's wisdom. In any case, the remark fits the situation and no doubt the Finnish record has confirmed the Soviet leaders in their cautious approach. But I would maintain that the principal reason for Moscow's restraint in Scandinavia is the basically defensive character of the Soviet posture there.

URBAN: Soviet intentions in Scandinavia as far as land forces are concerned may well be defensive, but the spectacular build-up of Soviet naval and missile power in the direct vicinity of Northern Finland—in Murmansk and the Kola area—betrays a different intention. Johan Jørgen Holst, the distinguished Norwegian defence analyst, discussed the significance of this build-up earlier in this series of discussions, and he concluded that the Soviet naval programme was both extremely ambitious and expansionist.

HALSTI: Clearly it has an offensive capability and a global role.

URBAN: Yet the Finnish Government does not seem to be disturbed. The build-up is thought to be a matter for Nato, and especially Norway, rather than Finland.

HALSTI: The Finnish concern is a little more immediate than that. The enormous increase in Soviet power in the Murmansk–Kola area has greatly added to the military importance of Norway's two northern provinces: Finnmark and Troms. Should the present détente policies for any reason fail to fulfil expectations, we cannot exclude the possibility of an East–West confrontation in Europe. In a crisis situation of that kind the Nato powers would want to hang on to Northern Norway because it gives them easy access to Murmansk and denies the Soviet Union Scandinavian bases, ports and other facilities it may find indispensable for its operations. However, the northern parts of Norway have too little depth for effective deployment; from the Nato point of view it would, therefore, make sense to deepen the theatre of operations by ordering Nato troops eastward, into Northern Finland.

The Soviets would, of course, want to prevent such a scenario from being put into action. They would probably invoke the 1948 Soviet-Finnish treaty, demand transit rights for their forces through Northern Finland and occupy the northern provinces of Norway, preempting any Nato move in the area.

URBAN: Doesn't Norway's great vulnerability—caught as she is in the whirlpool of rivalry between the Soviet Union and the United States—make her an early candidate for neutralization on the Finnish model?

HALSTI: It has always been an aim of Soviet policy to detach Norway from the Atlantic Alliance and to persuade the Norwegians of the advantages of a Swedish type of neutrality.

URBAN: The Norwegians are now visibly more worried about their security than they were in the past.

HALSTI: They have every reason to be.

URBAN: It is by no means certain that the Nato powers could arrive on the scene in time and in sufficient force to prevent an overland occupation of Northern Norway by the Soviet Union. And even if they did manage to put in an expeditionary force, it is an open question whether it could maintain itself in the face of overwhelming Soviet conventional power.

HALSTI: I entirely agree. I, for one, cannot understand why Norway continues to belong to Nato. Psychologically, Norway's membership makes sense, for the memories of the 1940 occupation still linger, but from the point of view of Norway's national interest, her presence in Nato is absurd: she is being tied to a military alliance that cannot assure her security. Norway has assumed certain responsibilities under Nato which have earned her the label 'anti-Soviet' in Russian eyes, irrespective of whether or not the Norwegian Government, or the Norwegians as a nation, harbour anti-Soviet sentiments. Yet, as we have both said, if it came to a confrontation between the West and the Soviet Union, Norway would stand very little chance of being helped. So I cannot quite see how the Norwegians expect to profit from their membership.

URBAN: Your assessment is shared by some leading Norwegian students of international affairs. Professor Nils Ørvik (now of Toronto University), for example, observes that the Scandinavian countries are confronted by increasing Soviet capabilities while the relative strength of their allies and supporters has decreased, thereby reducing the probability of effective and timely assistance. He concludes, quoting the opinion of 'some people who might feel . . .' that: '. . . on balance, the interests of their country would be better served by closer ties with the Soviet Union than the West.' Without in any way approving of such a development, he coolly observes: 'This pattern of political behaviour would move the Scandinavian countries closer to the Finnish model.'

HALSTI: I would not go so far as to say that the Finnish model is relevant to the whole of Scandinavia, but it is certainly true that the 1940-type of German invasion is most unlikely to be repeated by the Soviet Union so long as the general peace holds, and from that I would conclude that the security of Norway would be better served if Norway ceased to be a member of Nato and adopted a more flexible attitude to the Soviet Union.

URBAN: Could Norway's withdrawal from Nato be utilized to ease Finland's dependence on Soviet goodwill? 'In Finland the idea of a Scandinavian Defence Community seems attractive to some sections of opinion', Max Jacobson says in *Finnish Neutrality*. 'It is hoped that the Soviet Union might be willing to trade its Security Treaty with Finland for the exit of Denmark and Norway from Nato.' Do you regard this as a realistic possibility?

HALSTI: In theory an entirely neutral Scandinavia would be an ideal solution to all Scandinavia's problems. But the obstacles to be overcome to give such an idea practical currency are overwhelming. First, I do not believe that either the Danes or the Norwegians are now in a position to leave Nato. They have been bound up with the Alliance for many years, and although they are not, as it were, fully paid-up members because of the base-limitations they have unilaterally imposed on themselves as a gesture to Soviet sensitivity, their withdrawal from Nato could not be accomplished without great ructions internally and externally. Secondly, even if Denmark and Norway did leave Nato, I do not believe the Soviet Union would be moved to regard the Soviet-Finnish treaty as null and void. It would take more than a formal declaration of withdrawal to convince Moscow that Norway would not continue to serve as Nato's jumping-off ground for an attack on Murmansk and the Kola area. The Russians take a very long-term view of international relations, and they would hardly want to give up the firm and profitable connection they have with Finland for a concession that would strike them as incommensurable with it.

URBAN: Ambassador Max Jacobson argues that not only would the Russians decline to renounce the treaty but that the Finns themselves should, in their own interest, make a point of declining to renounce it. He uses an interesting argument. It is a fallacy to imagine, he says, that Finland's position would materially change if the treaty were declared void, for the provisions of the treaty are descriptive rather than normative—the treaty states what will happen to and around Finland in certain specified circumstances, treaty or no treaty. As the European situation has become more stable (he goes on), the likelihood that these circumstances would arise has diminished, but 'the purpose of Finnish policy must continue to be to prevent their occurring rather than to abolish the treaty—to remove any possible causes of fever rather than to throw away the thermometer'.

I can't see how this kind of argument would offer the Danes and Norwegians any incentive to leave Nato. Worse, it appears to lend gratuitous support to that unpleasing principle of Soviet foreign policy: 'What is mine is mine, what is yours is negotiable.'

HALSTI: I think we need not rack our brains over this problem (a) because it is most unlikely that Denmark and Norway will walk out on Nato, (b) because it is equally unlikely that there will be a Scandinavian defence alliance, and (c) because it is more unlikely still that Russia would, if (a) or (b) or even if (a) *and* (b) materialized, renounce the Soviet-Finnish treaty, whatever Finland would like to see done about it.

URBAN: The treaty provides for joint Soviet-Finnish military action if Finland, or the Soviet Union through Finnish territory, became the object of aggression by Germany or any state allied to Germany. What, one might ask, is the relevance of this treaty in the light of Germany's eastern treaties and détente? Not only is there now no danger of a German attack on the Soviet Union through Finland, but Germany is on extremely friendly terms with both the Soviet Union and several of its allies in Eastern Europe, and Germany's principal ally, the United States, is the motor behind détente. Doesn't all this make the treaty nonsensical?

I notice that the Finnish Foreign Minister raised this point recently but withdrew it after a few days' reflection, explaining that he had changed his mind. This was a curious incident, unlikely to reassure those who doubt whether Finland's external freedom of action is, as you say, really on the increase.

HALSTI: I cannot answer for our Foreign Minister's private thoughts, but as he had publicly raised the issue, it was an act of statesmanship on his part to take it back. I am convinced that in the Soviet perception détente and *Ostpolitik* will not invalidate the usefulness of the Soviet-Finnish treaty. I have already said that the Russians work to long time-scales—Marxism as well as their own national history have left them with that tradition. Let me illustrate the point with a Finnish example.

Our whole argument with the Soviet Union in 1939, leading up to the Winter War, turned on the problem of Soviet security. The Soviet Government insisted on having its Monroe Doctrine against nazi Germany, and Finland was part of the area covered. Stalin sought to impose a mutual assistance treaty on us similar to the ones he had imposed on the three Baltic states within a fortnight of the

Molotov-Ribbentrop pact. He demanded that Finland cede a number of islands to the Soviet Union, lease Hanko as a Russian naval base and push back the Finnish border on the Karelian Isthmus, among other things. Well, when Paasikivi met Stalin in October 1939 he argued—as you have just argued—that since Moscow and Berlin had signed a non-aggression pact, what need was there for Moscow's elaborate precautions, especially as Finland would not compromise her independence and neutrality? Stalin's memorable answer was: 'Everything in this world can change.' He said the pact with Germany was no eternal guarantee; whoever emerged as victor in the world war would attack the Soviet Union.

Much of Stalin's prophecy was soon to be borne out by facts: the Molotov-Ribbentrop pact did not last two years and Russia was attacked by Germany.

So when you look at the present Soviet-Finnish nexus through Russian eyes, bearing in mind Russia's historic experience, it is not so difficult to understand why Moscow would hesitate to sacrifice an institutionalized guarantee for some trend in international politics that hinges on the political survival of a couple of politically vulnerable individuals and may thus turn out to be ephemeral. Détente is not irreversible, and the Russians know it as well as the next man.

URBAN: Bearing in mind the lessons of recent *Soviet* politics, I am pretty sure, though, that Russia would not hesitate to exploit the German bogey once again if Soviet interests so required. She did so (as we have seen) in 1961 when Khrushchev, using the self-created Berlin crisis as his pretext, tried to exert pressure on Finland by demanding that the Soviet-Finnish treaty be activated. The Finns were told, as we know from a speech of President Kekkonen, that the threat of German aggression called for immediate Soviet-Finnish consultations, and the evidence the Russians produced was this: 'The increase of West German influence at the entrance of the Baltic, the visit by Mr Strauss, Minister of Defence of West Germany, to Norway, and the establishment by West Germany and Denmark of a joint command in the Baltic.'

HALSTI: A joint command comprising all twelve small ships the two countries then possessed! *Of course* it was ludicrous, and it is even more ludicrous in retrospect. Khrushchev must have had his fun with our straight-faced diplomats. But there it was. I am sure the German bogey will be painted up again, not least in Poland where the Russians are in a strong position to exploit the Polish people's justified anxiety that the Oder–Neisse border was acquired by means which will leave the Polish conscience vulnerable for many years to come and thus susceptible to Soviet pressure.

URBAN: One of the objectives of Moscow's détente diplomacy is the legitimation of Soviet hegemony in Eastern Europe. It is for us a little difficult to understand why the Russians should be so anxious to see the 'sold' label visibly displayed on their East European possessions for it is clear enough that they enjoy undisturbed tenure. But tenure is not the same as possession and it seems to me the Russians want to see the western seal of legitimacy firmly put on the *social transformation* which they have foisted—and with great difficulty maintained—in Eastern Europe since 1947. The Kremlin's unspoken fear is expressed by Milovan Djilas: 'Not a single communist state is a legal state in the true sense.'

HALSTI: You are implying that recognition should be withheld. I am not so sure. The Hungarians tried to break out of the Soviet embrace in 1956, then the Czechs tried to wriggle out of it in 1968. What was the result? Destruction and great suffering. The peoples of Eastern Europe have been systematically refused western help and they have no reason to believe that any future uprising or reform movement would be spared repression. The West has no East European policy—except an entirely passive one. My personal judgement of the matter is that so long as the Soviet Union remains the power she is, the situation of the East European countries cannot change significantly. Of course, one day the Soviet Union will fall apart as all past empires have fallen apart, but in the meantime Soviet power will continue to expand.

However, leaving aside the West's poor record in Eastern Europe for the moment—why should the East Europeans have any confidence in the United States on America's present showing? What do they see in the United States? An unprecedented moral crisis, a paralysis of leadership and a creeping isolationism. After Vietnam the Americans are in no mood and no position to undertake open-ended foreign commitments. What could be more shattering to East European morale than to see United States representatives sitting down to negotiate force reductions with the Russians, while back in America influential men in Congress demand a unilateral reduction of American troops in Europe? Has America gone mad?—the East Europeans may wonder. Do the American people realize that some of their Congressmen and Senators are pulling the rug out from under the feet of their own negotiators? *Cui bono*? My confidence in American power is utterly destroyed. A country that does not know how to use the enormous power it has, has none.

For the same reasons I believe that the West European countries are ill-advised to rely on American protection. I am a military man and I may have a military bias, but it takes no military expertise to see that the effectiveness of the American conventional forces is very low. An army that murders its officers and counts its deserters by the tens of thousands, an army whose men refuse to go into battle and get away with it—well, can that random collection of men still be called an army? I would not have thought so; I would call it a rabble, and anyone who relies on it for his protection does so at his own peril. The only effective but virtually unusable force the Americans have left is their nuclear arsenal. That can be activated by a few, highly-paid administrators who press buttons in air-conditioned offices well away from places where shots are fired in anger. But highly-paid civil servants tell us nothing about the morale of the American people, of the men who are supposed to be the backbone of Nato. And it is morale alone—as Mao Tse-tung rightly insists—that ultimately matters.

URBAN: It is not a happy picture you have depicted for us. Your fears may or may not be justified, but the American record in Europe is positive in the sense that the status quo has been preserved. Those highly-paid civil servants and military button-minders have, so far at least, kept the American nuclear umbrella pretty effectively over Western Europe.

HALSTI: The question is: for how much longer can Europe rely on American nuclear protection? Would the United States risk nuclear retaliation to protect Tromsø or Udine or even Paris, as the French have asked? I don't believe so. The American nuclear arsenal lacks credibility. I don't know if it frightens America's adversaries, but it does not reassure her allies, and this subjective factor has now assumed the force of an objective fact which weakens the impact of the whole Atlantic Alliance. The disintegration of the morale of the American political establishment and the crisis of self-self-confidence which is rocking the whole American people do not augur well for the outcome of America's détente policies.

URBAN: Before we condemn the Americans too much perhaps we should ask ourselves whether Western Europe is pulling *its* weight, and the answer to that is 'no'. Apart from Britain, the West European countries devote a very small percentage of their GNP to defence expenditure. Nor is military morale in Europe what it ought to be. Uniforms, discipline, patriotism have all been brought into contempt. European recruits spend twelve, nine and even as little as six months with the armed forces, whereas in the Soviet Union national service is two years or more. Army recruiting campaigns, the draft, military procurement are all ridiculed and protested against by every left-wing student organization worth its salt. During my recent visit to the North of Norway I was astounded to hear that one of the Norwegian Air Force's principal worries was to protect its bases against sabotage by servicemen belonging to extremist organizations. Détente has underpinned these anti-military sentiments with a sense of apparent realism so that, all in all, Western Europe has very little to crow about.

HALSTI: I entirely agree, but my contention is that Europe's unpreparedness and her unwillingness to see herself as she really is—that is: naked without American protection—is precisely due to the fact that it has been relying on American tutelage for over a quarter of a century and has therefore lost the will and perhaps the ability to protect itself. If the Americans left Europe, Western Europe would at once become extremely conscious of its nudity.

URBAN: It might or it might not. There will always be those in Western Europe who will argue that the American withdrawal, or partial withdrawal, is a sure sign that détente has come to stay; if the Americans can afford to send their troops home, there is clearly no need for us to worry about our security.

HALSTI: Did the chicken come before the egg or the egg before the chicken? I am convinced that the collapse (and later the non-revival) of the idea that Western Europe can and should defend itself relying on its own resources, betrays a failure of courage and political leadership. After the proposed European Defence Community had been defeated in the French National Assembly, the defence of Western Europe was simply relegated to the United States because that was the cheapest and politically least troublesome way out. But once you get used to being protected by a superior power and your own troops feel themselves to be little more than pawns in the service of some complicated game of power-politics run by American generals, it is a little difficult to ask them to fight for their country out of a sense of duty and patriotism. They may decide that the war will have to be fought without them.

But if Western Europe were made to face the fact that it is and will remain alone come hell or high-water, the realization would very quickly sink in that the price of West European independence is a high degree of political and military co-operation and pre-paredness.

There is, of course, another diagnosis of the ills of Europe and America—the 'ancient Rome' syndrome. This shows the West, and Western Europe in particular, to be falling apart because easy living, welfare, materialism and the absence of a higher social pur-pose are sapping the moral fibre of society. The western countries have, on this showing, played out their historical role and must now make way for Toynbee's 'universal states'. If this is true—and I don't believe it is—Western Europe will be Balkanized and there is nothing the Americans or anyone else can do about it.

URBAN: Mightn't your young non-conformist confront you

with the idea that the questioning of discipline, revulsion against regimentation and the refusal to sacrifice life and limb on the altar of nationalism were signs of a liberal conscience and political maturity? Mightn't he say that the American fiasco in Vietnam was a triumph of the heart and mind of young America over faceless bureaucrats and a mindless military machine?

HALSTI: He very well might, and I would respect his views, and I would even be prepared to live by them if the Soviet Union showed a similar tolerance. But it doesn't.

In the German Federal Republic an astonishing number, some 60–70,000 young men, evade military service each year by registering as conscientious objectors. No stigma is apparently attached to such evasion, which is equally astonishing. German officers I know aren't even surprised: 'Why should our young men behave differently?' they ask. 'What purpose does the German army serve? What reason has it to exist? If we put it to our national servicemen that Germany needs them, they will either answer "Oh, the Americans will take care of all that—that is what they are here for", or else they will just say that they will not be manipulated by power-interests. And it isn't easy to prove them wrong.'

URBAN: Both De Gaulle and Adenauer foresaw the problem. De Gaulle tried to answer it by removing France from the Nato command, and Adenauer attempted to create a new European identity.

HALSTI: He tried to create one, and the idea was and is right, but it remains to be translated into reality—Europe has not been exactly over-zealous in helping itself. If the Americans left Europe, a European identity should be less difficult to come by, but even then many decades would have to elapse before the consciousness of that identity seeped down to Sicilian peasants and Scottish miners.

The German armed forces—to come back to what is, after all, the lynchpin of Nato's conventional system—are in no way imbued with the idea that they have a worth-while target to defend. The German private soldier believes that his sole function is to provide cannon fodder for breaking up the first wave of Russian attack and deflecting it from the United States. He has no faith in the staying power of American conventional forces in Europe for he believes their morale—like his own—is low and their numbers entirely inadequate. Add to this the kind of sentiment Michel Jobert, the former French Foreign Minister, has uttered to the effect that France would use her independent nuclear deterrent to defend French territory against Soviet attack—that is to say, she would target it on German soil—and you can see why the central sector of the Nato Alliance does not inspire much confidence. As I say, Europe may have to go through the experience of being thrown in at the deep end. It will either sink or swim, but I am personally convinced that it will swim. Only we must first take the American life-belt out of sight of Europe.

URBAN: Would a European security declaration make it easier or more difficult for the Soviet Union to suppress a fresh East European uprising, or rein in centrifugal forces in the client states, such as Rumania's maverick course in her foreign policy? I don't think the East European nations can realistically hope to obtain anything approaching a Finnish type of internal sovereignty, but their chances of working themselves loose from some of the worst restrictions of the Muscovite model may improve under a security understanding.

HALSTI: The calmer the atmosphere in East-West relations, the more hope there is for a peaceful liberalization of the East European system from within. But here we run into the awkward and para-doxical problem of Soviet 'confidence'. There are two sides to Russia's political currency: the obverse side shows a traditional Russian politician of caution and realism; the reverse side depicts a millenarian communist. Soviet 'confidence' in the full sense of the word is unfortunately tied to the reverse side of the currency. Despite the hard realism of Russia's long-term policies, the link with foreign communist parties is never given up. Indeed, in many cases it is the touchstone of Soviet 'confidence'. We have never hesi-tated to tell the Russians that so long as they maintain their special relationship with foreign communist groupings—which are usually in bad odour in their own countries and unrepresentative of the thinking of the bulk of the electorate—co-operation with the Soviet Union at the state level will be lame and ridden with suspicion. But I cannot see how this missionary tradition can be weakened or eliminated without a thorough reform of the Soviet system itself.

The sort of 'confidence' a proselytizing Russia can advance to a foreign country can never be complete until and unless that foreign country adopts the Soviet system and subjects itself to Moscow's guidance. Neither the one nor the other will do in isolation. Now Eastern Europe has, under the force of circumstances, met both these conditions, and it would seem most unlikely to me that it would be allowed to escape from them. Therefore the parameters of reform in Eastern Europe are highly limited. Anything that smacks of systemic change will probably be suppressed, but within the system as defined by Moscow it should be possible to mark out a buffer-zone wide enough to accommodate national peculiarities, cultural reform and the like, but also inconspicuous enough to make it difficult for the Soviet leaders to justify its removal under the Brezhnev doctrine once a security document has been signed.

URBAN: You do not believe a Finlandization of Eastern Europe is a realistic possibility?

HALSTI: No, I don't. Even the sort of cautious liberalization I have just suggested would depend for its success on restraint shown on the part of the western powers. There must be no attempt to slice these states off the Soviet bloc and fit them into the western system. The attempt *was* made both in 1956 and 1968.

URBAN: But was it? Imre Nagy's Government declared Hungary's neutrality, and we know from the literature that the Hungarians would have been well content with a Finnish type of neutrality. Czechoslovakia did not even attempt to leave the Warsaw Pact.

HALSTI: But remember the millenarian communist on the reverse side of the coin: in Soviet eyes 'he who is not with us is against us'. This was the motto of Lenin's political philosophy and it has been taken over intact by the present Soviet leaders.

All of Moscow's troubles in Eastern Europe go back to Stalin's disastrous decision to impose the communist system on Poles, Hungarians, Czechoslovaks, Rumanians, Bulgarians and East Germans. These are freedom-loving nations, with a proud history and cultural traditions of their own. What fateful megalomania has forced these peoples into the Muscovite straitjacket! What willful ignorance of history!

We in Finland never tire of telling the Russians: 'If you want for a neighbour a Finland that hates you, that will reach for her weapons at the slightest provocation and will do her utmost to harm you in any way she can—impose the communist system on our country.' The Russians have never seriously tried to impose it.

URBAN: Not since the war, but in 1939, at the beginning of the Finnish Winter War, Stalin set up a 'Democratic Government of Finland' under the exiled Finnish communist leader Kuusinen. That it failed to rally the Finnish workers to the side of the invader is another matter.

HALSTI: Yes, the Russians tried it out on us, but they must have learnt their lesson for after the war the attempt was not seriously repeated.

It is a tragedy both for the Soviet Union and the whole of Europe that after the war the East European nations were not given time to hammer out in peace and at their own volition a balanced, realistic relationship with the Soviet Union. This might have allowed them to preserve, as we have preserved, their independent national institutions while giving Moscow the necessary guarantees about Soviet security. I once put all these points to the Soviet Ambassador in

Helsinki. 'You are absolutely right', he answered: 'in politics marriages of love are always the most dangerous and marriages of convenience the most fruitful.'

URBAN: But could the East European love-match (seldom has love been more one-sided) be turned into a marriage of convenience? In any case, would it not be an unconscionable time in coming?

HALSTI: It might be possible over a long period of time, but it would be difficult. The hatred of Russia runs deep in Eastern Europe. The East European nations have been subjected to too many indignities. Scratch the red surface anywhere in the client states and out spurts the loathing and resentment of Russia. You can't psychologically mishandle nations for decades, force them into a system that is alien to them and expect them to love you. I know no country that resents the Russians so much as Poland.

URBAN: Let me be cynical—wouldn't détente and a security accord deprive the Western Alliance of the leverage it enjoys by tacitly playing upon, or at any rate not discouraging, East European misgivings of Soviet rule? Wouldn't the West be throwing away one of its most valuable cards?

HALSTI: But can these misgivings be translated into the currency of political change? They can't for the reasons we have already discussed. The West has done and will do nothing to support East European dissent, and a fresh outbreak of anti-Soviet feeling would simply cause more suffering in Eastern Europe without achieving worth-while change.

URBAN: Isn't there, however, a difference between saying to the East Europeans: 'We are terribly sorry to see you in the situation you're in, but keep your chins up—you have our sympathy', and saying to them in fact: 'Sorry friends, you are in for it and we have no choice but to put our names to your death sentence'?

HALSTI: I don't think the East Europeans are under sentence of death; they are in a state of paralysis, but there are ways in which a paralytic can be made to walk again. The fact that the West is powerless to bring about any drastic change in the client states should not prevent it from putting a price on its co-operation with the Soviet Union. If I were asked to advise the western governments, I would say this to them: don't agree to force reductions, don't aid the Soviet economy, don't underwrite the status quo unless you can acquire meaningful and enforceable concessions for the East European states. As a very minimum, the western powers ought to hold fast to Basket Three and sit out the security talks, no matter how many years they might take, until they have wrung concessions from the Russians. Remember it is the Soviet Union that is in a hurry—it is the Soviet Government that has a rendezvous with China in the coming years, and it is the Soviet economy that cannot afford the arms race and is crying out for help. The West can—if we disregard the ghastly handicap of Watergate for a moment—afford to wait until the cows come home. And we must not stake western security on the political fortunes of one American President.

URBAN: It is a little too easy to say that Basket Three is non-negotiable when in fact the Russians regard it as being highly negotiable and the western side has already made important concessions such as changing the wording, under Soviet pressure, of the 'free' flow of people and ideas into 'freer' flow of people and ideas. 'Freer' may mean anything, and very likely it will mean next to nothing. It may mean stepping up the number of pictures exchanged between the Metropolitan Museum and the Soviet Ministry of Culture from, say, two hundred to three hundred, or swapping experts to study the production problems of magnetically levitated trains. This would be not merely watering down the third item on the agenda of the Security Conference, but bringing it, and its western originators, into contempt.

HALSTI: Whether or not Basket Three can be made to stick depends on the enigma of Soviet internal developments. I have already said that the Soviet leadership is a strange amalgam of realists and fanatics. Sometimes, indeed, the two are permanently locked in battle in the same Russian breast. The realists are as shrewd and unsentimental as the next man in the Quay d'Orsay, but the fanatics are heirs to the traditions of Byzantium and Orthodoxy. Their eyes are still fixed on the ikons on the wall; it is only the symbolism of the ikons that has changed.

The Soviet attitude to the free exchange of people and ideas depends on the balance between realists and ideologues. At the moment level-headed men like Brezhnev and Kosygin seem to be in command, but they are getting old and the next generation of leaders may be less pragmatic. As the politics of a dictatorship are impenetrable to the outside world, we just do not know whether these men are going to pursue a hard or a more realistic line. If the dogmatists come out on top, Basket Three will have an even smaller chance of being translated into practice than it has now, whatever agreement may be formally reached in Geneva and Helsinki.

URBAN: So reform by mini-steps is the most we can hope to get out of Basket Three?

HALSTI: I think that is unfortunately so. You must remember that under the doctrine of proletarian internationalism the East European countries enjoy no separate political identity from the Soviet Union. They are, both in terms of their social order and their military-geographic position, parts of the area of Russia's European hegemony. We could see that very clearly in 1968.

The Soviet leaders put an equation mark between the reform of the Czechoslovak political system and the security of their own system and decided that their own security would be mortally threatened if the Czechs got away with their reforms. This was another way of saying that Czechoslovakia and all the other client states are Soviet territory in fact if not in name. Soviet diplomats have made it clear to me on more than one occasion that in 1968 Russia had no choice but to take Czechoslovakia because she feared that a Czech defection would be followed by the rest of the satellite empire. And I believe this fear, though perhaps mistaken, was sincerely held.

The Russians were indeed so worried that during those critical days in August 1968 the Soviet fleet was on station just outside Helsinki (I saw their ships with my own eyes) and the Red Air Force was showing the flag above our heads here. Perhaps the Soviet leaders imagined that we too might make an ill-considered move. When you remember those MIG fighters and Soviet destroyers manoeuvering a few knots away from your main square, eloquent documents about the free flow of people and information do not strike you as being tremendously important or realistic.

URBAN: Looking at Russia's historic experience, haven't the Soviet leaders reason to worry about Soviet security? It was President Kekkonen who said in 1967 that Russia had been attacked 14 times in the last 150 years and that the capital of White Russia, Minsk, had been in enemy hands 101 times. If, he said, the Soviet leaders were not concerned with Russia's security in the light of this record, they would not be fulfilling their duty.

HALSTI: Kekkonen was probably right. If you look at Russian history over the last two to three hundred years you will find that Russia's position vis-à-vis Europe was almost always defensive. The Tsars' main concern was to secure their frontiers (in both the physical and the ideological sense, as one could see in 1849 when Nicholas suppressed Hungary), and it was only after Russia had been invaded that she went over from the defensive to the offensive, pushing ahead of her, and always a little further ahead of her, a protective zone to cushion the first impact of future invasions. This happened in the case of Charles XII early in the eighteenth century, then with Napoleon and twice with Germany in our own century. The buffer zone has become a tradition in Russian foreign political thinking. Today the Russian security belt is pushed much further to the west than it was at any time before; the Soviet Union is bloated, to the great discomfort of itself and its neighbours in Eastern Europe, but it is a little difficult—and quite useless—to quarrel

with the Russian perception that Russia needs a buffer along her
western perimeter.

URBAN: You said a moment ago that the Soviet leaders made a
mistake when they turned the East European countries into satellites, yet you are now admitting that Russian national interest requires, in the Russian perception anyhow, a security zone in Eastern
Europe. Moscow, you said, would have been better advised to construct a buffer zone on the Finnish model, without the ideological
rape of Eastern Europe. But would this really have met Soviet requirements? If the missionary streak in the Russian make-up demands, as it does, ideological satellitization as an additional
guarantee that the *cordon sanitaire* has been rendered entirely germ-
free, isn't it futile to argue 'But satellitization doesn't fill the
bill—you'd be so much better off with a sovereign Poland and Hungary co-operating with you as free partners'?

HALSTI: I think the Russians have a legitimate interest in seeing
themselves protected on their East European boundary, but it is
politically dangerous, morally wrong and most probably counter-productive to foist their system on states which they expect to
provide the first line of Russia's conventional defence. As things
are, the East European nations will not shield the Soviet Union.
They will, at best, opt out of the game if and when the crunch comes,
and they may do worse.

The problem boils down to one of style rather than substance.
The Soviet leaders could have achieved everything they have
achieved in Eastern Europe—minus the Yugoslav defection, the
Berlin uprising, the Poznan troubles, the Polish October, the Hungarian Revolution, the Prague upheavals and Rumania's partial
dissent—if they had acted with more tact, more circumspection,
and a greater understanding of what they were really about in terms
of European history. For us in Finland Russian behaviour is incomprehensible and I'm sure it is incomprehensible to most Central
Europeans too, but we simply have to make our peace with the fact
that the Kremlin is not Westminster and that the kind of policies
that provoked the Poles to rise against Russia in the nineteenth century will continue to be pursued by the Kremlin.

The Russian polity is, in the last analysis, an oriental polity.
Russian ways of thinking are not our ways of thinking; Russian
ways of making allies are not our ways of making allies; Russian
techniques of negotiation are not our techniques. Russia's image
smacks of a crudeness and brutality that marks it out for western
fears and, worse, western ridicule. We may complain that the
Romanovs are still in the Kremlin only they now go by the name of
Stalin or the name of Brezhnev; that communism has taken over

where the Orthodox Church left off in 1917; that Russification has stepped into the shoes of Pan-slavism. All this is true and most regrettable, but if these happen to be the characteristics of your most powerful neighbour, and if the United States does not want to, and Western Europe is not in a position to offer any effective counterweight to the policies of your most powerful neighbour, you have to learn to live with it. And that, for Eastern Europe, means a very slow inching forward within the framework of institutions sanctioned by the Soviet leadership, supported by whatever micro-aid may be gleaned from a security accord and any other Soviet-American political spectaculars that may come our way in the coming years.

URBAN: If Russian thinking, Russian mores, Russian attitudes to individual liberty and national independence are as different from our own as you say they are—if, in other words, the Soviet and western systems of politics are based on two fundamentally dissimilar views of the human condition—can détente and a security accord rest on anything but make-believe? Even if limited agreements are reached on arms control, force reductions and a modicum of crisis management, these differences will not go away and détente can never become anything more constructive than an anti-suicide pact.

HALSTI: That, in the present circumstances, is in fact all détente can amount to. But think how well the world would have been served if we had had an anti-suicide pact in 1939 or 1914.

URBAN: It is, to my mind, one of the marvels of contemporary politics how the Finnish people have come to accept compromise in their relations with the Soviet Union. Compromise is hardly a Finnish tradition; in fact, until after the second world war, it was held in contempt as unpatriotic and feeble; the Finns were always thought to feel that the most effective way of ensuring peace was summed up in the phrase: *si vis pacem, para bellum*. Yet today the Finnish people's attitude to their relations with the Soviet Union is, I believe accurately, encapsulated in President Kekkonen's remark: 'A good loser is often preferable to a bad winner.' 'I appeal to the Finnish people', Kekkonen said in a broadcast in 1961, 'and those who have not had confidence in Soviet friendship . . . to be "good losers".'

HALSTI: The Finnish nation is extremely tough and resilient. Finns like to compare themselves to the juniper—they will bend, they can be trampled upon, but they will not break. This resilience has been forced on us by Finland's national circumstances in the last hundred years. Let me give you an example from my personal experience.

We were, as you know, Germany's allies for four years during the war. I commanded a brigade which fought side by side with German

troops in the Karelian Isthmus. Such indeed was our co-operation
that for a long period of time my brigade alternated in the line with a
German mountain division. We got to know each other well, as
comrades in arms do, and most of us were on terms with the Germans.

Then, in the summer of 1944, Finland broke off relations with
Germany and signed an armistice agreement with the Soviet Union.
Finland undertook to ensure that the Germans would evacuate all
Finnish territory. But the Germans in the North of the country-
—some 200,000 men—would not leave voluntarily. One night I
received orders to move my brigade to the North and attack the
Germans in the rear. I issued an order-of-the-day explaining the
new situation and reminding my troops of their duty to Finland. I
told them that we had to carry out orders whether we personally
liked them or not. I was a little worried about the brigade's reaction,
especially the reaction of my officers; but I need not have been.

We were moving along the Swedish border, in loose formation, to
get into the back of the Germans and cut off their line of retreat to
the North of Norway. In the long nights of the Arctic autumn there
were opportunities galore for any of my 3,700 officers and men to
take himself over to Sweden where no questions were asked. We certainly could have done nothing about it—it was up to every man
either to go into battle against yesterday's comrades or to save his
skin by deserting to Sweden. I had exactly two deserters.

In the first twenty-four hours of our attack we lost eighteen per
cent of our force, but we broke through the German lines and
fought a desperate action for six more days with elements of a coun-
ter-attacking SS division. Then, east of Torne, we came face to face
with the mountain division we had shared a line with in Karelia.
There was fearful slaughter; the Germans lost eighty per cent of
their men. Their division was annihilated. None of my men
refused to fight.

I am recalling these terrible events because they illustrate the
patriotism and adaptability of the Finnish soldier and of the Finnish people. The great majority of my troops were simple peasants
from the North. They were, as I say, close to the men of the
German mountain division, but when Finland's interest demanded that they turn on their former allies, they did so without
hesitation.

URBAN: A rare display of discipline and patriotism.

HALSTI: Of patriotism or, as some have alleged, of apathy.
But my troops were not apathetic. I watched their reactions
closely: they considered their new situation very carefully and decided to respect my orders. They thought and fought as free men.

For all these reasons I believe that the Soviet Union has an entirely reliable ally in us at the present time. If the Soviet-Finnish treaty were activated, I have no doubt whatever that the Finnish soldier would do his duty—

URBAN: —fighting on the Soviet side?

HALSTI: —fighting on the Soviet side, but—and this is an important rider—only if we are left alone to run our affairs as a free and sovereign country. I have often told my Russian friends: 'Invade Finland and we'll make life hell for your soldiers: if you leave us alone, we'll carry out our contractual commitments to the letter, but don't impose your system on us or press us in any other way, for the Finnish Army will fight you to the last man, and the Finnish people will take to the forests and wage a people's war against you with no holds barred.'

It is, of course, anybody's guess how the Russians would actually behave if the treaty were activated. I, for one, have repeatedly warned them in my books: 'Keep your hands off Finland!'

URBAN: Your insistence that Russia must not interfere with Finland's internal affairs presumably goes the other way too: you do not, I take it, support Soviet dissidents such as Sakharov and Solzhenitsyn. How in fact does the Finnish public react to the idea that under the umbrella of détente the western democracies should forge friendly and irreversible links with the Soviet type of communism without trying to change the Soviet system? For over a quarter of a century Finland has successfully pioneered détente with the Soviet Union. What lessons have you to teach us?

HALSTI: We have, of course, many more years of experience of living in a state of détente with a despotic power—not only since 1917 but before 1917 too—than any of us would care to remember. The Finnish reaction to the problem as you have formulated it is twofold: the Finnish communists are blind to the truth and will go along with whatever the Russians want them to believe. For them Soviet dissent is a perversion, unrepresentative of the Soviet people and certainly no business of the outside world. These communist Old Believers in our ranks—for that is what they really are—represent about fifteen per cent of the Finnish people. The rest, that is, the great majority of the Finnish people, wonder, as the European and American critics of détente wonder, whether it is possible to build bridges with a system that tolerates no opposition, that suppresses the rights of the individual, that is contemptuous of the wishes of minorities and unrepentant about the crimes committed in its name in the very recent past. Can the civilized world, they ask, make friends with 'those strange gorilloids' whom Solzhenitsyn encounters on his way to Gulag Archipelago?

This is the *subjective* reaction of the majority of the Finnish people. But parallel with that there is a rational, political response which controls our feelings and governs our actions. 'Of course, we have a beastly system for a neighbour', the Finns would say, 'but it is not our system, and so long as no attempt is made to export that system to our country, our relations with the Soviet Union will remain correct. If the Russian people want to keep the communist system as it is, that is their business; if they want to reform it or get rid of it, that is their business too. We shall respect our contractual obligations, we shall trade with the Soviet Union and enter into friendly relations with it in any and every way as a sovereign, independent country. At the same time we expect our Soviet neighbours to respect those strange, for them incomprehensible and often chaotic goings on that make a democracy into what it is: opposition, the unrestrained conflict of opinions, irreverence, in-fighting, the public washing of political dirty linen and the rest.' So, although on the human level we do not at all approve of the Soviet attitude to dissent, we do not arrogate the right to ourselves to tell the Russians how they should deal with it.

URBAN: The 'free' flow of people and information has been a well-established practice between Finland and the Soviet Union for many years now. Has it produced the sort of results the western nations expect Basket Three to produce?

HALSTI: I am familiar with the problem for I have myself been heavily involved in Soviet-Finnish exchange. We have had this flow for about fifteen years now and the main lesson it has taught me is that as long as exchange is limited to technical and scientific matters, all is well: we both give and get something in return. The same goes for commerce and other morally and intellectually neutral, idea-free activities. But when it comes to ideas, social and intellectual history—*Geist*—the barriers come down and we talk at cross purposes. I have attended a great many discussions of the latter kind: we state our point of view, the Russians state theirs, there is no proper give and take, neither side has a visible impact on the other and the conclusions reflect the separateness of the two positions—nothing is resolved.

URBAN: But couldn't the West, under the auspices of a security accord, do better? Wouldn't the Soviet side have a greater incentive? The United States can equip Brezhnev with drilling gear for his Siberian hot air; Finland has given the Russians nothing but cold feet—before the war, during the war and since the war.

HALSTI: My answer to that is that the West might expect a more effective exchange with the Soviet Union only if the Soviet system changed, and changed pretty drastically. Without that the cross-talk will continue, this time under the wicker-work of Basket Three.

URBAN: But a drastic change in the Soviet system rather strains our imagination, doesn't it? It does mine. The scoundrel the Russian people will not put up with as Tsar, party leader or police chief has yet to be born.

HALSTI: Nothing in history is unimaginable. The Tsars fell, nazism fell, fascism fell—communism will fall too. Whether it goes down through revolution or whether it will change by peaceful evolution no-one can foretell. I would put my money on gradual reform. But one thing is absolutely certain: the Soviet citizen of the 1970s is not the muzhik of 1917 nor even of the 1930s. He has had his eyes opened by education—no-one will ever con him back into tolerating Stalinism.

I remember a conversation I had with a Soviet diplomat here in Helsinki not so many years ago about Russian attitudes to literacy. The old gentleman—a fine specimen of Russian conformism and rectitude—could not understand why we in Finland were at each other's throats all the time in our internal politics. The sneering between our political parties, the cacophony of voices, the sheer disorder of things upset him enormously. Where was the discipline he had been trained to obey? Where was authority? Well, I told him that he could not possibly understand our system because his schooling had been so terribly Russian. In a democracy, I said, we send a child to school to make him learn how to read and write and think for himself, but you in Russia send your children to school to make them learn how to believe, and a nation that has been trained to believe, not to think, is a captive audience for any dictatorship—Tsarist, communist, nazi, whatever.

The problem for the Soviet Union is that modernization requires literacy and numeracy; you cannot learn how to read and write and follow a rational argument without acquiring a taste for thinking, and I am liberal enough to be persuaded that a thinking man will not tolerate a dictatorship. The Soviet system has already changed for the better since the oriental despotism of Stalin, precisely because concessions had to be made to the rapidly increasing masses of Soviet non-believers. Atheism is a double-edged weapon: it may undermine your faith in God but it will certainly undermine your faith in usurpers of divine power—Führers, generalissimos, social drill-sergeants and the like.

URBAN: History is having a little joke on the Soviet interpreters of Karl Marx. Yet I wonder whether humbug, Byzantium, Orthodoxy and the other unpleasant accoutrements of the Russian tradition are really losing their power over the Russian people. Can centuries of conformism be eradicated with the stroke of a pen?

Followers of one of the Cargo Cults in Dutch New Guinea accuse the Europeans of having hidden the fact that Jesus was a Papuan by tearing out the first page of the Bible. To repair the injustice, they have renamed their villages Galilee, Jericho and so on, and one of their leaders, whose name was, moreover, Moses, retired to meditate on a mountain renamed Mount Carmel.

Not to pursue the analogy too far, it seems to me that the Soviet incarnation of Marxism has more to do with the primogeniture of *Russian* socialism and nineteenth century visions of a Russophile deliverance of the defiled humanity of the West, than with those earnest texts Marx and Engels wrote. Dostoyevsky said shortly before his death: 'The future genuine Russian idea has not yet appeared among us, but the earth is portentously pregnant with it and is making ready to deliver it amid agonizing pain.' And it was, he said, this Russian idea that would 'prepare the final vision of the twentieth century'—the 'Third Rome' I suppose.

HALSTI: Ancient and modern certainly make strange bedfellows in the Russian mind.

In the late 1920s I was stationed, as a young lieutenant, with a mechanized batallion on the Soviet-Finnish frontier. We were so close to Kronstadt and Leningrad that one could see the towers of the old capital rising out of the Bay of Finland, and when at night the Russians fired their heavy batteries, we could feel the ground trembling under our feet. Among the exiled Russian families who had settled in the area there was a Russian nobleman, Prince Gallizin, and his wife, living in pitifully reduced circumstances. The Gallizins had found shelter in a frightfully dilapidated cabin, held together by the kindness of the elements more than any human design. Gallizin came from a very old, famous and wealthy family. He had been a landowner, but of course he had lost his property in the revolution and what assets he managed to save he had sold to keep alive. So here he was, living in great poverty, right on the boundary of the land that was his mother-country, but from which he had had to flee to save his life.

One day when he and his wife were walking in the park, I joined them, and soon we found ourselves talking about that inexhaustible topic: the decline and disintegration of Tsarist Russia. 'It had to come', Gallizin said, 'we were a dam blocking up the great river of the Russian people. Of course the dam created a most attractive artificial lake; the surroundings were pretty, it was a joy for us to live there, and our only concern was to keep everything exactly as it was. But it could not last: the tumultuous flux of the Russian nation rose higher and higher until it breached the dam and devastated the artificial landscape.'

'Do you think', I asked Gallizin, 'that the Russian people will do better under the Bolsheviks, or will the Bolsheviks build a dam of their own, stopping up the rivers of Russia once again until they, too, are chased away? Mightn't they', I added, 'adjust to the real wishes of the Russian people and avoid another cataclysm?'

'I pray that this may be so for the sake of the Russian people I love', he answered, 'but I doubt that it will be so. There is a curse on Russia, and the name of that curse is dogmatism. It is a poison we inherited with Byzantium and it pervades everything we think and do. I should *like* to think that Bolshevism will be westernized and civilized, but I cannot believe that it will, I can see the new dam rising—a new and intolerable despotism which the Russian people will sweep away as they swept away our rule. But, in the meantime', he added thoughtfully, 'I do believe the Bolsheviks will have enough time and energy to turn Russia into a world power.'

URBAN: Holy Mother Russia that kills you but can do no wrong—

HALSTI: —yes. Every night, as the sun was setting on those long, warm summer days in the Karelian Isthmus, I saw Prince Gallizin and his wife kneeling on the sea-front with their faces turned towards Leningrad, praying for Bolshevik Russia.

RICHARD PIPES

Détente and reciprocity

URBAN: I propose to begin this discussion by looking at the semantics and vocabulary of Soviet political articulation. My immediate purpose is to find out whether the manner in which words are used, and not used, in the Soviet Union can tell us anything about Soviet attitudes to détente.

I would hesitate to raise so obvious a point, were it not for an erroneous, but commonly held, western assumption that the image which totalitarian regimes offer of themselves and their policies to their captive audiences is governed by a set of rules barely related to that governing their 'real' policies: totalitarian public usage is thought to be 'evocative', 'irrational', 'ideological', whereas the policies actually pursued are 'realistic', 'down-to-earth' and bounded by 'national interest'. The first is all talk—the hard decisions are said to be taken at the second level.

However, on closer examination, the differences between base and top dressing look less convincing. While it is true enough that one of the functions of totalitarian rhetoric is to elicit support for policies the true nature of which cannot be frankly stated, it is also true—and equally important—that totalitarian usage creates its own momentum, setting goals which totalitarian regimes cannot afford to neglect, and ruling out others which they cannot afford to support, without losing their title to legitimacy. In other words, you make your own propaganda, but then your propaganda also makes you.*

* The following passage from Khrushchev's memoirs (Vol. I, pp. 342–43), describing the preliminaries of Moscow's ideological reconciliation with Yugoslavia in 1955, illustrates this point: '. . . we had been so estranged from the Yugoslavs and we had thought up so many accusations against them that we'd started to believe what we'd been telling ourselves. It's like in that old story about the mullah . . . who is walking through the village square telling people that back where he's just come from they're giving away free lamb and rice. Word quickly spreads through the town, and everyone starts running in the direction where he pointed. When the mullah sees everyone running, he stops somebody and asks, "What's happening?" "They're giving away free lamb and rice over there!" So the mullah hikes up his skirts and runs along with the crowd to get free food, even though he made the whole story up himself. It was just the same with Yugoslavia. We'd made

174

Is there a predominant mode in Soviet rhetoric that might offer us a key to Soviet thinking?

PIPES: The language of Soviet politics is permeated with the vocabulary of militarism. Every sphere of public activity becomes a 'front' which has to be 'stormed' by 'brigades' in a 'campaign'. All-out 'offensives' are launched to overcome initial difficulties, and peace itself becomes the object of 'struggle'. This tendency to borrow words from the vocabulary of military science has its roots in Lenin. Marx is many things to many people. You can, if you wish, lift out of Marx the liberal humanitarian element of the young Marx, as some modern Marxists do—Marx the Feuerbachian, Marx the author of the *Philosophical Manuscripts* etc.—and you can also do many other things. Lenin took out of Marx the idea of the class-war as an inevitable and pitiless concept. We are told by Peter Struve, who knew Lenin intimately in his early career, that Lenin was attracted by Marx's theory because he found in it 'the doctrine of class-war, relentless and thoroughgoing, aiming at the final destruction and extermination of the enemy'. Class-war is, of course, the common property of all socialists, but to Lenin it was a very tangible thing—a daily, hourly struggle between the 'camp of socialism' and the 'camp of capitalism'. What for Marx and Engels was a means became for him an end. Lenin was, indeed, the first political leader to look upon politics entirely in terms of warfare and to pursue this conception to its merciless end.

The second factor which accounts for the militarism in Lenin's thinking and vocabulary was General Ludendorff, whose masterful conduct of 'total' war has probably exercised as great an influence on communist practices as anything Marx and Engels had written. Lenin observed carefully how the Germans mobilized the home front for total war—a temporary measure in the case of Germany—and grafted the idea of total mobilization onto Marxism, the end result of which was Soviet economic planning. The Soviet concept of the 'art of operations' (and we may come back to this in a moment) is also derived from an analysis of Ludendorff's conduct of the war—the idea that victory requires a series of interdependent actions, based on solid logistic support and synchronized to produce on the enemy mounting pressure which eventually causes him to collapse.

Last, but by no means least, there was Clausewitz. Lenin read him rather late in life, in 1915, but the appeal was instantaneous. Lenin, as might be expected, especially admired Clausewitz's insistence that war and politics were not separate, antithetical activities, but

up a story about all the terrible things the Yugoslavs were doing, and we'd heard the story so often that we started to believe it ourselves.'

simply alternative methods pressed into the service of a single policy. Whether one or the other was chosen at any juncture in inter-state relations was determined by what the ends required and by no other consideration. Lenin felt that blurring and then erasing the boundaries between political tactics and military tactics suited his book well at home, and he urged communist party workers to study and apply the principles of Clausewitz. In this he was, incidentally, at one with the nazis, who apostrophized Clausewitz with equal vigour.

URBAN: I notice there is a school of thought in American political science which studies the Soviet Union in terms of the 'mobilization state'.

PIPES: Not a bad framework for such an enterprise, for militancy and military symbolism are, as I say, deeply embedded in every aspect of Soviet life. Soviet society is mobilized for war, not necessarily in the conventional sense (though it is mobilized for that too) but for class-war which may take on a number of forms, and militancy is nourished by continuous propaganda which sees to it that at no point is the human psyche allowed to relax. The techniques vary: you create a myth of encirclement which makes it easier to enforce discipline and to offer a semblance of justification for maintaining a siege mentality. You withhold consumer goods from Soviet society, because such goods have a way of satisfying the needs of the ordinary citizen and thus making him less pliable in the hands of the state. I am convinced that the failure to provide consumer goods is not just an economic but a political decision.

I don't normally stress the impact of ideology on Soviet society, but there is no doubt that the concepts of a universal militancy have become part of the mental equipment of the ordinary Soviet citizen. And can you blame him? He is being told year in and year out that the world is in a condition of permanent class-war and that, since the October Revolution, the class-war has become even more acute. This war, in the Soviet view, need not be a shooting war; sometimes it does break out in actual hostilities, at other times it takes the form of ideological combat—that is its irreducible minimum. The two ideological systems must never be reconciled, and that is why, even during the current phase of détente, Moscow insists on keeping alive the ideological conflict.

URBAN: The problem for the observer less steeped in the intricacies of Soviet ideology is that the Soviet Union has, in fact, successfully put into practice détente types of policies from Brest-Litovsk to the present day, without giving up ideological combat. So can we unhesitatingly say that ideological combat, and all it implies, is a surer index of Soviet intentions as far as inter-state relations are concerned, than the actual record of peaceful co-existence?

PIPES: Détente has been deployed—and Brest-Litovsk and, later, NEP are good examples—whenever the Soviet Union was militarily or economically weak and needed peace and western assistance. They were temporary expedients which the new Soviet state saw itself constrained to adopt in order to secure some breathing-space by coming to terms with a powerful enemy. Lenin was under pressure from the Zimmerwald-Kienthal programme to turn the war into international civil war, but he realized that Russia's internal situation did not yet permit this. His advocacy of a peace treaty with the Central Powers on any terms produced a savage conflict in the Central Committee and almost led to Lenin's resignation. The records of the discussions in the Central Committee have been published. The communist leaders were very frank in those days, so we have no excuse for not knowing what motives they had at the back of their minds with their earlier moves to achieve a breathing-spell.

URBAN: I suppose if you conceive of détente and the 'normal' Soviet attitude to the outside world—that is to say, the class-struggle projected onto the international arena—as complementary policies in line with Clausewitz, Soviet policy to this day must be said to have shown a remarkable consistency.

PIPES: It has, and the reason lies not in the innate force of Lenin's ideas. It lies in the fact that the Soviet Union of today finds itself in a situation in one essential respect still identical with the one Lenin had left on his death bed, that is, a government devoid of any popular mandate or any other justification of its monopoly of political power except the alleged exigencies of the class-war. The regime is locked in, and even if it wanted to extricate itself from its predicament by internal democratization, it would be prevented from doing so by the opposition of its powerful and conservative bureaucratic establishment.

URBAN: Any idea, then, of the Soviet system liberalizing itself under the pressure of the increasing sophistication, higher living standards and *embourgeoisement* of its establishment is chimerical. Indeed, the Kremlin has at its disposal tools for the conduct of a 'total' foreign policy.

PIPES: I think so. Soviet foreign policy is very 'total' indeed. It follows the principles of the 'art of operations' in that it draws no distinction between diplomatic, economic, psychological and military means of operation. The bureaucracy carries out orders and asks few questions. Militancy is so deeply entrenched in the mentality of the Soviet élite that I wonder whether the best way of easing

East-West tensions is by attempting the piecemeal resolution of specific disagreements. These disagreements aren't, after all, the causes of tension, but its consequence. After all, the last war wasn't fought over Danzig.

URBAN: Do we have an answer to the 'art of operations'?

PIPES: Although this is a time-honoured technique of Soviet foreign policy, I don't think we have as yet developed a sufficiently comprehensive monitoring system to deal with it. The technique is, after all, quite simple: you do not go in for a series of isolated jabs, but co-ordinate your tactical moves so that each supports the other and you subordinate them all to an ultimate strategic objective. The idea was borrowed, as I say, from the German military, but it was a concept favoured by some Tsarist generals too. The Bolsheviks are simply using it in a larger context, following Clausewitz. If we had a sufficiently sophisticated early warning system, we might be able to tell why the Russians are jabbing in one place rather than another, and, by fitting the pieces together, explain how the Russians go after their quarry. As it is, we are seeing each jab in isolation and respond accordingly, that is—very inadequately.

URBAN: Lenin's adoption of Clausewitz strikes me as natural: if class-war—which is international by definition—is the basic premise of your thinking, you have to adopt a 'total' foreign policy, i.e. one that cuts across 'domestic affairs' and 'foreign relations' and treats them as one.

PIPES: Communism views the sovereign state as a transitional phenomenon connected with the capitalist mode of production and, therefore, destined to disappear with it, and it is for that reason that neither Marx nor Engels nor Lenin had anything theoretically significant to say about foreign policy.

The Soviet Government does not recognize in theory, and only grudgingly in practice, the international system of sovereign states. It has bowed to the necessity of maintaining a Ministry of Foreign Affairs with its diplomatic corps because other countries it must deal with happen to do so, but the Ministry is not charged with the formulation of foreign policy. Every important foreign policy decision is made by the Politburo and often carried out by its own agencies.

But Soviet foreign policy also works on other levels, of which inter-state relations conducted through the diplomatic network is only one, and not necessarily the most important. Moscow maintains an extensive subversive apparatus. The practice of entrusting foreign policy matters to the KGB and military intelligence is widespread. We know from Soviet diplomatic defectors that at some Soviet embassies less than twenty per cent of staff work for the

Foreign Ministry and are accountable to the Ambassador. The rest are employed by other agencies, mostly engaged in intelligence activities and reporting directly to Moscow. Hence it should occasion no surprise that the United States found it necessary to counter this unconventional conduct of foreign policy by broadening the functions of the Central Intelligence Agency and pitting against the Soviet variety a 'total' foreign policy management of its own.

URBAN: The brunt of détente diplomacy is borne by the Soviet and American sides. Are there any specific sensitivities in the American psyche that the Russians can play on more readily than they might on those of other nations?

PIPES: I believe so. When the Soviet leaders talk to the United States President, the Secretary of State, senators, congressmen and presidents of large corporations from whom they want money and technology, then they argue that basically the two systems are much more alike than meets the eye. They suggest that the Americans should treat Soviet ideology as a rhetorical device and nothing more. They stress the convergence of industrial societies—a line they totally reject at other levels, but one which comes in very handy with high-level United States executives. This line can be extremely effective, because it appeals to the tendency of Americans to regard the whole world as aspiring to the state of being American, and prevented from being so only by poverty, ignorance or some inexplicable wrong-headedness.

Now, on the mass level abroad, the Russians project a very glossy picture. Soviet society, they say, while it still has problems, hasn't any of the problems that plague the ordinary American: no unemployment, no crime, no corruption, no inflation and so forth. This, too, has great appeal for the man in Atlanta who has no idea what really goes on in the streets of Novosibirsk or even Moscow.

URBAN: I would have thought the American psyche in its present state of disorientation would offer Soviet policy-makers a much wider scale of opportunities to exploit than those you have listed. When your adversary's will is undermined by a lost war (Vietnam) and a profound internal crisis (Watergate), he may well prove to be a walk-over, or so it might seem to the more sanguine minds in the Kremlin.

PIPES: I would not stress American disorientation and demoralization too much—though these exist—first, because the Russians have some outsize skeletons in their cupboards (hence their silence on Watergate and the reasons for Nixon's resignation), and secondly because the Soviet leaders know that, ignorant though the United States public may often be, it would hardly enjoy the sight of bailing the Soviet Union out of its economic predicament *and* being destroyed by the Soviet Union at the same time.

In looking at the Soviet estimate of the American psychological make-up, I would rather point to certain fundamental differences between how Americans and Russians habitually view the conduct of foreign relations and state-to-state negotiations in particular.

American culture rests on a tradition of give and take. The principal American preoccupation has always been commercial and therefore, predisposed toward compromise. Each commercial transaction must show some profit for both parties; the competition between them is over the division of profit—who gets this and who gets that—but not over the principle that both have to benefit. It is well understood that neither party walks away with the till.

On the other hand, in Russia you have a society which makes its living on the production and consumption of goods (agricultural and industrial) and which is, therefore, predisposed to the denial of compromise. Why do I say that? Until a century ago the main form of Russian wealth was owning land worked by serfs. When you own land and serfs, your idea in life is to grab as much as you can and as fast as you can and never mind how your economic activity affects your neighbour. I needn't remind you that the Russian tradition is so entirely non-commercial that the first Russian merchant bank was founded in the 1860s and that, until the nineteenth century, the predominant form of exchange activity was straightforward barter.

These traditions have had an important influence on the negotiating postures of the two countries. Whenever we approach the Russians with a proposal (and that is why we are at such a disadvantage in negotiating with them) our position inevitably includes provisions designed to make it acceptable to the Russians. We sweeten our suggestions with concessions before the Russians have had a chance to ask for any, because we assume that the other party will do likewise, since the first premise of any negotiation is that the other party, too, must benefit.

Not so the Russians. Their position always represents what the Soviet Government actually wants, weighted down with other unrealistic demands to be given up in exchange for American concessions. They give absolutely nothing to the other fellow for free. So any negotiation with the United States is bound to work.out in Russia's favour because the original American positions include concessions which need not be fought for. Splitting the difference between the two parties isn't, therefore, a fifty-fifty arrangement, but gives the Russians a disproportionate gain.

This straining for gross advantage is occasionally self-defeating. In 1972–73 the Russians had a wonderful thing going: they had the beginnings of détente plus massive financial and economic aid almost within their grasp, but they were so keen on making a fast killing that they went for the American wheat deal. They got their killing but the killing left a bitter taste in America and contributed heavily to delaying for the Russians infinitely greater advantages—such as clinching investment contracts worth tens of billions of US dollars. They risked their long-range interests for a paltry 300-million-dollar profit simply because they did not know where to call a halt. The 1974 and 1975 attempts to buy more American wheat has shown them hell-bent on aggravating their earlier blunder.

URBAN: You are suggesting that Soviet maximalist positions should be countered by maximalist positions of our own so that if any whittling down has to be done, we don't whittle down our conditions until the Russians have done some whittling down too.

PIPES: My position is that we should confront the Russians with our demands, just as they confront us with theirs, and not let ourselves be inhibited by unwarranted feelings of guilt, or complain that the Russians don't love us. The Russians know how to cash in on the American Protestant tendency to self-accusation. But as we are aware of the fact that *they* are aware of this weakness, we can surely protect ourselves accordingly.

URBAN: How, in fact, does the Soviet side press home a maximalist proposal, and how does it come about that we accept it?

PIPES: Let me give you an example. The administration of Berlin after the war was regulated by four-power agreements; hence any unilateral change of its status in one part of the city by one of the four powers was illegitimate, or should, at the very least, have been accompanied by similar changes in the status of other parts of the city occupied by the other powers. In 1957, the Soviet Union recognized East Germany as a sovereign state and gradually transferred East Berlin to the control of the GDR. The western powers neither accepted this act as legitimate nor did they follow suit by transferring sovereignty over West Berlin to the Federal Government. The Russians, however, regarded the incorporation of East Berlin in the GDR as a fait accompli. They have not allowed the future of East Berlin to be put on the agenda of any conference or summit meeting since 1958. At the same time, however, by putting intermittent pressure on West Berlin, and especially by threatening its communications with the Federal Republic, the Russians have transformed what, in fact, was a problem of Berlin as a whole into a West Berlin problem which is said to be a threat to peace and thus to require a negotiated settlement. In the 1972 four-power agreement, the Federal Government secured certain concessions from the Soviet Union. However, the cold fact remains that neither Bonn nor the western powers got any concessions on East Berlin, because the status of East Berlin was simply not on the agenda. The Russians ruled it out from the beginning as non-negotiable. This is the way the Russians usually proceed and, astonishingly, they get away with it much of the time.

URBAN: Is it your view, then, that at the Security Conference, for example, we should have insisted on putting questions such as the condition of Czechoslovakia, Poland, Hungary, Rumania and Bulgaria on the agenda?

PIPES: Yes, that is the sort of thing we ought to do for the sake of equivalence. Of course it would be very difficult to get western diplomats to agree to insist on maximalist demands of this kind. The immediate reaction would be: 'You must be mad. If you make any such proposals, the Russians will walk out.'

URBAN: Which is itself a telling sign how successfully the Soviet 'art of operations' has affected—one might almost say brain-washed—our side.

PIPES: It is, but it is also a sign of confused thinking. What our men forget or overlook for some reason is that the whole idea of having a so-called security conference came from the Russians. *We* didn't suggest it—they are the ones who have been peddling the idea up and down the world for many years. It is *their* security they want to talk about, not ours.

By now, of course, the Soviet side has got so accustomed to the fact that we never make 'unrealistic' demands that our diplomats may be quite right in saying that the Russians would be scandalized if we did. Here I must say a word about semantics. The word 'realism' is in great vogue in all Soviet foreign political articulations. 'Realistic' in the Russian vocabulary is what conforms to Soviet interests. For example, the recognition of the Oder–Neisse line is 'realistic', but any recognition of the present status quo in the Middle East would be 'unrealistic'. 'Realism' is when we recognize that the Russians are in Eastern Europe to stay. If we question it, we are not being 'realistic'. Now we in the West have fallen into this semantic trap: we don't, in fact, make 'unrealistic' demands, but take for granted that the Soviet side should make such 'unrealistic' demands on us—if I may, for the moment, use their language from our point of view. This semantic technique, and our lack of resistance to it, allows the Russians to make continued piecemeal encroachments on our interests.

URBAN: But why do we fall for this terminological subversion? We are neither innocents in this game nor are we excessively unintelligent.

PIPES: Basically the problem is that we are very affluent. We feel that we *have* so much that we can afford to give away a great deal without being any the worse for it, which is, in effect, an appeasement policy. One can also turn it around and say: we have so much, and therefore so much to lose, that it isn't worth our while getting into major squabbles over small issues. It is an attitude of mind the Soviets know how to exploit, having learnt from Hitler. Stalin has expressed on a number of occasions respect for nazi methods, but always with one reservation: Hitler was over-confident, Hitler was in too great a hurry, Hitler went for this great western weakness with enormous energy and ended up with war after three or four years.

The Russians are much more cautious and they dispose of a great deal of time. They encroach upon us in very small instalments. They would have pressed for Danzig (if they had been in Hitler's shoes) over a period of ten to fifteen years, until we got tired of them and *gave* them Danzig; they would certainly not have gone to war over it. What we don't seem to realize in the West is that there is a principle involved in our non-resistance to this Soviet technique of making inroads through the back door. If we don't stand up on one small issue because we think it is too insignificant, and then don't stand up on another and a third, we could end up losing everything we have, small and large.

URBAN: The Russians, on their part, are extremely conscious of the need to resist this kind of erosion and are highly legalistic in their interpretation of international treaties, frontier agreements and everything that might touch upon the status quo.

PIPES: This is why they do not give up the Kurile Islands, for example, and this is why the Russians do not yield to the Chinese demand that they agree that the present Sino-Soviet border is the result of unequal treaties, which of course it is. A piece of paper, you might say, and so it would be, but the Russians fully realize that any doubt cast on the legitimacy of *some* of their boundaries would involve undermining their entire hold on Eastern Europe. Now if *we* were in that kind of a position, we would have agreed to the Chinese demand years ago.

The trouble with our current attitudes is that we, and especially the European governments, take extremely short-term views of our problems. Why hold on to a couple of terrorists who might have killed a dozen people, when that might result in your oil supplies being cut off? Why not accept some face-saving formula at the Security Conference when that might buy you a surprise-free life for a year or two? There is very little leadership in the West and virtually none in Europe. European governments live from day to day and this is an enormous weakness, especially vis-à-vis the Soviet Union.

URBAN: But isn't this a congenital defect of the democratic

form of government? Democracies never take a view further than the next elections, and nowadays they are (as you say) happy if they know where they are going next week. And this weakness does not only handicap them in their dealings with totalitarian governments who work with global planning devices, but it also makes it virtually impossible for them to do justice to the world's ecological, environmental and demographic problems, all of which are extremely long-range.

PIPES: I grant that there is a problem here, but it need not be as bad as we have allowed it to become. After all, for twenty years we *had* a policy—a consistent policy—towards the Soviet Union. We had leaders in the West—Truman, Adenauer, de Gasperi, Spaak. These men, too, had to fight elections and nurse their constituencies and play to the gallery, but they knew where they were going. They were not just being dragged along by events. Our present leaders are. So, while I agree that democracy is, to some extent, intrinsically at a disadvantage, the disadvantage need not be of the kind and magnitude which we have, gratuitously as I see it, invited upon ourselves.

URBAN: You said earlier that one of the psychological soft spots of the American people is their need to be 'loved'. Clearly, if America had a policy—and by that I take it you mean a policy Moscow might find distasteful—Soviet stocks of 'love' (such as they are) would soon be exhausted. But even if we keep on muddling along without a policy, as we have done in recent years, playing détente from improvised positions and writing them off when they become a burden, our capacity to attract Soviet 'love' will still be extremely limited. The 'no-love' position in Soviet-American relations isn't something we can overcome by consular agreements or liquefied gas, for it is precisely what the Soviet definition of ideological conflict is about.

PIPES: Americans dread being hated. They never ask themselves who hates them and why. They don't seem to realize that to be hated can be an honour if you are being hated by the right sort of person. It is, I suppose, the self-accusatory tendency in the Protestant ethic that makes you feel guilty purely because someone hates you, the inference being that this hatred must to some extent be your fault because you have done your hater an injustice. The Russians play on this quirk of the American psyche. They exploit it by setting in motion a barrage of hostile actions accompanied by expressions of hatred. The natural American reaction is bewilderment followed by guilt. And so an atmosphere is created which leads to concessions to propitiate the allegedly injured party. The nazis used similar techniques vis-à-vis England, and the Russians have learned from them.

URBAN: But in the current phase of détente, this 'hate-you' technique is used with considerable restraint and sophistication. It is not on display, as it was not so many years ago, all the time and in all places.

PIPES: The 'hate-America' campaign is, at the moment, largely confined to domestic audiences in the USSR; and of course it is not in the Kremlin's interest to make the American public aware of the extent to which the Russian people are being incited to hatred of America, or that they are being incited at all. But the fact is that, détente or no détente, inside the Soviet Union, the United States is continuously depicted as the bastion of fascism, the citadel of world imperialism, the bloodthirsty supporter of Israeli Zionism and so forth. So what, in the Soviet Union, is known as 'ideological warfare' is a euphemism for 'hate-America'. Abroad, however, the Russians do play the game much more quietly at the moment.

For example, in the last year of the Vietnam war we did some heavy bombing in the North. Where two or three years earlier this would have brought upon us massive demonstrations in Grosvenor Square and the Champs Elysées, there was none this time. So the Russians are conscious both of the uses and limitations of the 'hate-America' technique.

At the moment they are guided by the limitations. Détente to them is a tactical move made necessary by the backwardness of Soviet technology and the desirability of attracting western aid and investment on a very large scale. They realize (as I said before) that they cannot have a series of bitter confrontations with the United States *and* get our money as well, so they must, for the time being, somehow come to terms with us, making certain, however, that, by keeping up the flames of the ideological war, their constituency at home is not so confused that when the time comes to revert to the 'hard line' it will baulk.

URBAN: The Soviet Union has always been in dire need of investment and technology. What is partly new is the openness with which, at least behind closed doors, this need is now admitted in international negotiations and American help sought. Domestically, of course, no such admission is made; even the 1973 wheat purchases have been kept secret from the Soviet public.

I am struck by a passage in the Epilogue to the second volume of Khrushchev's memoirs, where Khrushchev says that vast military expenditure is all very well for the Americans who can sustain it and profit from it, but it spells the ruin of the communist world:

The reactionary forces in the West know it's expedient for them to force us to exhaust our economic resources in a huge military budget thus diverting funds which could otherwise be spent on the cultural and material needs of our peoples. We must not let ourselves be caught in this trap. . . . The arms race has been part of a calculated plan to hinder the development of our economy, impede the growth of our standard of living, sow the seeds of disarray and dissatisfaction—and, if possible, bring about the collapse of socialism and a restoration of capitalism in our country.

This raises an important question: when we are asked by the Soviet leaders to find the money to support their economy, aren't we being invited to do what—if my reading of Khrushchev is right—he is implying we should not do in our own interest: channel funds to the Soviet economy as a whole, stabilizing the system and thus, directly or indirectly, boosting Russia's military potential?

Khrushchev makes it very clear that, when he was Chairman of the Council of Ministers, heavy arms expenditure forced him to suspend the construction of subways in Kiev, Baku and Tbilisi and to cut back on athletic stadiums, swimming pools and cultural facilities. Are we now to make it possible for the Soviet leaders to finance the expansion of the Soviet Navy, for example, by providing Russia with resources for the construction of football stadiums and underground railways?

PIPES: There is no question that western investments and technological transfer would greatly add to the Soviet military potential and make the system less unattractive than it is. The present Russian leaders are engagingly frank about this. Their problem is to justify détente to their domestic audiences, and the thrust of their argument is that American goods, investment and know-how will give the Soviet system a tremendous shot in the arm. This is true, and that is why I believe transfers of capital and technology should be carried out very carefully. I also believe that for every transfer and every commercial deal we ought to exact an immediate and commensurable price.

For example, we should say to the Soviet leaders: 'You are asking us to help you put up a plant. All right, we'll give you the licence provided that you stop jamming Radio Liberty. The moment you start jamming again, we will suspend, for one year, all further deliveries.' This kind of procedure would make good sense to me: it would leave it to the Russians to decide whether they want investment more than jamming, and it would put a very tangible premium on the reform of the Soviet economy. The assumption behind our present détente philosophy is that if we furnish the Russians with the massive assistance they want from us, the Soviet system will, through a number of unproven transmission belts, eventually change its character. But this is mortgaging the real present for a highly vague future. My conception of détente is, therefore, direct barter on the basis of periodic accounting: 'We give you this, you give us that—at the end of each period we draw a line and see whether both of us have met our obligations.' This is the sort of thing détente should be about.

URBAN: Now it is my turn to say with your western diplomats: 'But surely the Russians would have none of this': look at their reactions to the Jackson Amendment.

PIPES: Sometimes they would, sometimes they wouldn't. The pressure to accept this kind of arrangement would be very strong. At the moment we are being asked to give, give and give again. No payment is made; the returns will come later, the Russians assure us, in oil, gas and other resources. I'm not implying that the Russians are getting everything they want from us, but they are getting a great deal more than they should, and they are, in the process, contracting debts which they may or may not be able to repay. This is wrong. I would, as I have just said, simply put it to the Russians: 'We'll supply you with such and such items on your shopping list, but you must at once pay us A, B and C.' Let them, then, make the choice. In the case of the Jackson Amendment, they first decided in favour of concessions until the credit sums available to them were limited, at which point they decided to say 'no'.

URBAN: Let me take you back to the semantic differences which appear to make any understanding between the Soviet *Weltanschauung* and our own—in so far as we have one—so difficult to come by. The problem boils down to the question whether, in our view, détente is exclusively about inter-state relations or whether it is also predicated on certain changes in the domestic conditions of the Soviet Union.

The semantic hurdles are, as we have already seen, quite daunting. It is, in international politics, hard enough for men of the same culture to understand each other, even though words have a shared meaning in their vocabularies. But when neither of these conditions obtains, as is the case in Soviet-United States relations, isn't détente just an extremely costly way for us to underwrite the post-war gains and future stability of the Soviet Union? After all, we cannot even agree with the Russians on the meaning of the word détente.

Let me quote a few examples from one authentic witness, Andrei Amalrik (*Will the USSR survive until 1984?*):

The idea of self-government, of equality under the law for all and of personal freedom—and the responsibility that goes with these—are almost completely incomprehensible to the Russian people. . . . The very word 'freedom' is understood by most people as a synonym of the word 'disorder'. . . . As for respecting the rights of an individual as such, such an idea simply evokes bewilderment, . . . 'justice' is motivated by the wish 'nobody should be better off than me'. . .

PIPES: As you know, I have myself written about these semantic barriers, and they are, of course, a great impediment. However, the purpose of détente is not so much to make Russia change its system of government as to reduce the threat which it poses to Europe. To some extent it is true that a freer and better informed Russia is less of a menace, and it is for that reason that we are calling for internal changes in Russia and Eastern Europe under Basket Three and through other channels. But a complete internal transformation is not really what we are after—we are after stability and peace, and if the Russians, even while maintaining their present system of government, can demonstrate that they are doing all in their power internally and externally to live in accord with us and their neighbours, then we would certainly not press them for any change in their system. It is not our way. Personally, I wish that the system would change, but this is not a goal that a country can adopt as its foreign policy.

It would be preposterous (as well as hopeless) for us to demand that the Soviet Union become a democratic country before we can talk peace with it.

URBAN: Let me quote you Amalrik again: 'Collaboration takes for granted mutual reliance one on the other, but how can one rely upon a country [Russia] which over the centuries has been distending itself and disintegrating like sour dough. . . ? Genuine rapprochement can be based on a community of interests, of culture, of tradition and on mutual understanding. No such thing exists.'

What strikes me as significant in this passage is that, in Amalrik's view, the external posture of the Soviet Union is a function of such elusive and definitely 'domestic' factors as culture, tradition and understanding. Can, therefore, a minimalist conception of détente be anything more promising than a non-aggression pact?

PIPES: Détente implies no love relationship. The cultural and semantic barriers are, of course, there, but this need not affect state-to-state relations. After all, we have decent relations with countries which have totally different sets of values and traditions from our own—India and Japan, for example. Peaceful co-existence does not require that we all look alike and think alike. That would be an impossible demand; humanity lives at very different levels of development.

URBAN: You have not quite convinced me. I still feel—and I'll quote some more evidence in a moment—that a country's internal condition is a fair barometer of how we can expect it to behave in its external affairs, and that this is true for Russia *par excellence*. Consider Amalrik again, weighing up the character of Soviet Russia, and compare what he says with an observation of the Marquis de Custine, writing well over a century earlier.

> Amalrik: 'What does this people with no religion and no morality believe in and what is it motivated by? It believes in its own national strength which other peoples must fear and it is motivated by the realization of the strength of its own regime of which it is itself afraid.'
>
> The Marquis de Custine: 'This essentially conquering nation, greedy as a result of its hardships, atones in advance for the hope of exercising tyranny abroad by degrading submission at home; the glory and the wealth which the Russian nation expects distract it from the shame which it suffers at home; in order to clean itself of the ungodly sacrifice of all its public and personal liberties, the kneeling slave nation dreams of the domination of the world.'

These two readings of the Russian national character are strikingly and depressingly alike: there is no glory to be had at home, hence aggrandizement is sought from adventure abroad—from pan-Slavic nationalism in the nineteenth century, from proletarian internationalism in our own. How does all this augur for détente?

PIPES: I don't think there is a direct relationship between what the mass of people think and feel, and the international policies pursued in their name. The two operate on different levels—not totally different levels, I grant, but different levels all the same. In other words, we must not think of international relations as if they were human relations. If, for example, you went to Russia and tried to set up a business there, you would, I suspect, run into people—the ordinary people of Russia—who might make life very difficult for you. But if you are dealing at the international level, methods have been worked out a long time ago which make it possible for different civilizations to co-exist with each other in peace. That is what diplomacy is about. The rules of modern diplomacy were laid down at the end of the Thirty Years War, in 1648, in the Treaty of Westphalia. This Treaty (together with its predecessor, the 1555 Peace of

Augsburg) enshrined the idea that there can be a Catholic and a Protestant Europe, that the two can co-exist and have normal relations. This was a revolution in human thought, for, until then, it was always taken for granted that the condition of the survival of one was the extermination of the other. So, after 1648, you had a Protestant culture and a Catholic culture which—given the importance of popular religions at the time—were as different as ideologies are today and possibly much more important in the daily lives of the people. The diplomatic practices then established by these two, seemingly irreconcilable 'camps' of Christianity have made it possible to reconcile their interests—without abolishing their doctrines—in certain peaceful ways. We are the heirs to that tradition.

Therefore, while I agree with much of what de Custine and Amalrik have to say about the nature of Russian political culture, I don't think it follows that the Russian people must necessarily want to conquer the world, and even less do I believe that they will succeed in conquering the world. The tendency *is* there—the desire to show force abroad because there is weakness at home is clearly in evidence—but if you confront this with determined diplomacy in which sophistication is combined with strength, you need not be overwhelmed.

URBAN: You are, therefore, keeping détente as a pursuit of foreign policy, and détente as a device of cultural reconciliation, in separate compartments, in which case you could not have wholly supported the Jackson Amendment.

PIPES: Why? I approved of the Jackson Amendment. It was one of the very few tactical devices we tried to bring into being for making our economic support conditional on domestic reform in the Soviet Union. It fits in with my idea of barter, annual accounting, immediate returns and so on.

URBAN: But it does not fit in with what you have just told me about the Treaty of Westphalia: surely no Catholic ruler would expect a Protestant prince to make a concession on a point of dogma in order to qualify for a supply of linseed for his cattle.

PIPES: The Jackson Amendment did not touch on Soviet dogma. Co-existence does not mean that you accept the system as it is. Nor does it mean that, because the Russians *are* aggressive and expansionist (and their expansionism is attested by history), at no point shall we be able to come to terms with them. We will—but only provided that we show half the determination in stopping them as they show in trying to outwit us.

We must remember that the Russians are immensely responsive to power: they know how to use power, but they also know how to yield to it. To this day, the entire mentality of the Soviet

Government is rooted in peasant experience. If you study Russian history, you will find that the peasant was always surrounded by force; he expected to bully or to be bullied. This is a natural consequence of the virtual absence in Russia of a legal tradition—where there is no law to adjudicate disputes, force inevitably replaces law. Here we have a great asset which we have as yet not learned how to use. We can make a very strong impression on the Russians at both the personal and national levels, provided that we let it be known that we carry a sizeable stick. The Russians can recognize a superior adversary when they see one, and they are very good at backing down without feeling any shame—as we saw in Cuba and in our October 1973 alert. My point is that this healthy respect for power makes it entirely possible for us to stop them even in the face of everything you said and quoted about the Russian character.

URBAN: But who, I ask you, is going to do the stopping?

PIPES: But that is an entirely different question. What I am saying is that we *can* stop them if we want to stop them. Proper leadership in the West could do it. The exercise need not be futile—one could easily chart a whole series of positions we could recapture from the Soviet Union if we knew how to use the power we have and made the decision to use it.

URBAN: Khrushchev's memoirs bear out what you say. He makes the point time and again that during his incumbency the Soviet Union was, militarily and economically, terribly weak, but the weaknesses had to be covered up, for otherwise the United States might do nasty things to Russia. Hence the bluffing, the thunder and fury of Khrushchev's peregrinating statesmanship. And, judging from the Soviet eagerness for détente, this may, certainly in the economic field, still be the case.

PIPES: Luckily for us, Khrushchev over-estimated both our will-power and our political sagacity.

URBAN: There is certainly no reason why we should not take the Russians at their word and agree with them that in matters of ideology there can be no peaceful co-existence. But as soon as *we* act on that understanding, up goes the cry of Cold War, imperialism and the rest. So the motto 'in matters of ideology there can be no peaceful co-existence' is, in fact, interpreted by the Soviet side as meaning 'we are entitled to work for your destruction, because we are on the side of history, but hands off the socialist camp'. However, there is, as I see it, also a deeper reason which prevents us from making a matching effort. Whether we agree with it or not, whether we think it is bogus or not—the Soviet Union *has* an ideology; we haven't: how do you put an ideological scaffolding around something as amorphous and fluid as 'democracy'? I suspect, therefore, that even if we did have the will to take up the Soviet challenge, we'd be fighting with unequal equipment.

PIPES: I would not sell us that short. We do have an ideology, a very powerful ideology, much more powerful than those juvenile ideas, that sham religion, which the Soviet Union promotes under the self-contradictory title of 'Marxism-Leninism'. I haven't the slightest doubt that if free elections were held around the world and people were to choose between, say, a set of values which you and I put down on paper, and one that our opposite numbers in the Soviet Communist Party did, we would win hands down. The idea of law, the idea of freedom, the idea of human dignity are extremely powerful ideas. They have agitated humanity for centuries and their appeal is fresh and inexhaustible.

Our problem is: do we have the vision and the vigour to pursue them? It is here that our principal weakness lies. We haven't the will to use what we have. We are being mesmerized by the sheer determination and apparently overwhelming self-confidence of the Soviet side.

URBAN: Matched now by Soviet superiority in armed power, too.

PIPES: That is of very recent origin and is even now not convincingly established. But we have allowed ourselves to be hypnotized into lacking will even when we had complete armed superiority over the Soviets. And for this we must not blame them—it is entirely *our* fault.

URBAN: We are now coming back to a problem we have already discussed in a slightly different context: why are we unable to get a grip on ourselves in this battle of wits? You said earlier that we were too affluent, had too much to lose and so forth. Is that, I wonder, the whole answer?

PIPES: It isn't, and the rest of the answer falls into two parts—one has to do with Europe and the other with the United States. The lack of determination is much greater in Europe than in America and the reasons are straightforward. Two world wars have so debilitated the will both of the European peoples and their governments that they have become incapable of taking bold action of any kind. There is a feeling in Europe—not always articulated, but very prevalent—that almost any policy is better than war, for war only destroys without settling anything. Hence you choose the line of least resistance, you conceal your impotence, above all from yourself, by rationalizing your appeasement.

'The Russians', you will hear Europeans say, 'are terrible people who run a detestable system, but they will mellow as they get into closer contact with western civilization, as all barbarians of the past have (allegedly) done', and so forth.

The second factor, just as important, is the social revolution which Europe has undergone since the war. Until quite recently, Europe was governed—by the yardstick of the United States at any rate—by an upper class élite which ran foreign offices and military establishments, and set the tone of government internally and externally. The private ethos of Europe was entirely upper bourgeois, and even those who had not climbed the ladder to bourgeois status aspired to it.

All this has radically changed. The lower middle classes and the working class have moved into positions of power and influence—they are Americanizing the whole social and ethical climate of Europe. Their materialism, their acquisitiveness, their ability to win for themselves in a few years possessions and living standards which would have been beyond the wildest dreams of their grandfathers, would put any American to shame. Moreover, these people are just not politically inclined—unlike their American counterparts, they have never been involved in the political process and they appear to have no desire to get involved. They are European isolationists in the same sense of the word as their cousins in America were American isolationists fifty years ago. They can see no point in standing up to the Soviet Union or even wasting time thinking of such problems when time could be usefully occupied in the football stadium or watching television.

To sum up: weariness and disillusionment with war and politics and, second, the pursuit of material wealth as a by-product of the social revolution have, between them, sapped the political will of Europe.

URBAN: I would have thought that *embourgeoisement* and the acquisition of wealth would make people more, rather than less conscious of the need to safeguard their new status and property, and that this awareness would call for an active foreign policy. After all, the officer who has come up from the ranks is always a greater stickler for respect and discipline than the man from West Point or Sandhurst. So, unless we have changed overnight into a continent of mindless sybarites, bourgeois status should have given us an extra stake in the political process, rather than the reverse.

PIPES: You are right in saying that, from the psychological point of view, the *nouveau riche* should have more to worry about than people of established status. But here a third factor comes into play: for the past twenty-five years, the United States has assumed the task of the military protection of Europe. If the various Berlin confrontations, the suppression of Hungary and the occupation of Czechoslovakia, for example, had been European happenings, rather than moves on the Soviet-American chessboard, I am sure there would be a very different psychology in Europe. But as things are, the Europeans feel that their military power is so inferior to that of the Soviet Union that they could not begin to stand up to Russia, and that America's protective presence makes it unnecessary to do any such thing in the first place. So the new European rich go on concentrating on their personal ends, glutting themselves on the goods and the good life they have just discovered, and leaving the rest to the Americans. This, to my mind, is the kind of thing that accounts for the paralysis of the political will of Europe.

Now this is not true of America. Of course, there is in America a sense of tiredness after twenty-five years or so of carrying the burden of world leadership. There is, in particular, fatigue after the Vietnam war, and there is confusion and bewilderment about the Watergate affair, Nixon's resignation and the state of the Presidency. Nevertheless, there is a very strong political sense which pervades the whole population—a sense of what freedom is about, what blessings we Americans enjoy because of that freedom. I am certain that if the United States were ever to be challenged on some issue that truly mattered to its future, the President would have no difficulty in rallying the American people. The will of America is not sapped.

I am not saying this in any spirit of vindictiveness: America, unlike Europe, did not suffer the ravages of two world wars on its territory; its losses were not comparable with those of the European countries and, also, the social revolution which has unhinged the European social order has been continuously with us for a century or so. For this combination of reasons, the average American is very conscious that America is a blessed land, that he owes America a great deal and he is prepared to fight for it. The European, as I see it, isn't ready to fight for Europe. For the average European, politics have always been made by an élite or, in recent decades, by the Americans; hence he does not feel involved—a home, the television and a holiday are as far as his horizons will stretch.

URBAN: This is, of course, precisely the picture we used to have of the average *American* during the period of isolationism—

PIPES: —and it was partly accurate. Now Europe has caught the disease and caught it with a vengeance. But while the United States is geographically so placed that it could (though it can no longer) indulge its short-sightedness, Europe cannot.

I'm not saying that the United States has no responsibility for European apathy; the flaccidity of Europe is indeed a measure of the success of American foreign policy, for we have given Europe too much of a good thing for too long. America ought to have started withdrawing from Europe in the late 1950s when EEC was being put together. Our attitude should have been: 'You are building up your economic unity, we hope this will impel you towards political unity and the two will force you to have your own military capability. And, just to make sure that all this does happen, we will start taking our troops out right now and complete our withdrawal over the next five or so years.' This kind of thing would have given Europe a salutary shock.

URBAN: You would obviously not agree with Michel Jobert (the former French Foreign Minister) that America was in Europe exclusively to protect its own, not Western Europe's, interests?

PIPES: I hardly think I could agree with anything Jobert might say. The United States has stayed in Europe because American foreign policy was beset by a sense of inertia—a fear that if we showed the slightest weakening of the United States resolve to stay in Europe, the Russians would at once take advantage of it. As always in history when you have a good thing going, the policy of least resistance is to keep it going. The American decision to stay was an understandable but costly long-term blunder.

URBAN: I can sense two flaws in your argument, and they may very well be flaws in my understanding of the points you have made. First, why is it that affluence and *embourgeoisement* have a way of making *our nouveau riche* lethargic, egocentric and ineffectual, but seem to have no such impact on comparable classes in the Soviet Union? You said earlier on that higher living standards and a greater sophistication would not change the militancy of the Soviet establishment. This is an unusual judgment, for most western observers believe that any liberalization of the Soviet system will occur for more or less the same reasons which—according to your analysis—account for our own apathy and our unwillingness to take part in the political process: the mellowing and enervating influence of the consumer society and the rising expectations it generates. If this were to be the case, apathy would be facing apathy, and détente might assume a more pleasing aspect than it does. But this is not happening.

Is there any reason why the Soviet new class should be more resistant to the allurements of affluence than we are proving to be? Has that splendidly slothful figure, Oblomov, ceased to stand for the ruling vices of the Russian élite?

A Marxist might, of course, argue that the answer is very simple. He would claim that, having played out its role in the historical process, the European bourgeoisie, new and old, has lost its will to govern and is now propelling itself into the dustbin of history; not so the 'new class' in the Soviet Union (my Marxist would, of course, never accept that term), where the proletariat is being carried forward, under the guidance of its 'most progressive elements', by the wave of history.

PIPES: The two phenomena are totally unlike. *Embourgeoisement* in Western Europe is affecting virtually the whole population; the goods and gadgets and holidays are coveted by all and available to all. *Embourgeoisement* in Russia, in so far as it really exists, is the privilege of a relatively small élite which has never severed its umbilical cord with the state. Historical traditions play a role here, but without examining those in detail, let me simply state that the Russian élite shows a high degree of psychological continuity which manifests itself in nationalism and obedience, whatever other concepts may have been superimposed on that attitude in the name of ideology. I would go so far as saying that the Russian élite isn't a class or a pressure group in our sense at all. It resembles a self-perpetuating religious order, rather than what one normally thinks of as a governing establishment. Your idea, therefore, that détente might produce a convergence of apathies which would make Europe and the Soviet Union comparably impotent, is not a contingency I would personally put my money on. But nor, I take it, would you.

URBAN: The second inconsistency, as I see it, concerns your point that in the late 1950s, parallel with the building up of EEC, the United States should have pulled out some of its forces from Europe and signalled that, within a few years, it would take out the rest. At the same time, you said that Russian governments have an immense respect for power, and you also mentioned that, in the official view prevailing in Washington in the late 1950s, an American withdrawal from Europe would have entailed unacceptable risks. It is the latter point I want to argue.

The Soviet leadership can be astonishingly unsophisticated when trying to read and make sense of western political attitudes. We saw this in Korea, for example, where one of Dean Acheson's casual remarks was interpreted by Stalin and his entourage as meaning that the United States had ceased to regard Korea as being within its sphere of interest, and this gave Stalin the green light for the North Korean attack. Here is a very important precedent, and my view is that, had the United States gone home from Europe in the late 1950s or early 1960s, Moscow might well have taken that for a sign of either American weakness or an abdication of American responsibility or both. For what other reasons—Khrushchev might have asked—would a great power give up something it has got? If the Soviet leadership under Khrushchev was foolish enough to believe that it could get away with challenging the United States on its home ground in Cuba, might it not have been tempted into an even more 'hare-brained' adventure nearer home, once the United States presence had been removed from Europe? Khrushchev's tendency to project Soviet modes of thinking on to the 'enemy' was always evident and is clearly attested by his memoirs.

PIPES: I don't agree. In the late 1950s, the United States had a very large nuclear superiority over the Soviet Union—enough to make any Soviet move in Europe prohibitively expensive. Russia's withdrawal from Cuba under determined American pressure was a sign of the size of the problem Russia was facing. Therefore, if the United States had started moving out of Europe in those years of undisputed nuclear superiority (gradually, of course), it would have indirectly contributed to the aggregate power of the West by cajoling or pushing Western Europe into political unity, and hence also into making a substantial military contribution of its own. So withdrawal would have ultimately strengthened our posture militarily *and* politically: it would have jerked Europe into pulling its weight more in accord with its economic power and geographic position. We could have prevented it from becoming a drop-out, which it now is.

URBAN: I grant you this is a convincing reading of what ought to have been done if our politicians of the time had known what we now know—for example, about Khrushchev's inferiority complexes, the extent of his and his generals' bluffing to confound their adversaries and so on. But our politicians didn't, nor were they particularly far-sighted, nor did Europe want to abandon the Belloc principle: 'Better keep a hold of nurse, for fear of getting something worse.'

PIPES: If this discussion has demonstrated anything, it is that Europe has now landed itself both with 'nurse' and 'worse'.

ALFRED GROSSER

The French paradox

URBAN: The French attitude to détente is puzzling. In his *Memoirs of Hope* General de Gaulle said that from the early stages of his Presidency détente with the Soviet Union was one of the principal aims of his foreign policy—a policy objective which has not undergone significant change under Pompidou and Giscard d'Estaigne. Yet the outside observer may be forgiven for wondering: if France is for détente—why is she against it? Or is she opposed only to certain forms of détente—for example, the United States having *its* détente with the Soviet Union? Do the French fear that an American-Soviet dialogue restricts their chance of bidding for great-power status and independence? Has France been de-emphasizing her special ties with Eastern Europe in the hope of obtaining privileged status with Moscow?

And why should it be so difficult to decipher what *is* French policy on détente? Are we being faced here with a display of Gaulish gamesmanship, too subtle for Anglo-Saxons to understand, or are the French, as some suspect, so obsessed with prestige and the legacy of the past that it is, for the student of history, not always easy to see where French patriotism ends and hysteria begins?

GROSSER: There is unhappily no either/or answer to these questions. A look at the recent past might give us a clue why. The second world war ended with Western Europe consisting of two types of major powers—major, that is, in relation to one another but not, of course, in relation to the United States or the USSR. On the one hand you had the defeated Axis powers, Italy and Germany, who were more than content to be made members of the Atlantic Alliance. Far from seeing it as reducing them to dependence, they looked upon membership as a token of their return to a status of respectability and international acceptance. The Italians wielded no influence and did not want to wield any. The Germans were happy to be raised to the equality of those states which had themselves lost equality with the emerging super-powers. Also, they had their hands tied by their national problem.

When you are in this kind of a situation, one way of preserving some of your influence is to hitch your wagon to one of the super-powers. Britain decided to opt for a special relationship with the United States, and, in fact, after the Dunkirk Treaty (Western Union) one discovered that Britain's privileged status with America did confer on her a semblance of influence. This was living on bor-rowed time—borrowed time, moreover, which was unwisely used for, basking in the reflected glory of the United States and die-hard illusions of her own, Britain cavalierly rejected the opportunity to join the Common Market when the going was good.

The French situation was entirely different both for external and internal reasons. After the nazi attack on the Soviet Union in 1941 the French Resistance, which of course included the communists, was united: Germany was the common enemy. The Resistance movement was sustained by the alliance between the United States and the Soviet Union and it was, as it then seemed, open to France to take her place amongst the great powers after the war. However, the Cold War changed that perspective. After the disruptive strikes of 1947, France was one of the initiators of the Atlantic Alliance, but that, as it turned out, meant accepting the status of a junior part-ner in the American camp. France was never happy with that role. Under two republics and several governments, the French aim has always been to work for détente. It was de Gaulle's policy and Pompidou's policy and I think it is the present President's policy, too, to give France the highest possible rank and prestige among the western powers and to end her dependence on the United States. Hence the emphasis on détente and the ambivalence towards détente; hence the resentment of any mention of a return to the spirit of Yalta; hence the identification of France with Europe. There was a cartoon (in early 1974) in the *Frankfurter Allge-meine* showing a French politician shouting 'Me, Me, Me', and the caption said 'Europe speaks with a single voice'. I would sug-gest that none of this is unnatural or disreputable once you rea-lize—as the British for so long failed to realize—that when (in the words of Dean Acheson) you have lost an empire, you must find a new role for yourself. The French became aware of their changed condition early in the post-war game. They refused to be driftwood in the stream of events as the British appeared to be—passive or at best reactive but without a vision and without a policy. And as the French saw that they must have *some* cards to play, they decided that those cards would be Europe. It is a policy which has not been wholly unsuccessful—

URBAN: —from the French nationalistic point of view—

GROSSER: —no, from the European point of view—strongly aided, I might add, by a number of American psychological blunders. One of the worst of these was the United States attempt to defeat Caravelle. When the Russians had no colour television, they decided to come to France and buy our system. When, for once, we had a European aircraft in an advanced stage of development, the Americans immediately decided to build competing types of their own to defeat Caravelle. This was read in France as meaning that the Americans were not interested in partnership but were determined to dominate us in technology as well as in all other fields. The American move further incensed the French and helped us, by gratuitously providing an outside adversary, to hammer out a European policy. When Kosygin came to Paris in 1967, his visit assumed, thanks to the American blunders, the character of 'Technologically under-developed countries of Europe, unite!'.

URBAN: And yet a great many thoughtful Europeans and, in America, men of the calibre of George Ball, have seen in France's European policy nothing but disaster for Europe, and it is a fair estimate that had the French not insisted on shaping Europe in their image and prevented any effective unification, they would themselves have had a much more significant European card to play at the time of the oil crisis and now that so much of the détente discussion is a dialogue exclusively between the United States and the USSR. But I fear you are right in saying that successive French governments had French rank and prestige uppermost in their minds, only you give us no clue as to the stridency of their commitment. To get the full sense of French nationalism and its particular flavour in de Gaulle's thinking, one has to go to the source itself. General de Gaulle wrote in his *Complete War Memoirs*:

> The emotional side of me tends to imagine France, like the princess in the fairy stories or the Madonna in the frescoes, as dedicated to an exalted and exceptional destiny. Instinctively, I have the feeling that Providence has created her either for complete successes or for exemplary misfortunes. If, in spite of this, mediocrity shows in her acts and deeds, it strikes me as an absurd anomaly, to be imputed to the faults of Frenchmen, not to the genius of the land. . . . In short, to my mind, France cannot be France without greatness.

It is this touchingly naïve, lyrical but extremely dangerous faith (imagine the outcry if a contemporary German or Russian leader uttered any such sentiment) which has robbed France of what she wanted most: a European card, for Europe cannot be France any more than she can be Germany or Italy or England. I would concur with George Ball when he says (in *The Discipline of Power*): 'most students of de Gaulle's prose and conduct would certainly agree that he looks out over the centuries. The relevant question, however, is whether he is gazing forward or backward.'

However that may be, why do you say that France wants détente while at the same time her attitude to détente is ambivalent?

GROSSER: This, like most things in French politics, is extremely complicated and paradoxical.

URBAN: With all due respect, I wonder if our understanding of these complications mightn't be best served if we decided to resist, as the first condition of shedding light on what really goes on in France, the French scholar's penchant for working in paradoxes. I must admit to a personal bias: I find paradoxes are too easy a way of substituting wit for judgement. They leave too many options open and encourage Dodonean utterances of the 'neither-nor' and 'yes-and-no' variety which are not always helpful.

GROSSER: This is a point of methodology. What you suggest will not make the genuinely tricky and self-contradictory nature of much of French politics go away. When you describe a paradoxical situation as a paradox, you are not superimposing on it an extra dimension—a paradox of your own—but simply underlining the multi-polarity, the openness of the situation you are observing.

The French feel détente is important, but it is important only in so far as they are themselves involved in the discussions. If détente is a purely Soviet-American dialogue, France is diminished in status. If, on the other hand, there is no dialogue between Moscow and Washington, there is increased tension in the world, in which case France has no choice but to close ranks with her western allies, even though she is no longer militarily integrated in Nato. And this puts her back among the ranks of America's junior partners. Here is one paradox.

URBAN: When did the French discover that the world was safe enough to pursue an anti-American policy even though they had to rely on the United States for their ultimate protection?

GROSSER: I would not agree with the phrasing of that question, but my short answer is: at the time of the Cuban crisis. In the eyes of de Gaulle the Cuban affair had greatly changed the balance of power in the world: the Soviet Union had acknowledged the superiority of the United States, and therefore Europe had little to fear from the Soviet Union by way of an armed attack. Consequently one could loosen the Atlantic ties and make overtures to the USSR.

The cry '*Pas de retour à Yalta*', of which so much was heard at the 1974 presidential elections, must be heard with all these overtones. Yalta is a dirty word in French political mythology, but not for the reasons which have given it a bad name in America and Britain, that is, not because Roosevelt made too many unjustified concessions to Stalin, especially in Eastern Europe. In France, Yalta means the division of the world into two spheres of influence, each under the tutelage of a super-power in which no other power can play more than a servitor's part. The French cry against Yalta, which is common to the rhetoric of all French political parties, is directed against this American-Soviet condominium and—because France is a western country—it means, in the first place, France's assertion of her independence vis-à-vis American supremacy. At the same time, France is very conscious of the fact that Europe is powerless, largely because she is unable to defend herself without American nuclear support. So at times of world crisis, as for example at the time of Cuba, in 1962, France under de Gaulle was a model ally—at least as loyal, I would have thought, as London or Bonn. But while the other European states do not resent their enforced dependence on the United States for their ultimate protection, the French do. They resent it very much. And this resentment, in turn, gives—in French eyes in any case—extra force to their claim that the French alone are truly European, for if the others accept and even welcome American protection, they are clearly in league with big brother.

France has never ceased scolding the Germans for the fact that, when the chips are down, Germany always comes out in favour of American leadership. The body and only the body of Europe is European, the French say; her soul is that of the United States.

The French feel that the other European countries are far too oblivious of the circumstance that while Europe, including France, surely needs America for her protection, America needs Europe just as much. The American stake in Europe—both as America's first line of defence, and in terms of prestige, partnership and economic interest—is enormous, therefore, the French insist, it is wrong for us to pay the United States for our protection because Europe's protection is, in reality, America's protection. Michel Jobert was the most articulate spokesman of this view. It may not be so loudly proclaimed under Giscard d'Estaing.

URBAN: But why is France's protest against the condominium (if that is what it is) of the super-powers so lopsidedly directed against one side? Is it due to some perverse 'help a man and he'll never forgive you' type of collective psychology? Is it a reaction to the slights de Gaulle is alleged to have suffered at the hands of Churchill and Roosevelt during the war? If so, why is the chip on General de Gaulle's shoulder so gamely carried by his successors?

GROSSER: This problem, again, has many facets. One has to do with the whole political culture of France. In French eyes the two super-powers are equally guilty of throwing their weight about, but the incursions and infelicities of one—the United States—are more keenly felt precisely because France is part of the West, than those of the Soviet Union. In France the Soviets are only very reluctantly looked upon as a potential adversary. In the traditional French view Russia serves as a natural makeweight to Germany (and you might remember that whenever de Gaulle was on good terms with Moscow, he always spoke of 'Russia'; when relations were bad, he referred to the 'Soviet Union'). Today we are, of course, Germany's partners and allies. Nevertheless, defying the logic of our situation, French fears of Germany—and the United States—stubbornly persist in the background, and therefore the promotion of good relations with the Soviet Union is definitely considered prudent and beneficial.

What is remembered about Russia, especially on the Right of the French political spectrum, is the Franco-Russian alliance of 1891–94, the 1914–18 war, the Laval-Stalin agreement of 1935 and the second world war. For most Frenchmen the major war effort against nazi Germany, and all the major sacrifices, were made by the Soviet Union. For most Frenchmen Stalingrad is the name of a great collective victory of the whole of Europe over Hitler's Germany. Indeed, the concept of partnership between France and Russia was asserted not only vis-à-vis Germany and the United States but Britain too.

In December 1944, when General de Gaulle was in Moscow negotiating the Franco-Soviet treaty with Stalin, Churchill telegraphed: 'May I be a third party?' De Gaulle became indignant and told Stalin: 'Between France and the Soviet Union there are no matters of directly conflicting interest. With Great Britain we have always had such matters, and we always will.'

URBAN: The French share at least this with other nations that they, too, have selective memories. In 1891, when France, emerging from her long isolation, found an ally in Russia against Wilhelmian Germany, Russia's credentials to serve as an ally were as little questioned as they are today in respect of détente. France signed a treaty with a government which de Tocqueville described as 'the cornerstone of despotism in the world'. There was no country in Europe in which the principles of 1789 were so little respected as the empire of the Tsar. However, power considerations prevailed. But in 1891, Russia, though internally despotic, had no global designs on the rest of the world. The Soviet Union has.

GROSSER: Here again the French story is peculiar to itself. If you look at the French Left and scan the horizon up to the middle of the Right, you will find a willingness to perceive the 1917 October

Revolution as related in spirit to the French Revolution, even though not many would claim that there is a direct link with 1789. But the affinity is felt to be a thousand times more real than any link with the decolonization of America in 1773–79 on the issue of American resistance to English duty on tea.

'Revolution' in France is a word that carries an aura of approval; as the French see it, the October Revolution has been the only successful uprising in Europe since 1789. There is a sense of continuity, a feeling that revolutionary ideas should not be condemned ab initio for they may bear useful results. Unlike Germany and Britain, France has never supported any systematic repudiation of revolution. The curious thing is that the French approval of 'socialism' in Russia and Eastern Europe is not limited to the Left or even the centre of the Right. As one could observe during the 1974 presidential elections, a large part of conservative opinion is extremely critical of western institutions and unsure whether our democratic system can, as it is, cope with the complex problems crowding in upon us. And although everybody except the communists deplores the lack of political freedom in the Soviet Union and Eastern Europe, a lot of people on the conservative Right readily admit that in certain fields, such as school reform, the social and medical services and the like, the East has something to teach us. Their image of the communist states is by no means uniformly black. At the same time—and here is another paradox—from Left to Right the domestic values and life-style of French society are extremely bourgeois. For every call for egality there is a matching cry for legality, and I rather suspect that the revolutionary romanticism of French society is an apology—a psychological over-compensation—for its fundamental conservatism.

URBAN: That may be one reason why the French Communist Party has found it so difficult to shed its Stalinist heritage, for isn't Stalinism the outstanding example of dyed-in-the-wool conservatism dressed up as revolution?

The picture that emerges from what you are saying is that both the French Left and the French Right have sound historical and ideological reasons to be on good terms with the Soviet Union: the past prior to 1891 is forgotten, so is the Ribbentrop-Molotov Pact, so is the French Communist Party's attitude to the war before Hitler's attack on the Soviet Union, so is the 1947 violence. Moreover, May 1968 may be presented as evidence that the Communist Party will not rock the boat of the establishment, and détente has made the Party politically respectable to the extent that at the 1974 presidential elections Mitterand, the socialist-communist candidate, polled over forty-nine per cent of the vote.

GROSSER: Well, for the reasons I have just given—and I dare say they are an odd mixture of rational analysis, fear, wishful thinking and a selective reading of history—the Soviet Union has managed to retain a certain attractiveness in French eyes. To be anti-Soviet or anti-East Europe is just not the done thing: it is worse than to be unwise or even unsophisticated—it is unfashionable; and, as I say, this great reluctance to be branded anti-Soviet runs right through the political spectrum.

URBAN: How much of this can be ascribed to national pique against the United States? If de Gaulle's *Memoirs* faithfully reflect the psychology of the French public (or vice versa), the sheer resentment of not only what the United States does, but what the United States is, would account for a great deal.

GROSSER: It does. If I were to mock the political idiosyncrasies of my countrymen I would say: one is full of political morality and therefore one is anti-American. The suppression of Czechoslovakia in 1968 is, of course, deplored, but what about Allende; what about the Dominican Republic, what about American machinations throughout Latin America? And after President Ford's exoneration of the CIA in Chile, who in France would undertake to condemn the Brezhnev Doctrine, seeing that the United States has not only always had a very similar doctrine of its own in the Monroe Doctrine, but that it is still being actively and openly applied in defence of the 'middle classes', as one high CIA official put it? 'I don't see why we need to stand by and watch a country go communist because of the irresponsibility of its people', Kissinger said to the Forty Committee on 27 June 1974. That takes some beating.

Some of this attitude is, again, a transfer of political romanticism: you cannot live out your revolutionary dreams in a French bourgeois environment, hence you transfer them to Cuba or Chile, but whereas in Germany and Britain this transfer is limited to the extreme Left, in France it is much more general, crossing otherwise impenetrable ideological frontiers with relative ease.

Another side of the same attitude is France's uneven-handed rejection of blocs. We are—to indulge in some more self-mockery—against blocs, but we are especially against blocs formed by our friends; we accept the blocs of our enemies. Thus we must do nothing to undermine the cohesion of the communist bloc. If Rumania has got itself into difficulties with Moscow, we must deal with Moscow, not Bucharest. If the oil-producing countries form a cartel, we accept it and live with it even though it hurts us more than most. But we cannot approve of any pulling together of oil consumers, for that would mean creating a bloc, albeit in our own interest, but under American leadership. And that is intolerable, especially if one remembers, as we do, that France's own proposals for a common European energy policy have been ignored over the years.

This double yardstick (to veer off from our point for a moment) shows itself in French policy towards EEC too: we have indicative planning in France; the state watches over, guides and controls the economy. We advocate, in theory, a similar policy for the Nine—a common European economy, monetary union and the like—but because we will not tolerate any curtailment of our national sovereignty, we do not allow a European decision-making authority to be created. Here again is one of those contradictions you dislike so much.

URBAN: To hear you say—even though you are saying it tongue-in-cheek—that the French are 'full of political morality' bothers me a little. Isn't France's acceptance of the tyranny of the Soviet state as 'socialist' a cruel joke, well recognized to be such by most of the French Left, including and especially the students who occupied the Sorbonne in May 1968? Why, one wonders, does French political morality stop short of the streets of East Berlin, Warsaw, Budapest and Prague, despite Captain (as he then was) de Gaulle's fine and much advertised war-record on the side of the Polish Army fighting Soviet troops in June 1920? And is the 1917 Revolution in backward, semi-oriental Russia really closer to the French experience and French sympathies than Czechoslovakia in 1968, and more worthy of respect? Also, I find the anti-American aspect of French 'political morality' a little hard to square with the American part in saving France both in the first and the second world wars. How hostile to France do you have to be to earn the respect of the French leaders?

GROSSER: I am describing things as they are in France, not recommending them for acceptance. These, as I see them, are the facts. Your disapproval of them will not change them.

The French attitude to Eastern Europe is the function of France's attitude to the United States. For Gaullist France the ultimate target of foreign policy was the United States. This had priority over everything else. The same could not be said of Germany. The Germans saw their relations with the Soviet Union as their principal problem and acted accordingly. They feared and tried to pacify the Russians, and their reliance on the United States was, and is, a reaction to their continuing exposure (as they see it) to the Soviet Union.

Ever since de Gaulle's visit to Moscow in 1944, the aim of French policy has been to promote, whenever there was an opportunity (and we must remember that there were also periods of serious strain between France and Russia), constructive relations with the Soviet Union—not as an end in itself, but in order to strengthen the French hand in our dealings with the United States. French attitudes to the USSR, and therefore also to Soviet interests in Eastern Europe, have been entirely governed by this consideration. We do not approach Eastern Europe except through Moscow.

De Gaulle did not reach this decision without heart-searching. He had to make a simple choice: is it better to give priority to relations with Moscow at the risk of perpetuating the Soviet hold over the satellites, or should one aim at loosening the East European bloc by aiding Rumania and others in their attempt to gain greater independence at the risk of Soviet displeasure? The second alternative would have been the logical one for the man who had caused France to leave the integrated command of NATO and thus set an example of the dissolution of blocs, and who seemed to want to build a Europe capable of counter-balancing the two great powers. After a period of ambiguity, however, the first alternative was chosen. De Gaulle visited Moscow, and although French efforts to improve relations with Eastern Europe were by no means given up, they were clearly subordinated to the interests of détente with the Soviet Union. And this limited the scope of French leverage in Eastern Europe, despite de Gaulle's visits to Poland and Rumania and all the other contacts and links that have been built between France and the East European states.

URBAN: At the time of de Gaulle's visit to Latin America, in 1964, there was talk of launching a proclamation, during one of the General's forthcoming trips to Eastern Europe, on the value of national independence. But when, in 1967, the visits were made, de Gaulle's silence on the subject was conspicuous. To call for a free Quebec and for freedom south of the United States border, in 'America's game preserve', was all right with de Gaulle because that was hostile only to France's friends; but, as you say, the General shrank from doing anything that might irritate America's adversaries. So de Gaulle didn't achieve anything for Eastern Europe, florid language to the contrary notwithstanding.

GROSSER: But he didn't want to achieve anything for Eastern Europe! He wanted to get out of what he considered to be an American straitjacket. Opposing Soviet interests in Eastern Europe would have weakened his stance towards the United States because it would have deprived him of Soviet support, or, shall we say, suspended his periodic and qualified immunity from Soviet attack and propaganda on issues such as the French atomic bomb and, earlier, Algeria. The Russians were and still are treating France with extraordinary tact, certainly by Soviet standards, especially where the

French have an exposed nerve.

You are, of course, right in saying that the proclamation on East European independence was never made, but then the French were always uncertain whether, with the exception of Czechoslovakia, communism wasn't a good thing for the rest of Eastern Europe— whether, after the right-wing authoritarian regimes from which these countries had been freed in 1944–45, even liberation by the Red Army didn't mean progress for them. This was certainly the view, in 1947, of the French Socialists, including people like Guy Mollet.

Well, shortly after his tour of Canada, de Gaulle visited Warsaw in 1967. *Le Figaro* carried an excellent cartoon showing de Gaulle getting out of his plane at the airport and a crowd of welcoming Poles shouting '*Vive la Pologne libre!*' The general was depicted as putting his fingers on his lips: 'Silence, please.' This sums it up.

When, under Gerhard Schröder as Foreign Minister, the first outlines of Germany's *Ostpolitik* began to take shape, de Gaulle was furious with the Germans because Schröder's first step was to approach Bucharest, not Moscow. This, he thought, was all wrong; one must not hurt Soviet interests. De Gaulle himself had gone to Moscow first, ostentatiously not stopping in Warsaw either on his way to the Soviet capital or on his way back. Eventually the Gaullist line was privately accepted by Brandt; he too decided to respect channels, he too made Moscow his first port of call, leaving Bucharest last.

URBAN: None of this, however, prevented French (and German) public opinion from reacting vigorously to Soviet moves in Eastern Europe.

GROSSER: It didn't. The French Communist Party had a heavy price to pay for the occupation of Czechoslovakia, as indeed it nearly had its back broken over Hungary in 1956.

URBAN: Yet as far as official France was concerned, Czechoslovakia provoked no reaction apart from the customary obituaries, although the Soviet-led invasion did, at the time, look menacingly like a change of tack in Soviet policies. The Rumanians and Yugoslavs were alarmed and both the Germans and Austrians thought they had reason to worry.

GROSSER: The occupation of Czechoslovakia threatened no-one in Western Europe, and it was not perceived to be a threat, least of all by the United States Government. The heartbreaking thing was precisely that, from the very beginning of the Czechoslovak crisis, the Russians knew that the Americans would not move. They had, to put it quite plainly, America's authorization to do with Czechoslovakia exactly what they liked, and in that sense America behaved more objectionably in 1968 than Daladier had done in 1938. The United States did nothing, economically, politically, psychologically or in any other way, to cause the Russians to pause in 1968. America's significant silence was broken only by Michel Debré's unfortunate—and equally significant—remark that Czechoslovakia was a mere incident on the way to détente. So Czechoslovakia was taken because both the United States and France were incapacitated by certain conceptions of détente which they had imposed on themselves and which, though built on different and conflicting assumptions, nevertheless agreed on one point: Eastern Europe was a Soviet preserve with which we must not, and in fact cannot, interfere.

And this is, of course, the great shared weakness of the American and French détente policies—

URBAN: —and indeed of the détente policies of the whole of the West. Eastern Europe is in a 'no-win' situation: all Brezhnev has to do is to keep the smile on his face.

GROSSER: Quite—there would not have been a single step taken towards European unification without Stalin and the 1948 coup in Prague. Even now, for example, a renewed pressure on Berlin would definitely upset détente and re-unite the West. Brezhnev knows this and that is why he is not doing it. He also knows that if the West were seriously threatened, France would again be the exemplary ally she was at the time of Cuba.

URBAN: Why is it that Warsaw, Budapest and Prague have had no lasting appeal to the revolutionary mystique of French society despite the fact that, in one way or another, all three were repercussions, via 1848, of the French Revolution? I am puzzled: the link, you tell us, with the 1917 Russian Revolution is cherished in France notwithstanding the ghastly farce into which 1917 has degenerated in the hands of Lenin, Stalin and the present Kremlin bureaucrats, but the East European nations' struggle for democracy and national independence is passed over, if not in complete silence, certainly without any action that might hurt the Kremlin. In one moving passage of her memoirs (*Hope against Hope*) Nadezhda Mandelstam says: 'By his screams [man] asserts his right to live, sends a message to the outside world demanding help and calling for resistance. If nothing else is left, one must scream. Silence is the real crime against humanity'. Well, the East Europeans scream and the Russian people scream, but if our political mythology binds us to their oppressors, will the victims ever be heard?

GROSSER: There are two points to be made here. First it is not true that the East European upheavals have made no inroads

into French communist territory. As I have already said, the repercussions of Budapest and Prague were enormous. After Hungary
the intellectual wing of the French Party went through a deep crisis,
and in the first post-Budapest elections, in 1958, the Party lost a
quarter of its support—1.5 million votes. Prague had an equally
traumatic effect, changing the whole complexion of the Party. For
the first time in its history the Party disowned Moscow by publicly
dissociating itself from the occupation of Czechoslovakia.

URBAN: There was some thunder, some heart-searching, and a
good deal of protest, but they have gone and left few traces: on 19 May
1974 France very nearly landed herself with a socialist/communist
President—a poor sign that the nature of communist tactics, in
Eastern or Western Europe, has been understood and heeded by the
French electorate. Whether Mitterand would or would not have
been able to out-manoeuvre his communist backers neither of us can
tell, but the fact is that he polled just over forty-nine per cent of the
vote, even though the electorate was familiar with the deeply Stalinist and Moscow-centric record of the French Communist Party.
The Party's sudden conversion to constitutionality and its siren call,
since the elections, to disenchanted Gaullist nationalists are surely
too transparent to deceive.

GROSSER: You over-estimate the political sophistication of
the Frenchman who votes Left. The linkage with Eastern Europe or
even with the Soviet dissidents is seldom made. Millions of Frenchmen vote communist—as German workers in Wilhelmian Germany voted socialist—not as a matter of careful political choice but
because voting Left is an expression of political and social belonging.

In any case, the French experience with the Communist Party
has not been as disastrous as you make out. The French communists were an important part of the Resistance and, between 1944
and 1947, responsible members of the government, which they
then left peacefully. With all the tergiversations of their policies
between the two world wars, and between 1939 and 1941, they are
still considered eligible by a great many French people, though
others, of course, suspect them for the reasons you have mentioned.

The second point of my answer to your question is that, even if
the French Left or Right, or any Left or Right, would have
responded more clearly than they have done to the screams of
Eastern Europe, the result would have been the same, namely inac-
tion. We have touched on this before: nobody in the West believes
it is possible to prize loose Eastern Europe from Soviet domination short of war, and that is why neither President Eisenhower in

1956, nor President Johnson in 1968, nor President de Gaulle, nor Chancellor Adenauer showed the slightest inclination to help Eastern Europe. These were not idle bystanders lacking sympathy, but the practical possibilities of effective help had all been foreclosed. Remember that when, on 17 June 1953, the East Berlin workers rose, Adenauer himself did everything he could to prevent an anticommunist revolution from taking hold in the GDR, and whenever in later years there was any hint of a similar threat, he did his utmost to ward it off. He did so because he was a responsible statesman and knew well enough that no help would be forthcoming. The principal shared assumption of détente is the recognition of the status quo, and on this point there is no difference between American, French, British and German attitudes to Eastern Europe.

URBAN: So any emancipation of Eastern Europe—and indeed of Russia herself—will be a long and uncertain process, a by-product of trade, cultural contacts and perhaps an increasing sophistication of Soviet society, rather than the result of rapid reforms which we may exact from the Soviet leaders in exchange for our economic and technological co-operation.

GROSSER: That is what I believe to be the case. Our only hope of opening up these countries to some extent is through channels which their governments themselves accept. There cannot be a free flow of peoples and ideas if the Soviet and East European governments are simply not prepared to allow it. So, apart from securing small and un-monitorable concessions, we are wasting our time arguing our case on Basket Three. However, official exchange, particularly at the scientific, technological and commercial levels, can still be effective. The more Soviet scholars and students we have at western universities, and the more time our scientists and technologists spend at Soviet universities and other Soviet places of learning and production, the better our chances that something will get through in both directions. Exchanges of this kind carry their own momentum. They lead to not only improved understanding on the human level—though that is important enough—but eventually to interdependence in trade, science and other forms of interaction. Also, I have no doubt that the technological development of Soviet society will bring with it greater sophistication in the whole tenor of Soviet life, and I venture the generalization that when a society grows prosperous and sophisticated, its external behaviour becomes more predictable and less adventurous than it had been before it crossed the threshold from under-development to space probes. However much we may regret the absence of civil rights in the Soviet Union, we cannot make domestic reform a condition of détente. Internal liberalization, if and when it comes, is a bonus; certainly we must press for it but we cannot expect it.

URBAN: These are unexceptionable sentiments. Let me, however, add that I find French aloofness towards internal liberalization in Russia and Eastern Europe easier to understand when I remember that for ten years under de Gaulle, France herself put up with—indeed she embraced—a policy and an ideology which were themselves internally illiberal and externally arrogant. Consider, for example, this passage from General de Gaulle's *Memoirs of Hope*:

> . . . in order that the State should be, as it must be, the instrument of French unity, of the higher interests of the country, of continuing national policy, I considered it necessary for the government to derive not from parliament, in other words the parties, but, over and above them, from a leader directly mandated by the nation as a whole and empowered to choose, to decide and to act.

No Duce or Vozhd could find fault with this prescription.

Or consider de Gaulle's account of his part in leading France out of defeat in 1940 to 'victory' in 1945:

> The authority with which, in the depths of disaster, I in my turn was invested during the course of our history, was recognized first of all by those Frenchmen who refused to give up the fight, then gradually, as events took their course, by the population as a whole, and finally, after much hostility and bitterness, by every government in the world. It was thanks to this that I was able to lead the country to salvation.
>
> She was seen to have re-emerged from the abyss as an independent and victorious State; in possession of her territory and her empire; receiving the surrender of the Reich alongside Russia, America and England; formally accepting, on an equal footing with them, the capitulation of Japan; . . . .

My impression is that a nation which places its fortunes in the hands of a 'leader' and consequently surrenders its critical faculties to the leader's fanciful account of its most recent history, must, in some ways, be inhibited from seeing why another great nation, in this case Russia, should not have a right to *its* 'salvation' in the way best suited to *its* genius, especially when the national interests of the two are felt to be complementary rather than conflicting. Here perhaps is another element to account for France's highly sui generis attitude to détente.

ADAM ULAM

Why the status quo in Eastern Europe
is a threat to Soviet security

URBAN: When former United States Ambassador Jacob D. Beam handed his credentials to President Podgorny in April 1969, he was told that 'Soviet action in Czechoslovakia had prevented the beginning of another world war'. In an article he wrote for the *Wall Street Journal* (July 1974) Beam examined the validity of Podgorny's words by setting them side by side with West European attitudes. The question he asked himself was: 'Why has the satellite cause failed to evoke sustained world indignation?', and his answer may be roughly summarized as follows: the Central and East European countries are the traditional hotbeds of parochial nationalisms and instability; they strongly contributed to the outbreak of the second world war as well as the first, and could cause a third were it not for the over-powering presence of a peace-keeping Soviet Union. 'There are even some in European official circles', Beam wrote, 'who say that the West is well quit of Eastern Europe, including East Germany, despite its accretion to Soviet strategic power'. Of course, Beam is far from agreeing with this view; indeed he stresses that the unresolved state of Central and Eastern Europe remains the second world war's 'most monstrous legacy'. At the same time he thinks that President Podgorny's view of the Soviet occupation of Czechoslovakia expresses an attitude sincerely held by the Soviet establishment.

ULAM: It is a constant theme of Soviet conversation—though not of open propaganda—that Russia is doing world-peace a service by sitting tight on a hundred million unruly Central and East Europeans. But I find it a little difficult to believe that Podgorny was entirely serious when he said that if the Russians hadn't marched on Czechoslovakia there would have been world war. What is, of course, true is that the Czechoslovak example might have spawned similar developments and worse in Poland, Hungary, Rumania and East Germany, and this would have put the cohesion, and perhaps the survival, of the Soviet bloc strongly in question. But this is not at all the same thing as saying that if Moscow had not intervened, Nato would have used the situation in Czechoslovakia to break up the Warsaw Pact. Nobody in the Soviet leadership can possibly believe that. The problem Podgorny's words really pose is: what constitutes war-like change for the Soviet Union?

In 1968 the fear that the bloc might fall apart if Prague were allowed to proceed with liberalization was at least as much Ulbricht's and Gomulka's—both of whom were rightly anxious—as a fear held by the Soviet leaders who were, for a period, undecided how they should exorcise the Prague evil, though not whether they should exorcise it. If one discounts the double-talk, Podgorny's words to Beam indicate what the Soviet leaders were—and probably are—prepared to do if a Czechoslovak type of heresy were again to attack the bloc and threaten to upset the status quo: they would presumably see it as war-like change and react accordingly.

URBAN: At the same time Beam makes a strong point when he stresses that the Russians are not alone in thinking that the East European melange of quarrelling nations, rival languages and long memories is better kept under firm control—even despotic control—for fear that Eastern Europe might push the world into nuclear war. The view that the Russians ought to be congratulated for keeping the lid tight on simmering pots such as the Bulgarian-Yugoslav quarrel over Macedonia, or the Hungarian-Rumanian feud over Transylvania, *is* pretty widespread in the European chanceries. It *is* difficult to fault the argument that the world can do without adding nationalist confrontations to the existing ones in the Near East and Cyprus.

Where this argument falls down is in implying that Nato and the Warsaw Pact are the same kind of organization—more specifically, that they have comparable means of controlling their members. It overlooks the fact that Nato can be wrecked if its members decide to wreck it, either by simply leaving the Organization, or by making themselves so unco-operative as to paralyze it. They are indeed free to go to the brink of war with one another as we saw in the case of Greece and Turkey. The Warsaw Pact countries have no such freedoms. When Czechoslovakia tried to depart in its domestic policies from the Moscow model without at all renouncing her membership of the Warsaw Pact, she was promptly invaded and occupied. In other words, the view that the Soviet Union is useful to all of us in her role as the *gendarme* of Central and Eastern Europe, tilts the scales automatically in favour of Soviet hegemony.

ULAM: Beam's reference to the thinking of 'European official circles' intrigues me. Perhaps we ought then to take the logic of 'European official circles' a step further and ask that not only Eastern Europe but all of Europe should enjoy the blessings of firm rule by one of the super-powers, and that would mean rule by the Soviet

Union. Without a doubt, a *Pax Sovietica* over Western Europe would offer an impressive array of instant solutions: our urban guerillas and Maoists would vanish overnight, the Irish killers in Great Britain would find themselves up against something much more unpleasant than Roy Jenkins's 'emergency legislation', the troubles at the German universities would evaporate at the approach of the first batch of KGB men, and the British miners wouldn't strike or else they would find themselves mining in Kolyma or worse.

In any case, I would not go along with your suggestion that if the Central and East European nations were given their freedom, they would engulf themselves in fratricidal wars. Any conflict that I would see arising would be limited and easily contained, precisely because the Central and East European peoples have long memories. Their historical experience tells them that the surest way of inviting the oppressive presence of a great power is by squabbling among themselves, and this they would at all costs want to avoid.

Instability in the centre of Europe arises from the fact that the Russians *are* sitting on the Central and East European nations, and therefore any conflict in their ranks is automatically upgraded and enacted on a much larger stage than the nature of the conflict would merit. With the Russians in occupation, all Central and East European problems acquire the sharp edges of fundamental, message-laden issues which the Soviets cannot afford, and cannot afford to be seen, to ignore. For example, a Rumanian shift in foreign policy would not be an earth-shaking event if the Soviets did not regard Rumania as their protectorate. The same goes for the Prague Spring, the Polish food riots and so on. Therefore the best service the Soviet Government can render to world stability is gradually to relinquish its control over these countries. The root cause—to repeat—of European instability is the Soviet occupation of Central and Eastern Europe and not the explosive potential of petty issues such as the languages used in Transylvanian universities—though I concede that, when there is no overwhelming common enemy, even problems of that size can breed trouble.

URBAN: Alexander Solzhenitsyn was forcibly expelled from the Soviet Union because the Soviet leaders thought that Solzhenitsyn abroad would be a less dangerous force than Solzhenitsyn at home. At home he acted like a dynamo, criticizing, irritating and frontally challenging the Soviet Government. Abroad Solzhenitsyn would die of irrelevance—that, anyhow, was the Soviet thinking behind his deportation. By the same token: if the Kremlin were to do as you suggest, putting the East European states outside the Soviet sphere of interest as it did Solzhenitsyn, would this eliminate

Central and Eastern Europe as a security risk for the Soviet Union? Assuming for a moment that my analogy is valid, isn't it at least extremely probable that the former satellites would be no more content simply to *be* outside Soviet control than Solzhenitsyn is—that they would, like Solzhenitsyn, go on fighting?

ULAM: Solzhenitsyn was an embarrassment because the regime could not take the kind of measures it wanted to take against him, so he became a very serious problem internally and externally, and the easiest way of trying to deflate him was to get rid of him. Now in my conception the shedding of Eastern Europe would be a much less drastic, a much more gradual affair than was Solzhenitsyn's expulsion, if indeed the two are comparable. My first objective would be a Finlandization of Eastern Europe. Finland is, after all, in the Russian sphere of interest in the old, imperial sense of the word: the Finns cannot do certain things in their foreign policy, in their defence policy and even in their economic policy if the Russians don't want them to do them. On the other hand, the Russians do not meddle in any directly offensive way in Finland's internal affairs. They tolerate the Finnish democratic system and they do not use their influence to secure special advantages for the Finnish communists. The Kremlin is therefore not saddled with the awful and undoubtedly hateful responsibility of watching over what the Finns read in their newspapers, how they order their religious affairs, what they see in the theatre and so on.

But these are precisely the kind of things they have to do in Eastern Europe as the legacy of Stalin's East European policies. My point is that the Russians could loosen their grip on the Eastern European states, giving them a 'Finnish deal', without in any way damaging Soviet interests, and with a very good chance of *enhancing* Soviet interests. A move of this sort would immensely promote Soviet prestige in the world and relieve the Soviet Government of having to allocate vast economic and military resources to what is, after all, a highly unprofitable and, in fact, counter-productive enterprise.

When you privately tackle Soviet leaders and diplomats on this point they tend to answer: 'But the non-alignment of the smaller socialist states wouldn't end with that; they would demand that we return the territories we recovered from them in 1939 and 1945— territories which had been taken from us after the first world war when the Soviet state was weak, and this we could not tolerate.'

I don't think there is much to this argument. The peoples of Central and Eastern Europe are too sophisticated to imagine that they could encroach upon the interests of a super-power bristling with nuclear weapons. My impression is that if Moscow loosened the reins and allowed these nations to go their ways, the reaction would be an appeasement of anti-Soviet feeling and possibly even friendship and gratitude.

URBAN: Let me pursue the analogy with Solzhenitsyn a bit further. Talking to Walter Cronkite in a television interview (in 1974), Solzhenitsyn said that the West was a little too concerned with getting people out of the Soviet Union and not sufficiently concerned with the lot of those who stayed behind. This is perfectly true as far as it goes, but does it go far enough? From a western, and arguably from a Russian national, point of view, the emigration and expulsion of Russian 'dissidents' is not a development we ought to welcome, for once out of the country, they cease to engage the regime's energies. The Jews who have emigrated to Israel, and individual 'dissidents' such as Kuznetsov in England, Sinyavsky in Paris, Litvinov in New York and possibly even Solzhenitsyn in Zurich, have been largely neutralized. Their lives have been spared (and this is something we have undoubtedly to thank détente for) but their leverage has been lost.

Wouldn't the release of such restless and dynamic irritants as the Polish and Hungarian and Czechoslovak people relieve the Soviet system of a great deal of internal tension and thereby foreclose its chances of reform?

ULAM: I don't think so. Neither Solzhenitsyn nor any other Russian dissident I know believes that the Soviet system can be changed within a generation or even two generations; nor do many of them think that Russia could or should become a multi-party democracy. So the seeding-power of the East European countries to effect change in the Soviet system would be very limited and bought at too high a price.

No, the Soviet Union should allow its present satellites to leave the Soviet camp for two rational reasons, both very much in the Soviet interest. First, if Moscow means what it says about détente, a gradual withdrawal from Eastern Europe would be the most convincing demonstration of the seriousness of its intent. I stress the word gradual, for the Soviet leaders couldn't be expected to do it at one fell swoop. But even a small move, such as granting Rumania the status of Yugoslavia, would give us some concrete proof that détente is not just a temporary phase which the Soviets can switch off at will, but that the Soviet Union, too, has come to terms with the modern world and that it realizes that even the Soviet form of imperialism is no longer feasible.

The second reason that would make me anxious to let the satellites float on their own follows from what I have just said: keeping them in may have catastrophic effects. Until now Russia's troubles with her satellites have come one at a time: there was Hungary in 1956 and Czechoslovakia in 1968 and less explosive upheavals in East Germany and Poland. But supposing several of these happened at one and the same time—and this is far from being impossible—and the Soviet Government found itself embroiled in military action in various parts of Europe: could anyone foretell where that kind of situation might lead us? In 1968 the Soviet Union was extremely lucky because the Czechoslovaks chose not to fight. But had they decided otherwise, the ensuing military confrontation might have had incalculable consequences.

URBAN: I cannot see why. Since October 1956 the Soviet leaders have had ample opportunities to satisfy themselves that the West, and especially the United States, will not violate the East-West divide, no matter how much it may admire East Berlin building workers, Hungarian freedom-fighters and Prague reformers.

ULAM: I don't think western help or inspiration would be needed to make a coincidence of upheavals in Eastern Europe an extremely serious matter for the Soviet Union. How would Moscow react if Poland and Czechoslovakia and East Germany gave trouble all at once? What effect would such an event have on the Soviet system? Would it revert to out and out Stalinism, would it crack under the strain, would Russia be engulfed by permanent crisis from the River Amur to the Danube? We have no answers to these questions, and the most effective way of ensuring that such questions do not arise is for the Soviet Government to recognize that it is in Russia's own interest to give its present satellites growing autonomy and independence. This is not asking for very much. One would not be saying to the Soviet leaders: you should be prepared to put up with the kind of regimes that existed in Central and Eastern Europe between the two world wars. One would be asking for much less.

URBAN: Why, then, are the Soviet leaders so adamant in refusing changes that would apparently benefit them so much? Would they be right in suspecting that your argument is a subtle way of trapping them?

ULAM: From time to time the Soviet leaders *were* tempted to release the satellites. Khrushchev was toying with the idea and, curiously enough, Beria too, though I will not go into either man's motives. The present élite is hamstrung by its conservatism. It will not change Soviet agriculture, it will not even make changes in marginal areas—not because power-interests or ideology are involved, but simply because the Soviet élite fear that any change is heavy with the possibilities of incalculable trouble. So the easiest way out is to sit tight and do nothing.

URBAN: There is a great deal of consistency in Soviet foreign policy. For example, the Russians never give up territory they have conquered. You have yourself pointed out in one of your articles that for the Soviet leadership the possession of Eastern Europe is (apart from being a buffer zone) a symbol of the legitimacy of communism. It represents the inexorable march of history and the ever growing power of the 'socialist' camp. Now if the Soviet leaders said to the Poles and Czechs and Hungarians: you can have your full internal autonomy, but you will please respect certain strings we will attach to your external affairs, by mutual consent, on the Finnish model—wouldn't that undermine the legitimacy of Russia's whole post-war political posture? Wouldn't that be an admission that Moscow is not the sole legatee of history, that history is not set in the direction in which Moscow said it was—that history can, in fact, be reversed? I would not be happy arguing such a case in conference with Ponomarev or Suslov.

ULAM: It is difficult to say. My feeling is that if we had the Soviet Politburo's off-the-record answer to Solzhenitsyn's famous letter to them, there would be very little in it about Marx and historical determinism, and the Soviet Government's appointment with history, but a great deal about hard-nosed Russian self-interest. But even if the Soviet leaders did feel that they could not openly turn their backs on their mission, the emancipation of Eastern Europe would not, in my view, undercut the rationale of their system. To some extent the Soviet leaders are, of course, prisoners of their propaganda, but on a more realistic level they can surely see that by risking a little now they would stand to gain a great deal in the longer run. The present relationship between Moscow and its satellites is mutually harmful. If the latter were allowed to disengage themselves from the Soviet embrace, the resulting rapport would be mutually beneficial.

I do not deny that the Russians have their own domino-theory; they undoubtedly feel (and we have evidence of this in the memoirs of Khrushchev) that any communist party dislodged from power spells the ruin of all: for Prague read Warsaw and Budapest and Bucharest and ultimately perhaps Moscow. But this fear is (as I say) ill-founded, and the policy based on it short-sighted. Nevertheless, we have to take note that the present Soviet leadership—old in years and rigid in attitudes—will not perceive Soviet interests as we perceive them.

URBAN: I am still curious to know whether you seriously think that there is any likely combination of internal upheavals which Soviet power could not adequately cope with if western intervention were withheld—as we know that it would be.

ULAM: I do seriously think that. I invite you to look at the recent past. Did we suspect that Khrushchev would be a liberalizing influence when he first began to dominate the leadership? We didn't, because Khrushchev didn't know it himself. He was a man with impeccable Stalinist credentials: he had been appointed to high office by Stalin and willingly co-operated in putting Stalin's most brutal orders into practice. But when Khrushchev began to take the pulse of the Party as its leader, he began to sense that the bureaucracy as well as the population at large wanted more liberal policies. So he began to liberalize—not in absolute terms, but relative to the hell which Stalin had created around him, Khrushchev's measures represented relaxation of a significant kind. Well, Khrushchev's secret speech at the Twentieth Party Congress and the de-Stalinization which followed had an immediate impact on Poland and Hungary, and we know that the Polish October and the Hungarian Revolution severely tested the whole Soviet system.

Now let us imagine that in two or three or ten years from now some individual or group in the Politburo makes a bid for leadership: there is a crisis, there is in-fighting, and finally a coterie, or an individual, emerges with the avowed intent of laying to rest all remnants of Stalinism and starting the Soviet Union on its way to the twentieth century. Modernization, rationalization, economic reform, political relaxation, and the proper observance of the Soviet constitution would follow. In the political and cultural climate created by such a change, I cannot see how Rumanian, Polish, Czechoslovak and Hungarian claims for independence could be resisted, or indeed why this or that Soviet leader would not himself suggest that the Central and East European countries henceforth be treated as equals rather than satrapies. My point is that the Soviets have everything to gain from starting these countries on their freedom now, that is to say, before a crisis or a combination of crises forces their hands. *Now* the price to be paid for their release from the bloc would not be high; indeed it would not be a price at all, for release might (as I have said) gain the Soviet Union certainly the neutrality and probably the friendship of its present satellites. The price to be paid under less auspicious conditions might be rather different.

URBAN: Let me return to a question we tried to answer at the beginning of this discussion and approach it from another angle: why is it that at a time when a great deal of western concern is expressed over the fate of oppressed minorities—Soviet dissidents, Soviet Jews, Soviet ethnic minorities, Palestinian refugees, Greek and Turkish Cypriots—we are not similarly exercised about the captive nations of Eastern Europe?

Our unawareness of the problem does, of course, hang together with our wish not to be reminded of Russia's post-war record, so let me briefly rehearse it. The Soviet Union is the only major European country which has added to its territories since 1939 and used military force to invade other European countries (exclusively its 'allies') since the end of the war. The acquisition of the eastern territories of Poland and Rumania, of the Carpatho-Ukraine of Czechoslovakia, of the Baltic states, of a large strip of Finland, and control over the whole of Central and Eastern Europe, mark the expansion of Soviet power. Yet if the proverbial man from Mars were to take soundings of the mood of Europe, he would find our silence on the Soviet record deafening, and he would go away thinking that the guilty men of Europe were Greek colonels, Salazar, Caetano, and those East European nations that were tactless enough to embarrass the Soviet Union, and the West, by asking for their independence.

Who, apart from George Kennan, knows and bothers to remind others that the Soviet record in Central and Eastern Europe is in stark contradiction with the very first official act of the Soviet government—Lenin's famous Decree on Peace? In it Lenin proposed to all belligerents a just and democratic peace 'without annexations and indemnities'. Let me quote a paragraph from this Decree for it has a traumatic relevance to the Soviet invasion of Hungary and Czechoslovakia and, indeed, to the Soviet control of the whole of Central and Eastern Europe:

> If any people is held by force within the borders of a given state, if such a people in defiance of its expressed wish—whether this wish be expressed in the press, in meetings of the populace, in the decisions of a party, or in uprisings against the national yoke—is not given the right of decision, free of every form of duress, by free elections, without the presence of the armed forces of the incorporating state or any more powerful state, what form of national existence it wishes to have—if these circumstances prevail, then the incorporation of such a state should be called annexation, i.e., an act of seizure and force.

ULAM: After the lost war in Vietnam and the traumatic effect of Watergate, the American public is in a masochistic mood. Europeans may find it hard to understand this, but the man in the street in the United States has in his heart of hearts always believed that God was an American and the puritanic ethic of universal application. Both myths have been shattered. America is tired and this expresses itself in a self-accusatory stance toward foreign policy: 'So much has been our own fault!' There is a feeling, not only on the Left but also among sensible people, that the Pentagon is the greatest danger to world peace, that we have aggressively surrounded the Soviet Union with our bases and that, in any case, it isn't our business to police the world.

We are using up so much of our power of indignation on ourselves that there seems very little of it left for the Soviets.

The theme of 'sinful America' was very prevalent after Vietnam, and there is still a lot of breast-beating and self-mortification. Therefore Poles, Czechs and Hungarians are barely within the realm of consciousness even of people who read the *New York Times*, not to mention the general public.

URBAN: Vietnam is ten thousand miles away from the United States. Racially, historically, culturally, linguistically the American people share nothing with the Vietnamese. Yet Vietnam has had a profound effect on the American psyche. American solidarity with the suffering of the Vietnamese has changed history. By contrast the misfortunes of Poles, Czechs and Hungarians, with whom the American people share just about everything, have utterly failed to stir the American conscience, and this despite the influence enjoyed—but hardly ever used—by large numbers of ethnic Poles, Czechs and Hungarians in the United States.

ULAM: But don't you see, it is precisely because the Vietnamese aren't part of us—because they are brownish and not white—that our guilt-complex induces us to love them? Wasn't Vietnam the crime of the white man—of European civilization—against the coloured man? Well, then—what if part of the European continent suffers discomfort at the hands of another part of the European continent! Isn't it time the sins of western civilization were visited upon western civilization itself? So roughly runs the argument.

Then there is the factor of sheer inertia. The Russians have been in Central and Eastern Europe for so long that their presence is taken for granted. Even sophisticated Americans can't conceive of change in Eastern Europe: 'What do you want—drop the atom bomb on Russia?'—that is the sort of question they ask. Of course it isn't a question of dropping nuclear bombs; it is much rather one of combining subtle moral, economic, political and military pressures—not even necessarily open pressures of the Jackson type—to effect change. Unfortunately the average American finds this kind of procedure too sophisticated to understand and support. He sees our options encapsulated in the bomb/no-bomb alternative which is a poor guide to an effective foreign policy. Remember that between 1815 and roughly 1900 the British Navy policed the world without firing a great many shots in anger. Yet the *Pax Britannica* was secure; the Royal Navy's mere existence was enough to impress upon friends and foes alike that British diplomacy was supported by a massive reserve of power.

URBAN: This is precisely the kind of position the Soviet Union is now trying to achieve, not least through its large naval building programme. The expansion of Soviet sea-power and the superiority of Soviet conventional land-power, combined with nuclear parity with the United States, may, in a matter of five to ten years, put Europe in a position where Soviet demands may have to be complied with or even anticipated without a single Soviet tank appearing in the streets of Bonn or Paris.

ULAM: Precisely.

URBAN: Why then should this entirely realistic scenario not make an impression on the American people?

ULAM: It is too complex. Détente is popular precisely because it is easy on our nerves. Having got 'concessions' from the Russians on one small issue or another, we like to go to bed feeling that we are having friendly talks with them and that all these horrible weapons in our arsenals are not going to be used. A determined stand would disturb this illusion, and, I might add, it would disturb similar illusions in Western Europe too, because I can see no evidence that Englishmen, Frenchmen or Germans are any more interested in the future of Central and Eastern Europe than Americans. The *dramatic* points register: Solzhenitsyn and Sakharov make good copy, therefore they get enormous coverage, but the issues they stand for fall by the wayside.

URBAN: An idealistic—or naïve—conception of what the Soviet Union is about is no new thing in American history. Roosevelt's trust in the goodwill and co-operativeness of Stalin is too well remembered to need rehearsing here. But American illusions go further back in history. In his speech to Congress, asking for the declaration of war in April 1917, President Woodrow Wilson pictured the February Revolution in these words:

> Russia was known by those who knew it best to have been always in fact democratic at heart. . . . The autocracy that crowned the summit of her political structure . . . was not in fact Russian in origin, character, or purpose; and now it has been shaken off and the great, generous Russian people have been added in all their naïve majesty and might to the forces that are fighting for freedom in the world, for justice and for peace.

You know as well as I do that the belief in the democratic instincts of the Russian people, the belief that the Tsarist government was an imported regime, and that the Russian Revolution would help to bring freedom and justice to the world were based on a misreading of both Russian character and history, and the nature of events that had just taken place in Petrograd. And the misreading stemmed from the American predilection to see the world through American eyes and to read American motives into other people's actions. To Wilson and the American public the Russian Revolution seemed, in the words of George Kennan, 'to be a political upheaval in the old American spirit: republican, liberal, antimonarchical'. Nothing could have been further from the truth.

Mutatis mutandis, America's present détente policies would seem to be in line with Wilson's and Roosevelt's misjudgments. Isn't the world's leading power becoming a little dangerous to itself and the rest of the West if it puts illusions, idealism and a popular craving for anaesthesia repeatedly before the empirically testable realities of international politics?

ULAM: The American psyche as it is at the moment cannot do justice to the international situation. No doubt, as time goes on, some of the hard lessons of history will rub off on the Americans, but it will be a slow process. Today even Kissinger's policies are widely held to be sinful because they are balance-of-power politics. He is accused of ignoring the United Nations. *That* (he is told) is where he ought to conduct his diplomacy—a laudable sentiment, but not a very smart one.

American foreign policy vis-à-vis Eastern Europe is a reflection of this attitude. We want a peaceful life, therefore we acquiesce too easily. Clearly, we cannot force a European solution with military means, but we could exact a much better deal from the Russians than they are now prepared to give us if we kept Eastern Europe on the East-West agenda. I am sure the Soviets are the first to be puzzled by our lack of interest. They must wonder why we show so little unwillingness to legitimate their hegemony.

What saddens me most is the history of our great ineptness and missed opportunities over the last thirty years. Twenty-five or so years ago, when we had all the cards in our hands, and the Soviet Union was militarily weak and economically exhausted, western recognition of the territorial changes wrought by the war in Central Europe could have brought us significant concessions. The German problem, too, might have been differently decided: in the first postwar years Moscow regarded the threat of a re-armed West Germany as serious enough to consider surrendering East Germany in exchange for the removal of that threat. We might, if we had exploited Moscow's fear, even have saved Czechoslovakia. Now, of course, the Russians are firmly in possession and our opportunities are virtually all gone. So détente is simply giving the Russians what they want in exchange for face-saving concessions.

URBAN: My impression is that we have, since the war, almost constantly misinterpreted both the real strength of the Soviet Union and the thrust of Soviet policies. Faulty evaluation would seem to be as much responsible for our predicament as lack of will-power.

ULAM: There is something in that. In the 'forties and 'fifties we did have a realistic picture of Russia's strengths and weaknesses, but at the same time we were so impressed by the recklessness of first Stalin and then Khrushchev that we thought our material and military advantages offered no protection against it. As we now know from Khrushchev's memoirs, we were, in fact, frightened into passivity by the sheer stridency of Soviet rhetoric.

Then there was our inability, which lasted until our reconciliation with China under Richard Nixon, to exploit the split in the communist world. From about 1960, the Sino-Soviet split was handing us all the instruments of leverage we could desire, and it was up to us to summon the will to use them. If the opportunity had been recognized in 1962 or 1963, Vietnam might have been avoided. But the recognition came much too late. Using the Sino-Soviet conflict as a tool of United States foreign policy would, of course, have been a very clear exercise in power-politics, and undoubtedly it would have been condemned by part of the American public in much the same way as Kissinger's mild form of triangular diplomacy is being branded immoral in the mid-1970s. Well, with our nuclear supremacy relinquished, a balance-of-power policy will soon be the only policy we'll be able to pursue in a sinful world.

The third memorable example of faulty evaluation was our belief in 1970 and 1971 and 1972 that the Soviet Government carried decisive influence with the North Vietnamese. We advanced concessions at the SALT negotiations and in commercial deals on the mistaken assumption that if we were nice to the Russians they would help us to get out of Vietnam. The concessions were pocketed but the Russians were powerless to fulfil their side of the bargain.

URBAN: Are we going to act on imperfect knowledge once again by signing an instrument on European security and cooperation with the Soviet Union on the terms discussed at Helsinki and Geneva? Could such an instrument change the political realities in Central and Eastern Europe?

ULAM: I don't think so. Nothing said in any security declaration alone can change the social and political status quo in Eastern Europe. The Soviet Union will not give up its right to intervene in Eastern Europe if Soviet interests are threatened. Also, while some of the East European governments may well want to *restrict* Soviet interference, they will not want to eliminate the threat of it, because, in the last resort, they need Soviet protection to stay in power.

A reduction or even the removal of Soviet forces from, say, Czechoslovakia or East Germany, would not affect this picture either, for the Czechs and East Germans know from recent experience that if there occurred another Prague-like situation, the Soviets would again act exactly as they did in Prague. It is the memory of past action rather than the physical presence of Soviet troops that is the inhibiting psychological factor in Eastern Europe.

The theory that increased contacts between East and West would loosen the Soviet hold by a kind of osmosis is also unfounded. There are, to be sure, forces of economic and social change—characteristics common to the so-called post-industrial societies, such as consumerism, etc.—pushing against the walls of the totalitarian state, yet the controlling factor has always been, and will always be, political. We can avoid a faulty assessment of the situation in Eastern Europe if we bear in mind that it will take more than four 'baskets' to empty communist society of its despotism. What political purpose there is in the four baskets—and Basket Three has some—is too vague to make an impact. The Soviet Government has a thousand ways of neutralizing it at the first signs of trouble.

URBAN: The Soviet Union, you said a little earlier, ought to shed its satellites in its own security interest for otherwise it might not survive the combined impact of a future Warsaw, Budapest and Prague all happening at the same time. In other words: keep the satellites in, and you are asking for trouble. What you are now implying is that if the Soviet tutelage of Eastern Europe is legitimated by détente, Eastern Europe will become a placid backwater of the communist world. Where, then, is the explosive potential of Warsaw, Budapest and Prague?

ULAM: It isn't an either/or situation. What I am concerned to refute is that the mere lessening of international tension and the increase in East-West contacts can or must bring about a fundamental change in Central and Eastern Europe. However, such change may be triggered by certain political events if these affect the balance of power in the world and thereby play upon the balance of fears and hopes under which the East Europeans now live. For example, a drastic deterioration in the Sino-Soviet conflict, a struggle for power in the Soviet leadership after the retirement or removal of Brezhnev, a revival of the unity and therefore of the magnetism of the European Community could set the winds of change in motion. It is only then that the expanded relationship between East and West would come into its own and add to the momentum of change.

URBAN: We have, in this series of discussions, assumed perhaps a little too uncritically that the Soviet leaders are really rather monstrous, self-centred and unscrupulous men whose one concern is to acquire power and stay in power. But while in one sense it is true that 'power corrupts and absolute power corrupts absolutely', it is, I believe, also true that even the most unscrupulous holder of power is saddled with some sense of responsibility for those millions of men and women of whom he has, rightly or wrongly, become guardian and spokesman. I am reminded of George Kennan's perceptive observation: 'However despotic [a ruler] may be, and however far his original ideas may have departed from the interests of the people over whom he rules, his position of power gives him . . . a certain identity of interests with those who are ruled . . . One cannot, therefore, just exploit one's power over a given people for the exclusive purpose of pursuing ideological aims unrelated to their interests and concerns.' We have certainly seen this to be true in Khrushchev's case, and I suspect that the Soviet leaders' ultimate objective with détente must, in one way or another, also be related to the greatest good of the greatest number, even though their definition of 'good' may be at variance with ours. Otherwise they would be confining themselves to sitting on a powder keg in perpetuity.

ULAM: We must not underestimate the strength of the tradition of despotism in Russian history. From Ivan the Terrible in the sixteenth century to this day Russia has, with the exception of a few years, known no other form of government than autocracy combined with varying degrees of repression. Soviet rule is, by and large, a continuation of that tradition.

At the same time it *is* true that the Soviet leaders are, by the logic of their position, obliged to think of the public good as they see it. In the matter of external affairs, however, the public good coincides with Russian national interest, or so it is easily represented. The Soviet leaders believe—sincerely as I see it—that they are acting in the Russian national interest by curtailing the kind of freedoms their satellites should be allowed to attain under détente, and I fear that the majority of the Russian people may well support this particular piece of Soviet policy for old-fashioned nationalistic reasons. Here, then, are the makings of conflict between the public good as conceived by the Kremlin, and the public good as conceived even by some of the communist leaders of Eastern Europe, for your point that despotic rulers must in some ways identify with the ruled goes for Eastern Europe as much as for Russia.

The Soviet aim of détente, as far as the future of the satellite belt is concerned, may be summed up in a sentence: the reaction of the people and governments of Central and Eastern Europe should be a harmonious balance between resignation and hope—resignation that their political status is unalterably frozen, and hope that in other respects life will become internally freer and materially more rewarding. The big question is whether or not more freedom and more wealth will burst the Soviet-approved political framework, especially if the people of Central and Eastern Europe conclude at some point that an outside political event, or a combination of such events, has made the time ripe for them to bring their simmering discontent to the boil. If the Kremlin were wiser than it seems to be and used détente to rid itself of its increasingly unsupportable burden in Central and Eastern Europe, this question need never be put to the test.

GEORGE W. BALL

Europe without a unifying adversary

URBAN: Those who oppose European unification from the ground up use a simple argument. They say that there isn't, and there never has been, such a thing as Europe; Europe is a spot on the map that has been dreamed into a myth by European idealists. André Malraux, for example—one of the most persuasive critics of European unification—not only believes that Europe is a myth, but he is also a spokesman of those who are especially upset by any suggestion that European unification could be modelled on the American experience. The justification he gives for this view brings us to the principal theme of this discussion: détente and the prospects of European unification.

Why, then, is it wrong to imagine that the methods which permitted the creation of the United States are also applicable to Europe? The United States, Malraux says, 'had a common adversary. . . . The United States was made in opposition to the British Army. If tomorrow there was a common adversary called Russia, which does not at all appear realistic, or a country in Asia, then perhaps there would be a European possibility.'

Is détente depriving Europe of the beneficial threat of a common enemy—is an outside enemy really necessary for unification?

BALL: The question is: can you have unification without a unifying state—a unifying state such as Prussia which was able to unify the German principalities by force of arms, or a unifying influence such as a common adversary? Until quite recently, the Soviet Union played the role of common enemy. I assured my European and American friends at a conference I attended in Amsterdam in March 1973 that they would be making a great mistake if they thought that the United States could ever play the role of common enemy and thus be a unifying factor, for though the United States might annoy, it would never terrify. On the contrary: as the resentment one experiences in Europe of the United States stems far more from pique than fear, an estrangement between the United States and Europe (or vice versa) would be far more likely to cause Europe to fall apart than to unite.

Therefore I feel that Europe has to face up to the problem of moving towards unity without the compulsion of a common enemy. Moreover, the concept of a common enemy as a prerequisite for unification is rather losing its relevance in the 1970s because the inner logic of European unity has become absolutely compelling: one simply cannot organize a modern economy effectively without a high degree of unity. This was, of course, one of the assumptions underlying the whole effort to bring about EEC; it is, if anything, more relevant today than it was in the 1950s. So even if the common concern of an aggressive Soviet Union disappeared, there would be good reasons for thinking that Europe is inevitably going to be forced toward unity even though there may be periods of retrogression.

But I do not myself believe that the common enemy—Soviet influence and expansion—*has* disappeared. What we rather glibly call détente represents little more than a tactical decision on the part of the Soviet leaders to achieve, by different means, the aim which remains central to their thinking, and that is the expansion of Soviet power and communist ideology. Whether communist ideology precedes or follows the expansion of Soviet temporal interest may vary from case to case, but ultimately the two are in common harness.

After the occupation of Czechoslovakia Moscow came to a frustrating dead end: there was nothing more that could be materially gained or redressed without taking great risks. There was the problem of Yugoslavia, outside the bloc and Comecon, holding a heretical version of communism which was a threat to Soviet hegemony; there was the menace of a new eastern Church in the communist establishment in Peking which was pursuing a doctrinally schismatic and politically antagonistic line; and there was the economic situation: the Soviet leaders realized that they were not going to be able to keep their economic place in the world without a very drastic infusion of technology and capital from the West, and specifically from the United States. Nor were the Russians able to get very far in trying to assume the leadership of the Third World. So everywhere they ran into one frustration after another. For all these reasons they came to recognize that a tactic of showing a scowling face to the West was inhibiting their ambitions rather than assisting them.

The decision to adopt a different tactical line was already taken after the fall of Khrushchev by the new collegiate government, but, as I say, I don't believe this decision represented a departure from basic Soviet objectives. If one reads the explanations which the Soviet people are given of détente by their leaders, this becomes perfectly clear: they say again and again that détente for them is useful to the advancement of their ultimate goal, which is the spreading of communism, and this is, of course, what peaceful co-existence has meant in the Soviet vocabulary since its first application by Lenin in 1920. 'Communists do not conceal the fact that the elimination of the rotten capitalist system and the building of socialism on a world-wide scale is their ultimate objective', V. Kortunov wrote in the August 1974 issue of the Soviet journal *International Affairs*.

In the early 1970s there was a danger that the European nation-states would respond to American unilateralism with a unilateralism of their own, making bilateral arrangements with Moscow from what would be essentially positions of great weakness. I myself feared at one time that, parallel with a partial withdrawal of United States forces from Europe, the European nation-states, far from further merging their sovereignties in EEC, would resume their rivalries and leave the field to be dominated by a powerful Soviet Union. We did have the beginnings of a bilateral diplomacy between Bonn and Moscow which resulted in *Ostpolitik*. I viewed the initial proposal for such a policy with concern, because it seemed to me that it could lead to a wishful belief in Germany that the menace of an expansionist Soviet state has passed, that the Cold War has finally ended, and that a permanent détente has settled like a cosy blanket over the whole of Europe.

I don't think that has really been the effect of *Ostpolitik*. There has been a 'normalization' of German-Soviet relations—although to consider the German situation as 'normal' is absurd—and the status quo has been recognized. But the debate took so long, and the Soviet moves were so tortuous, that the initial German euphoria is dissipated and the Germans are, by and large, much more realistic about their situation than they were in 1970 or 1971. It is well understood in Germany now that the Soviet threat is not so much the naked use of military power, as the application of political pressure reinforced by military power.

URBAN: I am still stuck with the idea of a unifying enemy. It seems to me that we have not only lost the benefit of having one but we may now go, or indeed we may be pushed, to the other extreme of admitting communist parties to West European governments. If this were to happen, no amount of tactical reassurances by the French or Italian Communist Party could allay my suspicion that the unifying enemy has become a Trojan horse. For while we have to all intents and purposes accepted the permanence of communist governments in Eastern Europe, the Soviet Union has never accepted the permanence of non-communist governments in Western Europe.

BALL: There is no doubt that the talk of détente, all the to-ing and fro-ing between Washington and Moscow, the showmanship of the summit conferences and Kissinger's jovial diplomacy have tended to give a false impression of the actual objectives of Soviet policy, and that this *has* tended to make the communist parties in the West more respectable than they were before. It was certainly a very near thing between Mitterand and Giscard, and I personally think that had Mitterand won, the implications would have been very serious. But Mitterand did not win, and if the French leadership is able to cope with the tough problems of inflation and balance of payment difficulties—and it seems it is—then the menace of communist participation in the French government could be regarded as a passing phase. In any case, it would not be the first time that this has happened in French politics—France had a spell of communist participation in government in the immediate post-war years and survived.

Italy is a different problem because the Italians are in considerable economic trouble. They will have to go through the painful experience of reducing their standard of living, and I can't see that they have the political restraints or the institutions to do so. This poses some very grave problems.

URBAN: You *are*, then, saying that the ostensible disappearance of a unifying adversary and his metamorphosis into an ostensible internal ally have had an impact on the state of European politics?

BALL: I would not suggest that they haven't. The Soviets made a shrewd tactical move in adopting the appearance of a more benign attitude, and this has had its consequences. In the meantime, however, there are (as I suggested) plenty of other compelling reasons why Europe should unite, and (not to ignore Malraux's point) I'm not sure that the historical precedents of America or Switzerland, for example, are determining because the circumstances have totally changed; we are now dealing with an industrialized and highly sophisticated set of countries which face entirely different imperatives from what any other combination of states had to face in the past.

URBAN: I agree with you that Moscow's long-term objectives have not changed, but I would go a step further and say that these objectives owe their unchangeability to communist ideology. This surely is the red thread running through everything the Soviet leaders do and say. And if one thinks of the condition of Soviet power in 1918 or even 1939, and compares it with what it is today, then communist universalism cannot be said to have been a failure.

One of the great handicaps of democracy is that it hasn't a comparably universalistic appeal—and I am aware that you do not regard this as a handicap but, on the contrary, as a virtue and indeed the very justification of democracy. In *The Discipline of Power* you say that it is quite wrong for a democracy, and especially for the United States, to promote a universalistic philosophy—first, because democracy and freedom cannot be codified on pain of ceasing to be democracy and freedom and, second, because there are all sorts of things wrong with the kind of universalism that is, or was until very recently, current in the United States. 'Wilsonian' universalism, you argue, rests on the arrogant assumption that America has a mission because American principles are the principles of all liberated mankind. On this view, you say, there is no reason why the rest of the world should not be made over in the American image. You condemn American universalism also on the practical ground that the United States has not been able to practise, and really had no intention of practicing, what it was preaching. You argue that even Dulles's panegyric to 'liberation' in 1952, though sweet music to certain minority groups in the United States, was a fraud, and a fraud quickly exposed in 1956, because when the Poles and Hungarians revolted it was revealed to the world that the United States would not interfere when the Soviet Union used brutal force in its sphere of influence in Eastern Europe. Hence, you conclude, American universalism is a hypocrisy.

American universalism may well be a hypocrisy, but I think it is a useful hypocrisy, certainly a forgivable hypocrisy, and perhaps even an indispensible hypocrisy, for if one gives that up, what does one pit against the ideological appeal of communism? After all, the latter too is at best a hypocrisy, yet it has been used to great advantage. The only trouble with political hypocrisy is that it is the most difficult and nerve-racking vice that anyone can pursue, for it needs (as Somerset Maugham once remarked) an unceasing vigilance and a rare detachment of spirit. It cannot, like adultery and gluttony, be practised at spare moments; it is a full-time job. In other words, it is something totalitarian governments practise well but we, wayward and easily bored western bourgeois that we are, would practise very badly.

BALL: Universalism in the Wilsonian conception has simply proven quite ineffective, and I don't see any chance of it being made effective. The depressing conflict in Vietnam was the dead end of American universalism. In that unhappy land we let ourselves be drawn, year after year, and deeper and deeper, into a situation where our power could not be effectively employed to achieve any objective clearly in our interests. We have learned through experience that international politics is the art of the practical. The Soviet Union recognizes South America as our sphere of influence and we recognize Eastern Europe as theirs because in each case the staking out of interests has been legitimized by the preponderance of military power. Cultural traditions and affinities do not enter the picture; clearly most Americans are more at home with Czechs and Poles than Latin Americans. Therefore one has to fall back on working with materials that are at hand, having to deal with realities as we find them, and that means having to cope with a world in which adjustments have to be made between power systems simply because it seems impossible in the foreseeable future to supplant them with a universal system. In other words, as long as the world's future is decided by the competing power of the United States and the USSR, I can't see universalism as offering a solution. If the Soviet Union had remained simply the Russian state, even though it might have been aggressive but lacking ideological drive, then we might have been able to make a universalistic system work. We certainly can't make one work under present conditions. Mind you, in breaking away from an unreflecting universalism we must not be swung towards an even more outworn isolationism, for our power exists, and it is necessary for the world's security that we continue to use it provided that we develop a sense of its limitations.

URBAN: But if America is giving up its universalistic appeal while the Soviet Union clearly isn't, aren't we putting ourselves at great disadvantage? I can sense a renascent psychological need both in the United States and Europe to come out of our inhibiting defensiveness and say: 'Here is what we believe in, and here is how we are going to go about enforcing it.'

BALL: Part of the equation consists of the recognition of what the Russians are up to; this has to be factored in. We don't proceed as though the Russians were behaving in exactly the same way as we are behaving or might be behaving in their place. The success of the Soviet ideological drive in the 1970s is far from clear to me. Détente is the Soviet leaders' recognition of bankruptcy, and I am not at all sure whether it will remain their permanent policy. After a period of time it is quite possible that they will revert back to something closer to at least the Khrushchev type of militancy, if not to Stalinism, and we have to be prepared for both. Whether they will succeed with détente any better than they did with their openly Cold War tactics remains to be seen. To answer that question will be one of the crucial challenges to our expertise and judgement in the coming years.

URBAN: One question I keep asking myself is whether some of the East European governments are clearly aware of the American refusal to give practical effect to American universalism—in other words, whether or not they think the United States would use its influence if contingency A or B came up in Eastern Europe. My impression is that, for example, Nixon's and Kissinger's visits to

Belgrade and Bucharest did not make it any easier for the Yugoslav and Rumanian leaders to form an estimate what the United States would do in an East European emergency. But then it may well be an American tactic to keep some of Eastern Europe, and especially the Soviet leaders, guessing.

BALL: I cannot speak of the future but I can tell you what happened in the past. I was United States Ambassador at the United Nations at the time of Prague. I had my Yugoslav friends calling on me day and night. They were scared to death. We were trying to give them reassurances, and we were making certain noises to Moscow. Manescu was also constantly making enquiries, and he, too, was extremely worried. I didn't think there was much we could do in the case of Rumania, for a Soviet move on Rumania would have been a geographically internal affair. Yugoslavia might have been a different matter. The psychological and political repercussions of the Soviet armies arriving on the Adriatic would have been enormous. Think of the devastating effect this would have had on Italian politics.

Fortunately, we did not have to face either the Yugoslav or the Rumanian contingency.

URBAN: Presumably Kissinger's package of détente policies contains some reassurance that Moscow does not grab Yugoslavia, or else détente is off.

BALL: I think détente *would* be off, but so what? I should think the Soviet leaders would much rather have Yugoslavia inside the bloc than détente. For us to keep saying that détente would be off means nothing. How serious a threat is it? The Russians are constantly taunting us: 'You are destroying the spirit of détente', but are we talking about anything real? We have already gone too far in trying to create a spirit of détente, whatever that may mean. Think of the Middle East where both sides are feverishly building up their respective allies' military strength, and the Russians have consistently frustrated our efforts for peace, with the resulting awesome possibility that the Middle East may become another Balkans involving the United States and the Soviet Union in nuclear confrontation.

Détente could mean something if it enabled us to come to grips with nuclear weapons control, but the advances we have made on arms control have also been exceedingly small. SALT I was a very tentative step which depended on SALT II. Limited to five years, it was simply a way of moving in the hope that one could move further. SALT I as a permanent arrangement would have been quite unsatisfactory to the United States. SALT II did nothing to improve the earlier agreement. In the meantime, the Vladivostok guidelines notwithstanding, both the United States and the Soviet Union are going ahead with their strategic arms programme.

For all these reasons I have a very qualified view of how far we are going to get with détente. If one looks critically at what has been accomplished in concrete terms, it's very tenuous stuff. Détente has certainly deprived us of a great deal of propaganda advantage—for example in the context of the so-called European Conference on Security and Co-operation—in return for extremely small benefits.

URBAN: I would have thought our performance at the Security Conference is another piece of evidence that because we lack a universalistic principle—an 'ideology'—our policies are fragmented and our counsels confused. The one bit of 'ideological' stiffening we have managed to get on the Helsinki-Geneva agenda—Basket Three—has been resisted tooth and nail by the Soviet Union.

BALL: I always thought the so-called Security Conference was a trap. Initially the United States Government was quite wary of it. However, Soviet pressure was strong and many of the European states seemed anxious to go ahead. When the United States finally agreed to the Conference—which, in my view, was a mistake—I thought it essential that we insist firmly on a quid pro quo which might well result in the destruction of the Conference. In other words, it seemed to me essential that we stand resolutely for an unequivocal statement of the freedoms contained in Basket Three. I thought it would be a tragic mistake, if, as a result of the Soviet technique of negotiating by erosion, we were to weaken our position and agree to legitimize the Soviet Eastern European Empire—including by implication the Berlin Wall—without at least getting something real and substantial in return.

URBAN: Do you think we are going to accept a much watered down version of Basket Three for the sake of ending the ordeal and coming up with an agreed document?

BALL: It looks very much like it and I think it highly unfortunate. I had proposed some time ago that the President should agree to attend the summit conference to sign the European security declaration only after he had obtained a firm Soviet agreement to a solution of the Middle Eastern problem. Kissinger, however, apparently did not accept that advice. Thus I feel that we are going to give Brezhnev a triumph by signing a document that is in effect a substitute for a World War II peace treaty without gaining anything substantive for the West.

URBAN: But even if we did get an agreement of the kind you suggested, the provisions written into Basket Three are not enforceable. How does one encourage the free flow of ideas if one side is, in fact, determined to discourage it?

BALL: Anything that comes out of the Security Conference is likely to be utilized by the Soviet Union for its own propaganda purposes. Brezhnev certainly looks forward to the declaration emanating from that Conference and the summit meeting that follows as vindicating his policy of détente. He can effectively use that at the Twenty-fifth Communist Party Congress in February 1976—which will presumably be the climactic moment of his career. Perhaps the best we can do is to make sure that the propaganda is not too disadvantageous for the West. That is one reason why I feel that our information dispensing media, such as Radio Free Europe and Radio Liberty, are performing an indispensible task.

URBAN: The Russians ascribe great significance to the successful conclusion of the Security Conference. They see it in a totally different light from ourselves.

BALL: They have always seen the security talks as the thin end of the wedge with which they hope they can ultimately bring about the dismantling of Nato and the dissolution of western unity.

URBAN: My impression is that the American public have been rather successfully sweet-talked into accepting détente as an agreeable way of composing our differences with a much-reformed Soviet Russia.

BALL: The American public is soft on détente primarily because they have been led along by a government that saw political advantage in being seen to be the peace-makers. Also (as I've already said), the propaganda effect of state visits back and forth has been disastrous: Brezhnev comes to the United States and appears to be a rather boisterous, attractive fellow and becomes a personality, just as Stalin appeared to Roosevelt—and through him to much of America—as Uncle Joe. These symbols are important; ambulatory summitry has had a gravely softening effect on the American public. Summit conferences are iniquitous; we should have a constitutional prohibition on them.

URBAN: I could never quite understand why the United States Government overcame its original reluctance and agreed to participate in the Security Conference. The Soviet objectives behind it have always been transparent and the voices warning against it many and clear both inside and outside the United States.

BALL: The Security Conference was accepted as part of a general move in trying to make some progress towards a relaxation of relations with the Soviet Union—part, that is, of a fundamental tenet of the Nixon-Kissinger policies. It fitted in with Kissinger's concept of 'linkages'—the idea that you give a little on many fronts and expect progress on many fronts. But that is not what appears to be happening.

As I say, the general effect of all the talk about the status quo and the 'normalization' of things in Europe has had an undesirable influence on the American public, and not the American public alone. There is, after all, nothing normal about the European situation; there is nothing normal about making a cage for seventeen million people in East Germany, or about the whole concept of the Iron Curtain. These are abnormalities of nauseating proportions. The East-West bonhomie is distorting our perspective. Instead of focussing on the monstrosity of the Berlin Wall, we focus on the fact that the Soviet Government is allowing a trickle of people to cross it. This worries me.

URBAN: That is why I cannot quite go along with you when you urge the United States to repudiate its remaining universalism. If the United States had an effective 'ideology', and the Soviet Union and the Soviet leaders were seen through the corrective lenses of such an American 'ideology', the American public would not be so easily deceived.

Wouldn't you ascribe to the same lack of ideological backbone the fact that the whole problem of Eastern Europe has dropped out of the East-West dialogue, or that the possibility of a Finlandization of Western Europe is being spoken of only in highly muted tones, if indeed it is being spoken of at all?

BALL: No, I would not ascribe it to that, though it may be that now our pragmatism has run away with us and we have de-ideologized ourselves a little too thoroughly. I would ascribe our attitudes to Eastern Europe and Finlandization to a combination of lack of leadership and the tendency of democratic societies to get bored with, and therefore to ignore, issues which do not seem to be susceptible of solution within a reasonable time-span.

On Eastern Europe there is a feeling in the United States that we crossed those bridges in 1956 and 1968. More recently, the American public saw that the country most closely concerned—West Germany—took a lead in the recognition of the status quo through its *Ostpolitik*. Hence there is great reluctance in America to insist on doctrinal rigidities that bear no relation to the realities of power: if (Americans argue) the United States is not going to move in and correct the situation in Eastern Europe, we'd better not make Eastern Europe a big issue.

Giving Eastern Europe higher priority in the détente negotiations than it has now would, of course, be an interesting forward position, but I don't think we could hold it for long. A stance of that kind could stir false hopes in Eastern Europe and that, in turn, would expose any American government that took such a position to attack for irresponsibility. It is hard in a democracy to stick out for a tough bargaining counter.

Our nonchalance in respect of the threat of Finlandization stems from the same apathy and lack of leadership which have made it possible for the Soviet leaders to give themselves a new image on our television screens. America is a country of short-distance crusaders. Our public want to escape the tensions of the last twenty-five years. They want to like people and to be liked, and to think that at least one of their worries can be safely written off. This, you might say, is wishful thinking, and so it may be; nevertheless it is a factor we must reckon with.

URBAN: In *The Discipline of Power* you discuss and dismiss any thought that democracy may be formalized and employed as a weapon to counter communist proselytizing and subversion:

I have even heard proposals for a Democratic International but, of course, that is a grotesquerie. Democratic principles are too subtle and various to be merchandised like cornflakes or cigarettes, and those who . . . argue for a formalized 'doctrine' or 'credo' of the West miss most of the point. . . . I am aware that the West has no analogue to the Moscow International, but it needs none. Blatherings about the 'world struggle for men's minds' that would put democracy on the same plane with Marxist-Leninist-Maoist dogma is intellectual rubbish. They misconceive the tolerant nature of western political theory, which cannot fit men into absolute moulds but which raises the protection of human diversity to nearly an absolute value; and they dignify the opportunistic patchwork of Marxist textual exegesis by implying that it is an intellectually defensible alternative to freedom.

I agree with you that the Soviet and Chinese interpretations of Marx do not represent intellectually defensible alternatives to freedom as we understand it. Nevertheless, as most people in the world are not intellectuals and thus much more likely to be captured by blatherings than by rigorous argument, shouldn't we think twice before dismissing the case that the principles of democracy can be shaped into something more coherent and more easily understood than they are now, especially if we want democracy to look attractive to that vast majority of the world's population which isn't, and perhaps never will be, educated and sophisticated enough to understand the finer points of western political theory? I am inclined to believe liberal democracy may go by default unless we can bring it home to people in simple language that democracy *is*, in fact, a more civilized, more effective and more prosperity-producing social system than the Marxist-Leninist alternative.

Furthermore, I sense a discrepancy between your rejection of the idea that democracy could, or should, be codified, and your strong support of EEC. You have stated on many occasions that while EEC has created a vast market and greatly increased the living standards of its member states, it has made no parallel progress on the political front. The question is: why has it made no progress on the political front? One answer is that Europe does not fire the imagination and inspire loyalties. It has not been able to progress beyond the Brussels bureaucracy and the game of institutions to legitimize its existence in political terms. In other words: it has no 'ideology'.

But one cannot quite accept this argument for it is not true that Europe is without an ethos of its own. By its very nature, the Treaty of Rome is a piece of 'ideological' codification because the agreement of nine like-minded, democratic and law-abiding nations to relinquish parts of their sovereignty for the greater good of all is, without a doubt, a piece of 'ideology', democratic ideology, and potentially a very powerful piece of ideology. The fact of the matter is that, for a variety of reasons we need not go into, the Treaty of Rome has never been made explicit and inspiring enough for the rank and file to understand.

BALL: When I say that democracy cannot be codified I simply mean that you cannot impose on democracy a single set of principles without causing it to cease to be a democracy. Marxism is not a very formidable body of thought, but, like some other badly written religions, it has—when reinterpreted by later prophets—become a great political force. As applied by communist parties and governments, it is a tool of political repression, justifying rule by an 'enlightened' minority. This flies in the face of the humanist enlightenment which carries a more optimistic view of man than the concepts of oriental despotism papered over by Marxist verbiage. Its essence is the idea that political freedom is paramount and requires a number of elaborate procedures—free elections, constitutions, independent courts, competing newspapers, limited sovereignties—to assure individual freedom and control over rulers. Such a principle does not belong to any one western nation or party, but to each and all. It is the common possession of all free men and the hope of men not free. Its strength and appeal derive from the fact that it need be accepted only voluntarily; force is its self-contradictory negation. That is why I find any talk of a 'gospel' of democracy or of a Democratic International quite absurd.

But the creation of political institutions in EEC is very different from the imposition of an ideology. In the first place, common institutions of the kind we have in EEC are not the work of some external agency—they are internally generated. While EEC may create certain institutions with supranational powers, the relinquishment of sovereignty to those institutions is done by the free expression of government and people. A unified Europe does, of course, have to be much more than a customs union. It has to move towards a posture where independent political power is vested in it—power that represents something more than the unanimous decision of member governments. But this is a question of the pattern on which federal societies are organized by democratic means. One pattern is that of the United States, and I am very conscious that you can only carry the American analogy up to a very limited point.

America's support of European unification has never stemmed from a simple-minded belief that Europe could, or should, slavishly repeat the American experience of federalism. Anyone who makes much of the resemblance between the fragmented American states of the 1870s and Europe in the 1960s or 1970s shows up his own ignorance of history and his innocence of the world today. We had better reasons than bogus historical analogy for supporting Europe's move towards unity—compelling considerations of national interest. The United States was convinced that a united Europe would be stronger than it was in the past and no longer a seed-bed of war. Combining the strength and talents of a great body of peoples, a united Europe could take over some of the burden of its own defence and well-being, otherwise carried at great cost by the United States, as well as become a like-minded partner of the United States in upholding the world's stability.

Having said this, I would add that when one thinks of European unification in institutional and juridical terms, there is some validity in the American parallel. Both the federal structure of the United States and the confederal structure of Canada, offer obvious lessons for Europe or any other group of states that wants to move towards unification. So it would be foolish of EEC not to look at and benefit from the juridical experience of these models.

Coming to the problem of packing punch behind the flagging spirit of European unification and reawakening the once powerful idealism of the young, especially in Germany and France, this is a function of leadership and a clear understanding of what Europe should be, and could be, and isn't, though I'm confident that it will be. We ought to have men willing to speak loudly and clearly on the future of Europe with conviction behind them. I'm not sure that we have such leaders in Europe at the moment. In Germany we had Willy Brandt who always seemed to be caught between the competing priorities of East and West and was never quite sure just where the brunt of his policies lay. Helmut Schmidt is as much an Atlanticist as he is a European, and the French leadership, though a great improvement on the old-fashioned and, for Europe, quite tragic chauvinism of de Gaulle, hasn't a clearly European programme.

The task of a new European leadership would be to recognize and to profess with unmistakable clarity that the European nations must unite in their own interest and in that of the whole world—whether there is a unifying enemy to prod them to do so or whether there isn't. Such a leadership would have to see Europe as a second western great power, capable of sharing with the United States the burdens and decisions of the West in a way the individual European nations can never do. It would have to assume that Europeans have the desire and the will to return to the world stage, and that once they begin to feel the heady sense of strength and power engendered by a growing unity, they would overcome their current lethargy.

There is no reason to think that this would not be so. The energy crisis has already forced the Nine to act in much greater unity vis-à-vis the Arab countries than they would have done otherwise, and at the European Security Conference the nine governments have been speaking from common positions. At the United Nations, too, EEC has begun to speak with one voice on an increasing number of problems, though not on all. These are small beginnings, but they are steps towards turning the world's dangerous bipolar power structure into a more differentiated structure in which Europe might eventually become the world's third great power. There are, I know, all sorts of arguments why this is no time to talk with much optimism about a united Europe, and we have listed some of them in this conversation. Yet, at the end of the day, it is clear that the United States is unwilling and probably unable to play a more and more lonely hand in the difficult tests of the coming years. It needs the partnership of a strong and self-confident Europe. Europe, on its part, cannot be content for much longer with a state of affairs where détente, the arms race, war and peace in the Middle East, and all the other dangers and dilemmas of modern power and their implicit threat of mass death, are discussed and decided without it.

So, while I do not think that Europe's unifying adversary has disappeared, it might be as well for Europe to act as though it had, and to proceed towards unification under the inexorable logic of Europe's own, internal and external imperatives. Between them they provide both the necessary and sufficient conditions of unification.

DEAN RUSK

Co-existence without sanctimony

URBAN: During his visit to the United States in the summer of 1973 Leonid Brezhnev addressed a number of leading American businessmen. Looking back on the Cold War, he asked: 'Was that a good time? No, a thousand times no. We will never return to it.'

You were United States Secretary of State both under President Kennedy and President Johnson and thus directly concerned with the American conduct of the Cold War. Would you agree with Brezhnev that the Cold War was a bad thing; if so, bad for whom: the Soviet Union, the United States, the peace of the world? Was there, in fact, such a thing as a Cold War in clear contradistinction from the kind of East-West relationship that exists now?

RUSK: Let me try and answer these questions by casting my eyes over the origins of the Cold War. In 1945 the United States disarmed almost completely and almost overnight. By 1946 we didn't have a single division in our army and a single group in the United States Air Force ready for combat. Our naval vessels were being put into mothballs, and those remaining in service were manned by skeleton crews. Stalin, who remarked at one of the war-time conferences: 'How many divisions does the Pope have?', looked out across his western boundaries and could see no divisions. So what did he do? He tried to cash in on his enormous superiority. He attempted to keep his forces in Azerbeidjan; he demanded the two eastern provinces of Turkey and a share in the control of the Straits. He ignored those parts of the peace treaties with the East European states which called for free elections and sovereign governments and turned these states into Soviet satellites. He encouraged the communist guerillas in Greece, supplying them from Albania, Bulgaria and Yugoslavia. Counting on economic chaos as his ally, he sought to extend his dominion into Western Europe. In 1948, in violation of the agreements with the western allies, Stalin blockaded Berlin, renounced the quadripartite control machinery for Germany, and set about making the Soviet-occupied part of Germany a political and social segment of the Soviet Union itself. Then came the aggression in Korea, and, in 1956, the suppression of

243

Hungary. One incident after another indicated that the Soviet Union was not prepared to work for a world of law. As one Soviet spokesman put it: 'The law is like the tongue of a wagon: it goes in the direction in which it is pointed.'

The so-called revisionist historians in the United States can write all the books they want, but they can't change the fact that those were the events that launched the Cold War. We did not declare it—we ourselves cannot end it.

Serious attempts to defuse the East-West tension were being made throughout the Cold War period, and in that sense détente is as old as the Cold War itself. For example, in 1946 the United States, Britain and Canada went to the United Nations with the Baruch Plan under which all fissionable materials would be turned over to the United Nations to be used solely for peaceful purposes and there would be no nuclear weapons in the hands of anyone, including ourselves.

There is no room for sanctimony here: I have to say that if the Soviet Union had first developed the atomic bomb and had made a similar proposal in the United Nations, I'm not sure whether the executive and legislative branches of the United States Government would have accepted that proposal, for it would have debarred us from acquiring nuclear know-how. In any case, the Soviet Union did not accept the Baruch Plan and went ahead with its nuclear programme. Then, Secretary Marshall, in complete good faith, included the Soviet Union in his invitation to participate in the Marshall Plan, and it was the Soviet Union that walked out of the Paris meeting and insisted that Czechoslovakia and Poland do the same although Czechoslovakia had accepted the American invitation.

URBAN: I do not want to cast doubt on Secretary Marshall's good faith in inviting the Soviet Union, but there is evidence that the Policy Planning Staff of the State Department, on whose paper the Marshall Plan was very largely based, was quite a bit worried how the United States should react if the Soviet Government and the East European Governments did accept the invitation. George Kennan, then head of the Planning Staff, says in the first volume of his *Memoirs*: 'It would be best, the staff thought, to stimulate initiative . . . in such a way that the Eastern European countries would "either exclude themselves by unwillingness to accept the proposed conditions or agree to abandon the exclusive orientation of their economies".'

RUSK: I do not doubt that such considerations had entered the calculations of the Planning Staff. However, the fact remains that the Soviet and the other East European Governments were invited by George Marshall and offered aid and co-operation on exactly the same terms as the other European countries. In presenting his Plan, Marshall said: 'Our policy is directed not against any country or doctrine but against hunger, poverty, desperation, and chaos', and I believe this is exactly what Marshall meant. It was only after the Soviet Union had refused to participate that the Marshall Plan took a West European direction and became the foundation of West European prosperity and unification—one of the most successful initiatives, I might add, ever taken by the United States. Again, we must not be sanctimonious because it may well be that if the Soviet Union *had* decided to accept Secretary Marshall's offer, the United States Administration might not have been able to obtain from Congress the necessary appropriations.

What else would I list under earlier attempts to reach a détente? In 1955, during the Eisenhower Administration, the Austrian State Treaty was signed. It was a momentous step towards the relaxation of East-West tension. Then, in 1959, we took a very important preventive measure by putting our name to the Treaty of the Antarctic which removed this vast part of the world from great-power competition. In 1961–62, Khrushchev presented President Kennedy with some very severe tests of statesmanship—first with the Berlin crisis, and then the Cuban missile affair—but both President Kennedy and after him President Johnson concluded from these crises that it had become far too dangerous for two great nuclear powers to pursue a policy of total hostility across the board and that we should probe and find points of agreement with the Soviet Union on large matters as well as small. These, it was hoped, might broaden the basis of common interest and reduce the range of issues on which violence might occur. So, during the 1960s, we had the Test Ban Treaty, the Civil Air Agreement, the Consular Treaty, the Treaty on the Non-Proliferation of Nuclear Weapons, two important space treaties, and an agreement not to put weapons of mass-destruction on the sea bed. Also, President Johnson proposed legislation to Congress which would have authorized bilateral trade agreements between the United States and the countries of Eastern Europe but, given the atmosphere of the time, Congress did not even hold hearings.

The Nixon Administration continued these efforts to find points of agreement with the Soviet Union. There was the four-power agreement on Berlin, the small beginnings of agreement to control strategic arms and another attempt to expand trade and economic relations.

I hasten to add that the moves towards détente in the 1950s and 1960s were not purely American initiatives. During the 1960s there were private discussions between us and our friends in the Federal Republic of Germany and in other western countries which eventually led to *Ostpolitik*—another major element in détente.

I believe myself that, despite far-reaching differences in political aims and social systems, the thousands of megatons that are lying around in the world in the hands of frail human beings compel us to look for agreements which can reduce tensions between us.

URBAN: These are sobering words from one who has been looked upon as a protagonist of the Cold War.

RUSK: Well, I am, after all, one of those relatively few people who shared highest responsibility in a world of nuclear confrontation. At the time of Cuba I looked down the abyss and I didn't like what I saw. The Cuban missile crisis deepened the sense of prudence in the world's capitals, but it would not be possible to say that had the crisis not been peacefully settled. The avoidance of such confrontations, which come far too close to the edges of human survival, must be the major objective of foreign policy.

At the same time we must be quite clear how far we have come with détente. I suppose each administration wants to put its best foot forward and picture its achievements as favourably as it can— but we haven't really settled any of the major problems that exist between the two sides: not in Berlin, not in the Middle East, and not in the strategic arms race where I understand Brezhnev has made it clear that the Soviet Union was going full speed ahead on those aspects of nuclear arms production on which agreement has not been reached—and we have no agreement on the number of warheads, megatonnage, mobile and stationary launchers, missiles fired from surface vessels and so on. So what we have done so far is to build a dam one-eighth of the way across the river. But unless we can get beyond that, just as much water is going to flow in terms of nuclear competition and conflict in other fields as it did before—if in slightly different channels. My point is that all these difficulties notwithstanding, we should continue to probe with prudence and intelligence but without giving way to wishful thinking. We must not allow an illusion to develop that all our problems will be solved by détente, because they will not. I note, for example, that various Soviet leaders and the Soviet press are continuing to speak of the deepening crisis of capitalism, pointing to significant new opportunities which might be opening up for the communist states and parties. This is very dangerous thinking.

URBAN: You are on record as having said on many occasions as Secretary of State that the Soviet Union was basically aggressive, that it was using its modern weapons to make terroristic threats and sow confusion in the world. 'Communism is not the wave of the future,' you said in January 1962, 'communists are only ex-ploiters of people's aspirations—and their despair. They are the scavengers of the transition from stagnation into the modern world.' 'The objective', you said on another occasion, 'is not national liberation but entrapment within the communist bloc. This method . . . is designed to bypass American nuclear strength' (December 1961).

A decade and a half have passed since you spoke the words I have quoted. Have you in the meantime revised your position?

RUSK: I do not believe that the leadership of the Soviet Union or of the other communist countries have changed their commit-ment to world revolution. This is part of their basic doctrine, just as the Declaration of Independence is central to our thinking. At the same time, I do think that there is a little more prudence in the world in terms of how one goes about pursuing one's objectives. Some of the Soviet leaders have come to recognize that the hazards of nuclear power have made for certain overriding common interests between the Soviet Union and the United States. They know as well as we do that a full nuclear war would be mutually suicidal, and they, too, can see (or so one would like to think) that there are possi-bilities of agreement that would reduce unnecessary friction between us. But I have seen nothing that causes me to believe that the Soviet leadership has abandoned the idea of world revolution.

My feeling is that détente has not reached the point where we can 'trust' the Soviet Union in the way in which we trust Canada, for example. But 'trust' at this stage is not what we are talking about. The most effective agreements with Russia would be those where performance on both sides can be easily checked and where the question of 'good faith' does not arise, and such agreements are the ones which the present Administration seems to be looking for. For example, if the Civil Air Agreement does not work effectively for Pan American Airways in Moscow, we can take that into account in the way in which we handle Aeroflot in New York.

URBAN: I think the Soviet leaders expect 'good faith' from us as little as you expect 'good faith' from them. Indeed—as you know much better than I do—their idea of peaceful co-existence is coter-minous with the 'international class-struggle', which they say is in-tensifying parallel with the development of détente.

RUSK: There is, of course, an ugly contradiction here. The Cold War was the expression of the announced determination of the Soviet Union to help along the allegedly inevitable world revolution by any means short of major war. It is, to my mind, far from clear whether the Soviet leaders aren't, under the slogan of 'détente'—much more cautiously and much more cleverly than they once did—

still pursuing basically the same objective.

If 'peaceful co-existence' means competition by *peaceful* means—and I'm not fully convinced that it does—then I would welcome it because I happen to believe that there is something in the nature of man that causes him to respond to the elementary idea of freedom and human dignity—and it is interesting to see the extraordinary measures which totalitarian regimes take to deny people this freedom and dignity. Man has a mind and a soul. He is capable of being terrorized into submission, but only to a limited extent and for a limited time. We can see that even the unparalleled terror of Stalin failed to make a lasting impact on the Russian people. Pasternak, Solzhenitsyn, Nadezhda Mandelstam, the dissident movement, are evidence that the communists have not succeeded in turning men into robots and that there are more and more men and women in the Soviet Union who are reaching back into the rich and long Russian tradition, focussing their thoughts on the meaning of man and the worth of the individual.

But there is also another aspect of 'peaceful competition': the capacities of the two systems to improve the material well-being of men. The Soviets have made great progress in developing their physical resources, which is not particularly surprising. They inherited a vast land with immense wealth, a considerable and fast-growing industrial establishment and a gifted people. There are those who say that the Russians could have achieved much more under a political system that did not fetter individual initiative and subject the entire economy to a command structure governed by ideology. The Soviet state has never been out of dire economic trouble. From East Germany to North Korea the communists have not solved even the elementary problem of food production and of supplying their population with consumer goods, to say nothing of housing, of which Khrushchev has given us some appalling evidence in his memoirs. More than half a century after the October Revolution the Russians are coming to us to help them put things to right in their economy.

Now contrast all this with the amazing economic progress of Western Europe, the United States and Japan under non-communist systems of government. I think we can say without being vindictive that—despite our present economic problems, which I do not wish to underestimate—the economic and social performance of the non-communist nations has knocked the bottom out of Marxist dogma. Marx said the poor would become more numerous and ever poorer and the rich would become fewer and ever richer. But nothing of the sort has happened in our societies. The non-communist nations have devised methods of directing income and the utilization of resources to improve the life of the ordinary man. It is precisely in the formerly poorer sections of our population that we saw an immense rise in well-being equitably distributed—all this, I might add, at a time when Europe and Japan were recovering from the devastations of war and were simultaneously shedding their overseas empires.

In a word: I have no fear that in a truly peaceful competition with the Soviet system we in the West would have much to worry about.

URBAN: Are you satisfied that the Soviet record of the early 1970s—the years of incipient détente—has been one of 'peaceful competition'?

RUSK: I am not sure that it has. Despite the four-power accord on Berlin—to mention one example—the western powers have repeatedly had to protest against the violation of this potentially very significant agreement. Nor can one say that the Soviet Union has played a pacifying role in the Middle East. My impression is that the Soviet leaders will assess their opportunities with great pragmatism, but will not hesitate to promote 'world revolution' if they can find ways and means to do so without exposing themselves to war-like dangers. If the Soviets do compete peacefully—that is one thing: both in the West and in the Third World we can well take care of that sort of competition, but there is always an underlying possibility of violence—open or covert violence—and that is very much another thing.

URBAN: It isn't really necessary for the Soviet leaders to resort to violence. I can envisage Portugal, or Italy gradually sliding under communist control through democratic or ostensibly democratic processes. The Soviet Union could afford to—and did—invade its allies in analogous situations. The United States and the other Nato countries cannot, and will not; or will they?

RUSK: If it is found that the communist states are pouring propaganda and money into countries like Portugal or intervening with them in other ways, then we in the West must consider how to respond. In general, it is not in accordance with our tradition to intervene in other people's domestic affairs, but the question is: what do we do if someone else is intervening? This would present us with a serious problem, and I would hope that the members of the new government in Portugal, for example, would be very much alert to the nature of the problem. Whether or not to call for outside assistance would be up to them.

URBAN: You said that our economic success has knocked the bottom out of Marxist dogma, but you qualified that by pointing to our present economic difficulties. I take it you were thinking of the oil crisis which has begun to undermine both our economic performance and our political self-confidence. The question we are now asked to answer is whether freedom and democracy can survive a sustained period of economic and political disorientation.

The reverse side of our freedom—which you so rightly emphasized—is a certain unresponsiveness and waywardness of our institutions. Free societies have always found it difficult to bring a sense of crisis home to the individual and to co-ordinate efforts to overcome it both nationally and internationally. It is the resulting fear of falling living standards, social conflict, and ultimately chaos that prepares the ground for totalitarian expedients.

RUSK: The West is going through a period of disarray which exposes us to the dangers you are talking about. For a variety of reasons, we have not yet called upon our best talents to find answers to inflation, the food and energy crises, international trade, investments and the balance-of-payment problems. But I am confident that in a reasonably short period we will, through a number of concerted actions, be able to put our house in better order. After the second world war we subjected Stalin, by our self-imposed weakness, to irresistible temptations. My concern now is that we may be doing the same thing again through the sheer disarray of our affairs. Therefore our first priority must be to re-create a sense of restraint, cohesion and success in the western world; this will, I am confident, reduce any expectation in Moscow that opportunities are beckoning.

There is also another consideration: the American people have not grown up, as the British did in the nineteenth century, thinking of themselves as playing a world role. If you scratch the thinking of most Americans, you will find them isolationist at heart. There is, in the United States, a growing mood of withdrawal from world affairs, and there is a danger that this mood will continue to grow. We must therefore keep our wits about us and be very careful lest we withdraw so much from the world scene that we again tempt the other side into adventures which both it and we would come to regret.

I am concerned about the possibility of miscalculation. It is very easy for an authoritarian government to misjudge the mood of a democracy because the multiplicity of our opinions and our divisions are constantly on public display. We voice and listen to every opinion, including the deep concern which ordinary people throughout the world feel for peace. It is easy from there to jump to conclusions—to think that we are effete, that the fight has gone out of us.

It is very important that we do not allow the Soviet leaders to make the mistake Hitler made about Britain. The democracies in

Western Europe caused Hitler to believe that Britain would not fight. I was in the Oxford Union on the night it passed the resolution: 'This house will not fight for King and country.' We allowed miscalculation and misjudgment to occur which cost fifty million lives. Counting missiles and 'throw-weight' is important, but it is the perceptions in people's minds that decide the destiny of mankind.

URBAN: A view you share with Chairman Mao.

RUSK: Maybe I do.

URBAN: Let us now move from a parallel with the past to a contrast with the past. You emphasized the continuity between the détente policies of the Nixon and Ford Administrations, and the policies pursued by President Kennedy and President Johnson, that is to say, during your own tenure as Secretary of State.

Two points of contrast strike me as important: German reunification, which was held up, certainly in the early 1960s, as a precondition of détente with the Soviet Union, and the future of Eastern Europe which, though not accorded anything like the same priority, was nevertheless from time to time considered as one element in any basic East-West reconciliation. Both have utterly vanished from the détente discussions.

RUSK: The items may have vanished from the agenda, but the two problems are still there. I don't think we made German reunification a precondition of détente in so many words. What we did say was that no permanent peace in Europe could be achieved until the German people had the right to determine their future. I did myself say on a number of occasions that although German reunification continued to be our political objective, neither the West nor the East had any intention of using force to achieve it. As it happened, the Soviet Union under Khrushchev did bring serious pressure to bear on the German problem through Berlin, but no violent action was taken to back up the Soviet threat.

The problem of Eastern Europe, too, is still with us. The feeling of national identity is strong and irrepressible in all East European countries. There is a nostalgia to rejoin the great community of Europe in science, and art, and literature, and the East European nations are never at a loss to find ways of expressing their traditional association with western civilization. Probably the best we can do is to let these associations grow quietly, without precipitating issues which might invite suppression. It may take time—it may take a considerable amount of time—before these nations are re-integrated in the community of Europe. Meanwhile we have to learn to understand why these matters have fallen off the top of the table. But they are still there—under the table.

URBAN: You were Secretary of State both at the time of the

erection of the Berlin Wall in 1961 and the invasion of Czechoslovakia in 1968. Although in 1961 American strategic superiority
over the Soviet Union was very large, and although, in 1968 too, it
was still considerable, the United States Government remained
totally inactive in both cases. Few people expected the United States
to start a war on either issue, but there were, as I see it, reasonable
expectations that the United States Government would, through
diplomatic and military pressures, through trade sanctions and all
the other means a powerful government has at its disposal, flex its
muscles and make it at least extremely expensive for the Soviet
Union to act as it did.

We know from the record that Khrushchev wanted to turn access
to Berlin over to the East Germans, and at the 1961 Vienna talks
with President Kennedy and yourself he said: 'If the Western
powers interfere with the control of this access by the East Germans, there will be war.' President Kennedy left Khrushchev with
the message: 'Well, then, Mr Chairman, there will be war.' But what
actually happened when the East Germans, at Soviet instigation, instituted a system of visas for passage in and out of East Germany,
and, on 13 August 1961, the Berlin Wall was put up? An American
military convoy was sent in, General Clay was ordered to Berlin,
and there were some tough words from Washington. That was all.

I cannot help feeling that Khrushchev's decision to 'lance the blis-
ter of Berlin'—to resort to 'sharp instruments, now that diplomatic
means had failed'—did, as he claims, pay handsome dividends. 'I
still remember Kennedy telling me in Vienna', Khrushchev says in
his memoirs, 'that according to the Potsdam Agreement, there
existed only one Germany and therefore if a peace treaty was
signed, it would have to create a government for a united Germany. . . . Well, whom has time borne out? Haven't things worked
out differently from what Kennedy said? Now Brandt himself has
found it necessary to recognize the GDR. . . . We set the stage for
this development [in 1961]. . . . In so doing, we forced Kennedy and
the Western Allies to swallow a bitter pill.'

I realize that some American 'revisionist' historians now accuse
President Kennedy and yourself of not having been co-operative
enough with Khrushchev; I notice that one of the participants in
your television interview with William Buckley (23 January 1974)
put it to you that 'all Mr Khrushchev wanted was to have the United
States sit down and talk about it' [Berlin], and I saw that you very
quickly disabused him of that idea.

My questioning comes from the opposite direction. My impression is, with all due respect, that President Kennedy and yourself were perhaps not tough *enough* with Khrushchev—that the

strong words President Kennedy had uttered in Vienna turned out to be without much substance. True, Khrushchev did not frontally challenge the West on the point on which the President had said there would be war, but Khrushchev did get away with enough to convince me that the West was, indeed, made to 'swallow a bitter pill'.

RUSK: You must not flex muscles if it is a bluff and you are not prepared to fight a general war with the Soviet Union. Long before the Berlin Wall went up, the East Germans and the Russians had complete control of East Berlin, so that the situation Khrushchev created with the Wall was not, from the foreign political point of view, formally different from the one that had existed before. The Wall was put up not, as the Russians claimed, to keep spies and sab-oteurs out, but to keep the East German people in. It was a dramatic demonstration to the entire world that the people of East Germany found the Soviet-imposed system quite intolerable. They voted with their feet in their tens of thousands day after day, and it was this drain Khrushchev was determined to stop.

URBAN: Writing from his retirement, Khrushchev did, to give him his due, recognize this. In an exceptionally frank passage of his memoirs, he says: 'If the GDR had fully tapped the moral and material potential which will some day be harnessed by the dictator-ship of the working class, there could be unrestricted passage back and forth between East and West Berlin. Unfortunately the GDR— and not only the GDR—has yet to reach a level of moral and ma-terial development where competition with the West is possible.'

RUSK: It is, of course, gratifying to see Khrushchev's admis-sion. We never had any doubt that this was the case, and I myself said so, rather more forcefully than Khrushchev does in his reminis-cences, a few hours after the Wall had gone up, on 13 August 1961.

In any case, the Wall was in direct contravention of the four-power agreement of 1949, and we protested vigorously. President Kennedy paid a memorable visit to Berlin to reassure West Berlin-ers of America's firm commitment to their freedom, but short of going to war over Berlin, there wasn't much else we could do.

After the occupation of Czechoslovakia and the announcement of the so-called Brezhnev Doctrine I spoke as directly as I could to that point at the General Assembly of the United Nations in October 1968, making it clear that we did not accept the authority of the Soviet Union over the East European countries as a matter of international law or international politics, but when you come up against the question of using force to back up your opinions, you have to decide whether, if you take the first step, you are also pre-pared to take the second and the third and the fourth, and, quite frankly, we were not prepared to fight a war over the Berlin Wall or Czechoslovakia.

URBAN: The understandings reached at Yalta and then enshrined in the European status quo were, in fact, respected.

RUSK: I would not necessarily ascribe our policy to Yalta, but certainly with the creation of Nato and the Warsaw Pact a demarcation line was established which we did not transgress.

URBAN: If I were to argue the Soviet case on Czechoslovakia I would say the Soviet Government did no more in 1968 than enforce its variety of the Monroe Doctrine and apply the principles you had yourself applied to Cuba in 1961–62, when Cuba was excluded, at United States initiative, from the Organization of American States, its trade was interrupted and its activities were watched over by a special security committee of the Inter-American Defence Board. And the arguments you used (at the Punte del Este Conference, on 25 January 1962) were these: 'What we cannot accept—and will never accept—is the use of Cuba as the means through which extra-continental powers seek to break up the inter-American system, to overthrow the governments of other countries, and to destroy the autonomous democratic evolution of the hemisphere. . . . The Castro regime, by repudiating the principles and philosophy of the inter-American system and making itself the American agent of world communism, has created a clear and present danger to the prospects of free and democratic change in every country in Latin America.'

A cynic might say: 'The Americans will no more tolerate incursions into their military and ideological empire than the Russians will into theirs; Cuba and Czechoslovakia are two sides of the same coin—for "capitalism" read "communism", for "proletarian internationalism" read "the principles and philosophy of the inter-American system" and for General-Secretary Brezhnev's doctrine read that of Secretary Dulles, or Rusk, or Kissinger.' Would you accept this analogy?

RUSK: Not completely—the form of the two attitudes may be superficially similar, but in substance they are different. In 1962 a considerable number of countries in the western hemisphere felt themselves threatened by Cuba. Castro was preaching subversion and intervention in their affairs at every opportunity. He had landed men and arms in several Latin American countries and, in 1964, he again landed a band of guerillas and weapons in Venezuela, and therefore the hemisphere imposed all the sanctions that were available to it under the Rio Pact, with the exception of the use of armed force for the direct invasion of Cuba. However, Castro was warned that if these depredations did not stop, the use of armed force too might be considered.

I am not a man from Mars. I am an American. I am on our side. I think it is one thing for several countries of this hemisphere to put troops ashore in the Dominican Republic in order to *permit* the Dominican people to choose, by free elections, their government, and quite another thing for the Soviet Union to invade Czechoslovakia to *prevent* the Czech and Slovak peoples from choosing their own government. Of course, people on the other side of the ideological fence will—as you have just indicated—take a different view, and a seasoned cynic may very well say that there is little to choose between the two political attitudes. But I am—and I was as Secretary of State—on our side of the line, and to me the two are utterly different.

URBAN: You said that the matter of Eastern Europe has fallen off the top of the table. Might I add that it has fallen off the top of the table because the West, and especially the United States, hasn't, and never has had, a concrete policy towards Eastern Europe? Let me be thoroughly obstinate and ask you again: can there be no middle ground between holding the gun against the Soviet Union—which no-one wants—and inactivity which demoralizes our own side almost as much as it demoralizes Eastern Europe?

RUSK: That depends on what one thinks that middle-ground policy ought to be. Let me ask *you* a question: if the Soviet Union were to launch a clear, unprovoked aggression against the Nato countries, would you add the forces of the smaller Eastern European countries to the Russian strength, or would you subtract them?

URBAN: I would subtract them, for they would either not fight or not fight effectively.

RUSK: That's a very important point.

URBAN: I believe the Russians would have to guard against their allies as much as against their enemies.

RUSK: If that is so the situation in Eastern Europe is not as desperate as some people think.

URBAN: But is that, I wonder, a policy? Does Kissinger have a policy towards Eastern Europe? I can see no evidence of it except in the negative sense that he is trying to discourage Soviet expansion to the Adriatic via Yugoslavia. Now if and when a European security document is signed, two things may happen (and I believe they are not necessarily mutually exclusive): through the legitimation of the status quo, Eastern Europe may find itself even more rigorously cut off from the West, and from any hope of early liberalization, than it is now; or the East European states may start working for a measure of greater independence, assuming, as the Rumanians for example

clearly do, that a European security declaration would be guaran-
teeing their integrity against *Soviet* incursions too—an expectation
which I do not, incidentally, share.

RUSK: I don't think we should leave the Soviet Government
with the impression that our interest in détente is a product of John
Foster Dulles's policy—'roll-back' through other means. Nevertheless, I do believe that under conditions of relaxed tension the smaller
nations of Eastern Europe will gain growing independence from
control and massive interference by the Soviet Union. Part of the
Soviet interest in Eastern Europe turned on the Russian fear of and
hatred for Germany; hence, soon after the war, the Russians created
this very large buffer zone between themselves and the Germans.
Ostpolitik, and various agreements signed between the United
States and the Soviet Union, have reduced the Soviet apprehension,
and I believe that, with the passage of time, one of the consequences
of détente will be the improved status of the smaller members of the
Warsaw Pact.

The case of Yugoslavia is rather different. But before I say any
more on this subject, let me put on record a disclaimer: I am now a
private citizen, I do not carry responsibility and I do not make
decisions any more. So I want it to be understood that my views are
not those—certainly not consciously those—of the present United
States Administration.

Well, if after the Presidency of Marshall Tito a crisis should arise
in Yugoslavia and the Russians should feel tempted to intervene or
play games there internally, this would create the gravest possible
crisis because the Nato countries would not be able to accept the
imposition of Soviet influence in Yugoslavia and the extension of
Soviet power to the Adriatic. Soviet intervention might create a
crisis as dangerous as the Cuban missile affair.

URBAN: What if a crisis of this kind and a subsequent call for
fraternal help were engineered purely internally under the mantle of
legality and with a show of popular support?

RUSK: Some of these questions are up to the people of the
country concerned. I'll remind you that Gandhi, who has always
been looked upon as a great idealist and a prophet of non-violence,
was very much a realist in terms of power. To him non-co-operation
too was an exercise in power. I spent a fascinating evening with him
in a small private group in Oxford in the early 1930s, and I heard
him elucidate some of his ideas. If I may apply the thrust of his
thinking to the question we are discussing: there are certain things
you cannot force anybody to do—there comes a point where the
people themselves must decide; there comes a time when the ordinary men and women must be prepared to put their lives on the line

for what they believe in. If they simply sit back and expect us to put our lives on the line for them, then there is not much we can do.

URBAN: But would the United States be prepared to put its soldiers' lives on the line even if Turks, Norwegians or Yugoslavs *did* take up the fight? In your conversation with William Buckley you quoted a recent American poll which listed twelve of America's allies, ranging from Britain, Germany, France and Japan to Israel, and asked the question: if such-and-such a country were attacked, would you be in favour of using the armed forces of the United States to come to their assistance? No ally scored fifty per cent; Israel's score was eleven per cent. Given the passionate commitment of influential sections of the United States public to the survival of Israel, these are sobering figures. The isolationism which you mentioned as a growing threat earlier in this discussion seems to have arrived already.

RUSK: There are two fatal flaws in such statistics; one is that they are based on questions asked in the abstract, without any actual situation in front of us; the second is that they are based on questions asked in the absence of leadership by a president or prime minister. I am personally convinced that if such a situation were to arise, the attitude of the American people would be different. If Berlin were involved, if Norway or Turkey were attacked, there would be plenty of support, provided, of course, that these countries themselves fought back. The poll I quoted was simply an illustration of the American mood of withdrawal which may be a purely temporary phenomenon. I certainly hope so, for in the present world situation isolationism in the United States could be suicidal for us, and I should imagine for all democratic countries in the world. But we must take note that the mood exists.

URBAN: Isn't it nevertheless a fair assumption that, when the chips are down, and an American president has to balance the destruction of New York, Washington and Chicago against letting Berlin or Munich slip under Soviet control, he would be very unlikely to push the nuclear button? The credibility of the American nuclear deterrent is widely questioned in Western Europe, not only by France, and I believe this questioning will seriously increase as the Soviet Union draws level with the United States in strategic capability and more SALT agreements are signed.

RUSK: At the time of the Berlin Wall there wasn't a single European country that was prepared to lift a finger to undo it, and I can assure you that at a moment of crisis the heads of the European governments are not going to rush to reduce their countries to a cinder pile if they can avoid it, for a full nuclear war will leave nothing of Europe, and perhaps very little of the United States or the Soviet Union. A decision to pull the nuclear trigger will be the last decision made by organized governments anywhere in the northern hemisphere. A nuclear war will not only remove all the answers; it will remove all the questions too; this conversation too will be of no significance, for there will be nothing left.

The notion that we would not keep faith with our allies is often kicked around in the free discussions we have in our democratic societies, but it would be a great mistake if certain capitals in the world drew false conclusions from it. Whatever one thinks of Vietnam, the United States went half way around the world, invested 50,000 killed and 200,000 wounded and over 100,000 million dollars in an effort to meet its security commitments to a very small country.

URBAN: Has the consciousness of the unselective disaster of nuclear war fully sunk in with the present Soviet leaders? Khrushchev was aware of it, yet he took calculated risks.

RUSK: I don't think any existing nuclear power would make a carefully considered decision to initiate nuclear war. That would be suicidal. You might have it, however, if a man or a group of men were backed into a corner from which they saw no escape—where they would elect to play the role of Samson and pull the temple down around themselves and everyone else at the same time. That is why President Kennedy gave Khrushchev several days in which to take the Soviet missiles out of Cuba. You might have a nuclear war also if there is a basic miscalculation about the reaction of the other side, and a chain of events is started which gets out of control, and there is eventually no way of pulling back from a situation in which neither side wanted to be involved. Now—to repeat a point I have already made, and I am doing so intentionally for it can never be over-stated—my concern today is that the Soviet leaders might, by looking at our disarray and by selectively reading some of the utterances they can hear in our turbulent public discussions, misjudge our morale and let themselves in for some grave military miscalculation. It is therefore very important for the President of the United States always to make clear that such miscalculation is out of bounds—that it just must not happen.

URBAN: I take it you are not one of those who believe that our chances of ruling out nuclear war and of having a genuine détente with the Soviet Union would be improved if the Soviet Union ordered its domestic affairs more in accord with our ideas of freedom and democracy?

RUSK: I'm not. I yield to no-one in my concern for human rights, but the United States, the American people, are not embarked on a crusade to establish throughout the world the human rights we guarantee in our constitution. If you look through the list of all the countries with whom we have diplomatic relations, only about twenty-five per cent have given their people human rights of the sort we are talking about in this country and Western Europe. We in the United States have never taken much interest in the doctrine of communism as such; all we have been concerned about is its translation into aggressive action, action in pursuit of ideology. Détente is a probing operation for possible points of agreement in the international field. No more.

URBAN: Nevertheless you do, I suppose, welcome the changes that have taken place in the Soviet Union since Stalin's day, upgrading as they probably do the eligibility and credibility of the Soviet Union as a partner for détente.

RUSK: There have been small changes in the Soviet Union that are of *some* significance, but not yet of historical significance. For example, apparently it is now possible for a high official of the Soviet Union to retire and continue to live. Solzhenitsyn and other Soviet writers and intellectuals were exiled to the West and not shot. These are achievements of a kind. Then, Soviet nuclear and space scientists, and now Soviet agricultural scientists too, are no longer under the day-to-day control of the Communist Party. I understand that plant managers in the consumer industries have become slightly freer to take into account the actual needs of their customers. That too is an achievement when I remember that Khrushchev used to complain to me about having billions of rubles' worth of consumer goods lying about in warehouses which the consumers weren't interested in—tropical sandals when the need was for winter boots, army-sized cauldrons when the housewife wanted frying pans, and so on. Khrushchev knew (and he says so in his memoirs) that one can't make soup out of propaganda.

So I would concede that small changes have been introduced to make the Soviet economy responsive to the market—as we would say in America—but it would be quite unjustified to infer from these piecemeal improvements that the Soviet system has changed its character. The Soviet Union is still ruled by the Communist Party which insists upon a monopoly of political power. It permits nothing like a free discussion of the world's common political, economic, military and cultural problems. It is still a prison by all standards except, perhaps, Russia's own. In other words, the differences between East and West are still fundamental but, I repeat, these must not prevent us from trying to find the minimum agreements which would permit us to live together on this speck of dust in the universe and gamble on the healing power of time as it works on human beings. This is an article of faith—I cannot prove it.

URBAN: The conflict between Christianity and Islam, too, was eventually dissipated, but the process took several centuries. Meanwhile a large area of Europe, in fact partly the same south-eastern segment of the continent which is now under Soviet control, was laid waste, its population decimated and its development held back with effects which are still with us today.

RUSK: It is not a happy reminder, but in the fast-moving milieu of our century no past analogy can be appropriate. In the last twenty years or so the ideas of freedom and democracy have penetrated to the remotest corners of the earth. The Roman, Spanish and Portuguese empires shrank and collapsed over a period of centuries—the British, Dutch and French empires of our own day took only some twenty years to complete the same process. The idea of liberty has always put great pressure on despotisms, but the idea of liberty boosted by electronic communication has made that pressure a pretty fast-acting as well as a very potent agent. I am confident that with time and some luck we may reach a point where, though lip-service will perhaps still be paid to world revolution, the actual challenge of revolution will be confined to its ritual.

URBAN: 2,300 years ago—to go even further back in history—Thucydides wrote: 'Not now for the first time have I seen that it is impossible for a democracy to govern an empire.' What you have just said about the fall of the British, Dutch and French empires bears this out. But Thucydides did not say that it was impossible for a *tyranny* to govern an empire, and if we look at the history of the totalitarian dictatorships of our own time, it is clear that fascist Italy and nazi Germany collapsed as a result of war, not domestic disintegration, while the Soviet Union and communist China show no signs of being ungovernable, and probably will show none as long as the will and the ability to maintain a faultless totalitarianism exist. Therefore I wonder whether the dissipation of differences between the West and the communist world will really be a much speedier affair than was Christianity's détente with Islam.

RUSK: In the last decades of the twentieth century it is no longer possible to maintain a sound-proof and germ-proof totalitarian system. Freedom and emancipation are in the air. Radio, television, tourism, sports, Olympic games, cultural and scientific exchange, trade and personal contacts are bound to temper and perhaps even to break up the monolithic features of the Soviet type of communism. Hence the importance of the free flow of people and ideas under Basket Three. Thucydides, if he were our contemporary, would probably say that in the electronic age *neither* democracy *nor* dictatorship can for long govern an empire. So I don't somehow think that history will confirm the relevance of the Christian-Islamic example.

URBAN: This is a highly libertarian attitude which I respect. However, let me play the devil's advocate and put it to you that détente will come our way—whether we like it or not—by the reverse process: the 'totalitarianization' of the western democracies. My thesis (with which I'm sure you are familiar because it is common currency) is this: as the world's problems become increasingly indivisible and 'total', only 'total' solutions can cope with them—in which case the communist totalitarian countries are way ahead of us in the race, and détente will pop out of the *Gleichschaltung* of our system with theirs.

RUSK: No, I don't feel or fear that. The arguments for greater controls and more authoritarianism are rather tempting short-term answers to the problem you have mentioned, but in the longer run I do not believe that totalitarian or authoritarian societies can succeed, either on the moral or the purely material level, as well as societies where individual thought, imagination and initiative are given full play. Moreover, as I've just said, I do not believe that governments can, at the end of the day, impose their will completely on human beings without stimulating opposition and violence.

Thomas Carlyle in *Sartor Resartus* once commented that the worst that a government can do to you is to kill you; you've got to die anyhow, therefore you are a free man.

ZBIGNIEW BRZEZINSKI

From Cold War to cold peace

URBAN: President Johnson's attempt to 'build bridges' to Eastern Europe and his whole programme of 'peaceful engagement' were, I believe, the results in concept as in name of your consultancy with the United States Administration and the President's considerable reliance on your advice for the conduct of his foreign policy, especially in the field of East-West relations.

How does the 'Johnson-Brzezinski programme' look to us in the light of détente?

On the face of it 'building bridges' and 'peaceful engagement' strike me as being more active concepts than détente, which carries rather passive connotations. Yet, détente, as it is being pursued by the Ford Administration, betrays many similarities with President Johnson's—and your—programme, but it also betrays many differences, certainly in emphasis, and I suspect in substance too.

For example, one important point in your concept of peaceful engagement was the reunification of Germany. You said that the Berlin Wall would increase the long-range prospects of reunification because a secure Soviet bloc would be more willing to make concessions than an insecure one. You urged the Federal Republic to initiate a new policy towards the Soviet Union and Eastern Europe—an *Ostpolitik*—for that, you thought, would isolate East Germany. You believed that only communist fanatics attached any ideological importance to the continued existence of a communist East Germany, and that the ostracism of East Germany could be advanced by treating the East European states as if, in fact, they were independent. You were hoping that, while we should encourage no defections from the Soviet Union, the slow democratic evolution of Eastern Europe would bring liberalization to Russia. These are some of the points on which peaceful engagement and détente, or, at any rate, the kind of détente it has been politically possible to pursue, part company.

On the other hand, you suggested, for example, an East-West standing committee to promote European security. You advocated a joint United States—West and East European development plan which would cut across partitions, narrow disparities in

living standards, promote human contacts, diminish the importance of frontiers—a Basket Three idea almost a decade before the
European Security Conference. On these points your strategy and
détente appear to be converging, but only to a limited degree for,
unlike Kissinger's concept of détente, 'peaceful engagement' envisaged a linkage of the Jackson type between trade and internal liberalization in Eastern Europe, though not in Russia. Trade and aid,
you insisted, have to be given in politically clearly defined conditions. Whenever an East European country extends external or
internal liberties, it should be rewarded, and vice versa.

The establishment of this kind of leverage through trade and
credits may, for all we know, be Kissinger's unspoken purpose, too.
This is certainly what the Russians fear it may be. If so, the broad
concept of détente isn't perhaps as different from 'peaceful engagement' as would appear from the Administration's public articulations. However, even if this were so, the differences on Germany
would remain. Reunification has been overtaken by Moscow's determined stand on East Germany, the Western countries' unwillingness to pursue the sophisticated policies you advocated under
'peaceful engagement', and the German Federal Government's
conclusion that, in the circumstances, any linkage between *Ostpolitik* and reunification has to be ruled out for the foreseeable future.

BRZEZINSKI: The similarities between our programme and
the détente policies of the Nixon and Ford Administrations are
easier to detect than the differences, and they are, therefore, rather
misleading. There is an obvious element of continuity in the sense
that both set out to improve East-West relations, notably American-Soviet relations. Within that context both policies attempt to
widen the range of relationships—to have trade where there hasn't
been any, and to develop more extensive collaboration in science,
technology and culture.

With that said, it is fair to point out, however, that the Nixon/
Ford/Kissinger approach is that of a highly compartmentalized
and essentially static, even conservative, détente, one in which ties
are forged very selectively, especially in the strategic and economic
fields, and one which seeks to perpetuate the status quo with all that
entails. Our view was that the ideological and political cleavages
which divide the advanced world are anachronistic, that they reflect
the past rather than provide guidance for the future, and that it is
therefore in the interests not only of our two societies and political
systems, but of the world community as a whole to repair those cleavages and change the status quo. To do so one must move forward
on a broad front; one must bring the two societies into much closer
contact with each other than they are in now, and one does this by

first diluting and eventually by eliminating the ideological hostility between them. Simultaneously one proceeds to create a web of co-operative relationships so that the two societies are increasingly inter-meshed and inter-dependent.

German unification, for example, which you mentioned as a cardinal point in our programme, wasn't in fact seen by us as a *sine qua non* of a European settlement. Up to about 1966 it was the conventional American view that German reunification must be the point of departure for the resolution of the East-West problematique. In October 1966 President Johnson made a speech—and I might as well add, as you have already hinted at it, that I had quite a bit to do with that speech—in which he reversed the sequence and said that a gradual change in East-West relations would have to *precede* the resolution of the German problem. In the meantime, of course, the problem has been removed from the agenda.

You can see from what I have said so far that, although there is a sense of general continuity between the policies pursued in the 1960s and détente, the content of 'peaceful engagement' was rather different from what Kissinger is doing and this difference expresses itself in conceptualization and style too. In some ways Kissinger's idea of détente is closer to that of Brezhnev than to the one the Johnson Administration was trying to pursue, and therefore probably easier to bring to fruition. Brezhnev, too, prefers a limited, strictly compartmentalized, non-basic détente, especially in the economic and strategic fields which are, of course, inter-related, and in which the Soviet Union is extremely vulnerable. Moreover Brezhnev and Kissinger agree that demands for domestic change in the Soviet Union must not be a precondition of the pursuit of relaxation.

The Soviet leaders and the Soviet press have spent quite a few words attacking 'peaceful engagement' and 'bridge-building' as refined plots to undermine the Soviet system. Indeed, they have attacked me personally to a degree which is quite disproportionate to my role: during the tense years of the Cold War the Soviets wasted more ink abusing me than they did any other American with the exception of the President and the Secretary of State. And the explanation is that the Soviet leaders fear a truly *comprehensive* détente. They see in it a challenge to their legitimacy and thus to their very existence, and I must say their fears are justified. They are right in diagnosing the danger to them, they are wrong, however, in not realizing that their resistance to change is at odds with the facts of life at the end of the twentieth century: if détente is to become more than a transient and fundamentally unstable relationship, it will have to be much more comprehensive than it is envisaged to be at the present, and that means a possibly gradual but nevertheless fundamental change in Soviet positions at home and abroad.

URBAN: The Soviet leaders' fear of the snowballing effect of détente is well attested. Khrushchev, for example, is remarkably frank about the alarm inspired by that relatively innocuous internal détente, the 1954–5 'thaw'. 'We were scared', he writes in his memoirs, '—really scared. We were afraid the thaw might unleash a flood, which we wouldn't be able to control and which could drown us.' And he adds: 'From the point of view of the leadership, this would have been an unfavourable development . . . Our people had a good expression for the situation you were in: "You want to scratch where it itches, but your mama won't let you".'

BRZEZINSKI: Brezhnev and his colleagues are just as conscious of the dangers flowing from a comprehensive détente as Khrushchev was, and that is why they view the prospect of a *compartmentalized* détente with quiet satisfaction. The present thaw in East-West relations will release no floods in the Soviet Union.

URBAN: To come down to specifics—what changes would Kissinger's conception of détente have to undergo to conform with President Johnson's and your programme of 'peaceful engagement'? We know from the example of Czechoslovakia that the liberalization of Russia via Eastern Europe cannot work, and we know from the example of the Twentieth Party Congress, and its impact on Hungary, that the liberalization of Eastern Europe via Moscow cannot work either beyond certain narrowly defined limits. So it seems to me that your bridge-building programme would have to make do with one rather than two bridgeheads. But no bridge other than a pontoon bridge has yet been built in that way, and pontoon bridges are not usually put up under peaceful conditions.

BRZEZINSKI: If I were in Kissinger's position I would do much less than has been done up to the end of 1975 in extending American credits on concessionary terms to help the USSR import advanced American science and technology, and I would do more in demanding that the Russians accept the kind of conditions we have built into Basket Three. I would insist on reciprocity, pressing more rigorously for what Kissinger has recently also stressed as being important: the linkage of the economic, political, strategic and cultural elements of détente. I suspect that because of the Watergate scandal and, until Nixon's resignation, the shaky state of the Presidency, there was pressure on the Administration to come up with quick foreign policy results, especially in American-Soviet relations. This has permitted Moscow to shape détente according to its own needs and to dictate the pace. As a consequence, certain sectors of détente, where rapid movement is beneficial to Soviet interests, are being strongly cultivated, while others have been frozen or gradually eliminated. Obviously this kind of détente does not get to the root of our problem with the Soviet Union and is bound to remain an uncertain blossom.

URBAN: Isn't it the case that the western notion of détente is totally at odds with the Soviet concept of peaceful co-existence? If so, aren't we incurring certain risks by giving the Russians too much, too soon?

BRZEZINSKI: It is one of the sad facts of political life, and a poor reflection on democracy, that despite the many volumes written on the subject on both sides of the East-West divide, the western public is still unaware of what exactly the Soviet leaders mean by peaceful co-existence. Some of the blame for this must be laid at the doorsteps of former President Nixon and Secretary Kissinger, who advised him, for the joint American-Soviet statement issued after Nixon's first visit to Moscow included the phrase 'peaceful co-existence' as the foundation-stone of the East-West relationship. In more recent American-Soviet statements, too, Soviet phraseology has been accepted, which means that the Russians dictate the semantic framework of the relationship. In this age of instant and universal communications, words are politics. The use of phrases and concepts structures the way in which people perceive the world and act on it.

The Soviet leaders are quite forthright about what they mean by détente. Détente, they tell us, is a limited and expedient arrangement which in no way terminates ideological conflict. On the contrary, we are told over and over again that peaceful co-existence is a form of class-struggle and that ideological conflict, far from abating, is to intensify during détente. This intensified ideological hostility, however, is not to stand in the way of economic co-operation. Indeed, as Marshall Shulman has argued, economic co-operation is a substitute for internal reform, for if the Soviet leaders can obtain from us massive investments and technology, they need not face up to the politically risky alternative of instituting fundamental economic reform.

I am not arguing that such a limited détente is worthless. It is better than no détente, but if we do agree to the massive investments and concessionary credits which the Soviets request from us, we must be quite clear that we are letting ourselves in for considerable risks. Ideological hostility can itself become a source of great tension. There is no way in which the Russians can make us feel that they want to co-operate with us so long as they are simultaneously telling us that they want to destroy us.

URBAN: This was the point on which Kennedy and Khrushchev crossed swords in Vienna, and the dilemma has not gone away.

BRZEZINSKI: It hasn't because 'peaceful co-existence' as an intensified form of the class-struggle is an article of faith with the Soviet leaders.

I have just said that ideological hostility can itself become a source of tension; add to this the possibility that changes in the Soviet leadership may bring to the fore groups and individuals less well disposed even to the existing limited détente than is the present leadership; clearly, in such a case, détente is susceptible of easy reversal. If that should happen after a period of sustained American investment in the USSR, with heavy Soviet indebtedness, a very undesirable situation might arise. I would not like to say whether the United States would, then, find itself more dependent on Soviet raw materials than the Soviet Union on American markets, but it is certainly a possibility that a Soviet leadership might be tempted to use both its debts to the United States and American dependence on Soviet raw materials for political ends. In other words, we could be blackmailed.

That is why we must, in the interests of the West and of world peace, move from compartmentalization to a global concept of détente in which economic co-operation is not offset by an artificially sustained ideological antagonism. We must urge upon the Soviet leaders the adoption not only of the principle but also of the practice of a true reciprocity in our relations. Until that happens, we would be wise to cultivate détente cautiously, not allowing it to be concentrated on American investments, and credits, and know-how, for these would, as I say, simply perpetuate the existing Soviet system and the prevailing ideological attitudes by reducing internal pressure for economic and political change.

URBAN: How do you explain the fact that the American Administration has been so weak on Basket Three and the policies associated with it? American tradition would seem to demand a strong commitment to moral issues. Indeed, until very recently, American governments have always been criticized for allowing their conduct of international relations to be governed by an *excess* of moral sentiment: the Soviet Union, it is often pointed out, was not recognized by the United States until 1933, and a similar American refusal to deal with unsavoury governments delayed, for an even longer period than it did in the case of the USSR, the admission of China to the United Nations. Has the pendulum now swung in the opposite direction?

BRZEZINSKI: It has. The moral indifference you mention was inherent in the Nixon Administration's whole philosophy of foreign affairs. Nixon and Kissinger prided themselves on being less ideologically motivated and more pragmatic than the Kennedys. They have, in my judgement, elevated amorality to the level of principle. This is not in keeping with fundamental American traditions. It denies American foreign policy an asset which has made that policy so appealing to many people throughout the world. The moral stature of the United States has been an influence every bit as important as our economic and military power.

This lack of concern with moral issues has penetrated into every corner of the East-West relationship: it has translated itself into an American negotiating posture which likes to deal with the concrete and the specific as an excuse for neglecting more fundamental issues; it claims to be hard-nosed but is, in fact, failing to do justice to those less visible but extremely important factors—the flow of ideas, the interaction of social forces, the impact of communication—which shape the contemporary world to a degree that was not possible in a traditional international environment, where compartmentalization corresponded to the existence of nation-states.

It is sometimes said that Henry Kissinger's model of the world as it *ought* to be is Europe after the Congress of Vienna. If so, this is a false analogy. I do not believe that a Congress of Vienna type of order can be, or should be, built on the basis of a contrived arrangement with our adversaries, especially at the cost of weakening hard-won relationships with our allies in Europe and Japan.

URBAN: Are you, I wonder, doing justice to Kissinger's policies? It is clear from his recent (1974–75) statements that his concerns have become universal, embracing not only détente, but also the exploitation and distribution of the world's energy and food resources, world trade, and the co-existence of regions, societies and civilizations. In his interview with James Reston (*New York Times*, 13 October 1974), the Secretary of State painted an apocalyptic picture of a world 'delicately poised' on the verge of a new historic era. He called for a new spirit of interdependence in order to avoid uncontrollable political, economic and social chaos. It seems to me that if you take as panoramic a view of human destiny as Kissinger is now taking, then détente must be subsumed under 'survival' and that makes the balance of concessions made by this or that side in the détente relationship look insignificant.

You make a very strong point when you appeal for a reassertion of morality in American foreign policy, but I can't help being impressed by Kissinger's answer to that plea, and to arguments of a similar nature that have been used against his conduct of détente. In his statement before the Senate Foreign Relations

Committee (19 September 1974) Kissinger said: 'Where the age-old antagonism between freedom and tyranny is concerned we are not neutral. But other imperatives impose limits on our ability to produce internal changes in foreign countries. Consciousness of our limits is recognition of the necessity of peace—not moral callousness. The preservation of human life and human society are moral values too.'

This is an impressive point, and it is very difficult to argue with it. It is moral at a high level of generality, but it is also very vulnerable precisely because it is so general: the 'survival of mankind' is a faultless excuse for not doing anything to help Soviet dissidents, Czech reformers, Hungarian revolutionaries and whoever else you have decided you cannot, or do not want to, help.

I am, incidentally, intrigued to see that my anxiety about the uses to which Kissinger's reasoning might be put runs parallel with the Chinese critique of détente as pursued by the Soviet Union. It is nonsense to claim, Chiao Kuan-hua said at the United Nations on 2 October 1974, that détente has ushered in, as the Russians claim, a 'world without war'. '"Détente" has become a quack medicine hawked by the Soviet leaders everywhere. . . . So long as imperialism, and social imperialism exist . . . genuine détente and lasting peace will be impossible.'

BRZEZINSKI: I am delighted that the Secretary of State is now taking a large view of the world's problems. However, the argument you have quoted makes sense only if we accept Kissinger's premise that the alternative to détente is, or is most likely to be, nuclear war. And this, as I see it, is not the case. The Soviet Union is not in a good position to wage war against the United States, and I do not believe that the present Soviet leaders want war any more than Khrushchev did. The United States certainly has no taste for war with the USSR, and the same goes a fortiori for Western Europe. War is a luxury which only the poor and weak nations can now afford, and the history of the last ten years or so shows that the wars waged by them can be controlled. The Soviet leaders want the fruits of war without taking too many of the risks of war, and an effective United States foreign policy must be able to frustrate this Soviet design without itself risking the peace of the world. But if you predicate your entire foreign policy on the assumption that any determined move you make in American-Soviet relations is fraught with the dangers of nuclear war, you are, in fact, declaring yourself unequal to the game Moscow is playing. I'm not saying that this is quite the case at the present time; what I *am* saying is that too easy a recourse to the argument that the only alternative to détente is war may render our foreign policy ineffective. I entirely underwrite Kissinger's global concerns. I have myself advocated them for a long time, but a genuinely reciprocal détente, with the elimination of ideological conflict written into it, is in no way antithetical to peace and the survival of civilization.

URBAN: The key word in your argument is reciprocity, so let me see if we can get a closer definition of the conditions which the Soviet side would have to meet before you would agree that a state of genuine reciprocity exists.

You said in an article published in 1965 that when Marshall aid was offered to the Soviet Union in 1947, Molotov's response was that the communist states would accept it if they could use it freely. But this Soviet condition was unacceptable to the United States; there is no reason, you added, why a similar Soviet attitude should be acceptable to the United States in 1966 or 1970. If American aid and trade are now to be extended to the Soviet Union, you would clearly want to attach certain strings to them. What would they be?

BRZEZINSKI: It seems to me we should insist that certain forms of Soviet behaviour, none of them strictly economic, are themselves incompatible with better economic relations. Extensive American credits, investments, and transfers of technology would only be justified if progress towards greater accommodation were made on five specific issues.

First (and we have already discussed this): ideological hostility. This contradicts the spirit of détente and is a threat to it.

Second: the secrecy surrounding Soviet strategic planning. This is a source of anxiety in the United States and is incompatible with strategic stability. It poses the question whether détente is not viewed by some Soviet leaders merely as providing breathing space in which the Americans are lulled into a false sense of security while the Soviet Union moves from parity to strategic, and from there to political, superiority.

Third: indifference to global problems. Russia remains remarkably insensitive to global issues which cry out for greater co-operation among the advanced countries. The inflated costs of food and energy have seriously afflicted the Fourth World, but the Soviet Union, though itself a key beneficiary of higher commodity prices, has given no practical sign of any willingness to help.

Fourth: the Soviet disregard of human rights outrages a significant section of the American electorate and thereby complicates and exacerbates Soviet-American relations.

Fifth: reciprocity of treatment for our diplomats, businessmen, journalists and scholars. United States diplomats, journalists, etc. are subjected to incomparably greater restraints than their Soviet counterparts in the United States. American scholars are often not only harassed but excluded from the Soviet Union, in marked contrast to the welcome extended in the United States to Soviet specialists. The Soviet side is free to lobby in America and even to promote joint American-Soviet lobbies in America, whereas American access to the Soviet élite is strictly circumscribed.

These, then, are some of the areas of strain in American-Soviet relations, and it is here that we could use our economic leverage to best advantage. The Russians will not accommodate us willingly, but if the adjustments we suggest are not excessive, if they do not bite into the structure of the Soviet system, the Russians may find that the risks entailed by the conditions we set them are balanced by the advantages accruing from American credits and investment. My hope would then be that, over a period of time, the adjustments gained would have a cumulative impact on the nature of the Soviet system.

URBAN: To pursue further the notion of reciprocity: what conclusions would you draw from the fate of the Jackson Amendment?

BRZEZINSKI: The Jackson Amendment did not achieve its purpose, yet its domestic utility cannot be denied for it has strengthened the Administration's hand in its negotiations with the Soviet Union. Going by the record of the last few years I rather fear that, without Congressional pressure, the Administration would not be using the power it has. The Jackson Amendment has carved out for Congress a share in the responsibility of making and policing American foreign policy. Of course, this co-responsibility can be put to good use, or it can be misused, and Congress has already shown its capacity to do both.

Why am I saying that the Administration's record is not encouraging? Take the outrageous case of the lie-detectors. It was not until an intense Congressional outcry that the Administration decided to do something to prevent United States industrialists from selling voice-print-detection technology and lie-detectors to the Soviet Union. I find that not only poor politics but also very amoral, in fact, immoral, and such immorality weakens (as I have already stressed) our position internationally, quite apart from adding to the efficiency of the KGB. Until Congress raised a·howl, the position of the United States Commerce Department was that *its* job was to promote American-Soviet trade. There was to be no discrimination, no differentiation. Take another example: the United States Commerce Department is actively engaged in modernizing Soviet civil aviation. This will materially advance the Soviet airlift capability against China. I fail to see an American interest in that, but the position of the Commerce Department is that the modernization promotes American business and is therefore good for America.

There is, of course, a general problem involved here. American-Soviet economic relations are calibrated on the Soviet side because all Soviet economy is state economy. For us, with our relatively free market economy, it is difficult to infuse a sense of political purpose into our economic relations with Moscow, yet if we do not make such an effort, it will always be the Soviet side that benefits economically and politically.

URBAN: If you were appointed Secretary of State, where would you pick up the threads of détente?

BRZEZINSKI: I would certainly continue the strategic dialogue, I would certainly want to go on with the trade relationship, but I would hope that in that case Congress would give the Executive full authority to negotiate trade arrangements on the basis of the extension of most-favoured-nation status to the Soviet Union. Of course, both the military relationship and the trade arrangements would have to conform with the five principles of reciprocity I have mentioned, that is to say, I would develop American-Soviet relations in a much larger context than they are being discussed in at present. I would put more emphasis on creating organic links between East and West in the social and cultural spheres. This would probably mean a lengthier process, with fewer expectations and no immediate pay-offs—a process in which Western Europe would take a greater part than it does now, but one which might prove more enduring than the piecemeal détente we are now pursuing.

There is, of course, always the possibility that this slow cultivation of interdependence, of continuing discussion, of mutual involvement may not succeed. It may be that we are going to remain ideologically divided for a long time to come, but if that is the case, then it is better to face that reality head on rather than delude ourselves that we can create, through the balance of power approach, a structure of peace which will be lasting.

URBAN: Let me take a bird's eye view of détente as Brezhnev might see it. Challenged by Marshal Grechko or Suslov, would Brezhnev be able to claim that détente is a success for the Soviet Union?

BRZEZINSKI: If I were Brezhnev facing Marshal Grechko at the conference table I would have no difficulty in defending the proposition that détente is a Soviet success story. 'We have got', I would say to him, 'American acknowledgement of Soviet strategic parity and maybe superiority: we have quantitative parity which lends itself to be translated into qualitative advantage. We have done remarkably well in obtaining American aid and trade and we have not had to pay a price for this socially, culturally or in any other way that would threaten our system. We have had no price to pay in Eastern Europe or Western Europe either. In fact, we will soon have the status quo guaranteed by a security declaration. I would say that is not a bad record.'

URBAN: Brezhnev may well claim even more than that. He could point to the fact that the spectacle of repeated summitry, diplomatic hobnobbing, protestations of goodwill and the like have vastly increased the eligibility of some of the West European communist parties, notably, of course, those of Italy and France. We saw in the 1974 French presidential elections that Mitterand, the communist-socialist candidate, polled no less than 49.3 per cent of the vote. In Italy, too, there is, after the success of the Communist Party in the 1975 local elections, a growing willingness to draw the communists into government as a parliamentary party that will presumably respect the rules of parliamentary democracy. These, too, are facts Brezhnev might well chalk up on the credit side of his détente-account.

BRZEZINSKI: I would not agree that the sudden rise of the Italian and French Communist Parties is predominantly due to détente; it has a great deal to do with the domestic destabilization of West European society, but I would concede that détente has probably created a climate in which certain, otherwise internal, processes have been reinforced. There is no doubt that the Italian and French Communist Parties seem more legitimate, more respected, and suddenly closer to attaining some form of power than they were perhaps ever before.

URBAN: If things are going as well for the Russians as you say they are—and I agree with you that they are going well for them—why should they be so keen on obtaining a piece of paper from a summit spectacular?

BRZEZINSKI: If you take a long-term view of Europe as it must seem to a Russian observer, it is clear that the successful conclusion of the security talks is the conclusion of only phase one, and the simultaneous beginning of another phase in a continuing process. The conclusion of phase one puts the seal of legitimacy on the status quo, that is to say, the division of Europe. That is an important Soviet goal in itself, but it is not the only goal the Russians are after. The Russians' next objective is a step-by-step qualitative readjustment of Soviet-American and Soviet-West European relations.

URBAN: Finlandization?

BRZEZINSKI: That, I should imagine, would be the ultimate goal, but I think the Russians would move very slowly and settle for less—a 'Swedenization' perhaps—as their interim objective. This second phase would mean a gradual dilution of political interdependence between Western Europe and America: armed neutrality to start off with, though not a very well-armed neutrality; radical internal policies which would be the more likely to be attained if the West European communist parties became members of coalition governments; normal relations with the United States but no political and cultural intimacy. Finlandization would follow from these. Such a Soviet strategy would, of course, not be unconnected with the Soviet concern with China, and therefore with the desirability of transforming Europe not merely into a more stable but also into a more docile instrument.

URBAN: Can all this be prevented from happening? You said earlier in this conversation—and you have said it in several of your articles in the 1960s—that the division of Europe is a dangerous anachronism which must be gradually eliminated. But is it likely to be in the light of past evidence?

For several years after the war, when the United States had nuclear monopoly and then undisputed nuclear superiority over the Soviet Union, when American moral authority flourished and the American economy was the wonder of the world, nothing was done to translate these enormous assets into political policies to change the status quo in Europe. And it wasn't that the *Soviet* leaders had any doubt about their helplessness in the face of American power. 'I would even say the Americans were invincible at that time', Khrushchev remarks of the Truman-Acheson period in his memoirs.

In the 1960s you warned that, for any profitable give-and-take to be set in train with the Soviet Union, we must maintain our military superiority. Now that we appear to be settling for strategic parity and conventional inferiority, aren't we throwing away our ability to prevent a Finlandization of Europe, let alone to restore the unity of Europe? We are pursuing détente from a position of increasing weakness, whereas your policy, as I understand it, was to go after peaceful engagement from a position of strength.

BRZEZINSKI: I would not want to argue that we must regain nuclear superiority before we can peacefully engage the Soviet Union, but we can certainly not pursue such a policy if the *Soviets* acquire nuclear superiority, for the Soviet leaders would without a doubt exploit it for political ends. It therefore behoves us to make certain that this does not happen.

What we do need, however, absolutely categorically for the creation of a new and stable relationship with the East—one which does not itself cause a weakening and perhaps even a collapse of democracy—is the reinvigoration of the moral authority of the United States. Watergate, the growing cynicism and indifference of Western Europe, and our universal permissiveness have shaken our self-confidence and robbed us of our former magnetism. This is a serious problem. For two decades we have over-estimated the importance of economic welfare and under-estimated the importance of moral and spiritual values.

On the question of the status quo: I never thought the status quo could be changed by the naked application of force. Change will have to be a process deliberately sought over a long period of time. If change had been sought from a position of military superiority in the early fifties, for example, one can confidently assume that the Soviet side would have resisted it because it was all too clear that the West was not prepared to go to war. Now that our moral stature is weakened (not, of course, in relation to that of the Soviet Union but to what we ourselves had before), and Russia has drawn level with us in strategic capability, we are, paradoxically, perhaps in a better position to abet change—

URBAN: —parity removing Russia's inferiority complexes and vindictiveness—

BRZEZINSKI: —that sort of thing. All this, however, requires an act of will and a sense of history. I must repeat that it is the anachronistic division of Europe that is the source of instability. If we contribute to its legitimation in the form of some security declaration, we are not contributing to European security but to its opposite. Hence the creation of an extensive web of relationships—far more wide-ranging than is envisaged in détente—must become our central concern. I don't believe we have to be particularly specific as to what eventually the outcome of this process will be. In fact, I don't think there *will* be a time when we can say that the process is completed. But this does not weaken my argument that commitment to a long-term goal is our best hope of regaining political influence and moral authority. The patchwork view of East-West relations—and that is all détente is at the moment—leaves us with a feeling of opportunism, passivity and lack of leadership. Morality is sometimes said to be the privilege of the weak; we mustn't be both weak and immoral.

URBAN: It has been suggested, especially by the Soviet side, that the black-and-white alternatives of the Cold War were more congenial to your intellectual temper than those fine distinctions we are now called upon to make among different hues of grey. While I would certainly not agree with that judgement, you did write, in 1972, that the Cold War, with its stability and clear bearings, 'would look calm in retrospect'.

BRZEZINSKI: I did make that remark, but I don't want it to be thought that I am hankering after the Cold War. Indeed the whole purpose of 'peaceful engagement' was to put an end to it. What I meant to say was this: the Cold War was Manichean, and under a Manichean constellation all questions are sharply put, all solutions are simple, and all contrasts are stark because Manicheism is the confrontation of good and evil, of darkness and light. Everything is crystal clear. We are now moving away from that period of easy contrasts, and the price we are paying is complexity. But to recognize and to do justice to the overlapping truths and fine shadings which characterize this new situation is a much more realistic thing to do than to seek refuge in the outdated certainties of another age. In Russia and Eastern Europe, too, and even inside the Soviet leadership, there are elements who are beginning to recognize that the Manichean world is dead or dying. We should encourage these, and not encourage those elements who would rather preserve the ideological past. Now détente is being used as a cornucopia to overhaul the Soviet economy while avoiding a political crisis.

URBAN: Let me focus my claim that the United States was unwilling and/or unable to use its post-war superiority on one specific problem-area, Eastern Europe: would you agree that western policy towards Eastern Europe since the end of the war has been a total failure, if indeed there has been a western policy towards Eastern Europe other than our acceptance of Soviet rule there? Yugoslavia's defection was given half-hearted support, but the upheaval in East Berlin, the Polish October, the Hungarian Revolution and the Prague Spring were left entirely unexploited. Thirty years after the war we consider ourselves fortunate if we can persuade the Soviet leaders ('breakthrough' is the fashionable word for it) to allow divided families to be re-united under certain conditions, to tell western journalists, as they are being expelled from the Soviet Union why they are being expelled, and to permit more ancient coins and meteorologists to move across the East-West divide; such is the measure of our failure. I find it a little difficult to believe that the multiple-mesh technique of peaceful engagement (to say nothing of détente) can undo three decades of missed opportunities.

BRZEZINSKI: When one speaks of western failure or success one has to bear in mind what the West is and what it is not and cannot be. The West has not been militant for a very long time; it is certainly not Manichean. A group of states which is neither militant, nor Manichean, nor held together by politically institutionalized links, cannot be expected offensively to exploit political opportunities in anything like the same way in which a Manichean system can and does.

The basic characteristics of the West are pluralism and defensiveness, and if one accepts the limitations inherent in these, then one can claim that the West has been successful. Where it has failed is not in failing to muscle in on openings in the East, but in failing to generate an attractive and morally compelling policy which would, in due course, render ineffective the bureaucratic-ideological system of Soviet communism. This is not a question of sending in tanks but of maintaining the kind of sustained attractiveness which, for a brief period, particularly under Kennedy, America did generate.

URBAN: I don't believe that philosophical infiltration or sustained attractiveness through moral example is likely to succeed where western military and economic power, combined with moral authority and severe restlessness in Eastern Europe, didn't. However, there is one card which western governments have so far, and rightly as I see it, shied away from playing: nationalism—both the nationalisms of the East European countries and the powerful separatisms of the ethnic minorities within the multinational Soviet state, where the Russian population is now beginning to be outnumbered by the non-Russian races. Your attitude to this problem was expressed in an article you wrote in the mid-1960s in which you warned that we should not encourage East European nationalism, for nationalism is a tiger and we don't know how to ride it. There is, however, a respectable school of opinion in both Western Europe and the United States which holds that if the Soviet leaders insist that détente brings with it a sharpening of the international class-struggle, then the West is perfectly within its rights to wheel out nationalism as one of its most persuasive weapons and deploy it in the ideological conflict as a counter to the class-struggle.

BRZEZINSKI: I am not against wheeling out secret weapons, but I am in favour of using weapons we know how to control. What makes me uneasy about the reasoning you quote is that I am not quite clear how we would use the nationalism we have helped to release. Would it be to promote hostility between Rumanians and Hungarians, between Poles and Czechs, between Poles and East Germans, between Poles and Russians? Would we try to pit Ukrainian nationalism against Russia, or that of Central Asia or of the Caucasus? What would we do if our encouragement were successful—as in many cases it probably would be—and national discontent broke out in violence? We could not possibly intervene in the Soviet Union (we haven't been able to do so even in Eastern Europe), and to provoke an uprising but not to support it would be morally reprehensible and politically short-sighted. I am making these caveats not because I am against encouraging greater national awareness, particularly inside the Soviet Union, but because I fear that we are dealing here with an unguided missile: once you have launched it you are not quite sure where it will end up and what effect it will have. I *would* like to see the non-Russian nationalities of the Soviet Union gain greater independence and indeed autonomy because this would be one important step towards the pluralization of Soviet society, but I feel strongly that we have to be extremely careful not to touch off a development which might, once it has acquired momentum, slip out of control and become dangerous even to ourselves. This having been said I would concede that some realistic encouragement of pluralism via nationalism and separatism may be our best answer to the Soviet challenge on the ideological front. It would certainly be within the rules of peaceful co-existence as the Soviet leaders have defined it.

URBAN: One could, of course, not appeal to the nationalism of the *Russian* people because that certainly appears to be inextricably mixed up with the Soviet system. I often wonder whether we are paying enough attention to the sheer Russianness of Soviet Russia. Isn't it true that the Soviet Union is at least as Russian as it is communist—that if the Communist Party of the USSR were chased away tomorrow, our power-problem with Russia would not automatically change for the better, for we would still be facing a very large and probably highly nationalistic super-power?

BRZEZINSKI: I am quite prepared to accept the proposition that a non-Soviet Russia might be a more formidable and more competent rival than a communist Russia. I have, in fact, myself written something to that effect. A strong case can be made for saying that the Soviet experience has been a historical calamity inflicted on an otherwise energetic and gifted people. But what about the future?

It does not follow that what might have been steps in and assumes real life once communism fails or loses its Manichean militancy. My hope would be that, after the disappearance of the communist state, a combination of residual socialism and internationalism would mitigate the power-oriented ambitions of extreme Russian nationalism. Already that nationalism is becoming stronger and is acting in some ways as a substitute for the waning ideology. In that sense there *is* the danger of which you have spoken but I don't think it is predetermined—that if Soviet communism fails, its successor must be militant nationalism. There is, as I say, at least a possibility that something else might emerge, and it has to be our objective to try to promote, no matter how marginally, that more acceptable alternative. I am not predicting that a nationally unmilitant Russia is a likely thing to happen after the demise of Soviet Russia but, thinking of the future to the extent we can, we ought to encourage in the Soviet Union processes that might make a future Russia a responsible partner rather than an adversary. In the interdependent world which is emerging before our eyes this is what the common interests of humanity require.

URBAN: Not many weeks before Nixon's resignation, Secretary Kissinger gave the former President a copy of Spengler's *The Decline of the West*. The ostensible purpose of the gesture was to draw Nixon's attention to Spengler's warning that the modern statesman must have the 'media' on his side or perish.* But I wonder whether that was the whole meaning of Kissinger's gift.

BRZEZINSKI: I don't know what else might have motivated Henry Kissinger to give Spengler's book to Nixon (he could hardly have expected Nixon to make it his bedside reading). I do hope that the title of the book was not the conclusion Kissinger wanted the President to draw, for there can be nothing more debilitating for a statesman than to permit himself to be dominated by a persuasive pessimism, and I trust that Spengler's book is not a key to Kissinger's own thinking. As it has turned out, Spengler was prophetic about Nixon's personal fortunes, for his inability to master his relations with the media cost him dearly.

The Decline of the West has a great deal to say that is relevant to the problems of our time. Not so—or so I like to think—the main thrust of its thesis: if the West is in decline then everything else is in decline too, for there is no-one to take over the management of global problems. If the West falters, the consequences will be world chaos and anarchy. The Soviet Union is strong enough to be America's rival but not strong enough to become America's successor.

Hence (to repeat) there is no alternative to the West and there simply must be no decline of the West.

URBAN: I wonder how Brezhnev would react if Kissinger were to present *him* with a copy of Spengler's book. Brezhnev would have no reason to quarrel with either Spengler's thunders against capitalism and democracy or with his historical determinism aptly expressed in that dark maxim at the very end of his book: *Ducunt fata volentem, nolentem trahunt*—those willing are guided by destiny, those unwillingly are dragged by it.

BRZEZINSKI: Brezhnev would, of course, object to Spengler, but I agree with you that he would have no logical reason to do so, for Spengler's apotheosis of socialism and his cognate criticism of capitalism and democracy—though of right-wing provenance—share a good deal of ground with Marx. What truth there is in Marx and Spengler has long been sifted out by scholarship and integrated in our common stock of knowledge. The rest, and especially their

* The reference is probably to pages 554–56, Vol. II of the 1923 German edition of *Der Untergang des Abendlandes* (C. H. Beck, Munich).

scenarios for the future, is fantasy, and I am very much against fantasy dragging us along a path we do not want to follow, and most assuredly do not have to follow.

FRANÇOIS DUCHÊNE and LEOPOLD LABEDZ

Rival perspectives

URBAN: One of the seemingly unanswerable arguments running through any discussion of détente is paraphrased in the proposition: because, in the nuclear age, the only alternative to co-existence is non-existence, the only alternative to a policy of détente is nuclear war.

The policy implications of such a formulation of the problem, frequently invoked by Henry Kissinger, have not found general acceptance in this series of discussions. Although the calamity of a nuclear confrontation has not been denied, the political wisdom of fashioning the nuclear dilemma into an either/or proposition and presenting it as such to the western public has been severely questioned. Thus, for example, Zbigniew Brzezinski has argued that Kissinger's détente-or-else philosophy is misconceived because 'if you predicate your entire foreign policy on the assumption that any determined [American] move . . . in United States-Soviet relations is fraught with the danger of war, you are, in effect, declaring yourself unequal to the game Moscow is playing'.

The history, the current thrust and the implications of Moscow's policy of 'peaceful co-existence' have, I believe, transpired with reasonable clarity from the preceding conversations, despite the confusion created by the equivocal use of both the word 'détente' and its supposed Soviet equivalent. What interests me at this point is some clarification of the strategy the West is pursuing. If Brzezinski is right—and I am assuming for the sake of argument that he is—why are western responses inadequate? Why are they responses, in the first place, and not initiatives of the sort we were capable of taking even twenty-five years ago? Does our deficiency stem from the difficulty liberal democracies have always experienced in attaining a consensus on foreign policy objectives and, once attained, maintaining the will to pursue them, or is it due to some temporary flaw in the conduct of western foreign policy under its present stewardship? And if the two are inter-related, how does one affect the other?

LABEDZ: The proposition that the type of policy which has

281

been described as détente is inevitable because the alternative is nuclear war is fallacious, and the fallacy springs from two premises. First, the Soviet conception of peaceful co-existence is not only out of step with the western view of détente but is directly opposed to it. Some of the participants of this symposium have amply demonstrated the differences between the two conceptions, therefore I will restrict myself to underlining that in the Soviet view nuclear war and political combat are not irreconcilable policies—choose one and you automatically repudiate the other—but a dilemma resolved by an expedient which recognizes that nuclear war must be avoided while insisting, under the tacit threat of nuclear devastation, that the long-range political and ideological campaign against the West must go on. This, in the Soviet vocabulary, is the meaning of peaceful co-existence. It takes no eagle-eyed analysis to arrive at this interpretation, for the policy is being proclaimed by the Soviet leaders up and down the country, and anyone who chooses to read it can read it. There are many official Soviet statements openly proclaiming that 'peaceful co-existence does not mean anything more than that the inevitable struggle of two opposing systems is confined within non-military bounds' (*Voprosy Filosofii*, No. 2, 1975).

The second premise has to do with the advent of nuclear power. In 1945 the facts of nuclear life were quickly absorbed by the western public. The bomb was rightly perceived as a fundamentally new historical fact which makes war between the nuclear powers no longer a rational means of foreign policy.

Not so (at first) in the Soviet Union. The Soviet leadership tried to resolve the dilemma—a much sharper dilemma than the one Lenin and, until Hiroshima, Stalin, had to face, when the alternative to peaceful co-existence was conventional war—by amending the books. First, during the last years of Stalin, it was enunciated that there would be no nuclear war but the possibility of nuclear war could, nevertheless, not be entirely discounted. Then, starting with Malenkov and leading up to Brezhnev, it gradually became part of the ideological canon that nuclear war equals universal holocaust.

The incorporation into official doctrine of the conclusion that nuclear war also means the devastation of the Soviet Union (which the Soviet leaders knew all along), and not only of the capitalist West, was undoubtedly a step forward. But while the West followed up the same perception by saying: 'As nuclear war is such a terrible danger, we shall renounce the political confrontation, too, because we must avoid a nuclear disaster', the Soviet leaders did no such thing.

They proceeded to incorporate the nuclear factor in their strategy of peaceful co-existence, leaving, however, the Leninist formula of ideological and political combat entirely intact.

The western realization that nuclear war was an unacceptable option seeded a great variety of pacifist movements, of which the British CND was perhaps the most typical. Under the slogan of unilateral disarmament it pressed, in effect, for western capitulation as the sole alternative to a nuclear exchange. I find it a profound historical irony that at a time when the Aldermaston marchers have shrunk to an insignificant group, important western policy makers have implicitly—though never explicitly—accepted the view that the only alternative to nuclear war is the unilateral renunciation of the political struggle, in the same way as military disarmament was conceived by the nuclear disarmers. Moreover, our repudiation of the politico-ideological combat under the portmanteau slogan of détente came at a time when the Soviet doctrine continuously stressed that peaceful co-existence in the age of nuclear weaponry means the sharpening of the political and ideological struggle. I find it a little hard to understand why the West should now accept the premise of the reasoning of the Aldermaston marchers instead of recognizing the premises of the Soviet challenge. The fact that Soviet doctrine explicitly rejects nuclear confrontation should be an additional argument for conducting the political struggle on a reciprocal basis, and that means taking into account the communists' own perception of détente. The latter could hardly be clearer: 'Détente is a political phenomenon with important social and political consequences, and it is also a point of departure in establishing conditions that will permit continued shift in the balance of power. The socialist countries' pursuit of peaceful co-existence has both an international and a class character: it strengthens the position of socialism, it promotes the world revolutionary process.' Thus the Hungarian Communist Party's official journal, *Párttörténeti Közlemények*, in September 1974.

DUCHÊNE: I have difficulty with the assumptions of this discussion if it is to be set exclusively in the framework of Urban's reference to the inadequacy of western responses, and Labedz's reference to the West's renunciation of the political struggle. I find the concentration on the Soviet Union in those remarks excessive at a time when many western preoccupations are elsewhere. One can, of course, say that the very fact they are elsewhere is dangerous, but one cannot ignore, as an aspect of détente, that political attention has partly at least moved away from East-West issues. It is less that our view of the Soviet Union itself has changed; it is much more that other issues have risen to the top which have no clearly articulated relationship to the Soviet Union or East-West politics. In these circumstances, if East-West relations are made the only yardstick of our political priorities, the attitude of the West is bound to appear dispersed, indeed purposeless. But if one no longer thinks of them as the only yardstick, then the burden of proof is on those who claim that it should be.

The Soviet Union is undoubtedly a profound problem, even more so for Western Europe than for the United States. The Soviet Union has very great strength both in terms of its present and potential military power, and in terms of its reserves of raw materials at the threshold of a period in which supplies of raw materials may become a major constraint on the economies of Western Europe and Japan. Also, Soviet policy objectives are extremely uncertain, and here I agree that the Soviet definition of peaceful co-existence casts a great deal of doubt on Soviet purposes. There are also many questions we have to ask ourselves because of the power of the Soviet bureaucracy vis-à-vis Soviet domestic opinion, compared with the weakness of the western establishments vis-à-vis western electorates or lobbies. This is the obvious basis of arguments about the cat waiting to pounce as the mice come out to play in the sun. From Mao to Labedz this is a view many serious people hold, and indeed it deserves to be taken seriously.

But the Soviet Union also has very great weaknesses in a number of fields—ideology, economics, and also something that is more pervasive, which might be called culture. During my recent visit to the Middle East I was struck by the number of young men who have been through American universities and will soon be rising bureaucrats. While these people are not necessarily pro-American, they have acquired operational priorities for their own societies which strikingly bear the trade-mark 'Made in the United States'. This is one of the invisible reasons why the relationship between the Moslem world and the West is growing, even under the strains of the energy crisis.

According to the stress you put on these strengths and weaknesses, you can look at the nuclear détente between the super-powers—and that, after all, is primarily what détente is—in quite different ways. You can see it as a ploy by the Soviet Union to nullify the strategic superiority which America was able to turn to political advantage throughout the 1950s and 1960s, and so be free to exert the political superiority that, if you are a Marxist, you ought to believe the Soviet Union possesses and must exploit. But if you think that this is an old-fashioned view of what the Soviet Union is about, and that the United States is really the country that has, of the two super-powers, the more political potential because of its economic and cultural assets, then détente through nuclear parity between the United States and the Soviet Union has the paradoxical effect of nullifying, or certainly reducing, the major visiting card of the Soviet Union, which is its military strength, and of making the competition move into the area where the United States has its greatest comparative advantage, which is the area of civilian process.

Obviously the issue of détente with the Soviet Union is of immense importance, but my own remarks in this discussion will be set in a different framework from the one assumed so far by Urban and Labedz. I do not think it is self-evident that the Soviet Union is the *légataire universel* of détente. Labedz's characterization of the motives of Kissinger in saying that 'we must go towards détente because we must avoid nuclear confrontation' cannot, without violently caricaturing Kissinger, be assimilated to the slogan, 'Better red than dead', which is itself a caricature of CND policy.

LABEDZ: Kissinger did not just say that 'we must go towards détente because we must avoid nuclear confrontation'. Kissinger and Nixon proclaimed that 'the era of confrontation is over', and although Kissinger is perfectly aware of the character of Soviet policies, he has nevertheless chosen to confuse the public by the whole tenor of his détente arguments. What I was therefore really driving at was not just the formulation of policy, but the perception of policy by the general public in the West. In his formulation of policy Kissinger does, naturally, work with careful qualifications, but when the debate reaches the market place, he falls back on the contention that the ultimate alternative to détente is nuclear destruction. This seems to me to be either a form of moral blackmail or an unserious approach to the dilemma, because if you release this kind of genie from the bottle—if the nuclear danger is said to overshadow all other relevant political considerations—there comes a point where you are left with no choice but to opt for prophylactic capitulation. Your ability to stand up to what is, after all, an aggressive Soviet policy, is then inherently vitiated.

This is new, for at the time of Kennan's containment policy we never heard it officially said that we should pull our political punches for fear of releasing nuclear war. The question was only whether the political struggle should be offensively or defensively conducted; but the sort of false choice that is now put before us: 'You must not protest against Solzhenitsyn's expulsion for you may be risking nuclear war', would have been out of tune not only with any resistance to Soviet pressures, but with the very idea of containment.

President Ford's initial refusal to meet Solzhenitsyn on the advice of Henry Kissinger fits into the picture. We seem to have reached a point where the Soviet Union has a veto on the visitors' list to the White House. The majority of the American press, including the

New York Times, was critical: 'The most eloquent contemporary Russian enemy of dictatorship was snubbed by an occupant of the White House who finds time to receive eminent soccer players and lovely cotton queens', while 'neither Leonid Brezhnev nor any other high Soviet official has ever been known to refuse to receive American Communist Party leaders for fear of upsetting détente'. Indeed, the occasion could not be more indicative. It has shown once again that the official American perception of détente implies the classic pattern of unilateral sensitivity to the attitude of the oppressor, and appeasement at the expense of the oppressed.

To repeat: I am not saying that western policy is a capitulationist policy, but capitulationism is the political psychology it breeds, no matter how carefully the policy is qualified at source.

The mass media inevitably carry the message in over-simplified form, and it makes little difference what semantic reservations Kissinger may make. As George Meany put it in his testimony before the United States Senate Foreign Relations Committee in October 1974: 'Détente [according to Kissinger] is the avoidance of nuclear war. . . . If this is the meaning of détente then . . . what is the difference between détente and Cold War? Isn't Cold War also an avoidance of hot war? . . . This is not what the man in the street thinks is meant by détente. And I contend . . . that this is not how détente was sold to the American people by Mr Nixon and Dr Kissinger.' But it was so presented everywhere.

The fear of war has always been a factor on which dictators tried to play. Hitler did it, and those who wanted to resist him were branded war-mongers; Stalin did it by enlisting western pacifist sentiments through the Stockholm Appeal; Brezhnev does it now with his Programme for Peace in which détente is a formula for Soviet ascendancy without the risk of war.

The verbal obfuscation employed is impressive: those who venture to suggest that 'ideological struggle excluding war' is precisely another phrase for Cold War, and that the Soviet Union should not be permitted to wage it unilaterally, are told that they are the enemies of détente. At the same time Moscow's policy of consolidating and extending Soviet power is presented as an act of peace. Those who inveigh against it are cold warriors.

There is, of course, nothing new about such Soviet dialectical casuistry. What is new is that it is now receiving western support through the assimilation of the Soviet semantics of détente, often at official levels.

Moreover, from the formula 'there is no alternative to détente' follows the need to accommodate Soviet demands unilaterally, if necessary. This is a case of what I would call the 'fallacy of misplaced concreteness', for it is clearly a substitute—and a poor substitute at that—for a rigorous analysis of current Soviet policies against the background of history, and specifically Soviet history.

But the formula provides an overall rationalization for other arguments too. For example, it justifies the duplicity whereby unconcern with the victims of Soviet oppression goes hand in hand with acute sensitivity to Soviet official complaints. It makes it possible to accuse those who do not display this particular combination of attitudes of interfering with the domestic affairs of the Soviet Union, or to raise the spectre of nuclear war as the likely consequence of speaking up for Sakharov.

It also makes it psychologically possible for the same people who raise the alarm at the slightest intimation that the western side may support those oppressed or unjustly treated in the Soviet Union, to be conspicuously silent when Czechoslovakia is invaded, when Moscow incites the Arabs to tighten their oil embargo, or fuels the passions of nationalism and racial hatred in the Middle East.

The 'conceptual breakthrough' of which Henry Kissinger has so often spoken, has indeed been achieved, but it is the Soviet side that has broken through our semantic—and political—defences.

DUCHÊNE: There can never be more than a one-to-one relationship between policy and public psychology relevant to that policy, and I don't think Kissinger's détente philosophy breaks that rule. There is a tendency in industrial society to secrete certain values peculiar to it. Industrialization leads to a better standard of living and this, in our tradition at least, means a much more critical attitude towards the principles and values of states, a criticism based in the last resort on the expectation that they should exhibit the values we assume in our private relationships and the normal conduct of civil business. This involves new domestic and foreign policy problems for the West. An advanced industrial society will be sceptical of any international behaviour that cuts across its domestic values. Treaties, commitments, above all, the traditional notions of national interest and patriotism will be—*are*—questioned. At the same time, radicalism demands more power to the base, not more to the top. This hits western governments hard, but the political magnetism of the Soviet Union even harder. Soviet defensiveness over Basket Three at the European Security Conference, or events in Portugal, show that the Jacobinism of the communists, their assumption that Big Brother knows best and the many know nothing, even in their own interest, is becoming anachronistic— even, and especially, on the Left. In this sense, the Soviet ideological appeal has never been weaker than today.

The Russians, too, have their own domestic problems. From random remarks by apparatchicks I have gained the impression that they are not that sure of their ultimate capacity to discipline and mobilize a deeply anarchic people and, as they industrialize, to keep away the 'corruptions' of the West. They are unsure about the ultimate political strength of the régime. This fear alone, we must recognize, is a potential source of international crises. If the Russians were to drop their security guard in the framework of some international agreement, I have no doubt that Western Europe, with its innate magnetism, would start impinging on the internal Soviet status quo. We would then be faced with a quasi-Czechoslovak type of situation, albeit on a much larger scale. This obviously entails risks, potentially very great ones, but they are not those of one-sided western self-delusion, self-indulgence and collapsed morale.

In general, one must not confuse public talk with state action. Labedz's view of the western posture does not square with the way in which Kissinger has been trying to exploit the situation in the Middle East to the full advantage of the United States. Nor do I think that the conclusion drawn from the case of Solzhenitsyn is correct. On the contrary, the Soviet treatment of Solzhenitsyn, Sakharov and other critics of the regime has been one of the factors which moved German public opinion rapidly to the right after the success of Brandt's *Ostpolitik,* and this, from the Soviet point of view, must be regarded as a serious flaw in Russia's *Westpolitik.* I would go further: one would think that it was the Soviet Union, not the United States, that mined Haiphong Harbour, or instituted the nuclear alert during the 1973 war in the Middle East. It is wrong to suggest that the Soviet Union is simply advancing and the West retreating. If you want metaphors, I offer another: when water pours from a dam, you get disturbances of waves in all directions, so it is very difficult indeed to see how the lake will finally settle.

In a similar vein, I accept that there are risks in over-rating the stability of the super-power military stalemate. But do the weaknesses of western defence policies all arise from the bland assumption that we can go on living our comfortable and quarrelsome domestic lives, ignoring the security problem? Or are western societies inclined, against the advice of their governments and bureaucracies, to put a low priority on defence because they are beginning to sense that the ways in which western governments have defined defence policy are no longer really well-tailored to current problems, and that a perfectly responsible politico-military analysis of the situation could lead to conclusions different from those of Nato's conventional wisdom?

LABEDZ: You said there must be some relationship between

political resources and foreign policy. This is an important point, and we all know that there are constraints on what a foreign minister can do, because he has constantly to look over his shoulder to see how far he can carry the country with him. But I would suggest that this relationship is not a static one, and that one of the functions of leadership is not simply to look at this one-to-one relationship between the reservoir of domestic psychological resources and foreign policy, but to formulate and to present foreign policy to domestic audiences in such a manner that a dynamic foreign policy can be sustained by popular approval. And here I'm afraid the policies initiated by Henry Kissinger have led to an emasculation of the political will of the West.

Of course, in principle, everybody is for détente, but what we are discussing here is not some ideal conception of détente in a games-theory situation, but current détente policies as they impinge on western political psychology. It is quite clear that we have, in this respect, put ourselves at a disadvantage both in relation to earlier western policies such as Kennan's conception of containment and, of course, vis-à-vis the Soviet Union which has not made the mistake of pulling the rug from under its own ideological scaffolding as we have. Optimistic expectations of the positive effects of détente on the human level ended in increased cultural repression in the Soviet Union and Eastern Europe, graphically demonstrated by the exile of the most prominent Soviet dissidents. If western public opinion spontaneously reacts against such reversions of the idea of détente this is hardly a reason to give credit to its architects, as Duchêne suggested in his reference to Solzhenitsyn and *Ostpolitik*. If the German public is disappointed with détente, this is no more a manifestation of its achievements than a similar clamour for a less supine policy in the United States is a proof of Kissinger's effectiveness. A Churchillian reaction cannot be taken as an alibi for a Chamberlainian type of policy.

URBAN: Wouldn't the natural imbalance between a dictatorship's ability to control public opinion and a liberal democracy's virtual inability to do the same explain, to some extent, why the presentation of détente in the West had to be so utterly different from the presentation of détente in the Soviet Union, where it is being simply shown as the latest, and most successful, phase of a continuously triumphant policy of peaceful co-existence?

LABEDZ: We do, of course, know at least since Tocqueville that, in a democracy, the conduct of a consistent foreign policy is one of the most difficult feats of statesmanship. But it would be an over-simplification to say that there is, therefore, no difference between one type of foreign policy and another in a democracy.

Tocqueville's diagnosis of the problem does not absolve us of the responsibility of searching for a more effective foreign policy than the one which has been imposed on us under the well-meaning but poorly-executed philosophy of détente.

DUCHÊNE: Is American foreign policy really as ill-considered and unsuccessful as Labedz is making out? Between 1961 and 1967 American forces in Europe fell by about 130,000 to 140,000 men, basically because they were needed in Vietnam. Since 1967 we have been talking of force reductions under the aegis of détente, but the combat forces of the United States in Europe have been increased while the total strength of the United States has not decreased. Furthermore, Senator Mansfield has not been much in evidence lately with resolutions to pull American troops out of Europe (though he wants to have them reduced in Korea), and Senator Jackson tried to use United States economic bargaining power to squeeze political concessions out of the Soviet side, and very nearly succeeded in doing so. None of this seems to me to indicate that American foreign policy is in the doldrums, despite Indo-China. On the contrary, since the Middle East War of October 1973, the United States Congress has become much more wary of the Soviet Union than it was three or five years ago.

Therefore your doubts about the psychological stamina of the western public seem to me much more relevant to Western Europe, excluding Germany, than to the United States. Why Western Europe—minus Germany—has become softer is related to a whole set of factors of which the détente-mentality is only one: there is the dependence of Europe on the United States for its security, which is an issue in itself now that the Soviet military threat is seen to have receded and United States priorities need not coincide with European priorities; there is the fact that the smaller European powers have enough room for manoeuvre to pursue their own purposes within a larger framework and to some extent have a free ride. Add to these that the German-American cover is, in effect, a cover for France too, and the French take full advantage of it, and add, furthermore, that forest of question-marks which now surrounds Europe's economic situation: the psychological weakness of Western Europe is the combined result of all these factors.

The United States, however, has a large number of advantages vis-à-vis the Soviet Union in bilateral relations. The Soviet Union used to have two visiting cards which it has lost. The first was ideological: it sprang from the feeling that the Soviet Union was in opposition to a system which had dominated the world for the previous hundred years, and often much longer, and built up great antagonisms in just about every non-white country. Moscow was in a position to harness these antagonisms to what seemed to be a global design. But the last twenty-five years have undermined Moscow's ability to exploit them. Soviet military power began to be severely limited by the nuclear factor, and the Soviet leaders had to come to terms with the consideration that the escalation of political conflict, too, is subject to the constraints of nuclear discipline.

Moscow's second visiting card was economic but that visiting card, too, has been lost. The collapse of industrial production in many western countries in the 1930s had created an assumption, which was still a powerful one in the 1940s and 1950s, that the only way to maintain production was through planning, and that a planned economy was inherently more efficient than a market economy. For reasons we need not go into, this belief in planning, and by implication in the Soviet approach to economic growth, has vanished in the intervening years. The fact that capitalist Japan, for example, has been able to have a growth rate much higher than the Soviet Union is devastating for the Soviet Union both economically and ideologically. Whether Moscow will have acquired a new economic visiting card by the 1980s through the mobilization of Soviet raw material resources is another question, but it has none at present.

Thus the United States, which has a political *and* an economic visiting card right across the range, is in a good position to exploit Russia's two great vulnerabilities, namely, that the Soviet Union is no longer the residuary legatee of every resentment created by Europe in the last hundred years, and that it has nothing to pit against American economic power. Therefore, although the strength of Western Europe vis-à-vis the Soviet Union may not be very convincing, the United States has, on the global level, a great structural advantage over the Soviet Union.

LABEDZ: May I ask the time-honoured question: 'If the situation is so good—why is it so bad?'

DUCHÊNE: The answer is simple: human nature abhors a good situation. As soon as things are going well, people strain at the limits and propel themselves into a more difficult situation. Also, I am not so sure the situation is so unrelievedly bad.

LABEDZ: But human nature also abhors complacency—or so it ought! I do not disagree with your analysis of the various factors which limit Soviet foreign policy. The constraints became obvious after the Twentieth Party Congress with the deflation of the Soviet myth, the arrival of polycentrism, the emergence of 'new' nationalism, and the weaknesses of the Soviet economy. However, my argument was not that the Soviets can, like some fairytale giant, implement whatever foreign policy they please—my argument concerned the asymmetry between the effectiveness of western and Soviet foreign policy in exploiting each other's weaknesses. There are, of course, limitations on both sides, but while the Soviet leaders are doing their best to turn their adversaries' weaknesses to good account, we are doing virtually nothing to make intelligent use of Russia's vulnerabilities which are, ultimately, more profound than ours. That is why the situation is far from being a good one for the West.

URBAN: When I raised a similar point with Zbigniew Brzezinski earlier in this series of discussions, his comments were Tocquevillian—rather along the lines which have just failed to satisfy Labedz. Brzezinski said: 'When one speaks of western failure and success one has to bear in mind what the West is and what it is not and cannot be. The West has not been militant for a very long time; it is certainly not Manichean. A group of states which is neither militant, nor Manichean, nor held together by politically institutionalized links, cannot be expected offensively to exploit political opportunities in anything like the same way in which a Manichean system, such as the Soviet, can and does. The basic characteristics of the West are pluralism and defensiveness, and if one accepts the limitations inherent in these, then one can claim that the West has been successful.'

LABEDZ: If one looks at this problem not *sub specie aeternitatis*, arguing that democracy by its nature is non-militant and therefore cannot be expected to support effective policies of survival, but as a pressing problem of our day, then one has very strong grounds for saying that, historically speaking, there has been a serious decline in the western position, and that the West has been culpably complacent about it, just as it was, in the 1930s, culpably complacent about the rise of nazi Germany.

A future historian, looking at the political map of Europe in the second and third quarters of this century, will observe that between 1945 and 1975 the balance has shifted against the West and in favour of the Soviet Union. This is a fundamental fact which Olympian theories may explain but cannot make less damaging or more palatable.

I am concerned here not simply with the military balance, nor simply with the fact that between 1945 and 1949 the Americans had a monopoly of nuclear power and that eventually the Russians caught up with them so that we now have an officially admitted nuclear parity. I am concerned with the effect all this is having on the American political will. If I could see a reassertion of political will in the United States, then I would not be too worried whether there were five or three or two United States divisions in Western Europe.

The purely military argument about the Soviet threat to Western Europe was misleading from the beginning. There was, strictly speaking, no such immediate threat, and Nato was not set up on that assumption. It was organized because we had to have a military card to support our hand in the political conflict with the USSR. The whole purpose of Nato was to make it possible for us not to have to face the choice between nuclear devastation and political capitulation. We obtained the military instrument, but we have failed to learn how to use our political weapons.

Not so the Soviet leaders. They, too, have come to understand that military irresponsibility is ruled out by the nuclear factor, but they are not allowing this to paralyze their political policies. The West has, as I say, never clearly understood the necessity to beat the Soviet system at its own game, that is, politically. It first exaggerated the military threat, conjuring up pictures of Soviet direct military action; when détente was enunciated, the realities of the East-West conflict were belittled, the political struggle was dismissed as a reprehensible legacy of the Cold War, and the western public naturally drew the only conclusion it was likely to draw in the circumstances, namely that we were well set on the way to a modus vivendi with the Soviet Union on the basis of give and take, live and let live. And that, in turn, tied the hands of the western policy makers.

In other words, this policy has been suffering from the beginning from a schizophrenic double impulse: on the one hand it was meant to be realistic, but on the other it induced conditions in which this realism could not be effectively implemented because it created a psychological mood which made any political response to Soviet policy extremely difficult.

As you have given some examples, let me do likewise. Until the late 1960s the unification of Germany was one of the conditions which we said would have to be fulfilled before we came to any long-term arrangement with Moscow. Today, German unification is not even on the agenda. We have, instead, the legitimation of the East German state and of the Soviet domination of Eastern Europe. In Indo-China, after an officially proclaimed 'peace with honour', we have had war and dishonour and the collapse of the United States position. Our situation in the Mediterranean is full of risks. The state of Portugal is not exactly an improvement in Nato's strategic posture, nor is the hostility between Greece and Turkey. I am not saying the Soviet Union will be able to exploit every difficulty we have, but the Russian leaders are trying; we are not.

DUCHÊNE: We are beginning to see some of the deeper differences but also the sources of agreement between us. The differences: as an ardent supporter of European integration, I know how important it is what mental image one carries in one's head, relative to which one is optimistic or pessimistic. It is clear that there is a difference, between Labedz and myself, in our mental images. But there also seems to be a point of convergence in our judgements; we both seem to feel that it matters much less what the Soviet Union is and does, than what our own priorities are, and how we deal with our problems. There is far too much emphasis on what the Soviet Union is aiming at, how well it is doing in various areas, and not enough emphasis on what *our* purposes and attitudes should be.

While there was Cold War, accompanied, on our side, by a great rush for prosperity, the underlying problems of our society expressed in foreign policy decisions tended to be much simplified: the world was Manichean or could easily be so represented. With the relaxation of external tensions, however, the problems of our society are now coming to the fore. Also, we are in the midst of a recession which seems too deeply rooted to disappear rapidly. In other words, there was a period after the war when there was consensus on what needed to be done, but as a reaction to the affluence and ease of the post-war years, that consensus has disappeared.

Since the middle of the 1960s, and especially since 1973, we have, rightly as I think, become less tolerant of certain social evils which persist in our societies—new forces and demands for income redistribution have appeared—and although these, and the sociopolitical tensions they generate, are primarily concentrated in the Mediterranean area, they are also evident elsewhere, and we in Britain are well placed to know something about them. The dramatic eruption of new social aims may also be responsible for the fact that the United States Congress and the American public are, in the 1970s, more concerned with internal problems than external ones. But we also have to contend with an external problem of a new kind. This arises from the world-wide restriction of raw material supplies and the cartelisation of raw material suppliers. This tendency is going to bear harder on the growth of raw material dependent regions, such as Western Europe and Japan, than Russia or the United States, and therefore it will have a more profound impact on Soviet-West European relations than Soviet-American relations, but it will affect the position of the whole of the West.

Yet, we are not on our knees. As soon as a crisis reaches a stage where it might become really damaging to us, western policy reacts with extraordinary flexibility and effectiveness. For example: I am encouraged, not discouraged, by our response to the energy crisis. Certainly it has hastened recession, but our actual reaction to the demands of the oil producers has been to move towards a system of co-operation-through-confrontation which is, strangely enough, analogous to the co-operation-through-confrontation we have at the nuclear level with the Soviet Union. Despite all the appearance of trouble and chaos, the area of dialogue between western countries and non-western countries is increasing faster than the relationship between the Soviet Union and the non-western world. The Soviet leaders are usually talking to people who follow the faith, whereas the West is coming to co-operate with the oil producers who are, after all, most of the Islamic world. On balance, the habit of dialogue implicit in our way of doing things is expanding in the world much more effectively than the operational dogmatism of the Soviet side.

What Labedz says about the decline of the West is certainly true in the sense that we no longer cover the world scene politically: we have to have dialogues with non-western nations. But the expansion of dialogues has been continuous since the 1860s: the Meiji reforms in Japan, the emergence of Germany and Italy as united nations, the Russian Revolution itself, the reappearance of China after the second world war, now the rise of the oil producing nations, with countries like Mexico and Brazil waiting in the wings—all this represents the filling up of the world scene with the actual actors of the world. This seems to me natural. The question is: can we live with the new balance? Will it benefit the Soviet Union at the cost of others? Why should it?

LABEDZ: Our mental images are indeed different. I wish this were not so, for if I could share your mental image, I could also share your presumably optimistic view of the present threats to what is vaguely known as western civilization. When I look at the state of Western Europe, I am struck, not by the flexibility of our policies, nor by the success of our dialogue with emerging countries, but by the question whether Western Europe is at all in a position to survive. I am struck by the fact that Western Europe is neither ready to assert its autonomy, nor to organize its own defence, because it lacks political will. The anodyne you offer—Europe making itself dependent on the goodwill of Sheikh Yamani—does not strike me as reassuring.

But supposing we could come to an accommodation with the oil producers—how reliable would that be? We would still be the prisoners of the will of volatile rulers who do not share our traditions. We may, as you say, well slide into a relationship of interdependence with the Arabs, but in that interdependence Western Europe would be a mere object of history. The Meiji reformers provide a clue to what we may expect. They were perfectly explicit about their intention: 'We want western technology but we will preserve our traditional culture.' The Soviet regime, too, made enormous efforts right from the beginning to assimilate western technology while proving impenetrable to the political culture of the West. Right now, we are, mutatis mutandis, witnessing the Meiji approach to the modernization of China: once again, an eastern country is trying to import western science and technology without also importing that whole, symbiotic cluster of ideas and traditions which makes western civilization into what it is. And that applies to all non-western modernizing countries.

DUCHÊNE: Is that a necessary danger to us?

LABEDZ: It is, because if—as you suggest—we come to live in a state of political and economic interdependence with a large number of countries which are unceasingly getting stronger by using our technological achievements, while remaining hostile to our entire civilization, then I am forced to conclude that our situation is weakening vis-à-vis the rest of the world. The modernization of these countries may mean that they adopt the technology of the West and then use it against the West. Modernization is a universal aspiration, westernization is not. This may be inescapable, but there is advantage in being clear about it.

DUCHÊNE: There is at least one big flaw in your argument: the Japanese fought both on the Anglo-American side, in the first world war, and against the Anglo-American side, in the second. They have been profoundly penetrated by western culture although they have also managed to preserve their own, but on balance they have changed out of all recognition from what the Meiji reformers expected.

Cultural philosophy *à la* Spengler and Toynbee does not explain too much in this context—practical politics do. Gilbert Murray said: people always ally with their neighbour-but-one against their neighbours. Japan and, a fortiori, China are, then, two sources of strength for the West rather than the reverse.

LABEDZ: I am not concerned in this argument with the general question how civilizations interact. My concern is the survival of the West and I know that this is very largely a function of political will. We have seen nations and civilizations survive against all odds and others go down although there was nothing in their situation to pre-destine them for destruction. There is no predetermined pattern in history. I am a follower neither of Spengler, nor of Toynbee.

Whether, after the collapse of Western Europe, the United States will have even much stronger reasons than it has now to court the People's Republic of China (as it well might on Murray's principle), and whether Japan, or any other country among the world's new 'actors', will fit this or that category of westernization, interests me very little as all this will, as I say, happen over our dead bodies. My concern is (and in this, if in little else, I agree with Marx) not just to study history but to try to contribute to determining its direction.

The proximity of one's execution, if we can believe Dr Johnson, concentrates the mind wonderfully; yet I can see precious little evidence that the possibility of the fall of Western Europe is spurring our leaders into anything more intelligent or energetic than economic nationalism and a resolute avoidance of the problem of European security under the misleading slogan of détente.

Thirty years ago we were talking of the survival of Eastern Europe—survival in the sense of avoiding Soviet domination—now, whether we explicitly formulate it like this or not, we are talking about the survival of Western Europe. Such is the measure of our failure.

URBAN: Isn't Marxist political culture also part of the West European tradition? And couldn't one say, in that case, that its survival is well assured throughout the world?

LABEDZ: This is a mischievous formulation, but I would not reject it out of hand. As Marx himself liked to stress, political victors are often absorbed by the civilization of the vanquished if the latter are culturally superior, witness the case of Greece and Rome. Defeated West Europeans would emancipate Soviet-Russian political hegemonists from their cultural inferiority—this, I take it, is Urban's implication. Let me say at once: I don't think the analogy stands. A generalization of this sort assumes that methods of control, including the transformation of psychological attitudes, are unchanging in history. But this is blatantly not so. The tools of psychological control of the twentieth century totalitarian state have been developed to a point where this alleged law can no longer hold, if indeed it ever did, which I would question. Secondly, assuming that this were a correct argument, I do not cherish the idea of several hundreds of years of Soviet domination at the end of which Soviet totalitarianism might, if the theory works, mellow in the glow of western rationalism and liberalism.

The price to be paid for such an experiment would be stupendous; the result, at best, uncertain, at worst—and most probably—disastrous.

DUCHÊNE: Clearly, we do not want to risk the political-cultural regression which Russian rule would mean. It is in part because I do not accept this perspective, that I firmly believe that we need a more integrated Western Europe to ensure a balance between the West and the Soviet Union.

A scenario for Europe

URBAN: So far we have been talking of the decline of Western Europe in rather general terms. Could we now refine our concepts and make them bear on Western Europe's relationship with the Soviet Union and the United States?

DUCHÊNE: Let me, once again, group my ideas around mental images of what appear to me to be our primary problems. The first image one can have is dominated by the Soviet Union. Our emphasis, since the war, on the Soviet menace to Western Europe has been entirely understandable because the Soviet Union is the most primitive political system in Europe. Neither the East Europeans, who have to live with it, nor the West Europeans, who feel threatened by it, have the slightest illusion about the political and cultural consequences of Soviet domination. The Soviet system is primitive even in comparison with the Chinese system because the latter—whatever its constraints, and whatever one's dislike of living in a permanent boarding school—seems infinitely more civilized than the Soviet model.

Hence, contrary to what Marxists would say, the real reason why West Europeans have always rejected Soviet influence has not been economic (although western industrialists on the Right would reject it on that score too), but profoundly political and cultural. To put it quite simply: they have repudiated the system because they want a great deal more personal freedom than the Soviet system would give them. The sort of regime in which state despotism, verging, at the (not infrequent) extreme, on state terror, are normal features of government, has been outlived in Western Europe since the sixteenth and seventeenth centuries and can, therefore, hold few attractions for West Europeans. That image leads to certain emphases which I take it are uppermost in Labedz's mind.

But one can also have another picture. Suppose you think the nuclear standoff between the super-powers has worked, is working, and will work, and that the daily bread and butter of politics will not be dominated by the Soviet relationship, which is, after all, infinitely less intense than the American-European relationship. Then the fear of Soviet domination is going to act, as it has acted, and is acting, as a major factor in giving the United States bargaining power on a whole series of issues vis-à-vis the West European countries which want to maintain American military protection. My second mental image, therefore, is the domination of Europe by the United States.

This is, of course, something much more subtle than the threat of Soviet domination because American society, unlike its Soviet counterpart, is not a primitive and alien political system. It is as diverse and complex as are our own societies, so that one finds contacts and communication between people in America and West European society at every level. Moreover, you may ask: when a government such as the United States Government finds it more and more difficult to control its own population, how can it possibly control the populations of other states? One can ask all kinds of other questions about the reality of the very notion of domination in compatible societies.

LABEDZ: In what sense are we American-dominated?

DUCHÊNE: For instance: it is inconceivable, at the present time, for Western Europe to define an independent defence policy vis-à-vis the Soviet Union.

LABEDZ: Has Europe ever tried?

DUCHÊNE: No, but why has it not tried? The basic reason is that no West European country is prepared to make any moves for fear of disturbing the American relationship—the Germans aren't, the British aren't, the Italians aren't. Nor, really are the French. The difference between France's independence and the other European countries' dependence on the United States is largely histrionic.

The long-term effect of all this is that the European countries are now part of a system of which, at every level, the United States assumes leadership. It is possible that, over time, the United States will, to some extent, abuse that leadership, as Nixon might have done if he had carried through his doctrine of linkages.

But even short of that, when you talk of the lack of political will in Western Europe, the primacy of the relationship with the United States supplies the fundamental explanation. In the long run, this primacy has unfortunate results, for it means, in negotiations for example, that the security of the European-American relationship distorts all other issues, and therefore it becomes virtually impossible for Western Europe to develop an independent political will.

My first image was: how do you protect yourself against the Soviet menace? My second image was: how do you protect yourself from your senior partner when the Soviet menace is probably not primary?

But one can also have a mental image of the European situation in which neither Soviet domination nor, in a completely different way, American domination, provides the main shaping thought. This picture, which is inherently a more optimistic, perhaps a too optimistic, image, is based on the idea that the net effect of American military power has been to create a garden wall which protects Europe from the winds and makes it possible for civilian relationships and politics to flourish. The nuclear standoff is making civilian relationships more and more important, and it is in this area that Europe could and ought to concentrate its ingenuity. This would mean concentrating on the economy, on our relationship with the oil producing countries and, more generally, seeing that Europe remains an attractive alternative to any other social or economic system.

Of the three images I have depicted I would, on balance, plump for the third, though with reservations. If the West Europeans are capable of getting together in order to solve their problems on the civilian level, they may be able to develop and to assert an effective political will. I readily admit that there are a lot of question-marks hanging over my third mental image. For example, which way is Italy going to go if there is such an erosion of the American will that the Communist Party of Italy no longer reacts to Kissinger's threats by saying: 'We are for the Common Market, we are in favour of the maintenance of Nato', etc., and chooses to go back to more orthodox communist perceptions? At the moment, the Italian Communists are in a heterodox position vis-à-vis Moscow, and they probably have far stronger reasons for not wanting to be within the radius of Soviet orthodoxy than you or I. So long as Nato and European unity maintain a framework of magnetism, the Italian Communists will tend to be attracted to it, but if there is an erosion of Nato and the European political system, the Italian Communists will be forced to think in different terms and we will find our internal and external policies moving eastwards.

This, then, is our central problem: making a success of the civilian relationships within the European garden. Though Nato is important, our principal intellectual and material resources must be invested in these civilian relationships.

URBAN: The three points you have made coalesce in the idea of European security. How do they relate to the European security document? Is this, in fact, the insecurity document of the Soviet Union?

LABEDZ: The Security Conference and the document drawn up in Geneva are give-away testimonials of the Soviet need to have Soviet rule legitimized both in Russia and in Eastern Europe. The minority government which has been in power in Moscow since 1917 has never shed its fear that its legitimacy may be built on sand. Its fear for the legitimacy of its rule is even more pronounced in Eastern Europe, where Soviet hegemony arrived at the point of the bayonet, and where profound cultural differences act as natural barriers to any thorough-going Soviet domination. This explains Moscow's repeated attempts to exact recognition from outside, for as long as such recognition is withheld, the Soviet leaders feel they must reckon with the possibility that the East European nations will not give up hope that at some point in the future they will regain their independence; in the meantime, they will deny the communist regime its title to legitimacy. This point is not always recognized in the West.

The birth and loss of legitimacy are slow and uneven and, in many ways, puzzling historical processes (only American behavioural scientists are naïve enough to imagine that cause-and-effect in history are a twenty-four hour affair): the consciousness of legitimacy can seep in and out of a nation's psyche over a period of years, decades or even centuries. Six hundred years of Turkish occupation did not extinguish the Serbian peasants' consciousness of their national identity and of the non-legitimacy of Ottoman rule, and the Russians know this.

I have, therefore, very little time for people who ask: 'But why do the Russians need a piece of paper from us? Why do they come again and again and want our confirmation? Haven't we already conferred on them security of tenure? Can we change the political consequences of the fact that they have twenty-two divisions in East Germany?' Questions of this kind betray a devastating innocence, which is especially prevalent in America and not confined to the uneducated mass of the people.

DUCHÊNE: The Russians do need legitimation. They know well enough that they are not wanted in Eastern Europe, and I should think they are rather pessimistic about their long-term future there. The structural facts between Russia and Eastern Europe contain for the Russians a great many dangers which are, moreover, growing, because Eastern Europe consists of a number of small states which depend economically and culturally on the outside world, and are going to get tied more and more to the outside world, whereas the Soviet Union is relatively well placed to go on pursuing a policy of economic autarky and cultural isolation. At some point these divergent tendencies will disrupt the uneasy symbiosis between the two.

LABEDZ: Western Europe conveys a message to Eastern Europe by its very existence. It makes Soviet insecurity in Eastern Europe permanent and all-pervasive. This, if nothing else, makes it imperative for the Soviet leaders to gain maximum de jure recognition for their hegemony over Eastern Europe, and to do what they can to remove the politico-cultural menace implicit, not in this or that piece of West European policy, but, as I say, in the fact that Western Europe exists. If we were not so influenced by Soviet-Orwellian double-think, we would have called the Security Conference by one of its two proper names—either Soviet Security Conference, or European Insecurity Conference. The two do not mix.

DUCHÊNE: Your emphasis on the impact of Western Europe merely by virtue of the fact that it exists is also the best argument for the maintenance of Nato: it is necessary to stop Russia being tempted to get rid of the 'bone in its throat'.

As to the European Security Conference: the idea was launched by the Russians; it is they who want a substitute peace-treaty to impart a semblance of legitimacy to their domination of Eastern Europe. The West went to the Security Conference only after considerable hesitation, and only because it is, for a democracy, always difficult to say 'no' to people who want to talk to you. But I don't see what interest we have in the Security Conference. We may well want freer contact with Eastern Europe on the cultural and human levels, but we don't need a European Security Conference for that. It may be that a security declaration will make Moscow more hesitant to use force in Eastern Europe, but we will not be able to enforce it. The future of Eastern Europe will continue to be a function of the world balance of power which no security declaration is likely to affect.

URBAN: The Rumanians make no secret of their hope that an all-European security declaration would reinforce their immunity (such as it is) from Soviet attack and interference.

LABEDZ: This is make-believe. It is perfectly clear that the security of Yugoslavia and the relative independence of Rumania are predicated (as Duchêne says) on the balance of power, of which Western Europe is a part, and on nothing else. The Yugoslavs are doing themselves a disservice when they suggest that the West should accept various Soviet proposals (under Basket Four) for a standing conference or some permanent secretariat. This would give the Russians an institutionalized leverage in the West European decision-making machinery without giving the West any leverage in comparable Soviet institutions. If the Yugoslav proposal were translated into reality, Yugoslavia's security would suffer at least as much as our own. Ideological double talk of this kind does not help.

DUCHÊNE: We can be as flexible as we like as long as we know what our interests are. The West has problems of cohesion as an alliance which the Soviet Union naturally does not have. If Russia were allowed to become one of the sponsors of contractual arrangements with us in such a way that she would divide Nato, we might find our whole system undermined.

There is one recent warning example: we have, since 1973, learned to our dismay that even where the initiative is ours, it is often difficult to safeguard our interests. I am referring to the Vienna force-reductions talks which were set in train in response to a western demand: we said we would not go to CSCE unless, parallel with CSCE, progress was made on mutual and balanced force reductions. Well, if various Soviet proposals at the force reductions conference were accepted, our freedom to pursue western military and political interests would at once disappear because the Soviet side would be handed an institutionalized leverage in our affairs. I am dead against introducing lasting arrangements which bring a Soviet voice into the Atlantic Alliance.

URBAN: What you are worried about is the Finlandization of Western Europe under some other name: force-reductions or a standing conference.

DUCHÊNE: I don't see Finlandization as a serious threat. I am struck by the solidarity of the EEC countries, for instance in seeing at the Security Conference that nothing should be agreed that might foreclose their option on common defence. In some ways East-West negotiations have tempered the West European sense of self-interest rather than weakened it. But the more we are frightened of being Finlandized, the more we become psychologically dependent on the United States in order to be protected from Finlandization—and the more we tend to sacrifice what should be our proper aims in negotiating with the United States.

As long as the West as a whole has a firm political purpose and the determination to pursue it, the Soviet Union will continue to assume that the western system works, whatever its internal politics, that the United States protects it and, moreover, that, in the last resort, the West can solve its problems. If we fail to be firm, we give gratuitous points to the Soviet Union, and if we exaggerate the danger of Finlandization, we give gratuitous points to the United States.

LABEDZ: I'm sure you are right about giving the Russians gratuitous points—it will not be the first time we will have done so—but I am not sure how your very original argument can be made to square with your earlier point that Western Europe is under American domination. Your first mental image was: how do we protect ourselves against the Soviet menace? The second: how do we protect ourselves against our senior partner, the United States? You are now saying that the Soviet menace is imaginary if we can keep our house in order, and that we are in fact *inviting* or perpetuating American domination by an exaggerated fear of what the Russians might do to us.

Let me focus on one vital detail: I can see why Federal Germany, with its special non-nuclear status and the delicate issues any massive increase in its armed forces would raise for the intra-European balance, has not taken the initiative to make Western Europe militarily independent, or more independent, from the United States; but whatever has prevented Western Europe from making its own defence arrangements on the basis of Franco-British military cooperation as a first step? If Europe fears Finlandization, this would have been at least a very effective partial answer to it; if Europe fears United States domination, it would have answered that, too. But nothing has been done because Europe lacks political will.

DUCHÊNE: The reason for the failure of France and Britain to come forward with a European defence plan is that the two follow radically different political strategies. The British say: we must follow the Americans in all circumstances; the French say: the American presence is so assured that we can reject American leadership in all circumstances, have a theatrical foreign policy and affirm our Europeanness to the point of dividing Europe and making any European policy entirely impossible. My view is that the only way in which the Europeans can obtain real political leverage on the United States is through the creation of an effective bargaining counter within the Atlantic system—not by denying the American relationship, nor by accepting every American priority as one's own. De Gaulle denied the American relationship to the point where Europe as a cohesive unit was unable to achieve anything at all.

LABEDZ: The implication of what you said in the first leg of your argument—before, that is, you contradicted yourself by shifting the blame for the lack of a European policy to Europe's 'unjustified' fear of Finlandization—is that the Europeans were somehow discouraged by the Americans from organizing themselves into a more effective military instrument. But this was just not so: year after year the Americans have tried to persuade the Europeans that the United States needs a more helpful, and therefore also a militarily and politically more powerful, partner than what Western Europe can offer in its present state.

DUCHÊNE: I am not blaming the Americans; I would be hard put to it to decipher who started the process. All I am claiming is that if we accept that Western Europe lacks political will, it must be very largely ascribed to the fact that Western Europe has not been made to face up to its situation because it could rely on American protection (this is a point Wolf Halsti has argued in this symposium), and there is every sign that it will go on relying on United States protection—

LABEDZ: —meaning that Western Europe will be able to go on affording its own irresponsibilities?

DUCHÊNE: Yes—in the security area Western Europe can afford its irresponsibilities, but the problem today is that the military fact is no longer *ultima ratio regum*—it is only a small part of the total socio-political activity of society. As things are, Western Europe is handicapping its own capacity to act as a coherent unit in the areas where it could be most effective, the civilian areas of economics and diplomacy, by its divisions over military security surrounding attitudes to the United States. Germany and Britain toe the American line too easily, while France is half neutral, and they do not cohere.

One could argue that if Western Europe had coherent economic and political policies but were, at the same time, totally disarmed, it might prove to be a most effective actor on the international scene under the American-Soviet nuclear condominium.

To sum up: the decline of Europe is not the decline of the West as a total civilization. It is decline in a particular political area due to a number of very specific circumstances: that Germany cannot be a nuclear power, that all the smaller powers in Europe are, in effect, traditional neutrals, and that the French and British have been trying to achieve status vis-à-vis all the other European countries and have not been in a communal sense truly European. If you add up these factors, the result is neither a coherent policy, nor anything one could describe as a European political will. Hence my inclination to opt for my third alternative.

LABEDZ: You want us to concentrate on civilian policies under the United States nuclear umbrella and not get too involved in defence. But the fact is that the American umbrella no longer covers the full range of military contingencies, and that, to my mind, is sufficient reason for the Europeans to do something about their defence—not necessarily in the sense of making a total effort, but contributing to American military power to preclude any shift in the political and military balance, should there occur a vacuum in Europe due to the diminution of American power. If, for whatever reason, there is a change in the western posture in Europe, the Europeans should be ready to step into the breach.

DUCHÊNE: If the Europeans want to take real responsibility for their affairs, they must have nuclear weapons, and that means having a German finger on the trigger. In practical terms, this is not a possible policy: for one thing, it would create a first-class crisis in which the Germans would be the first not to wish to be implicated. For another, it is not the direction in which politics are going at the present.

No, I would agree that Europe ought to maintain enough military power to redress the effects of any reduced American presence and to keep the Soviet inhibition out of the political consciousness of Europe when we negotiate with the Soviet leaders. I specifically do not agree with the tendency to think that defence can look after itself and we need not concern ourselves with thinking it through. But for the rest, we should emphasize our civilian capacities, recognizing that our protection under the nuclear standoff gives us a degree of freedom of manoeuvre. Concentration, then, on the civilian elements of influence, without ignoring the military pillar of security, could amount to a coherent policy. This would be my preference.

URBAN: Isn't this a prescription for European neutrality?

DUCHÊNE: I don't see it in that light. Western Europe, which is a politically sophisticated group of countries, could never be neutral towards the Soviet Union because Russia is (as I remarked earlier) a primitive political society. It also relies on military power in a way which would threaten all European states.

The Americans do protect us, but we must contribute something to American protection. We do not have to make a huge military effort in terms of outdated military concepts; it would be enough for us, Americans and Europeans, to arrive at a notion of what constitutes sufficient military security and deploy our political and economic resources coherently in the light of that assessment. A Europe of this kind could be perfectly effective both in a very close, symbiotic relationship with the United States (which is obviously necessary) and in a relationship of slowly increasing political confidence with the Soviet Union.

My Nato policy would be as follows: Nato was created in 1949 and 1950 basically to prevent a communist coup in France and Italy. However, once you have set up a military organization to stop a Soviet invasion, the military take over, and from then on the whole discussion is conducted in terms of a perceived military threat. But I would submit that a Russian invasion is not our real problem and that therefore we should carefully define what constitutes *effective* containment. We must simultaneously accept the fact that our societies, rightly, consider the risk of war to be remote, and, at the same time, build up enough military power of our own to make any exploitation of accidents and political temptations an extremely risky business for the Russians.

Labedz's position and mine are not far apart on this issue.

LABEDZ: What you are saying is that you see no contradiction between defence and deterrence.

DUCHÊNE: I am not saying that. I want to draw a distinction

between the forces we need to keep in active being at a time when war seems remote, and the reserves we would need to mobilize if it becomes clear that a crisis impends. There are problems in this, but the Russians themselves work a similar system.

The basic difficulty is political. The West European nations are deeply and rightly suspicious of the Soviet system, but their suspicion is dormant as long as they have reason to believe that military conflict with the Soviet Union is extremely remote—and I think they are right to think that it is remote. Therefore we have to design a security policy which makes a distinction between what is needed to provide a 'defence-deterrent' in a period when war is remote and acknowledged to be remote, and what is needed if war proves to be within the norm of probability. If we can generate such a dual security policy over the next ten to fifteen years, and if we can generate public confidence in it, then we may soon find ourselves relieved of a large number of excessively defeatist assumptions about Western Europe's situation vis-à-vis the Soviet Union which, in turn, react, as we have seen, on European-American relations. We could, then, start building on our very considerable political and economic assets. Thus, the externalization of the natural propensity of our society to think in civilian terms would not become a weakness; on the contrary—it would become the principal element of a new European buoyancy.

URBAN: You are saying '*if* we can generate public confidence'. But can we?

DUCHÊNE: This is one of the great problems, but I think we can. We have large forces under Nato which we find difficult to maintain, not because they are a tremendous strain on our economies—they are not—but because their justification in the name of an impending Soviet attack strains credibility. We have to get a deployment that corresponds to the psychological balance in people's minds. If we do that, we have European security.

LABEDZ: That, too, would be my hope and prayer, but between prayer and reality there is many a hitch. In other words, I cannot agree with your perspective. It is not enough to say that the western public does not believe that there is an immediate threat of war. Since 1945 there has, to my mind, never been a real threat of war in Europe. If there were occasional scares, they were due to a lack of understanding on our part of the role military power plays in promoting *political* change, and to a lack of understanding of how political ambition can push military postures to the threshold of war without pushing them *over* the threshold of war. I can see no sign that the nature of the game has changed. The dialectical relationship between political power and military power exists, as it did during the Cold War, no matter how many people in the West have been bamboozled into believing that détente has made it go away. The danger of nuclear war, too, exists now as it did in the past. Admittedly, it is remote, and as long as the two sides remain rational, the ultimate weapon will not be put into action; but there cannot be a shadow of a doubt that both sides will go on making political use of their military muscle wherever military preponderance lends itself to be translated into political advantage.

Therefore our problem is not that of persuading the West European public to adopt the sophisticated scenario you have put to us; it is much rather a simple question of whether Europe can regain the moral stamina and political will which it has lost, and without which, incidentally, your schema, too, would have no chance of being put into effect.

We can see in retrospect that all the voluminous discussions, in the late 1950s and early 1960s, about flexible response and limited war were also conducted in a vacuum because they failed to take into account the same characteristics which are also missing from your strategy: the willingness of the European peoples to recognize the dangers facing them, and to shoulder the requisite military burdens without either exaggerating the Soviet threat into a psychologically paralyzing vision of a nuclear holocaust, or posing our situation in such a way that détente and, at the extreme, capitulation appear to be the only cogent alternatives to a nuclear showdown. This is a misleading perspective, and I have already stated why I hold it to be misleading, but let me say it again: the real danger to us stems from military power being used to promote political ends without a shot being fired. Neither the finesses of diplomacy nor abstract scenarios can undo the disadvantage at which we have placed ourselves in this matter. The asymmetry in our positions can only be resolved if Europe is ready to carry its share of the defence burden, but that, in turn, is unlikely to be done unless the European people are clearly told the facts and shown leadership.

Emancipation and the status quo

URBAN: You are both exercised about the formation of political will: Duchêne bases his tightly argued 'civilian' scenario on the assumption that a European political will of sorts exists, whereas Labedz laments the absence of a European will and our consequent inability to respond to Soviet policies with the single-mindedness he thinks they require. I am interested in the process of will-formation. This need not be an abstract question. There may well be no easy answer to it, but let me put it to you all the same: how do we account for a society's morale—high and low—and what is the psychology of will-formation? The wild oscillation of United States morale and will-power on the issue of Vietnam, and the deepening demoralization of British civilian society since the war, are cases in point, although they are not our immediate concern in this conversation.

DUCHÊNE: Labedz and I differ in a manner which is philosophical rather than purely political. He is saying that political will is manifest only if it is conscious, clearly defined, immediately recognizable and readily translatable into power-terms. My position is more differentiated; I feel that political will is rooted in unconscious preferences which cannot be translated into clear, definable political choices operating along a single trajectory, but nevertheless add up to a certain, if you like, 'morale', and it is my impression that this kind of internal fibre does exist in Western Europe. Admittedly, this morale is taking a lot of risks with reality; it does tend to say: 'We prefer our quarrels with each other to any coherent assertion of will even though these quarrels make it impossible for us to maximize our bargaining power vis-à-vis the super-powers.'

Nevertheless, this unformed and badly defined political will can assert itself effectively, and there are precedents for it in history. For example, in the late seventeenth century it was generally assumed that England was a country of anarchy (and so, of course, it was) and France the country of order and future order. Yet, the eighteenth and nineteenth centuries did not exactly confirm that expectation.

Look at Europe's recent behaviour. It has shown considerable flexibility and capacity to react, exemplified, for instance, by our responses to the 1974 energy crisis. Putting aside Britain, which is suffering from severe divisions, the Germans, the Scandinavians, the French and even the Italians have shown impressive resilience.

Our proven capacity to prevent balance of payments strains from affecting relations among industrial countries, and thus to prevent a recurrence of the madness of the 1930s, when international financial policies turned recession into catastrophic slump, though not sufficient in itself, does show that we have learnt some lessons from the past.

We are not as weak as Labedz has made us out to be. In any case, over-emphasis on our demoralization and on the Soviet threat can hamper us, not so much in our relations with the Soviet Union, as with the United States, because our fear of the Soviet Union, outside times of actual crisis, reduces in effect our power to negotiate with the United States.

LABEDZ: Well, your characterization of Europe's behaviour during its greatest crisis since the war as its hour of triumph strains, at any rate, my imagination. The kow-towing of the European countries before the oil blackmail of OPEC is scarcely something to be proud of.

But let me go back to the question Urban has raised: how is political will formed? I will have to match your lack of hubris on this point and answer that I don't know either. But then nobody knows: no historian or sociologist or political philosopher was ever able to analyze the mysterious process of the ebb and flow of morale and the formation of political will. All one can say at the moment—and this is very unsatisfactory—is that it is either there or it isn't.

DUCHÊNE: Often it is merely an expression of a favourable contextual situation.

LABEDZ: It is more complicated than that—frequently political will does not exist in a favourable situation but does in an unfavourable context. No-one can intelligently generalize about this phenomenon.

But Duchêne has just shown us that there is a way of evading the problem by making it appear that one has actually tackled it. His sophisticated, rather Hegelian, design assumes that in the 'unconscious preferences' of the Europeans resides the guarantee of their long-term security. One can, of course, always assert without further evidence that the owl of Minerva flies at dusk, for we don't know when the owl of Minerva flies: if Hegel knew, I don't—that is the difference between his hubris and my lack of it—and so I don't pretend to know the answer to Urban's question. I don't know how political will is created, but I know when it isn't there, and that is—whatever our theories—the present situation in Western Europe.

DUCHÊNE: The psychological problem in Western Europe is that we do not, either collectively or as individual countries, feel that we are in control of our destinies. One may claim that this is not necessarily a bad thing for one's foreign policy. After all, did Holland suffer more between 1815 and 1945 than France or Germany? It had two wars less than they did.

LABEDZ: The perspectives of Vichy France or *La Kermesse Heroique*?*

DUCHÊNE: Well, one might argue that it is precisely because one is anxious to avoid a Vichyesque situation that one wants to behave more like Holland behaved in the last hundred years, and

* A film comedy made in the 1930s, depicting the Spanish occupation of the Netherlands in the seventeenth century as much more bearable and civilized than is allowed in most historical accounts of the time. Its message was that it is better to submit to the invader than to resist him.

less like France or Germany. But I am not arguing for neutralism; I am merely saying that the security argument is a very complex one and that neutralism is a possible position within that argument, although personally I would not take that position. So, the first problem is that Europe is not in charge of its destinies.

LABEDZ: Is any country?

DUCHÊNE: No, but there *are* societies, such as the American at the present time, which feel, rightly or wrongly, that they are in charge of their destinies and can influence others. The Americans think they have (or had until recently) the wind of history in their sails, and they are rather impatient if anybody says otherwise.

LABEDZ: I wonder; it has become difficult to find any American who argues in terms of manifest destiny.

DUCHÊNE: It has, but your American isn't prepared to argue in anybody else's terms either. One does not hear of many Americans in the cultural metropolis of the United States who would pay much attention to perspectives which fall outside the American point of view. There is definitely an intellectual-metropolitan view in the United States today, even if there isn't a philosophy of manifest destiny.

LABEDZ: A combination of arrogance and masochism.

DUCHÊNE: Arrogance—yes, but aren't we all a bit arrogant? Masochism—I don't know.

LABEDZ: Perhaps you have not met as many members of the New York intelligentsia as I have. Their arrogance is compounded by their masochism. As Midge Decter put it in her contribution to a *Commentary* symposium on 'America now—a failure of nerve?':

> The people in whose keeping has been given the social, economic, and political leadership of this society . . . no longer wish to assume the responsibility of defending and cherishing it. They certainly do talk that way; I can't remember when I last heard a millionaire, or a successful journalist, or a well-heeled academic, or even a politician, of the so-called liberal persuasion, say a genuinely kind word about the system that made possible his own considerable elevation in it. But what I would say is that they are spoiled, rotten, and cosmically greedy . . . anything less than an uninterrupted flow of success, accompanied by an uninterrupted round of applause, they call evil. They have, blessed Americans, forgotten what evil is.

DUCHÊNE: There is in America a self-obsession that tends to exclude consideration of the tangential views of third parties, which is, ironically, a sure sign of a metropolitan political culture. Mind you, one can see this phenomenon almost as much in Paris, which is a fossilized metropolitan culture of a century ago, as one can see it in the United States.

LABEDZ: I would quarrel with the word 'metropolitan'. One of the Americans' great impediments is precisely that, in their hour of history, they have been unable to rise above a devastating parochialism.

DUCHÊNE: Everybody is, in a sense, parochial, but some parochial people are listened to by others and become metropolitan as a result, while others think they are listened to but they are not, and that is the case of Paris or London, where the habits of faded great power live on as mere egocentricity.

But to return to Urban's point: my first contention was that the Europeans are no longer in charge of their destinies. My second contention is that Europe is faced with major social, political and, ultimately, metaphysical strains and that these have an impact on foreign policy.

Two hundred years ago ninety per cent of the European population lived on the land in conditions which precluded effective participation in civil society. In the eighteenth century, France, which was, apart from England, the richest country in Europe, had sixteen general famines excluding regional ones. The peasants, to put it mildly, lived an extremely concrete form of life: they starved or survived, but in either case they had a hard row to hoe. At the other end of the spectrum civil society consisted of no more than perhaps ten per cent of the whole of society. This ten per cent, too, although often fragmented into regional élites and far from being uniformly prosperous, lived in a sociologically concrete manner. In other words, both at the bottom end and the top end of society one found homogeneous groups and life-styles. At the bottom, society lived with necessity as a constant constraint, and between the bottom and the top there was hierarchy as the expression of that constraint in human relationships.

Then we come to the modern world where the bottom nine-tenths of society—the pure 'subjects'—officially become citizens (whether or not they *are* citizens is another question) and the constraints of necessity lose a great deal of their force. At the same time society is unified, communications are centralized, there is industrialization, urbanization and so on—in short, the large mass of the people are emancipated. What are society's psychological reactions to emancipation? Everybody has an aspiration to esteem in the eyes of others, or even eternity, and, of course, a lot of these aspirations cannot be fulfilled. There is the notion that everybody else is managing to do the things that you personally, by some extraordinary quirk of fate, are not able to do, that everything you have chosen is everything you have not preferred, and that life is, therefore, a series of ghastly failures. Even in sexual life the aspiration is to be a Don Juan, and you feel deeply frustrated if in the wear and tear of practical living your image of yourself does not match up to that of some contemporary cult figure.

But emancipation and the disaffections flowing from it are common to Western *and* Eastern Europe. In Eastern Europe they are, at the moment, less conspicuous than in our society because the controls at the disposal of the one-party system slow them down or hold them in check, and also because affluence, which is a precondition both of higher expectations and consequently of their frustration, is much more a West European than an East European achievement. But the two tendencies are basically hostile to the Soviet system because they involve individual choice which is, of course, not consonant with the ethos of a regimented polity. I suspect that the explosion of the time-bomb of emancipation is merely delayed in the Soviet Union, but the bomb has not been defused.

In Western Europe and the United States we have already seen a series of revolts both in the name of equality, which is a concrete political goal, and of personal freedoms which are a Dionysiac expression of a society no longer struggling on the breadline. The hierarchical order of society, which we have inherited from the eighteenth and nineteenth centuries, has been challenged, and all authority is under heavy attack.

We can clearly see this in Britain where the revolt against hierarchy has spilled over into a revolt against economic discipline; we can see it in the whole Mediterranean region where people are beginning to emerge, if not into the twentieth century, certainly into the nineteenth; but we can also see it in Germany and the Low Countries where neither British nor Mediterranean conditions apply, and yet there is profound unrest in society. Throughout Europe people have moved into a world of choice where they can think of *deferlement du moi*—where they demand free scope for their personality and imagination. Whether or not this should be rated as a decadent phenomenon, I do not know, but the phenomenon is there, putting great strain on the whole physical and metaphysical structure of western society.

To sum up: we are short of a coherent foreign policy because we lack a conscious political will, and we lack political will because of complex social and psychological reasons which are part of the total development of the culture.

LABEDZ: I have two questions to ask and one comment to make. Would Duchêne consider the possibility that the disruptive forces which are now active in western society pave the way for

Soviet domination?

DUCHÊNE: Yes, I think this is a possibility, but a remote one.

LABEDZ: Would you say that for every western anarchist there waits a communist to take his place when the time comes?

DUCHÊNE: I accept it as a possibility though I don't think it is the most likely one.

LABEDZ: My comment is this: it is perfectly true that western society is undergoing a profound crisis of which the Spenglerian, Toynbee-esque, Dyonisiac components may be a good part of the explanation. *If* so, we are dealing with a long historical process; if *so*, I cannot understand how Duchêne can square his long-term pessimism about the lack of cohesiveness and decision-making potential of western society, with his optimistic assumption that through the tangled web of unconscious psychological processes Europe will, in the near future, generate enough political will to support a security policy of its own. If the first assumption is true, the second cannot be true also. My own inclination is the reverse: short-term pessimism combined with long-term optimism.

DUCHÊNE: My basic position is that I do not know whether the ferment in western society *is* decadence. It certainly is by past standards, but I think part of the situation is that new standards are appearing as personal self-determination spreads from a small class to the mass of society. As for European political will, the major failures in energy, for instance, are partly at least balanced by progress in the Lomé Convention, or common positions on the European Security Conference and Portugal.

URBAN: Duchêne has expanded the argument to the socio-logical and cultural-philosophical fields. Let me keep it there for the moment and suggest that we consider the question of the status quo, but an enlarged, 'envelope' interpretation of it, because it seems to me that any realistic discussion of the status quo must include not only the situation as it is in terms of territory and the military balance but, much more broadly, in terms of opposing social systems too. In other words, it must include the inviolability of the social order as it exists at the present time in Eastern Europe and Western Europe.

But here we run into some difficulty, because whereas the Soviet Union regards the Soviet-East European status quo as sacrosanct both in the territorial sense and in terms of the existing social order, and expects the West so to regard it also, it sees the 'envelope' status quo in the West, and indeed throughout the rest of the world, as eminently subject to change—preordained change which the Soviet state and the world communist movement are pledged to support. Hence 'status quo'—like 'détente'—would seem to mean one thing to us and quite another to the Soviet Union.

LABEDZ: The Soviet notion of the status quo *is* a one-way affair. There is a passage in Khrushchev's memoirs where he says that status quo is the kind of change that leads to the triumph of communism. In the West this Soviet attitude has long been summed up in the sentence: what is mine is mine, what is yours is negotiable. Gromyko reproached Kissinger in 1975 for violating the spirit of détente; he said the American defence budget was incompatible with it. He did not raise the question whether the Soviet rearmament effort, which is now greater than the American, is compatible with détente. Is it not time for the West to ask whether, from Vietnam, through the Middle East, to Portugal, Soviet policy as a whole is compatible with the spirit of détente?

But before going into that: Duchêne holds that the structural change in western society and the structural change in communist society are basically the same kind of transformation, only in the West the process is more articulate because it has had more room in which to develop, whereas in Russia and Eastern Europe it has been hemmed in by the power of the totalitarian state and party. I would tend to be a little more cautious in reducing the two to a common denominator for, at the end of the day, the differences between them strike me as being more significant than their similarities.

The similarities presumably consist of things such as western and Soviet youth sharing a taste for pop music, jeans, sexual permissiveness, the possession of a motor car and other marvels of modern civilization; in other words, they refer to a superficial westernization or embourgeoisement of East European society. The idea, if not the phenomenon, has been with us since the beginning of the Cold War when an American sociologist, David Riesman, suggested that if nylon stockings were dropped over the Soviet Union, Soviet women would be so overwhelmed by this show of western opulence that they would become embourgeoisée; this would then lead to the political transformation of the Soviet system.

Today we have a slightly improved perspective on this problem. A ferment of sorts *has* taken place in Soviet society without the aid of American hosiery: western ways and the expectations of western affluence—though not affluence itself—have slowly percolated into Russia and Eastern Europe, but to infer from this very ambiguous development that social change in Russia and Eastern Europe is in any way comparable with those upheavals which are rocking the West today is, to say the least, a simplistic way of looking at the two phenomena. Twenty odd years after the death of Stalin Soviet society is still a totalitarian system with a command economy and a regimented culture. Such spontaneous social transformation as has managed to break surface is held within strict bounds by the power of the totalitarian machine. There has been no significant weakening of authority.

But what do we see on our side? From Berlin to San Francisco the social ferment has led to the weakening, and often to the dissolution, of authority, and I am, with reservations, prepared to agree with the reasons Duchêne has put forward in explanation of this process. Without, therefore, wanting to deny that *some* of the salient facts underlying the western ferment are analogous with those which tend (if allowed) to trouble Eastern Europe too, I would nevertheless assert that—so far at least—their political repercussions in Eastern Europe have been very different from what they have been in the West. In other words, if the notion of the status quo is interpreted in its broadest sense, as it must be, then it is obvious that the status quo in terms of the structure of existing Soviet society has not changed to anything like the same extent as our own, and consequently the impact of that change on Soviet foreign policy is in no way comparable with the impact which our own social upheavals are having on western foreign policy.

URBAN: I would underline the specificity of the East European, as distinct from the Soviet, form of the social ferment Duchêne has described, for it seems to me that while, for reasons of historical and cultural affinity with the West, the spontaneous thrust of social change is much greater in Eastern Europe than it is in the Soviet Union, it is inhibited, and frequently neutralized, by the Soviet presence. Emancipation, civil rights, workers' participation and so forth all run into the wall of Soviet power, so that the East European combustion assumes a one-dimensional, anti-Soviet, 'national liberation' character, which, insofar as it does not lead to confrontation on the Hungarian or Czechoslovak model, tends to fizzle out.

LABEDZ: I would go even further: some of the East European social revolt (it does not have to assume political colouring) provides a fairly harmless channel which dilutes political resistance to the communist system, for when it runs into the wall of Soviet power, it sees itself confronted by such a desperate perspective that the political message gets dissipated and the movement ends up in some ineffectual, *carpe diem* type of philosophy. To what extent this weakening of the original charge actually happens depends on that indefinable factor we have wrestled with before: morale and political will. If there is political hope (and here foreign broadcasting, for instance, plays an important role) the movement may go in one direction; if political hope is blocked, it peters out in political indifference, faddism, psychodrama and social apathy.

Let me take up one specific example to show that the analogies Duchêne has read into the social situation in the West and East are, in fact, not there. Between 1968 and 1970 we saw in the United States that various student movements, which were entirely non-political in their origins, were suddenly politicized either through self-combustion or some fusion with political movements. The result was political extremism of the Weathermen and Chicago Seven type. In the Soviet Union and Eastern Europe the social ferment has so far moved in the opposite direction: it mostly starts off with a disguised political purpose, but finding itself banging against the wall of the totalitarian state, it ends up in some politically innocuous, individualistic life-philosophy. Why? Because the movement lacks hope and political expectations.

DUCHÊNE: There is undoubtedly a contradiction in the western situation, for what we are in effect saying is that we feel ourselves to be so safe that we can play against the frontiers of safety until we make ourselves insecure—which is, in fact, what we have contrived to achieve. But the Soviet position is equally paradoxical, for if the whole of Western Europe went communist, Moscow would be in a parlous state—it would cease to be the *sanctum sanctorum*. In other words, we are not dealing with conscious political efforts, either in the East or in the West, to exploit situations to calculated advantage. The world is much more chaotic than that. In the West, the limitations on foreign policy stem from the emergence of social and cultural forces for whom the state is no longer a duty, but a service, for the citizen. What ingredients of thought and interests make up the Soviet alloy is less clear to me. In what sense can it be said in the 1970s that the Soviet Union is a revolutionary power? Has it, as the Chinese claim, become 'revisionist' in terms of the actual policies it is pursuing throughout the world? We don't know. Take the Inozemtsev report of 1970 which stated on the one hand that the western world would go on economically expanding, but asserted on the other that this expansion would cause great structural strains which the Soviet Union should exploit. Or take Boris Ponomarev's reference, in 1974, to a 'qualitative shift' in the crisis of capitalism, which raises the prospect of 'radical revolutionary transformation' and greater influence for the western communist parties, and set it against the assurances the Australian Prime Minister was given in January 1975 by Kosygin that industrial chaos in the West was not seen by the Soviet Union as being in its interest. How does one interpret such statements? Do they reflect conflict in the Soviet leadership between those who believe that a benign Soviet image is essential in encouraging Nato to lower its guard and make Europe more amenable to Soviet pressure, and the more militant leaders who have always had misgivings about détente and are, now that their quarry seems almost within reach, straining at the leash?

One is, I believe, on safe ground in making the minimalist claim that the *wilder* expectations of Soviet ideologues have, in the last thirty odd years, certainly been disappointed. For example, it was widely assumed after the war in the Soviet Union that if a Third World country gave up its relationship with the West, it would take one up automatically with the communist East. Well, the Soviet leaders had to learn by hard experience that, although the oil-producers may wreak their will on the West in highly expensive ways, they have no intention of cutting their umbilical ties with the West, whereas with the Soviet Union they can afford to have virtually no relationship at all. Another post-war Soviet expectation was that structural contradictions within western society and the politico-economic rivalries among western nations would lead to the violent collapse of the whole capitalist system.

But what has happened? The western countries have had twenty-five years of unprecedented economic boom and the European Community was created. This, of course, did not fit in with Soviet prognostications, so reasons to account for what could no longer be ignored had to be created *a posteriori*: there was, consequently, a great deal of rationalization in traditional language but, in reality, the ideological defeat was severe.

So, coming back to the present situation: do the Soviet leaders really want Soviet communism to become one of several competing communisms? They already have China on one side being extremely difficult—could they want a communist Western Europe, saddling them with another load of trouble? I can understand that the Russians need to legitimize their position by reference to an ideological antagonist. 'Out there', they may be saying, 'in the West, are our ideological enemies with whom we are in conflict.' But what advantage would the Soviet leaders have at the end of the process? Would a communist Portugal, a neutral Italy, a Britain torn by social upheavals, really suit Moscow's book?

LABEDZ: Duchêne is a philosophical rationalist. He asks: what role does rational calculation play in Soviet decision-making and—more generally—in the dynamics of Soviet policy-formation? But I'm not sure whether one should confine the questioning to so narrow a basis, for no political process, past or present, can be understood merely as an interplay of rational calculations. A large part of the political and social process is always irrational, and the 'normal' thing one observes in history is that it is the *combination* of rational and irrational factors that drives societies into unforeseeable situations, and therefore often into disaster.

My second point, very briefly, is this: Duchêne assumes that the emergence of western communism cannot be in the Soviet interest for it would further divide the world communist movement and add to the problems created by Belgrade and Peking. Supposing, though not admitting, that this were true—it does not at all follow that the expansion of Soviet power would be halted; it would only mean that the Soviet Union would have to brace itself to face new kinds of problems. This it has done in the past, and I have little doubt that it will do so again in the future.

Also, I have heard Duchêne's argument deployed before, especially by American Sovietologists. It was predicted soon after the Twentieth Party Congress—and it has, from time to time, been predicted since—that polycentrism would totally undermine the communist papacy and that consequently the Soviet leaders must be against any further multiplication of communist regimes.

It is certainly true that the spread of polycentrism *may* breed new difficulties for Moscow, but let us not feel too sorry for the Soviet leaders in their predicament—in a certain sense they *want* those difficulties!

They were, of course, always ready to sacrifice the interests of foreign communist parties to the Soviet raison d'état, but it does not follow that communist victories abroad automatically exclude the possibility of such victories coinciding with the Soviet raison d'état. One must also remember that the Communist Party of the Soviet Union is committed to the successes of foreign communist parties in terms of its own legitimacy, and that the communist parties abroad derive strength from Soviet support and may need it even more after they have come to power than they do before it.

In 1962 I published (with Walter Laqueur) the first book on communist polycentrism, so I am aware of its existence, but surely one should keep in mind not only its fissiparous tendency, but also its limitations; not only the divisions between communist parties, but also their common characteristics, such as 'democratic centralism', their need of external support, and their revolutionary mystique. True, their needs of legitimacy may not always coincide, but that does not mean that mutual political interest does not often tend to bring them together, as the case of Cuba and, even more, the case of the genuinely pro-Soviet communist parties, illustrate. I fail to see how a communist victory in Portugal or Italy could be seen as a drawback for the Soviet Union and a hopeful portent for the West, but that is the logical implication of exaggerating the disruptive power of polycentrism. One must realize that even such a revisionist party as the Spanish Communist Party (which condemned the

Soviet invasion of Czechoslovakia in 1968) has made its peace with the Soviet Party. How much more will it need Soviet support in the post-Franco situation?

Third, Duchêne's emphasis on the disillusionments which the Soviet regime has suffered since the war, and the conclusions he draws from them, are not justified. The Soviet leaders, trained as they are in the dialectic, are well used to setbacks and know how to turn them to good account. From the time when Lenin put forward his April Theses, Soviet history has been a long chain of frustrated expectations in terms of the received truths of Marxist ideology. But the defeats were—as Duchêne rightly said—rationalized and the sacred texts amended. This is a feature common to all millenarian movements: when the prophecy has failed, the ideocrats invent reasons to explain why they have failed and why they cannot possibly fail next time.

From Lenin to Brezhnev the Soviet Union has been led by very tough men who were, and are, conscious both of the need to maintain legitimacy and to re-write the canon whenever the situation so demands. After Vietnam, Cambodia, and Laos, I am not unduly hopeful that disillusioned Soviet leaders will go into a sulk and let slip their openings in Western Europe.

Fourth: the status quo, as far as the United States is concerned, is predicated on Henry Kissinger's premise that you create interlocking interests between East and West. Why should these secure the status quo? Because, says Kissinger, the Soviet establishment acquires vested interests in maintaining those elaborate relationships in international trade, technology, culture, and so forth on which it depends for its legitimacy and status. Once, he argues, we have the Soviet élite tied in with these arrangements, it cannot want to upset the status quo by promoting revolutionary change in Western Europe. Well, it is an idea—not, I would have thought, a very good one. It may offer an attractive perspective to those in the West who are anxious to avoid more difficult dilemmas, but I cannot agree with it, and my reasons are these.

Hopes of this kind were first raised very early in Soviet history, in 1921, and were later picked up by people like Otto Bauer, the Austrian socialist. After the war they were revived, *inter alia*, by various American 'Mensheviks', until they have now found expression in the reasoning of Henry Kissinger.

So far at least, the exigencies of the legitimation of Soviet power have always proved much stronger than the hypothesis underlying Kissinger's scenario. The question is: has Soviet behaviour undergone so drastic a change that it would suddenly be reasonable for us to assume that the Soviet élite will, in fact, respond to the Kissingerian device in the manner in which Kissinger expects it to respond?

Personally I can see no new facts that would justify such an inference. Those factors which frustrated earlier hopes are still there, and those which are new are insufficient to make a difference.

There is undoubtedly a greater degree of educational progress in the Soviet Union than there was in 1921 or in the 1930s. There is undoubtedly some discrepancy between the rationale of modernization and innovative technological thinking on the one hand, and the unquestioning acceptance of the rationale of a Byzantine politico-cultural system, on the other. But we know that, from the very beginning, the Soviet Union was facing the same kind of dilemmas and somehow it managed to ride both horns of these dilemmas. Admittedly, from time to time a price had to be paid, especially in tampering with economic planning, but the penalties did not bring about economic catastrophe, much less political upheaval. The interests vested in the preservation of political controls have (as I say) always proved much stronger than those allegedly pushing for social change. Therefore, in the short run, it seems to me unrealistic to bank on Henry Kissinger's perspective.

We cannot, of course, predict what will happen in the long run. It may well be that, at some point, the discrepancies will become unmanageable, and the legitimacy and cohesion of the Soviet system will prove highly fragile. It may well be that a regime which has successfully ridden the dangers of so many decades and maintained its domination over the mass of the population, will collapse the moment the élite has lost the will and ability to govern (here I certainly subscribe to Lenin's analysis of what constitutes a revolutionary situation). We have seen this happen, mutatis mutandis, in Eastern Europe where what one day looked like a formidable Leviathan turned out to be, under the first impact of crisis, very small fish indeed. There are many plausible denouements to the Soviet situation.

What I am arguing, therefore, is that the possibility of establishing what Kissinger calls a 'structure of peace' based on the hope that an intermeshing of self-interests will diffuse the activities of the Soviet establishment and turn that establishment into a guarantor of the status quo, is a very slender hope indeed.

It is a fallacy to imagine that one can have a modern version of the Holy Alliance between status quo powers and another power whose legitimacy is predicated on the *denial* of the status quo. The existence, and therefore also the political will, of the Soviet establishment depend entirely on Soviet legitimacy. The western world is a standing challenge to that legitimacy, therefore the Soviet establishment can have no interest in underwriting the status quo: its real interest is the profitable pursuit of *controlled* tension. This, while it may rule out nuclear war, rules out a fortiori any genuine accommo- dation with the West. To think otherwise is to persist in political judgements of the kind Henry Kissinger has, in the context of Viet- nam, but only *after* Vietnam, himself described as adolescent. Henry Kissinger may be 'systematically acknowledging [his] past mistakes', as Joseph Kraft has put it, but these acknowledgements fall short of admitting that the very premises of his policy were based on an intellectual fallacy.

A question of reciprocity

URBAN: Let me put to you an even more controversial formula- tion of the status quo than the ones we have just discussed. Its most convincing variant is the 'Don't rock the boat' thesis argued, in this symposium, by Claus Kernig. He advances the idea on two levels. On the first, Kernig asserts that we must not rock the boat because we might disturb the bipolar political and military balance, especi- ally through ill-considered cultural exchange; on the second be- cause we might disturb the world's ecological balance.

On the first point Kernig says:

> Our system today is centred on two poles, the United States and Russia, and the stability we enjoy is entirely due to the interplay between these two principal powers. Change the power or nature of one and you have destabilized the world system. . . . We have, as members of a precariously balanced world system, an interest in the preservation of stability in the Soviet Union. To pose the question of cultural exchange in isolation from this overriding necessity is to divert our attention from the real issue. In so far as cultural exchange might undermine the stability of the Soviet system, or even destroy it, we have no interest in promoting cultu- ral exchange, for we would, in fact, be promoting the destruction of the world balance of power. So we have a vested interest in the stabilization of the Soviet regime.
> . . . our own security is intimately connected with the interests of the Soviet leaders . . . we would risk our own security if we tried to foist a completely unrestrained kind of cultural exchange on the Soviet Government.

Kernig's second point takes the question of the status quo on much wider ground. He asks: 'Is it more important for the survival of humanity to accelerate political change in Russia and Eastern Europe than to maintain the equilibrium of the world eco-system and the world's present balance of power?' And his answer is 'no'.

We must deal with the world as a single system and subordinate to it all parochial considerations of power, nation, ideology, race, class and religion.

Kernig's technical reason for advising against precipitate change is that we have no reliable knowledge of how social systems work. We can muster a certain amount of predictive knowledge about homogeneous systems such as a business corporation, but, he argues, our present state of sophistication does not permit us to make predictive statements about anything as multivariant and complex as an entire social system, much less about relationships among social systems.

DUCHÊNE: If you want to start changing somebody else's regime, you must also want the consequences of what you are undertaking. Given the military power and despotic character of the Soviet regime, and seeing that in East Berlin in 1953, in Hungary in 1956 and Czechoslovakia in 1968 we respected our side of the post-war bargain and did nothing to interfere with the Soviet domination of Eastern Europe, I don't think it is very likely that we would want to, or that we could, shift the Soviet Union by means which go against the considered views of the Soviet leadership. That is also the lesson of the failure of the Jackson Amendment, and my feeling is that the West's inability to move the Soviets directly is also going to be reflected in the position the West will ultimately adopt on Basket Three, despite protestations to the contrary. Our only hope of making headway with the Soviet Union is by changing the context.

Kernig's contention that we must not change the equation, for there is no telling where change may land us, does not hold water. Change happens anyway: there can be no frozen stability between the United States and the USSR. For example, the Soviet side of the equation will undergo serious change in the coming years by virtue of the fact—and I spoke about this earlier in another context—that while the Soviet Union is one of the world's major raw materials producers and is virtually self-sufficient, Eastern Europe is going to need the international market. Therefore, unless the Soviet Union takes certain measures to forestall a heavy reorientation of the East European economy—and, knowing the Soviet way of doing things, these measures would be centralized on Moscow and thus create tensions in themselves—the Soviet Union and Eastern Europe will, under the pressure of outside events, have to part company in many important ways: Eastern Europe will have to get onto the world market, face the raw materials situation, inflation, competition and so on. In other words, the kind of strains that preceded 1968 may become evident again. All this, rather than any direct move on our part, might destabilize the eastern end of the present equilibrium and thereby the equilibrium itself.

One element that lends substance to Kernig's thesis is the fear of nuclear confrontation between the United States and the USSR. This is a powerfully limiting factor. It rules out inter-state war and circumscribes marginal instabilities in the political field.

But if that is the case, how do we change the context—how do we break the log-jam? If we are successful in creating an alternative model of society powerful enough to change people's minds, including people's minds in the Soviet and East European élites, then we have made a start in changing the context. Personally, I would have no compunction about setting in train provocative policies if these promised to serve our purpose, but I just do not think they would get us anywhere.

LABEDZ: Duchêne is right in saying that Kernig's argument is erroneous because, whether or not we want to introduce change into the East-West equilibrium, it is going to happen anyway. But quite apart from that, Kernig's theory reflects—I fear rather accurately—a refined form of self-destructiveness that has taken hold of a lot of people in the West, for what he says in plain English is that it is in the *western* interest to safeguard the totalitarian Soviet system from change, whereas the Soviet side never ceases telling us that *its* purpose is to change—not, of course, the internal status quo in Russia or in Eastern Europe, but that in the West. The irony is that the Soviet stance is a good deal more realistic than Kernig's construct, for undoubtedly there can be no stasis between the two sides; undoubtedly there will be change both in the external and internal status quo; and undoubtedly one side will get the better of the other in the political conflict for change. The question is: which side?

The second premise of Kernig's thesis is that the preservation of the world's socio-ecological stability must take precedence over all other considerations—political, military, economic and cultural. But if that is so, then his plea for the preservation of the political status quo is nonsensical. Why? Fifty per cent of the world's raw materials are consumed at present by the United States with a population of 240 million. Pending a reliable global sociological theory—which we shall probably never have—Kernig wants to put a moratorium on any attempt to change the world's present constellation in terms of power and social systems. At the same time, he denies any intention of wishing to keep the underdeveloped states poor, that is to say, to freeze their status as low consumers of the world's resources. If so, a country like China, with its ambitious programme of industrialization—which is the cornerstone of any communist system, and thus an essential component of the status quo expressed in terms of social and political systems—is bound to have a significant effect on the world's eco-balance. And when you consider that the Chinese population stands at 800 million in 1975, and is still growing, the disturbance which China alone will generate in the world's eco-system is bound to be extremely radical. In short: you cannot preserve the eco-balance and the world's political status quo at the same time. It's one *or* the other.

DUCHÊNE: It is the same fallacy as claiming that Japan is a status quo power.

LABEDZ: I'm afraid Kernig's conservative thesis is as utopian in its way as are some of the radical fantasies on the revolutionary Left. One can't perpetuate the status quo either ecologically or in terms of the political and military balance. The Soviet Union suffers from no such misapprehension. Its insistence that nuclear war must be avoided, goes (as we have seen) hand in hand with the insistence that the politico-ideological struggle goes on. And so it does, even if some of us in the West choose not to see it.

DUCHÊNE: The psychological impulse that makes us reject Kernig's thesis is a gut-reaction to the Soviet Union's institutionalized interference in our internal affairs through the communist parties. 'Let us do something', we tend to say, 'to balance the books with the Soviet Union.'

Sometimes this impulse takes a mild, almost neutral form: our attitude (we argue) is against all power politics, so let us try to civilianize relations between the communist and western societies by instilling into both a sense of those peaceful, 'suburban' values which dominate our cities from San Francisco to Vienna.

At other times our reactions take a more militant form. We then feel we must bargain from a position of strength because strength is the only language the Russians understand. This is what one might call the attitude of 'containment-plus'; it amounts to a feeling that if the Soviet Union is trying to change the West under the slogan of peaceful co-existence because it is (as the Russians tell us) the duty of the man on the side of history to promote such change, then the West must answer that interference with interference of its own.

There are two things that have to be said on the second reaction. One is that the Soviet Union has become very careful not to involve itself as a state in any overt support of communist parties in Western Europe. The Russians have traditionally backed communist parties, or dropped them, as Soviet interests required, and this policy is unlikely to change unless West European radicalism results—possibly as a consequence of a prolonged recession—in creating situations favourable to orthodox communist parties. But because of the democratic nature of western radical attitudes, I think successful meddling is unlikely.

The second point that has to be made is that it is very difficult for us to do to the Russians what they are doing to us in anything like the same manner. We are at a disadvantage because we are a democratic, pluralistic society. We are, to be sure, constantly tempted to *wish* to undo this disadvantage, but there is in fact very little we can do about it except, as I said before, change the context of the game.

LABEDZ: The western approach to the context suffers from a curious confusion of identities: we regard ourselves as both players and umpires in the contest to change the context. With one half of ourselves we are party to the conflict, but with the other we take a very elevated attitude, thinking that we can hand down just solutions because we have superior wisdom and authority and stand outside the conflict. These two attitudes, whatever historical explanations there may be for their co-existence (and the 'umpire-complex' is an offshoot of traditional concepts of western hegemony and cultural superiority), are incompatible and very damaging to our interests as an active party to the conflict.

Changing the context means, among other things, pitting our own political and conceptual framework against that of the Soviet side and assuming it to be universal. But we can't do that if we look upon ourselves as half player, half referee.

DUCHÊNE: The Soviet Union is much too powerful militarily and in other fields—in which our own societies are not powerful—for us to say: 'We are going to impose upon you changes that you are adamant you do not wish to have.' That was the policy of 1968.

LABEDZ: It wasn't to my knowledge.

DUCHÊNE: That was the policy of 1968. It *was* an 'aggressive' policy; it was not *intended* to be aggressive—though I yet have to find a Russian who would believe that it was not so intended—but there *was* a conviction on our side that through Czechs, Poles and Hungarians, who were more like ourselves in the sense of being heirs to political libertarianism, and were, in 1968, reviving elements of the market economy, we could achieve some loosening up—first in Eastern Europe and then in the Soviet Union itself. Not very surprisingly, the Soviet leaders got the message just as we did, and used force to reimpose Soviet rule on Czechoslovakia.

The lesson of 1968 is that we must induce change by a little sunlight—not by blowing too hot too soon. Of course, as I have just said, we are, as pluralistic societies, in a very difficult situation; our responses cannot be properly orchestrated, and therefore we are leaving ourselves open to indirect Soviet interference through the communist parties and in many other ways too, whereas the Soviet system is rigid and has no comparable chinks in its armour, though it has others.

What, then, can we do to balance the books? I'm afraid I have to revert back to a point I have made earlier and insist that we must concentrate on dealing with our own problems effectively. Once we have a society that can look after its social and economic problems, offering a prosperous as well as a morally and intellectually attractive alternative to the Soviet system, half the battle is won, because political leverage is a by-product of a vigorous society.

Even now, our socio-economic superiority over the Soviet system is, despite the hard knocks we have received, manifest. Take, for example, the case of Egypt: after Suez the Egyptians turned to the Soviet Union because Russia seemed an alternative power-base in Egypt's conflict with western imperialism. At the time it was not unreasonable to expect that this relationship would develop—and it did for a time, but not for long. Why? Apart from its misconceived diplomacy in relation to Israel, the Soviet Union had no economic resources to deal with Egypt's pressing problems. It's trump card was a military card, and this could not be used beyond certain limits for fear of creating an unwanted major conflagration. For all these reasons Egypt had to turn back to the United States. It wasn't that the United States was pursuing an active policy vis-à-vis Egypt from a position of overwhelming strength—it was the great economic weakness of the Soviet Union and its inability to change its tack from confrontation to a more adaptable and more sophisticated stance that sent the Egyptians back, or at least partly back, into the American embrace. The September 1975 settlement between Israel and Egypt under exclusively American auspices underlines my point.

We have, therefore, great possibilities for changing the context in which East-West relations are conducted. We *can* make the Soviet regime less powerful in its capacity to influence the world politically without making it less powerful militarily. In the last decades of the twentieth century it would be a great mistake to see a necessary equation between military power and political power.

LABEDZ: I am beginning to wonder whether my agreement with Duchêne goes beyond our shared criticism of the hypothesis of Claus Kernig. I do, of course, agree with Duchêne that we must take care of our internal problems, but it seems to me there is a certain residue of unspoken disagreement between us about how best to deal with the Soviet Union. Duchêne is saying that Soviet society is monolithic while ours is not, and that therefore the communist system has certain levers to unseat us while we have no comparable levers to unseat it. Hence, he argues, we are at an innate disadvantage in any attempt to balance the books with the Soviet Union.

What we can do is to revitalize western democracy but, in the meantime, we might as well give up any idea of establishing reciprocity in our political contest with Moscow.

But it is, to my mind, not the case that we have no leverage with the Soviet Union. The fact that the Russians are strenuously rejecting the free flow of people and ideas as embodied in Basket Three, and that, for example, they want to have television broadcasting by satellite internationally outlawed even before the technology for it has been developed, show how extremely vulnerable they are as far as the internal legitimacy and stability of their system are concerned, and Duchêne himself has acknowledged that the Soviet leaders are worried about the consistency and cohesiveness of their regime. And while I am not saying that free cultural contacts would at one stroke change the nature of the Soviet system, nor that the end-result of an evolutionary or revolutionary development in the Soviet Union would be entirely what we would expect, I *am* insisting that there is a decisive difference between encouraging those elements inside the Soviet Union who are vitally interested in changing the system, and abandoning them, as I take it we would have to, if we accepted Duchêne's strategy.

At the moment, we are incapacitated, and I am not unduly interested how we rationalize this self-imposed impotence—whether we excuse ourselves by saying that the liberal democracies have *no* spoons to sup with the devil, or whether we resort to the argument that the exigencies of the world's eco-balance impose total immobilism on our political relations with the Soviet Union.

Moreover, it is erroneous to delineate, as Duchêne appears to have done, the two systems as being entirely separate. The two do, and will continue to, interact on many levels. It is a *Soviet* ambition that there should be no interaction—witness the Soviet insistence at CSCE that each side should respect the other's 'laws, customs and traditions', which is a euphemism for *cuius regio eius religio*—but *our* job is to encourage and make the most intelligent use of interaction, and not take our hats saying: 'Ah, but if you don't *want* it, of course we shall not insist.'

Also, any acceptance by our side of *cuius regio eius religio* harbours additional dangers for us. The phrase comes from the Treaty of Westphalia which ended a long period of religious wars in Europe, diffusing the passions of the time by vesting supreme religious authority in the temporal ruler of each realm, so that religious interference by Protestants in Catholic lands, and Catholics in Protestant lands, was ruled out.

I notice the idea is discussed by Richard Pipes in his contribution to this symposium, but I submit that he uses it in a misleading context, for his case is that just as Catholics and Protestants hammered out, under the Treaty of Westphalia, a mode of peaceful co-existence, so can we have entirely normal state-to-state relations with the communist world without in any way jeopardizing our respective 'ideologies'. The parallel would only stand—in so far as any historical analogy does—if we had comparable dogma and comparable authority on both sides—communists one, liberal democracies another. But this isn't so. If *cuius regio eius religio*—that is to say: the Soviet rider on 'laws, customs and traditions'—were to be accepted, we would further endorse communist legitimacy in Russia and Eastern Europe by specifically underlining that the Soviet bloc is a doctrinal whole over which Moscow has unlimited ideological as well as 'temporal' authority. At the same time our own benefits would be precisely nil because a pluralistic system has no ruling ideology and thus no means with which to exploit the formula suggested by the Treaty of Westphalia. If we want to encourage gradual evolution away from dogma in the Soviet Union, *cuius regio eius religio* is not the principle I would use to do it.

It is not that I would doubt that, other things being equal, a pluralistic, flexible, liberal system such as ours would, in the long term, win any competition with a rigid, totalitarian system such as the Soviet system, but other things are not remaining equal, and we have to think very seriously of the possibility that the crisis of authority in western societies may, in the short run, so undermine faith in the legitimacy and viability of our system that the long-term competition will never take place. On that score, too, it does not make sense to me to think of the Treaty of Westphalia as offering a valid analogy.

DUCHÊNE: It is clear that if the western system lost internal legitimacy, then the sense in which we see ourselves as a society capable of competing with Soviet dogma and orthodoxy would collapse; one cannot base foreign policy on a system which has disintegrated from within. Assuming for a moment that this did happen and our system fell apart into various forms of totalitarianism—for that is undoubtedly what would happen—I am not at all sure that the Russians would relish the prospect, if, that is, Soviet ambitions can be assessed in terms of the *avowed* aims of Soviet ideology, and that, of course, is to some extent begging the question. I fail to see what the Soviet Union would stand to gain if, for example, the United States collapsed into a radically right-wing authoritarianism. I would have thought Stalin's costly miscalculations with Hitler and the German Social Democrats would have taught Moscow a lesson.

But let us assume there is no such collapse of western legitimacy; our problem then is: will the East-West relationship consist of two juxtaposed but non-communicating systems, or will it consist of two reciprocating systems. Reciprocal relations are going to become necessary for a whole series of reasons: we will be inter-dependent with the Soviet Union for food, raw materials, the exploitation of the resources of the ocean, the husbandry of global energy reserves, population, pollution, weather control and many other problems. I suspect that our political quarrels will become, not so much irrelevant, as a diminishing part of the daily preoccupations of the leaderships of major states. The old problems will slowly sink into the ground and will be covered over by new geological strata. Our relationship with the Soviet Union will, then, be conducted on the grid provided by these new problems—the game between us will be codified in increasingly non-political terms.

LABEDZ: There is nothing more political than making decisions about seemingly non-political issues.

DUCHÊNE: I agree—very often the political factor defines how you reach an agreement or don't reach an agreement. But it is also, and increasingly, true that the *kind* of problem you have to deal with defines the relationship. After all, the nuclear fact has profoundly changed the relationship between the two leading states and has played a large part in the conflict between Russia and China.

LABEDZ: The nuclear factor is *sui generis*; we have two recent examples—the Rome food conference and the Bucharest population conference—where two of your allegedly global problems were at once politicized or strenuously belittled by the Soviet Union and China.

DUCHÊNE: Over the years there will be areas, such as energy and minerals, where the Soviet Union will be in a relatively strong position vis-à-vis the United States; there will be others, notably food, where the Soviet Union will be in a relatively weak position. But these strengths and weaknesses will not lend themselves to exploitation—they are going to act rather like nuclear weapons: they will be so heavy with consequences that neither power will take the risk of allowing them to get out of hand. All this will happen very slowly—but don't forget that the Treaty of Westphalia, too, was only the belated codification of the spirit of the Peace of Augsburg which preceded it by almost a hundred years.

I would also submit that the East-West and even the North-South frameworks which dominate our thinking at the present will prove entirely inadequate to define the real network of interests. To take one example: 96 out of 122 of the Third World countries are—contrary to popular belief—not significant exporters of raw materials—that is 75 per cent, which makes nonsense of the North-South division. So there will be a completely different map of world-interests and power, based on reciprocity—cagey reciprocity at first, especially with the Soviet Union, which is not a transparent system, but (one can at least assume as a working hypothesis) more trusting reciprocity later, dictated by mutual interest.

LABEDZ: Once again, I must bring this argument down to earth and invite you to consider, not how the game may be codified in the year 2075, but how the world's powers actually behave in given situations and what we can infer for the future from their behaviour. We know—as I've already briefly mentioned—that at the Bucharest conference on demography, the Soviet and other communist representatives brutally politicized the whole problem of population-control in the Third World. Population control, they said, was an imperialist plot: the western nations wanted to stop the coloured races from multiplying.

We know perfectly well that in two or three decades mankind will be faced with the extremely serious problem of over-population and under-nourishment even if present plans for increasing world food production and curbing the fertility curve are successfully carried out. If not, the population bomb will hit us sooner and with much greater force. Yet the communist countries show no hesitation in using this terrifying problem as political and ideological ammunition; witness also their attitude to the Rome food conference where, by politicizing the issue of food production, the Soviet delegates simply avoided discussing it on its merits.

Of course, the Russians should really keep quiet about food production: as the Soviet Union has never been able to solve its own food problem, it is not in a very strong position to advise under-developed countries how to solve theirs. Russia, having been the world's greatest exporter of grain before the 1917 Revolution, has become an importer of food—and an exporter of military hard-ware—sixty years after the Revolution. This is hardly a perspective that would commend itself to hungry underdeveloped nations, though their appetite for guns is never to be underestimated. The irony is that although the Soviet Union has never been an exporter of grain from its domestic production to the Third World, and although it was the United States and Canada which have done the bulk of exporting grain both to the USSR and other food-deficient countries such as India, the United States did not only not reap any political harvest from its low-priced (and partly free) exports to the Third World, but was actually manipulated into a position where it could be *blamed* for its food shipments. The Soviet Union, which never attempted to help the Third World with food, has managed to maintain its image as a well-wisher.

I would conclude from all this that it takes two to codify the rules of the game, and that one side is just not playing the game. Judging by Soviet behaviour, Duchêne's prognostication that global issues, such as food and population, will imperceptibly forge reciprocal and less and less politically-loaded relationships between the West and the communist countries, seems to me highly unconvincing.

DUCHÊNE: A certain codification has already taken place, though the process is extremely slow. Reciprocation began with the thaw in 1953, which was the first political issue of the nuclear factor. In 1955 Bulganin, Khrushchev and Eisenhower went to the Atoms for Peace Conference in Geneva; there then ensued a quarrel between the Russians and the Chinese on the Soviet-American nuclear duopoly, and from that point on we have been moving, with great ups and downs—Cuba being the furthest pole in the opposite direction—to a more systematic codification of our relationship, with SALT I, the conference on force reductions, the Security Conference, SALT II and the Vladivostok agreement marking the principal stages of its development. Over the years, a number of new issues—economic, political, ecological—are bound to arise, each of which would, in the process of being tackled, add an element to the codification.

LABEDZ: You have sketched out a certain codification of the game since the death of Stalin, but I fail to see what the West has got out of it in terms of reciprocity. What I do see is the continuation of the old game, and the western side losing out in the old framework. The Soviet Union, when it goes to the conference table, does not spend half its time behaving like some self-appointed appeal judge adjudicating in the name of humanity—it goes in with a political purpose and uses everything at hand to drive home its purpose. I am not saying that the United States is not thinking in terms of the East-West competition—it is—but the United States side is inhibited by this umpire-admixture from taking full political advantage of western strengths, Soviet weaknesses or some combination of the two.

We are also suffering from an intellectual disadvantage. The Anglo-American tradition, which is empirical and non-ideological, has always tended to reduce our differences with the Soviet Union to technical questions. This is debilitating in itself for it neutralizes *ab initio* some eminently non-neutral issues, giving the Soviet side a head-start in negotiations. But it is also very naïve, for it frequently takes the form of a sophisticated but politically castrated analysis of some problem that goes, in reality, to the heart of fundamental political issues: the United States side would then try to convince the Russians that the political issue facing them is, in fact, a complex *technical* question, and that it is as much in the Soviet as in the western interest to look upon it as some accidental road-block which both parties must take a hand in removing if they want to travel along the same road.

Of course, the Soviet negotiators will not be lectured by us. They are perfectly aware of the technical aspects of our differences, but they also know how best to approach them in their own interests. One could see this non-meeting of intellectual traditions at work—greatly to our disadvantage—at the SALT I negotiations in Helsinki, where the American case was consistently handicapped by a negotiating and research tradition which prevented the United States negotiators from making up their minds whether they were playing the Soviet Union or playing at being Solomon. Richard Pipes has given a good summary of the American predicament in this matter in his contribution to this symposium, so I will say no more about it.

I can see no advance towards codification, slow or fast; what I can see is a creeping anaesthesia and the shrinking of our estate. To be specific: until recently the rule of the game was said to be the one laid down at Yalta—there was an invisible demarcation line between East and West which both sides were supposed to respect. In East Germany in 1953, Hungary in 1956 and Czechoslovakia in 1968, the West stuck to the rules of the game, depriving itself of leverage vis-à-vis the Soviet Union. Not so the Russians—in 1962 we had Cuba; now we have Portugal and other incursions across the demarcation line: gradually even this—allegedly real and binding—element of the Yalta agreement is dropped through the memory-hole and we are forced to swallow and indeed to legitimize now this, now that gain by the Soviet Union.

We have gone to the Security Conference which can be of no conceivable advantage to us; we have allowed the whole South-eastern flank of Nato to fall into disarray; in Portugal we are tolerating what may become, in effect, a Soviet grip on a vital sector of our defence system and an ominous political example; the four-power agreement on the control of Berlin is being eroded by faits accomplis in East Berlin and by Soviet diplomatic statements questioning its continuing validity; internally we have not only failed to exploit the collapse of the communist myth after Khrushchev's denunciation of Stalin—a political windfall if there has ever been one—but we are witnessing the political position of the western communist parties and of their ideological allies getting stronger and indeed directly menacing.

In short: reciprocity must be based on quid pro quo, and the quid pro quo must be political. If we give something to the Soviet Union, we must be perfectly clear that we get something in return. The Soviet Union reserves the right of total control and armed intervention in Eastern Europe, yet when Soviet power transgresses into other territories, the world resounds with the slogan of 'non-intervention'. In other words, there is a double standard built into the Soviet negotiating posture, and unless we explicitly reject, rather than implicitly accept, that double standard, new rules of the game will never be established—we will simply go on accepting the Soviet codification of the game as the yardstick for western political behaviour, and that spells defeat.

DUCHÊNE: I take your point that there must be a quid pro quo, but the question is: in what can we actually get reciprocity? Let me look at the leverage we appear to have by virtue of the Soviet need of western economic assistance, especially technology.

It is no doubt true that Soviet industrial productivity is very low, that the Soviet leaders have great difficulty in getting the population simply to work effectively (a problem we ought to know one or two things about in Britain), and that the defence sector is a great drain on Soviet physical and organizational resources. Nevertheless, the rate of Soviet economic growth *is* quite impressive; therefore I wonder whether technological transfers from the West will *go on* being considered by the Soviet leaders as the means of solving their problems, for the Soviet Union's real problems seem to me inherent in the kind of system it is rather than the state of its technology at any given moment.

The Soviet Union does need certain things from the West: food from the United States spasmodically, and technology from the United States, Germany and Japan.

But then the problem immediately arises: who wants what? For instance, we might be able to get a long-term raw materials agreement with the USSR, but such an agreement would be wanted by the West European countries much more than the United States— yet it is the United States that has the technological and economic bargaining power much more than the Europeans.

Are there other things we might get? I would not rule out the possibility of linking technological assistance with common ceilings for Nato and the Warsaw Pact forces.

Should we not insist on a common credit system? But here one comes up against the problem that it is the westerners themselves who are competing with each other to provide Moscow with cheap credits and the Russians are just playing on our disunity.

LABEDZ: I would stress one point: we must have absolutely no inhibition in asking for political concessions as a condition for technological co-operation.

DUCHÊNE: The Jackson Amendment has shown the limits of trying to force political concessions on the Soviet Union in exchange for technology. Nevertheless we should see what we can get for it.

What is the kind of reciprocity we can envisage? There are two kinds: the first regards every item in the East-West problematique as ultimately political: you work in package-deals across the whole range, and technology is part of the package. But there is also another kind of reciprocity (and I have already hinted at it), exemplified in the nuclear relationship. This relationship is not best looked at in terms of who gets the most out of it; its most important result is the constraint it puts on both parties. It has changed the quality of the game, which is more important than anything we might write down, in algebraic form, as the quantity of advantages accruing to one party or the other. The character of the East-West relationship is being changed for us by developments which neither principal protagonist can wholly control, and by which they have, in fact, been conditioned, separately and together. This, too, is reciprocity and, I would have thought, in the long run a more helpful kind of reciprocity than reciprocity by package-deals.

LABEDZ: I cannot match your passion for political futurology. *I* am talking of the situation as it is—abstractions and fine nuances about what may happen in a wholly unforeseeable set of conditions leave me slightly unconcerned.

It seems to me that reciprocity means, first and foremost, putting political pressure on the Soviet Union because that is the sort of game the Soviet leaders clearly understand. If we press them, they will be most unlikely to be able to put matching pressure on us— hence on this or that, possibly small, political issue, we are going to win marginally. But these small gains are extremely important because their cumulative effect determines the historical direction of the conflict. However, if we do not stand up for our principles, if we do not apply pressure as pressure is being applied on us, we will, sooner or later, be forced to our knees.

For example: we should not be too concerned whether or not Basket Three is to the liking of the Soviet leaders. We can leave that to the judgment of history. *Of course* it isn't to the Soviet leaders' liking; of course it might, logically speaking, undermine Soviet legitimacy; but in practice it will, at best, make a very small dent because the Soviet state is well able to take care of itself and control the flow of people and ideas. Nevertheless it is, for the reasons I have just stated, extremely important that we should insist on the letter and the spirit of Basket Three and not go along with anything that threatens to dilute them. It is not our business to worry about the survival of Soviet legitimacy.

DUCHÊNE: Our two interpretations of reciprocity reflect two western attitudes. Labedz is saying: 'We must do what we can to inscribe the priorities of *our* political system as they impinge directly on the Soviet system.' If, he argues, the Soviet leaders don't like it and refuse to sign Basket Three, for example, he would not be terribly upset: 'O.K.', he would tell them, 'in that case *we* will sign no European security document.' Now I would myself, as I've said, not be deeply disturbed if nothing came of the Security Conference, for I don't believe that it is going to change history, but I would not care to create a diplomatic crisis out of a Soviet non-acceptance of Basket Three. This is, for the Russians, an extremely sensitive issue. Our uncompromising insistence on it would be analogous to the Soviet leaders openly declaring that they were going to give vast credits to the French and Italian Communist Parties. That would go to the nervous centre of our system—Basket Three does to theirs.

But I would submit that the whole question of western leverage on the Soviet Union is more complex than Labedz has suggested. If we endorse Soviet positions, we renounce the leverage we should have; if, on the other hand, we insist too much on our own vision, we get no agreement at all, witness the Jackson Amendment. But if our political leverage on Russia is to have a fulcrum from which it can be exerted, there have to be inter-relations. One has to tread a narrow path between supine acceptance of the Soviet point of view and failure to interact.

Labedz would be talking to the Russians in terms of a positive policy, demanding one-to-one reciprocity in the whole range of relationships, whereas I would be more likely to say: 'Let's look at our own priorities, what *we* care about primarily, and build up a practice of reciprocity with the Soviet Union item by item as our separate interests produce issues on which we need to reach particular agreements.'

Admittedly, my view does not promise to have a rapid impact on the Soviet Union (nor, for that matter, does Labedz's). It may, indeed, have a smaller influence than the one which western culture and western societies would normally have on the Soviet system. But that is another reason for thinking that our principal problem is not our relationship with the Soviet Union, but, to repeat, our relationship with ourselves.

LABEDZ: I am a little uneasy about your priorities—they smack of moral rearmament, or perhaps political disarmament. *Of course*, on an abstract plane, we would all agree that the health, stamina, vitality of our system are highly desirable. But is so fine an abstraction not, in fact, an evasion of the real problem? I remember the argument used by Bertrand Russell in a book he wrote before the war (*The Road to Peace*) in advancing the idea of what was then known as 'integral pacifism': the peace of the world, he said, depended not on how we behaved vis-à-vis Hitler, but what we did ourselves in relation to India.

DUCHÊNE: I am not arguing from a pacifist position, and the Soviet Union is very far from being a pacifist power.

I would sum up our differences—and those of many Europeans and Americans who study these problems—in this: your fear is that, unless we match every piece of Soviet stratagem by one of our own, every move in the political or economic or ideological field with comparable counter-thrusts of our own, we will eventually grow so overpoweringly conscious of our own weaknesses and of the strengths of the Soviet Union that we will, as the Finns have had to do, abdicate our freedom to pursue an independent foreign policy.

I readily admit that, if the West disintegrates, the Soviet Union will be the beneficiary of it—there might be Finlandization. But it is at least as likely that we shall continue to have a super-power condominium in Europe, with the Soviet Union permanently in control of Eastern Europe, and the United States exerting a dominating influence in Western Europe. In this situation Western Europe could attempt to exploit its assets to terminate the threat of Finlandization by the Soviet Union, and also the possibility of anaesthesia by the United States. I know it is fashionable to be extremely pessimistic about the capacity of Western Europe to do any such thing. Both in America and in the European Commission in Brussels there is a tendency to write off West European collective initiatives. And yet, I repeat, the foreign policy positions which the Community countries have been taking since 1974, though embryonic, auger well for the future. And if I am wrong, it is not Russia but Atlanticism which will gain.

'Deaf-mutes'?

URBAN: Towards the end of 1920 or early in 1921 (the precise date has yet to be established) Lenin dictated his by now famous Memorandum on the tactics to be followed by the Bolsheviks when dealing with the capitalist world:

As the result of my own direct observation during the years I spent in emigration I must confess that the so-called cultured strata of Western Europe and America are incapable of understanding either the present position of things or the real state of relative power. These strata should be regarded as deaf-mutes, and our behaviour towards them should be based on this assumption. Revolution never develops along a straight line or by uninterrupted growth, but forms a series of spurts and retreats, attacks and lulls, during which the power of revolution grows stronger and prepares for the final victory . . . taking into account the long process which the growth of the world socialist revolution involves, it is necessary to resort to special manouevres which can speed up our victory over the capitalist countries: (a) To announce, in order to pacify the deaf-mutes the separation (fictitious!) of our government and government organs (the council of people's commissars etc.) from the Party and the Politburo, and especially the Comintern. The latter must be declared to be independent political groupings tolerated on the territory of the Soviet Socialist Republics. The deaf-mutes will believe this. (b) To express our wish to establish immediately diplomatic relations with the capitalist countries, on the basis of complete non-interference in their internal affairs. The deaf-mutes will believe us again. They will even be delighted and will open their doors wide to us, and through these doors will speedily enter the emissaries of the Comintern and of our Party investigations organs in the guise of diplomatic, cultural and trade representatives. Speaking the truth is a petty, bourgeois prejudice. A lie, on the other hand, is often justified by the ends. The capitalists of the whole world and their governments will shut their eyes to the kind of activities on our side that I have referred to, and will in this manner become not only deaf-mutes but blind as well. They will open up credits for us, which will serve us for the purpose of supporting communist parties in their countries. They will supply us with the materials and technology which we lack and will restore our military industry, which we need for our future victorious attacks upon our suppliers. In other words, they will work hard in order to prepare their own suicide.

These observations of Lenin were echoed at the time by other Bolshevik leaders—by Kamenev, at the Tenth Party Congress (15 March 1921)*, and in Chicherin's correspondence with Lenin

* 'The capitalist countries are at present more powerful than we are economically; they have more engines, more equipment, and a better organization, and they know how to manage their economy better than we do. . . . However, we are now in a position to prevent them from forcing us to give in to their strength. How can we do this?. . . While developing our natural resources, can we save and develop our economy without the help of foreign capital? . . . Our answer is no . . . we cannot develop it fast enough to prevent the capitalist countries from overtaking us, unless we call in foreign capital. We must realize this clearly: . . .

before the 1922 Genoa Conference. Is it legitimate, sixty years after the Bolshevik Revolution—at a time of détente—to think of Lenin's Memorandum as being still relevant to the policies of a mighty Soviet state which is no longer surrounded by hostile countries but has, on the contrary, advanced from 'revolutionary defeatism' to revolutionary expansionism and nuclear parity with the United States?

LABEDZ: I know it is not very fashionable to answer your question in the affirmative, so, to avoid being labelled a Neanderthal type of a cold warrior, let me explain why I think Lenin's words still apply. Obviously a great deal has changed since 1921. Obviously the Bolshevik Revolution has fossilized; obviously the ideology has become a ritual; obviously the Soviet Union is no longer the sole carrier of the sacred burden for there are many other states which also carry it.

But, with that said, the fact remains that Soviet speechifying along the lines of the Lenin Memorandum continues unabated. I could put before you a hundred quotations which explain the Soviet Union's current détente policies—both for consumption within the communist parties and for public consumption in countries where the communists are in power—in the same kind of terms as Lenin used when he first laid down a policy of temporary accommodation with capitalism. But, invariably, when one produces such quotations, there is disbelief—'The Russians can't possibly mean it'—so the question we have to answer here is: by what criteria can we dispassionately assess the relevance, or lack of relevance, of such statements to current Soviet practice?

It seems to me that the onus of proof is on those who do not believe that the Russians mean what they say. It is they who will have to find cogent evidence that the Soviet view of political reality—which is a Manichean view of reality—has fundamentally changed since 1921. It is they who will have to show that the Soviet leaders no longer believe that the children of light are called upon by the ineluctable will of history to do certain unpleasant things to the children of darkness. It is they who will have to convince us that the

---

In developing our natural wealth, we cannot receive help from foreign capital unless we pay for it. We shall have to pay a tribute. . . .

But we are convinced that the foreign capitalists, who will be obliged to work on the terms we offer them, will dig their own grave. Without them we cannot rearm ourselves (economically); this is the dialectic of history. But while strengthening Soviet Russia . . . foreign capital will fulfil the role Marx predicted for it when he said that capital was digging its own grave. With every additional shovel of coal, with every load of oil that we in Russia obtain through the help of foreign technique, capital will be digging its own grave.'

Soviet notion of peaceful co-existence is, in fact, identical with that modus vivendi, with that elimination of military, political and ideological tensions, which the western public associates with the word détente.

Soviet political behaviour belies all this. The fact is that the Soviet use of the word peaceful co-existence is no mere ritual lip service. It is one outward expression of a built-in perception of the world, and a means of impressing that perception of the world on others. That peaceful co-existence equals political struggle in the Soviet vocabulary is attested by our daily experience. If it did mean détente in the western sense, one would be hard put to it to explain Soviet political actions in Vietnam, Cuba, Chile, Portugal, and all the other evidence of Soviet-supported subversion of the western positions. Only the politically naïve believed that détente would motivate the Soviet Union to help the United States find some accommodation on Vietnam, the Middle East, or Portugal.

It has been argued that although the ritual is retained as a gesture of ideological rectitude, the gap between Soviet words and deeds is growing: the Soviet establishment, it is said, needs an outside antagonist to hone its militancy and endorse its legitimacy, but the militancy is purely verbal. I can see no sign that there is truth in any such supposition. The Manichean view and practice have not been abandoned; whatever the mix of intentions and emotions of the decision-makers behind the walls of the Kremlin, Soviet foreign policy continues to be governed by the principle that in the ongoing conflict between us and them, between capitalism and socialism, socialism will be triumphant, and that it is the Soviet Union's business to bring the triumph about with all means short of nuclear war.

Hence I retain my scepticism and my historically grounded view of the Cold War, past and present. The Soviet leaders have not turned their backs on Lenin's Memorandum.

DUCHÊNE: All revolutions begin with absolutist expressions and expectations of victory—they would not be revolutions if they did not. It is true of Christianity, of Islam, of Calvinism, of the French revolutionaries, and it is also true of the communists who have carried the methods of eschatology much further than others to give them a pseudo-scientific air. Undoubtedly, ideology continues to be part of the psychology of the Soviet Union. Undoubtedly, the Soviet Union is also a great military power which, for the lack of other assets, tends to emphasize the military component in political relations. Undoubtedly, there are enough elements of militancy in the conduct of Soviet affairs to justify extreme caution when dealing with the Soviet Union.

But I wonder if some of these judgements aren't too categorical. In some ways the Soviet Union has a less predatory record in its foreign policy than Tsarist Russia had; for example, Iran has been very vulnerable to Soviet attack and interference, but has not been interfered with since the surprising withdrawal of 1946.

Then, in a totally different context, I wonder whether there is not a certain element—ignored by us because we are anxious—of what one might call civilianization of motive in the Soviet Union, the beginnings of limited liberalism. I am not saying it is dominant; I am not saying it allows us to be less vigilant, but it does seem to me that though Sakharov (to take one example) is right outside the Soviet system, he has come from inside it, and one can, perhaps, more generally, sense a new, though embryonic, liberalism in certain sections of Soviet society. I don't know what weight to ascribe to it, but it does seem to me that one cannot entirely dismiss it as one variable in the détente equation. I realize that it may be dangerous to count on it—and it is one of the great drawbacks of the Soviet system that its opacity does not allow us to detect how important such a departure might be—but I also think it would be a pity to waste opportunities that arose from developments of this kind.

I repeat, we must proceed with caution when dealing with the Soviet Union; but this is precisely what our policy of containment since the war has been doing. We have, in fact, been telling the Russians: 'We shall be using a number of policies, including our determination to resist Soviet aggression as one—though not the only one—of our major instruments, in order to change Soviet revolutionary expectations into the relative expectations of other societies.' Containment has been successful to the point where we are entering a period when, precisely as a logical extension of containment, there is greater contact between the two sides: ideological expectations are low and there are discussions about the nuclear factor, security, trade and culture. I readily admit that the passage from two non-communicating systems to two reciprocal systems is a very difficult one, for the Soviet position is highly ambiguous. In other words, we are very much in the first stage of fashioning confrontation into reciprocity.

In the meantime, I can see no sign that we have been dropping our guard gratuitously or otherwise. Since negotiations have got under way with the Soviet Union, both the western public and the western bureaucracies have become more cautious, not less. The force reductions talks have led to more cohesion among the western governments than there had been among them before there was any talk of having force reductions; and on Basket Three, it is the European neutrals who are making most of the running.

What I am saying is that our new contacts with the Soviet side are being conducted in a climate of sober realism. It would be a great mistake to think of us as a bunch of innocents or political idiots who have been manipulated into a game of chess with a much better player. We are no deaf-mutes.

LABEDZ: If you are right and our policy is really conducted in a 'climate of sober realism', why, I wonder, does this climate still produce so many deaf-mutes?

DUCHÊNE: Whether or not the Soviet leaders echo in their pronouncements the tactics which Lenin laid down for them in his 1921 Memorandum—and, indeed, whether or not they are actually trying to implement Lenin's strategy—the changing facts of the world make it difficult for me to believe that, in the last quarter of the twentieth century, Lenin's Memorandum can possibly serve as a guide to Soviet action. It certainly does not explain the expansion of Soviet power in the second and third quarters.

The Soviet advance in Eastern Europe was due to the failure of Hitler's war with the Soviet Union, not to the success of Lenin's subversive tactics. Indeed, the Leninist tactics had led to the defeat of the German communists and the triumph of the nazis in 1933. Outside Eastern Europe the striking thing is how relatively little the Soviets have encroached on the world. In Latin America, East Asia, Africa, certainly in the Moslem world, the expectations of Soviet hegemony have patently declined since the mid-1960s. Even in countries with which the Russians have signed treaties of friendship and alliance, such as Iraq, there has been an erosion and, in the case of Egypt, a collapse of their influence. On the other hand, everywhere there has been a growth of nationalism, for which there is no provision in communist ideology, and it is a moot point whether Mao's victory is a triumph for communism or a defeat for the Soviet Union.

The tendency to see the energy crisis as a Soviet-directed conspiracy to destroy the West is another dangerous over-simplification. Of course, if the energy shortage were greatly to inhibit Europe's future growth, Europe would be much weakened vis-à-vis both the Soviet Union, which has abundant energy and raw materials resources, and the United States which can, if it wishes, be self-sufficient in energy, too. But the solution of this problem lies first and foremost in Europe's relations with the oil producers themselves, not the Soviet Union.

Nor would I blame the Soviet Union for the growth of European radicalism, or see the Soviet Union as the automatic beneficiary of European radicalism. Even in Portugal it will be a very new military regime indeed if it finally proves to play Moscow's game rather than a nationalist one of its own. In both Britain and Italy the demands for democratic expression come from so many diverse quarters that we are clearly facing developments much more complex than a straight communist-capitalist, East-West competition.

I do not wish to be misunderstood here. I am not saying that the Soviet Union poses no problems, and that every time we look at the debit side of the account we can ignore the East-West dimension. But Soviet ideology and political militancy can hardly account for our debit. In the decades to come the Soviet Union is quite likely to gain more from its position as a great raw materials producer than from its ideology, its military power, or its ties with communist parties in the non-Soviet world.

Perspective is important. It would be possible to paint a picture of the United States, with its economic power, cultural influence and unique position as the bread basket of the world, which would make the United States look just as overbearing and potentially aggressive as the Soviet Union is often depicted to be. We must not under-rate, but also not exaggerate, Soviet power; we must not exaggerate, but also not under-estimate, the positive aspects of the balance between the super-powers.

Finally, political will. What has happened in the West is not that our suspicions of the Soviet Union have disappeared, but rather that the relative success of containment has allowed other priorities to claim more of our attention. We may be taking risks with the Soviet Union in permitting this to happen, and in view of the power and uncertain motives of the Soviet leadership, we have to be extremely wary; but this is very different from perceiving a multi-dimensional world from the one-dimensional and, really, simple-minded perspective of East-West détente. The world has become polycentric in its preoccupations as well as in its power-structure.

URBAN: We have, in this symposium, repeatedly raised the question whether a declaration on European security would make any difference either to the present state of East-West relations, or to the internal status quo in Eastern Europe or Western Europe. The Helsinki document is now behind us. I will not ask you whether you think this has been a major step in the development of détente, for clearly neither of you feels that it has. I am, rather, curious to know in what way the Soviet and western sides are likely to harness the Helsinki document to their particular political strategies.

The interpretation of the masterly ambiguities written into the document is manifestly important. Barely two weeks after Helsinki, Brezhnev told a group of visiting US congressmen that different parts of the document required different interpretations. He said the inviolability of frontiers and non-interference in internal affairs were 'points of a binding nature', whereas those contained in Basket Three were subject to further agreements.

On Portugal, too, we have seen some surprising exegeses. Within three weeks of Helsinki, *Pravda* commented that the EEC countries' decision to postpone considering (until the autumn of 1975) whether to offer economic aid to the communist-dominated Portuguese Government was 'to interfere directly in the internal affairs of the Portuguese'. 'Is it not time', *Pravda* asked, 'to begin fulfilling the obligations undertaken by the representatives of the western powers at the conference in Helsinki concerning non-interference in the internal affairs of other people?'

LABEDZ: I am not sure that, from the western point of view, the ambiguities of the Helsinki declaration are as masterly as Urban has indicated. They are more likely to rebound against the West than against the East. Basket Three, which was the main western concern, is no more specific than the Universal Declaration of Human Rights, and can be no more effectively invoked. I am sure that Brezhnev would have readily signed the Ten Commandments if no specific clauses were to be attached to them on how exactly they must be expressed in concrete policies. The main Soviet concern—western confirmation of the existing frontiers of the Soviet empire—is also somewhat ambiguously formulated but easier to interpret as conferring international legitimacy on Soviet political and territorial expansion since the second world war. Solzhenitsyn called it the final betrayal of Eastern Europe by the West.

The western powers tried to limit the damage by stressing the importance of freer communications, but by putting on paper how little they were prepared to accept, they have also implicitly stated how much the Soviet side will be allowed to get away with. Also, the American apologetics of the Helsinki document would—if their logic were to be taken seriously—lead to some strange conclusions. For example, Ford assured the American public that the Helsinki document does not imply the recognition by the USA of the incorporation of the Baltic states in the USSR. But what then does it mean? The answer that it confers 'only' moral but not legal recognition amounts to saying that aggression is acceptable morally but not legally—which is like refusing to condone rape in law, while condoning it in morality. This is neither good ethics, nor good jurisprudence. Is it good politics?

Urban has rightly mentioned that almost immediately after signing the Helsinki declaration, Brezhnev applied to the document the usual Soviet double standard by announcing that some of its points, which he likes, are binding, while others, which he dislikes, are not. Historically, this is just another example of the Soviet interpretation of 'peaceful co-existence': you must grant *us* freedom on *your* principles—we will deny *you* freedom on *our* principles; *you* must not interfere in Eastern Europe—*we* will have a free hand in Western Europe; 'arithmetic majorities' apply to missiles but not to elections, and so on.

Nor is there anything unexpected in *Pravda's* invoking the Helsinki declaration in support of communism in Portugal. What amazes me are the reactions of those supposedly shrewd western politicians and publicists who, unmindful of the political experiences of recent history, still hope (or say they hope) that the Soviet Union will somehow conform to *their* interpretation of the Helsinki declaration. There is no excuse for such naïvety, self-induced or real.

Whatever uncertainties about Soviet behaviour after Helsinki some western observers may entertain, the fundamental question in the late 1970s and 1980s will be exactly the same as it was after Yalta: what opportunities will Moscow be permitted to exploit? Unless there is a general re-evaluation of our foreign policy, that is to say, unless our foreign policy stops being a record of unilateral western concessions to the rising Soviet power and an open-ended promise of more to come, the pseudo-détente which led up to Helsinki will eventually lead to the Finlandization of Western Europe as surely as Yalta resulted in the satellitization of Eastern Europe.

Should this happen, however gradually, the United States would find itself an isolated island in a hostile world in which the present problems of American foreign policy would retrospectively seem insignificant compared with the new international realities. But there is still time to regain at least some of our political will and to reassess the policy perspective which led, under the slogan of détente, to the Paris agreement, the Helsinki declaration and the Middle East arrangement between Israel and Egypt. Of these three achievements of Henry Kissinger we already know the result of the first. There is little doubt in my mind that, unless the western (and in particular American) public realizes that diplomacy is not a substitute for politics, that resistance to totalitarianism cannot be achieved without willingness to pay the necessary price for it, that there is no easy or painless way out of our contemporary predicaments, the other two agreements would prove to be as hollow as did the first. The western public has been rightly sceptical about official optimism, but unless its inchoate anxiety is given appropriate political leadership no realistic alternative to the present drift can emerge.

DUCHÊNE: I believe Helsinki has changed very little. I suspect that everyone—the Soviet Union, the United States, and the West

Europeans—have discreetly dabbled in the internal Portuguese struggle, though as a matter of course such interference can only be documented in retrospect. There could hardly be a more flagrant contrast with clauses of the Helsinki agreement enshrining non-interference in the internal affairs of countries, at the very time that the document was being signed. Declarations of this general character hardly ever have much effect on deep-rooted political processes. They may, and in the case of the Helsinki document it probably does, punctuate changes that have already occurred. But they do not make them occur; they are not the political process itself. The ambiguities built into the Helsinki instrument are relatively unimportant except as evidence that, after two years of hard work, the two sides were unable to settle for unequivocal formulations even though the declaration moves in very broad generalities and is non-binding. This tells its own tale.

Helsinki will be used for propaganda, and it is precisely because it can be shown to vindicate almost any policy, as well as its opposite, that it is an ecumenical instrument for propaganda. But I do not believe that it will in any other respect make a great difference, for instance, to a crisis in Yugoslavia. It might have had a more substantive impact on the political process had Basket Three been more far reaching. But—apart from withholding western agreement to respect Soviet 'laws, customs and traditions', as the Russians first demanded—Basket Three is far from being remotely radical; and because Basket Three was, as originally conceived, the only potentially new element in the security negotiations, Helsinki leaves things substantially where they were before.

At the same time, the fear that the 'Final Act'—as the Helsinki declaration is rather disturbingly called—will also prove to be Europe's 'final solution' has not been borne out by the facts. On the contrary, the western reaction has been one of caution, scepticism and, in many cases, outright hostility. What we do not know is how Helsinki will impinge on the Sino-Soviet conflict. This, too, is ultimately a European problem in the same sense as the endorsement of Soviet security in Europe via Helsinki is, and is very actively seen to be, a problem for Peking.

*   *   *

URBAN: Most of the contemporary debate on the future of East-West relations, and especially the controversy in this symposium, seems to fall into two clusters of ideas.

The first sees the struggle between the USSR and the West as global and continuous. Every change in the world, whether or not inspired by one of the two protagonists, is automatically entered in their books under a plus or a minus sign. No move is wholly neutral or apolitical, and security itself is a competitive, rather than shared, quality. Bipolarity assumes global dimensions, reinforced, on the Soviet side, by the universalistic claims of communist ideology, but matched by the West only hesitantly and parochially. Détente (on this showing) is a misnomer for one phase in the East-West power struggle, which the West is ill-equipped to win because pluralistic societies find it inherently difficult to do justice to a neither-war-nor-peace type of situation, and consequently lack purpose and political will. Paradoxically, it is, in this view, especially as expressed by Labedz, a pre-condition for the eventual de-ideologization of the East-West conflict that the West should effectively resist the expansion of communist power and influence. Any form of accommodation is, on this showing, not only immoral but ineffective and indeed counter-productive too; any unilateral acceptance of the Soviet rules of the game would both weaken the West and also remove any incentive for the long-term evolution of the communist system from ideological totalism to political pluralism, internally and internationally.

The second cluster of ideas consists of a number of disparate arguments which nevertheless share a common denominator in denying that the East-West axis is, or could again become, the formative relationship in the world. One of these arguments is grouped around the equalizing role of nuclear arms. Another stresses the world's interdependence in terms of energy resources, food supplies, population growth, and environmental problems. A third sees the emergence of the majority of the world's population from tutelage to adulthood as annulling the primacy of the East-West axis, or at least shifting it from its central position to a more peripheral position. One could add others.

One of the decisive questions the last quarter of the twentieth century will have to answer is whether the problems arising from the world conceived as a single system will, in fact, de-politicize and de-ideologize the East-West relationship, as Duchêne suggests, or whether there are other ways of transcending the conflict between East and West which threatens to imprint *its* particular imperatives on the world's diversified preoccupations, suffusing with political and ideological bias precisely those new problems and relationships which should, by their nature, exert a de-politicizing and de-ideologizing influence. The observation that human nature abhors chaos much more than its abhors unjust government is as old as it is poignantly relevant to our condition. If the world's ecological and demographic problems prove intractable to the kind of order which the libertarian societies of the West can impose on them or inspire by their example, then the promise of a harsh but orderly world, coming not necessarily from the Left alone, may well prove to be irresistible.

Notes on Contributors

GEORGE W. BALL is a former United States Under-Secretary of State and author of *The Discipline of Power.*

FRANÇOIS BONDY is a Swiss writer and journalist and the former Editor of *Preuves.* He is author of *So sehen sie Deutschland; Der Rest ist Schreiben.*

ZBIGNIEW BRZEZINSKI is Herbert Lehman Professor of Government and Director of the Research Institute on International Change, Columbia University. His publications include *Political Power: US/USSR* (with S. P. Huntington); *Ideology and Power in Soviet Politics* and *Between Two Ages.*

ROBERT F. BYRNES is Director of the Russian and East European Institute and Distinguished Professor of History at Indiana University, Bloomington, Indiana. He has published *The United States and Eastern Europe.*

FRANÇOIS DUCHÊNE is Director of the Centre for Contemporary European Studies, University of Sussex, and a former Director of the International Institute for Strategic Studies, London. He has published *The Case of the Helmeted Airman: A Study of W. H. Auden's Poetry,* and *The Endless Crisis* (editor).

ALFRED GROSSER is a Professor at the *Institut d'Etudes Politiques de Paris* and Director of Studies of the *Fondation Nationale des Sciences Politiques.* His recent publications include *Germany in our Time; L'Explication Politique;* and *The Colossus Again.*

WOLF H. HALSTI is a Finnish contemporary historian and a former President of the Paasikivi Society. His best-known recent publication is his history of Finland in the second world war, *The Finnish War.*

SIR WILLIAM HAYTER is Warden of New College, Oxford. He was British Ambassador to the USSR from 1953 to 1957. His publications include *The Kremlin and the Embassy* and *Russia and the World.*

JOHAN JØRGEN HOLST is Director of Research at the Norwegian Institute of International Affairs. His publications include *Norwegian Security Policy in Strategic Perspective* and he has also edited and contributed to *Five Roads to Nordic Security* and *Norway and Arms Control in Europe.* Since 1971 he has been Editor of the Nordic journal *Co-operation and Conflict.*

CLAUS D. KERNIG is Professor of Political Science at the University of Trier, Germany and Editor-in-Chief of the comparative encyclopaedia *Marxism, Communism and Western Society.*

LEOPOLD LABEDZ is Editor of *Survey* and a Visiting Professor at Stanford University. He has edited *On Trial, the Case of Sinyavsky (Tertz) and Daniel (Arzhak)* (with Max Hayward); *Solzhenitsyn, A Documentary Record,* and *International Communism after Khrushchev.*

RICHARD PIPES is Professor of Russian History at Harvard University. He has published *The Formation of the Soviet Union: Communism and Nationalism 1917–23;* and *Struve, Liberal on the Left.*

BRUNO PITTERMANN is Chairman of the Socialist International. He was Vice-Chancellor of Austria from 1959 to 1966 and Chairman of the Austrian Socialist Party from 1959 to 1967.

DEAN RUSK is Professor of International Law at the University of Georgia. He was United States Secretary of State between 1961 and 1969. A selection from his speeches and statements was published in *The Winds of Freedom* (Ernest K. Lindley, editor).

ADAM ULAM is Professor of Government and Director of the Russian Research Center at Harvard University. He is author of *Lenin and the Bolsheviks; Expansion and Coexistence: The History of Soviet Foreign Policy, 1917–67;* and *Stalin: The Man and his Era.*

G. R. URBAN is a writer on contemporary history. He has recently contributed to and edited *Can We Survive Our Future?; Toynbee on Toynbee;* and *Hazards of Learning.*

Index

détente, 9; states news black-out in USSR, 18; views on China's attitudes, 21; questions ideological possibilities, 23; advocates changing of Soviet status quo, 24; questions how far moral principles appropriate to conduct of foreign policy, 26; asks rights and wrongs of tying foreign policy to moral considerations, 27; interprets negotiating from strength, 28; revulsion at Soviet dictatorial system, 30–1; dilemma faced in pursuing détente, 32; states in Soviet thinking détente is Cold War, 32–3; ideological declaration and purpose of USSR, 33; questions Hayter on American public's self-respect, 41; views on cultural exchange, 49, 59; distaste for apparatchiks, 50; poses question to Soviet intellectuals, 53; questions Bondy's attitude to contact with Soviet intellectuals, 53; reluctance to accept Soviet laws, customs and traditions, 56; suggests fear of Soviet leaders, 57; asks connection between détente and domestic climate in USSR, 67; cites one-sidedness of exchange agreements, 72–3; compares cultural exchange in Germany, 74–5; fragility and backwardness of Soviet system, 77; questions collision of interests between USSR and USA, 79; avers USSR's spectacular achievements in space technology due to exchange agreements, 82–3; assumes Russians possess first-rate system for translating western publications, 83; questions possibilities of channels of communication being opened up without opening Soviet system, 84; is West restricting work of Soviet scholars in comparable fields?, 89; American predilection

to show Russian visitors America, 90; states reasons for USSR's failure to inspire confidence, 99; awareness by USSR of implication of scientific or scholarly work for humanity, 102; states scholar's or scientist's social responsibility inherent in ethic of work, 103; states Soviet regime deplorable, 104; USSR trying to make world monopolar, 108; European unity is in parlous state, 110; argues that French and British desire Europe not to be satisfied with second-class citizenship, 113; concerned that Scandinavian interests are coinciding with USSR's, 118; lessons learned from Chicherin's speech, 121; comments on size and sophistication of Soviet forces facing Norway, 128; questions Norway's refusal to have nuclear weapons, 130; opinions regarding showdown between USSR and China, 134; states Soviet leaders unable to understand how free press works in West, 143; USSR would exploit Germany bogey in own interests, 156; unpreparedness of Europe, 158–9; questions worth of a European security treaty, 161; states remarkable consistency in Soviet policy, 177; views on democracy, 183–4; urges agreement with Russians in matters of ideology, 191; comments on 'new class' and 'most progressive elements' in USSR, 195–6; states unsophistication of Soviet leadership, 196; asks French policy on détente, 198, 201; states USSR has global designs on rest of world, 203; says USSR's non-involvement in Eastern Europe viewed favourably in European chancelleries, 214; asks reason for refusal of